TRANSLATION EFFECTS

TRANSLATION EFFECTS

The Shaping of Modern Canadian Culture

Edited by

Kathy Mezei, Sherry Simon, and Luise von Flotow

McGill-Queen's University Press

Montreal & Kingston • London • Ithaca

ISBN 978-0-7735-4316-4 (cloth)
ISBN 978-0-7735-4317-1 (paper)
ISBN 978-0-7735-9058-8 (ePDF)
ISBN 978-0-7735-9059-5 (ePUB)

Legal deposit second quarter 2014
Bibliothèque nationale du Québec

Printed in Canada on acid-free paper that is 100% ancient forest free
(100% post-consumer recycled), processed chlorine free

This book has been published with the help of grants received from Simon
Fraser University, the Faculty of Arts at the University of Ottawa, and Concordia University's Aid to Research Related Events (ARRE) Program, administered by the Office of the Vice-President, Research and Graduate Studies.

McGill-Queen's University Press acknowledges the support of the Canada
Council for the Arts for our publishing program. We also acknowledge the
financial support of the Government of Canada through the Canada Book
Fund for our publishing activities.

Library and Archives Canada Cataloguing in Publication

Translation effects : the shaping of modern Canadian culture / edited by
Kathy Mezei, Sherry Simon, and Luise von Flotow.

Includes bibliographical references and index.
Issued in print and electronic formats.
ISBN 978-0-7735-4316-4 (bound).–ISBN 978-0-7735-4317-1 (pbk.).–
ISBN 978-0-7735-9058-8 (ePDF).–ISBN 978-0-7735-9059-5 (ePUB)

1. Translating and interpreting – Canada – History – 20th century –
Case studies. 2. Translating and interpreting – Social aspects – Canada –
History – 20th century – Case studies. 3. Translating and interpreting –
Canada – History – 21st century – Case studies. 4. Translating and inter-
preting – Social aspects – Canada – History – 21st century – Case studies.
5. Canada – Civilization – 1945– – Case studies. I. Mezei, Kathy, 1947–,
author, editor of compilation
II. Simon, Sherry, 1948–, author, editor of compilation III. Von Flotow,
Luise, 1951–, author, editor of compilation

P306.8.C3T76 2014   418'.02097109045   C2014-901228-4
                                               C2014-901229-2

To Barbara Godard (1942–2010) whose enthusiasm, courage, scholarship, and dedication to translation have greatly inspired us and this collection.

CONTENTS

Part Four **Translating Drama**

Part Five **Performing Translation**

TABLES AND ILLUSTRATIONS

ACKNOWLEDGMENTS

We would like to acknowledge the following for their invaluable assistance in the preparation of this manuscript: Sorouja Moll, Sophie Cardinal-Corriveau, Dennis McKearney, Maria Mirassol, Dorine Sosso, Kate Baltais, Inken Kaumann, and Margaret Manery. We are especially grateful for the support of our editor, Jonathan Crago, at McGill-Queen's University Press. For providing funding and support for this project and making publication possible, we express our sincere appreciation to the Fonds québécois de recherche sur la société et la culture, the University of Ottawa Faculty of Arts, the Office of the Vice-President, Research and Graduate Studies, Concordia University, the Department of Humanities at Simon Fraser University, the Simon Fraser University Publications Fund, the Simon Fraser University Faculty of Arts and Social Sciences Retirees Research Fund, and the Social Science and Humanities Research Council of Canada.

TRANSLATION EFFECTS

INTRODUCTION

Kathy Mezei, Sherry Simon, and Luise von Flotow

A judicial debate regarding the admissibility of oral histories in First Nations treaty claims negotiations, the diffusion of the FLQ Manifesto, *coureurs de bois* exchanging furs with the Wendake, a Japanese Noh play written and adapted in present-day Vancouver – all these events involve translation and all have had important effects on Canadian life and culture. Yet these acts bear little resemblance to the mirror-image paragraphs with which Canadians are familiar, the symmetrical double texts required by the Official Languages Act and produced by an efficient cohort of professionals across the land. Much of Canadian cultural life is sustained and enriched by translation on the streets, in movie theatres, on stages, in hospitals, in courtrooms, and across café tables. Paradoxically the very prominence of official translation in Canada has restricted our sightlines and diminished awareness of the variety and impact of other forms of translation.

This volume starts from the ubiquitous nature of translation in Canada, and explores events that mark the presence as well as the effects of this activity that underlies and touches so many aspects of Canadian society. It shows that many of the translation activities most vital to Canadian cultural life take place in zones that lie outside the realm of government and mobilize energies of a very different nature. The law decrees equality of English and French, and seeks to create a level playing field; however, the realities of cultural life are saturated with the conflicting forces of inequality and violence, resistance and redress. The translation activities to be considered here not only comprise the many languages of Canadian culture, including immigrant and First Nations languages, but they also focus on the unequal terrain upon which they are enacted. This book seeks to capture this diversity of interactions as well as their continuing impact on

Canadian cultural life. As a process through which ideas and styles are incorporated into Canadian life, translation can have crucial and often unacknowledged effects. And so, this book's mandate and impact extend far past that usually assigned to translation by official bilingualism, and the subsequent traffic between French and English that has been institutionalized through federal government agencies such as the federal Translation Bureau or French immersion programs and schools, bilingual signage, and the translation grants section of the Canada Council for the Arts.

Methodologically, this book uses "cultural" approaches developed in Translation Studies, a young academic discipline in which Canadians have gained international reputations in the past decades. Moving beyond the analysis of linguistic transfer – the traffic between two languages – Translation Studies, emerged internationally as a field in the 1980s. One important area of this new field of studies emphasizes the cultural and social aspects of translation and the contexts in which translation occurs (Bassnett 2). An interdisciplinary field, it draws not only upon linguistics, but also upon sociology, philosophy, gender studies, post-colonialism, and literary theory. Driven by the pervasiveness of translation in this country over the past centuries and the demands of the present, Canadian scholars have explored many practical aspects of translation, examining and describing the contexts that affect the production and outcome of translation, and developing a range of theoretical insights that derive from the Canadian situation of multilingualism and multiculturalism, and the constant exchanges across and with many languages.

The essays collected in this volume offer a fresh picture of translation practices through several decades of Canadian life, exposing activities that are often restricted from view. They work towards an alternative history of translation in Canada that incorporates and moves beyond the rich literature on Canadian translation practices already available on a number of specific topics. Such previous studies include, for example, Jean Delisle's 1987 overview of official translation, *La Traduction au Canada / Translation in Canada: 1534–1984*; Annie Brisset and Louise Ladouceur's examinations of theatre translation, *Sociocritique de la traduction: Théâtre et alterité au Québec (1968–1988)* (1989) and *Dramatic Licence: Translating Theatre from One Official Language to the Other in Canada* (2012); Susanne de Lotbinière-Harwood's 1991 feminist study, *Re-belle et infidèle: La traduction comme pratique de réécriture au féminin / The Body Bilin-*

gual: Translation as as Rewriting in the Feminine; Betty Bednarski's discussion of the revolutionary Quebec novelist, Jacques Ferron, *Autour de Ferron, littérature, traduction* (1989, 2011); and Patricia Godbout's 2004 analysis of cultural exchange between Quebec and anglophone Canada in the 1950s, *Traduction littéraire et sociabilité interculturelle au Canada (1950–1960)*.[1]

Rather than attempting a linear history and survey of translation in Canada in this volume, the editors chose a format that concentrates on detailed case studies that highlight specific events and examine the reverberation and spread of their effects. Addressing the period from the 1950s to the present and including a deliberately wide scope of examples from medical interpreting to film dubbing, *Translation Effects* creates a panoramic view of the creation of modern culture in Canada. The book is modelled upon the now classic *New History of French Literature*, edited by Denis Hollier (1989). His collection of essays proposed a radical approach to French literary history, eschewing the traditional encyclopedic presentation of a "simple inventory of authors or titles" or "continuous historical narrative or alphabetical 'dictionary,'" presenting instead "a historical and cultural field viewed from a wide array of contemporary critical perspectives" (Hollier xix). Each entry is an autonomous essay taking as its point of departure an "event" which is defined as an exemplary moment in the evolution of French literary culture and which is signalled by a "headline." This approach gives rise to a layered and expansive discussion; for example: "1536 Summer: Clément Marot Imports into French the Petrarchan Sonnet." While Hollier's collection as a whole makes no claim for exhaustive coverage, it nevertheless accomplishes a complex, textured, and diversified view of French culture over several centuries. Following Hollier's method, the essays in this volume also begin with a significant date and an evocative headline that capture specific moments in time and specific happenings in order to suggest a dynamic, multifaceted view of translation as a precise vehicle of cultural transfer in Canada that can be located in a particular time and place and whose impact can be traced. Through their imaginative, at times unusual, investigations, the contributors have succeeded in unveiling the simultaneous invisibility and omnipresence of translation moments.

The entries in the volume are presented in five broad categories: Translating Media and the Arts; Translating Politics; Translating Poetry, Fiction, Essays; Translating Drama; and Performing Translation. To view translation effects through these categories is to propose a cross-cut of Canadian translation experience, defining practices not by language but by the varied finalities of translation events. The chronological arrangement of the pieces within these categories corresponds to our wish to situate translation events within the context of Canadian cultural history. But readers are invited to skip across categories and time to make their own connections. For instance, six of the essays in the collection (Ellenwood, Lang, Cardinal, Moll, McCall, Gaertner) discuss translations of First Nations languages. These six essays, taken together, demonstrate the range of effects – from domination to resistance – that play through contemporary engagements with First Nations culture. This broad range of interactions cuts across traditional distinctions between literary and non-literary texts, between textual transfer and transculturation. All point to moments at which some kind of reversal or redress becomes possible through actions as different as the legislative acts of judges or performative practices in poetry, cinema, and theatre. These acts draw attention to shifts in the burden of translation. Who carries the responsibility for the acts and outcomes of language transfer? Two entries discuss issues of gender (Capperdoni, Mossop), two essays are devoted to Acadie (Merkle, Nichol), two to Yiddish (Anctil, Margolis), several address the question of *joual* (Lane-Mercier, Ladouceur, Mezei, Reid, Margolis). Questions of geographical region, of language categories (immigrant, First Nations, Quebec), of social movements, of literary genre, and of medium are all represented through the lens of translation and from the perspectives of translation scholars.

A Fresh Perspective on the Past

Two chapters in the volume can serve as examples of the kind of methodological "re-vision" the volume proposes. In "1885, 1998: Translating Big Bear in Film," Ray Ellenwood discusses a remarkable use of translation in the 1998 made-for-television movie *Big Bear*. Directed by Gil Cardinal and written by Rudy Wiebe, the movie tells the story of the ill-fated 1885 rebellion in the Canadian northwest. What is most important to the experience of the film is the unusual sound track. The Aboriginal characters speak in idiomatic English, while the white soldiers of the North-West Mounted Police utter an incomprehensible babble. This means that the viewer sees and hears the tragic events of 1885 from the perspective of the Aboriginal populations because they speak a familiar language (idiomatic English) while the soldiers are depicted as foreign and incomprehensible. The viewer is forced to enter into the subjective position of Big Bear's followers, forced to understand the repressive power of language. No subtitles accompany the barkings and babblings of the soldiers, and so the viewer can only guess at the meaning of what is being said. This reversal and accompanying revelation bring the burden of translation into sharp focus. Who is obliged to translate and who will suffer the consequences of the inevitable miscommunication that will result? The rebellion of 1885, initiated by the Métis Louis Riel and Gabriel Dumont, ended with the crushing defeat of Big Bear and the First Nations peoples on the prairies, and put an end to the very polyglot culture that had prevailed. The movie tells this story, but with a linguistic innovation that is crucial. The enacting of non-translation in the film, as Ray Ellenwood explains, demonstrates the compelling and decisive effects of language as the Cree are made to capitulate to the power of English. Whatever acts of translation are shown in the film are unable to reverse the negative effects of language and its power to exclude and silence. This silencing extends into the film itself from which the sounds of the Cree language are absent. But, at the same time, the film works to overturn this silencing, calling on English to provide a new sort of power to Cree.

The movie *Big Bear*, and the historical events on which it is based, remind us that the responsibilities and effects of translation are intensified in times of conflict, and redoubled again when translation takes place across the gaps of power. It also very effectively shows that the *performance* of language relations within specific media can have important pedagogical effects. While journalism, theatre, television, legal proceedings, documentary film, feature cinema, and political speeches all rely on translation for the spread of information, the process is rarely acknowledged.

The absence of attention to translation is highlighted in what was probably the most dramatic and widely broadcast incident in Canada's history – the crisis between languages as they clashed during the 1970 October Crisis. It would be difficult to overestimate the effects generated by the publication and diffusion of the FLQ Manifesto in 1970. In "1970: The October Crisis and the FLQ Manifesto," Robert Schwartzwald shows that the biggest domestic news story Canada had ever experienced was received by the majority of Canadians through the filter of French-to-English translation. Yet the document at the centre of the crisis, the FLQ Manifesto, never received an official translation (although it received many improvised versions), and the crisis was marked by many divergences in interpretation – both of the actions and of the words that fuelled it. Schwartzwald's account of the many differences of perspective that were brought to bear on these events makes for a powerful counternarrative to the official story of Canadian translation as objective and neutral. Instead of the seamless transfer of a message into the other official language, the events of 1970 highlight the obstacles that hinder communication, demonstrating that strain to the federal system will inevitably express itself as a translation issue.[2]

Translation Events and Effects

To highlight the active role that translations play, this volume introduces the twin notions of *event* and *effect*. Translation *events* pinpoint the moments at which books, performances, films, or concepts enter into the life of the culture and make themselves known. This event is an occurrence that draws attention to the translation and to the trend or movement of which it is a part. We are aware that the concept of "event" has been much debated by philosophers and historians. The "Annales" group, led by Fernand Braudel, were highly critical of "event-centered history," preferring to focus on "perennial problems" and "serial patterns" (Jay 144). By the late twentieth century, however, following discussions by Roland Barthes, Gilles Deleuze, Jean-François Lyotard, Michel Foucault, and Jacques Derrida, the "event" re-entered work in the human sciences as part of a philosophy of history that resisted linearity and coherence. Our historiography of translation in Canada is affected by this resistance, by the changing conceptions of the event, as was the model for this volume, Hollier's *A New History of French Literature*. Focusing on recent Canadian culture, our volume aims for the same kind of multiple and "thick" perspectives. Each essay hones in on a single cultural artefact or event, exploring its history, explaining its significance as a translation, and analysing its effects on the Canadian cultural scene. "Event," in this sense, recognizes the impossibility of a coherent narrative of history, instead retaining the idea of a "pivotal moment" that itself is the effect of multiple causes (Jay 145). The contributors have all chosen a significant date to highlight moments in the life of a translated play, book, political speech, or testimony. Anchoring the translation in the world to which it contributes, these events emphasize the fact that translations circulate, are performed, viewed, and consulted. Replicas of an original, they are not identical to these originals, and as separate cultural artefacts they have specific, often powerful lives.

While the idea of a "translation event" has not been explicitly theorized in Translation Studies, the idea of the "translation *effect*" underlies a great deal of recent thinking in the field. An early study by Andrew Chesterman offered a tentative definition of an effect as a change of mental state (emotional, cognitive, etc.) in the reader or recipient (219). Such effects can be intended or unintended, and can range from the personal to the intercultural; they can be directly observable (e.g., conversion to Christianity as a result of biblical translation), but also less easily observable (an aesthetic experience, an increase in knowledge). Effects can be heterogeneous (translations have different effects on different people), changing (effects can change over time), and multiple (translations can have more than one effect) (220–1).

After several decades of intensive Translation Studies, we see that the inevitable discrepancies between original and translation can develop the potential of the original text, offer new surfaces of understanding, and contribute to what Edith Grossman calls the "revivyfing and expansive effect" of translation, infusing a language with "influences, alterations and combinations that would not have been possible without the presence of translated foreign literary styles and perceptions, the material significance and heft of literature that lies outside the territory of the purely monolingual" (16). Among the examples of such exchanges is the connection between William Faulkner and Gabriel Garcia Marquez: "Someone once called Faulkner the best-known Latin American writer in English, a description that may be more than mere witticism. He seems to have inherited and then transferred into English the expansive Cervantean style that has had so profound an influence, both positive and negative, on all subsequent Spanish-language writers" (21). In other words, one translation effect is a broadening of horizons, affecting not only readers but also writers: "The more a language embraces infusions and transfusions of new elements and foreign turns of phrase, the larger, more forceful and more flexible it becomes as an expressive medium" (23). At the same time, translation augments the works on the bookshelves, adding to the repertoire of expression (Casanova). This dynamic is especially relevant for a language tradition perceived as minor or marginal to a more central tradition. One of the most important effects of translation, therefore, is to draw attention to the multiple differences, the polyvocality, of contemporary culture.

Much of the remarkable research generated by the influential move to Descriptive Translation Studies since the 1980s has been premised on the fact that translations are a significant presence in literary systems, and that they have effects that are linguistic *and* cultural. Reversing the stubborn prejudice that the effects of translations are negative (that they diminish the impact of the original), thinkers such as Gideon Toury emphasized the ways in which translations introduce new ideas and styles into the receiving language, expand the repertory of forms and capacity of expression, and challenge readers' expectations. Often large bodies of translations (rather than single, exceptional works) are studied for their effects on particular styles of literary genres, in particular, for the ways translations contribute to stylistic innovation, strengthen new literary and social movements, or influence opinion and open horizons. For example, the French translations of Edgar Allan Poe inspired Charles Baudelaire and the French symbolist movement, while Rabindranath Tagore's self-translation of his poetry from Bengali to English reinforced British colonial views of Indians and Indian culture. In other words, rather than lamenting the fact that translations can never be identical copies of a source text, Translation Studies has shown that the difference between the original and the translation is a space that has substantial revelatory power. For theories that foreground the political dimensions of translation, this space heightens awareness of power differences. Post-colonial perspectives, like feminist studies, have accentuated awareness of political effects as they operate between languages of unequal prestige or historically dissimilar experience. While the political implications of translation are most often associated in Canada with the relations between English and French as they are regulated by official bilingualism, the essays in this volume deal with the broader sphere of power relations. The power imbalances between the First Nations and the rest of Canadian society are notably acute, and so the *effects* of translation effects can be illustrated, in particular, through entries relating to First Nations languages and culture as demonstrated by our first entry.

Part I: Translating Media and the Arts

It is particularly appropriate to begin the volume with Ray Ellenwood's discussion of the made-for-television movie *Big Bear* since this essay foregrounds the political impact of translation for First Nations communities. But Ellenwood's piece also addresses the prevalence and effects of translation in and by Canadian media, an issue that came briefly to the fore in 1992, for example, when Canada's news broadcasters recognized the powerful role of translation and proposed that French-language newscasts be played on English-language television *with subtitles*. The rationale was that English-speaking Canadians should have access in an unmediated fashion to French-language news, and vice versa. This idea, which responded to what was considered an urgent political imperative at the time, was short-lived; the focus on the ubiquitous although largely invisible role of translation in Canadian media is, however, once again on the upswing.

The history and politics of translation at important cultural (media) agencies like the National Film Board have had crucial effects on the interaction of francophone and anglophone Canada, and how each views the other. Christine York's essay on translation practices during the 1950s, "1950–1956: An Interventionist Approach to Versioning at the National Film Board of Canada," is a valuable window onto that institution. During its early years, translation into French at the NFB was largely left – remarkably – to the initiative of one individual, Jacques Bobet. Because the administration of the national agency saw no need for a separate French-speaking production unit (one that was indeed formed several years later), English-language films were simply given French-language versions. York shows how Bobet took his work seriously, in some cases actually transforming the content to create a more suitable French version. What is most peculiar about this period of NFB history is that translation was given so little consideration and oversight, and relegated to the efforts of one person who was free to provide the kinds of versions he personally considered most relevant.

The vocabularies of art criticism, and of the social movements that sustain artistic production, are deeply embedded in local cultures. In her essay, "October 2006: *Territoires et trajectoires* Is Launched in Montreal and 'Cultural Race Politics' Are Introduced to Quebec," Sherry Simon discusses the difficulties of finding equivalents in societies that have not seen the same conscious articulation of struggles. Simon takes as her example the French version of a series of interviews focused on artistic production during the intensely identity-conscious 1980s and 1990s in English-speaking Canada. The preface by the interviewer and editor, Monika Kin Gagnon, to the French-language version highlights the dilemma of the translator: whether to confirm the distance between these cultures or use new terms that will create connections? How can the translator turn her work into an enactment, a performance of new linkages? That Gagnon was obliged to invent a neologism for the term "cultural race politics," the movement that had gained currency in English Canada, reveals the absence of a similar organized movement in Quebec – and of the separate and parallel evolutions of social discourse in Quebec and English Canada.

In "June 2007: Quebec Politicians Debate a Bill to Impose Strict Controls on Audiovisual Translation, and Fail to Pass It" on the dubbing of popular American films and television series dubbed and shown in Quebec, Luise von Flotow outlines the effects of practices and laws concerning film translation in Quebec and how they reflect anxieties about language and identity. What idiom of French is most appropriate for the translation of popular programs, or of children's programs? Experiments with local variants of French in Quebec have often been met with controversy, but so have imported versions from France. The debates, as von Flotow shows, have political implications as national governments try to maintain protected language markets.

The final contribution in this part, by Glen Nichols on the cultural translation of an Acadian theme park, "Summer 2008: Pays de la Sagouine: Cultural Translation at an Acadian Theme Park," introduces the idea of spatial translation and the field of Tourism Studies. Nichols describes how a tourist showcase village built around the fiction of Antonine Maillet celebrates and perpetuates a folkloric vision of what has become a model of Acadian identity. The tourist site becomes a full-body, "lived" experience, whose mediation effects are similar to theatre performance. Through its spatial and temporal translation of Maillet's fictional worlds, this theme park thus performs "easily consumed and homogeneous impressions" of Acadian culture and "reinforces the clichés of Acadie as a simple, old-fashioned, and non-threatening myth that more sophisticated 'come-from-aways' can safely indulge in" (Merkle et al. 105). The goal of this kind of tourism is to welcome the visitor into a new cultural text through gestures that have been rigidly choreographed in order to produce a preconceived effect.

Part II: Translating Politics

The idea of translation as a neutral and symmetrical exchange between two equal cultural forces is challenged throughout this volume, but the essays on the politics of translation and the translation of politics between English and French demonstrate this idea with particular force.

Denise Merkle's description of the battle to preserve Acadian language and culture in the Maritimes, "February 1968: Acadian Activism and the Discontents of Translation," traces a particularly polarized moment in the history of the city of Moncton in the 1960s when the mayor rejected official bilingualism. Merkle's account of the struggles over translation in New Brunswick, while emphasizing the always unstable and conflictual relations between languages, also shows how these unequal relations led to the galvanization of the citizens and to an extraordinary renewal within Acadian culture and literature.

Robert Schwartzwald's essay on the politics and omissions around the translation of the FLQ Manifesto, as discussed above, explains how crucial political texts and their effects circulate in sometimes paradoxical ways.

In "1971: Pierre Vallières Comes to English Canada via the United States," we encounter another case study of how translation operates during heated political periods, and how causes are transported through ideological channels in paradoxical ways. Julie McDonough Dolmaya discloses the little-known story of the ways in which Pierre Vallières' revolutionary *Nègres blancs d'Amérique* came to appear in English. Vallières' revolutionary *White Niggers of America* was first translated and published in the United States by the leftist Monthly Review Press, which only later sold the rights to McClelland and Stewart. Although copies in French were banned and seized in Quebec during the October Crisis, the English translation was available, albeit in an abridged version, a version that, however, Vallières approved.

The effects of translation in the arena of official party politics are evident in the account, "January/February 1977: Independence, Secession, Political Duels or Lévesque and Trudeau in the United States," by Chantal Gagnon of the translation of political speeches during the same period of political tension. Gagnon shows how the imperatives of political partisanship had the upper hand during the famous "duel" of ideas between Quebec Premier René Lévesque and Canadian Prime Minister Pierre Elliott Trudeau. Gagnon's study of two speeches by these political enemies delivered in New York and Washington in 1978 effectively exposes how political leaders in Canada can use the two official languages to their benefit by subtly redirecting meanings towards their new American audiences.

Renée Desjardins' discussion of the "2007: Translating Culture during the Bouchard-Taylor Commission" is a most appropriate follow-up to the previous pieces, in that it brings the discussion of difference in Quebec closer to the present, and indicates how translation developed into a complex and embattled arena within Quebec itself. In an attempt to describe and regulate Quebec's response to diversity, the term "accommodement raisonable" – itself a translation from quite a different English context – became open to interpretation from many constituencies in Quebec life. Desjardins outlines the context for this debate and the various forms of cultural translation it triggered. The effects were multiple and mixed: the Commission gave voice and agency to citizen-translators from all walks of Quebec society and encouraged exchange between different community groups; it set a precedent for methodologies in dealing with multicultural policy and discourse; and it encouraged a retranslation of the Québécois "nous." It also fuelled the debate that launched the Commission in the first place through inciting cultural stereotyping and visual representations of the "other" in the media.

Part III: Translating Poetry, Fiction, Essays

One of the principal ways in which translation has nourished and sustained Canadian literature is through the languages of immigration. Since there is a direct relation between translation and immigration, the writings of the first generations of immigrants to Canada convey or translate through new languages the experiences of displaced populations. The effects of the symbiosis between translation and immigration are addressed by Daisy Neijmann in "1923: 'Foreign' Immigrants Write Back: The Publication of Laura Goodman Salverson's *The Viking Heart*," a novel that depicts the struggles of the Icelandic community to retain its values while adapting to the new world. Issues of immigration are also addressed by Hugh Hazelton, who sketches the history of political persecution, arrival, and translation among Latino writers in Canada and their effect of expanding consciousness of North and South America in his essay, "11 September 1973: Latin America Comes to Canada." Similarly, in "1978: Language Escapes: Italian-Canadian Authors Write in an Official Language and Not in Italiese," Joseph Pivato examines the language choices made by Italian-Canadian writers, especially their resistance to a form of Italian-English called "Italiese," which has the effect of replicating stereotypes of Italian speech. And in "1992: Translating Montreal's Yiddish Poet Jacob Isaac Segal into French," Pierre Anctil describes how the translation of Yiddish literature, beginning in the twentieth century, has had the effect of expanding and enriching Quebec culture beyond the two official languages. All of these examples show how these languages of immigration continue to stimulate English- and French-speaking cultural production not only through conventional acts of translation, but also through less formal acts – which can be called "creative interference" or "cultural translation." Yiddish offers a particularly interesting case study, as the moments and circumstances of its translation first into English and then into French illustrate the story of Jewish experience in Canada. While the passage from Yiddish into English followed what Pierre Anctil has called the "natural incline" of Jewish assimilation into the anglophone population, translation into French signalled an important deviation in this trajectory. A new route opened when the work of Montreal Yiddish writers was recognized as part of the history of French-language Montreal. The effects of the translation of the poet J.I. Segal and many other Yiddish writers into French are incalculable if one considers that this translation heralds a new understanding of Montreal cultural history and the role of Jewish writers in this history. Where translation traditionally took place within the Jewish community, from Yiddish to English, the switch to French signalled a new era of literary and cultural history – in which the literature of an earlier period would take up new citizenship in an arena both familiar (because belonging to the same city) and foreign (because living for a long time in separate spheres).

Turning to the effect of translating a very different language in Quebec, Gillian Lane-Mercier offers an extensive overview of *joual*, a form of urban slang, and the different approaches to its translation in her "1984: Disquieting Equivalents: David Homel Retranslates *Le Cassé* by Quiet Revolution Novelist Jacques Renaud." *Joual* had become the flashpoint signalling the difficulties of translation in the highly politicized 1960s and 1970s. Translations from and into *joual* were instrumental in drawing attention to the ideological power of the urban slang and its flowering as a creative idiom. The literary rehabilitation of *joual* in Quebec was an important chapter in the events of the Quiet Revolution. Analysing David Homel's 1984 retranslation of Jacques Renaud's *Le Cassé*, Lane-Mercier explores English-speaking Canada's reception of revolutionary writers of the 1960s from Quebec. She also discusses the political implications of retranslating this radical novel after the failed 1980 Quebec referendum on sovereignty.

The effects of translation between Quebec and English-language Canadian literatures have displayed multiple trajectories. With their legendary 1970 *Dialogue on Translation*, the poets, Frank Scott and Anne Hébert, became a kind of literary "poster couple" for official bilingualism. Their dialogue symbolized a dignified poetic engagement, sustained by mutual respect. With no intention to diminish the importance that this exchange represents, Patricia Godbout in "September 1970: Publication of a 'Monologue' on Translation," reveals through careful archival research that many aspects of the exchange were manufactured. Godbout demonstrates how the "dialogue" was a staged event, theatricalized by the astute academic Jeanne Lapointe who saw the political potential of this epistolary exchange. This oft-cited series of transactions is less a dialogue than a monologue, pursued more assiduously by Frank Scott than by Anne Hébert. Scott's intelligent and sensitive pursuit of meaning in Hébert's poems received gracious acknowledgment by Hébert, but each remained in their assumed roles and separate spheres: Hébert the inspired poet, Scott the devoted translator. The fact that the exchange was published on the eve of the October Crisis would emphasize its symbolic import as subsequent contact between the two cultures became fraught.

Julie McDonough Dolmaya's research into the translations of Mordecai Richler's impassioned text into French and their negative reception in Quebec is an equally instructive tale about cultural exchange and one very different in temperament and character from that between Scott and Hébert. The story of Mordecai Richler's voyage through the American press into French as outlined in "1992: Through Translation, Mordecai Richler's *Oh Canada! Oh Quebec!*" Generates Controversy in English and French" is a telling episode of cultural history via translation in and by the media. Indeed, the effects of translations are not always linked to the accuracy of the version produced, and this volume cites several other examples of translations, that – for different reasons – neglect cultural meaning in favour of other kinds of objectives.

There is a close link between translation and social movements. As currents of opinion that attempt to reverse or transform perceptions and that are sustained by the spread of ideas, social movements rely on translation. Through her analysis of the 1989 translation issue of the journal *Tessera*, in "1989: The Heyday of Feminist Translational Poetics in Canada: *Tessera*'s Spring Issue on *la traduction au féminin comme réécriture*," Alessandra Capperdoni explores how translations of feminist texts, primarily by experimental women poets, affected feminist consciousness in the literary avant-garde of English- and French-speaking Canada during the 1980s and 1990s. This moment of exchange has been noted and followed internationally.[3]

Two entries in Part III are devoted to the translation of First Nations languages and literatures. While asymmetries are present in the exchange between English and French, they occur even more glaringly in the case of First Nations languages. In "1998: The Artefactual Voice Within: Terry Glavin's "Rain Language" Is Published," George Lang's reflections on a bilingual text, Wawa (Chinook jargon), and English introduce a new set of considerations into the question of translatability, in particular, in relation to the question of the "source" language. Like Ray Ellenwood in his discussion of the 1885 rebellion, Lang is speaking to two time periods – the time of the flourishing of Wawa as a trade language in the late nineteenth century and the time of its revaluation through a modern-day retranslation. Wawa is a language that is already mixed. As the default lingua franca on the northwest coast during most of the nineteenth century, Wawa was spoken fluently almost exclusively by Aboriginal peoples or those in close and frequent contact with them and was therefore a language emphasizing the interdependence of settler and Aboriginal communities. The poem "Rain Language," published in 1998, is a co-translation that aims at restoring knowledge of a dead language not as scholarship but as poetry and no doubt intended to be performed. But the translation takes the language one step further, bringing the older language into the idioms of the poetic present. The effect of the translation is to draw attention to the source language and to reaffirm its possibilities, turning English into the foreign, intrusive language of the Pacific northwest. Lang's discussion of Terry Glavin's bilingual poem demonstrates the performative nature of translation. The translation is a speech act, one reflecting west coast cultural history and beliefs. By speaking itself it affirms its existence.

In the long history of negotiations between First Nations languages and the colonial languages of French and English, the negative effects of translation have been undeniable. The political implications of translation are evident in the very techniques of translation as Philippe Cardinal implies in his analysis of the double tradition of literary and ethnological translations of First Nations stories in "1999: Cross-Purposes: Translating and Publishing Traditional First Nations Narratives in Canada at the Turn of the Millennium." Cardinal shows how in each case translations shape narratives according to the rules and conventions of the receiving culture. Whether it be the masterfully crafted verse of Robert Bringhurst, or the more eclectic renditions of the ethnographer Dominique Legros, versions of First Nations narratives will face issues of betrayal. Although translations explicitly attempt to take account of previous mistakes, striving towards what is perceived as greater authenticity and respect, the structural divide remains: it is the receiving culture that dictates the terms for the reformulation and circulation of these cultural artefacts. This basic issue will not be adequately addressed, suggests Cardinal, until First Nations poets and scholars themselves take charge of translation.

Non-Canadian authors are the focus of Hélène Buzelin's entry, "22 February 2001: Les Allusifs Enter the Publishing Scene," on a Quebec publishing house that initiated a bold program of translation from languages other than English and French. Breaking with the tradition that has long kept Canadian publishers tied to translation grants handed out by the government (and which restrict publishers to Canadian authors and therefore almost exclusively to translation between English and French), Les Allusifs sought to broaden the variety of authors published in Quebec by publishing translations from a wide range of languages.

Part IV: Translating Drama

It is no accident that Michel Tremblay figures prominently in this part of the volume. It would seem that the very challenge of translating Tremblay's plays has inspired numerous candidates for the task, and his plays have been as successful around the world as they have been in English Canada.

The group of entries related to Michel Tremblay (Louise Ladouceur, Kathy Mezei, Gregory Reid, Rebecca Margolis) is emblematic of the broad influence that Tremblay's work has exercised over the years both locally and internationally. In "31 March 1973: Michel Tremblay's *Les belles-soeurs* in Toronto: Theatre Translation and Bilingualism," Louise Ladouceur demonstrates how English translations of Tremblay purged markers of vernacular speech and slang (*joual*) that were so revolutionary at the time, noticeably increased the number of swear words, and imported the use of Gallicisms with the result of perpetuating a certain fantasy of a pre-revolutionary, quaint Quebec for anglophone audiences.

Kathy Mezei describes how a small press on the west coast, far from other Canadian publishing centres, developed an active translation line, became the publisher of Tremblay in English, and influenced the creation of a canon of Quebec literature in translation in "1974: Small West Coast Press Talonbooks Makes a Bold Move and Publishes Four Quebec Plays in Translation." These effects can be empirically attested. Translations ensure accessibility of texts for general and specialized readers; they allow the entry of works into a new canon, create the possibilities for a greater readership, and permit the staging of works in the theatre. Studying the histories of particular publishing houses, as Kathy Mezei and Hélène Buzelin do, allows for a better understanding of the material circumstances as well as the ideological forces that promote the spread of translations. Gregory Reid's "1977: Michel Tremblay's *Bonjour, là, bonjour* at the Saidye Bronfman Centre Theatre: Jouissance, Translation and a Choice of Taboos" outlines the history, controversy, and subsequent significance and ramifications of the first English production of Tremblay in Quebec. Reid describes how *Bonjour, là, bonjour*, which deals with incest, "marked a new level of radicalism in both style and content" in Tremblay and in Quebec theatre. The translation of Michel Tremblay's *Les belles-sœurs* into Yiddish, according to Rebecca Margolis, in "1992: *Les belles-soeurs* and *Di shvegerins*: Translating Québécois into Yiddish for the Montreal Stage," signalled a new era of Jewish-francophone relations during the 1990s. Here the interaction between the déclassé languages of *joual* and Yiddish had strong political resonance.

As Jane Koustas explains in "1984–2009: Robert Lepage Meets the Rest of Canada (ROC)," Lepage's performance work has been important in addressing issues of translation through the years, as well as devising innovative ways to integrate translation techniques into theatrical performance. Lepage's 2009 production of *Lipsynch*, for instance, highlights the idea of "voice" and therefore implicitly introduces translation issues. Koustas analyses the ways in which the internationally renowned dramaturge skilfully incorporates multiple languages and media into his productions, with what Andrew Chesterman described as the "intended effect" of exposing audiences to a multilayered theatrical experience (222).

Translations can be acts of reparation as Beverley Curran shows in her treatment of Japanese in a British Columbia theatrical production, "May 2006: East Meets West Coast in Canadian Noh: *The Gull*." The careful preparation of the play written by Daphne Marlatt, its translation techniques, its recognition of past injustices, and its implication with Japanese communities and actors in British Columbia were designed to deploy translation as an attempt to recognize and recover elements of the past. The specific circumstances and venues of encounter are important. Produced by the Pangae Theatre in Vancouver, this Noh play is a stunning example of the ways in which a history of Japanese exclusion in Canada is transformed into the welcoming of Japanese cultural forms. Encounters with the Classical Haida language, as well as with Chinook jargon, explored here by Philippe Cardinal and George Lang, are similar examples of the ways in which the Pacific coast of Canada shows itself to be a contact zone.

The use of the term "translation" to describe the processes of adaptation in *Death of the Chief* as described by Sorouja Moll in "February 2008: *The Death of a Chief*: Translating Shakespeare into Native Theatre" further strains the conventional definitions of the term. Moll's essay on First Nations adaptations of Shakespeare investigates the indirect movements through which Native languages are processed through English and become elements of theatrical performance. While translation is usually examined as *transfer*, as the passage of a text from one language to another, as the replacement of one text by another, there are also forms of translation that are unruly or incomplete. Such practices can be referred to as cultural translation, as transculturation, or as creative interference. In a tradition termed by Brazilian cultural theorist Haroldo de Campos as "antropophagia," or cannibalism, the previously dominated culture consumes the cultural artefact and infuses it with its alternative aesthetic. In this play directed by Yvette Nolan, sections are delivered in Native languages but the production does not aim to salvage language as much as to expose the absences of language within Indigenous culture today. The effect of this adaptation is to assert newly claimed cultural authority.

Part V: Performing Translation

This final part of the volume includes acts of translations in venues such as protest movements, medicine, and law that produce broad social effects. In "1974: The Weimar Republic Comes to Gay Toronto," Brian Mossop discusses the pivotal moment of translation that saw the first era of sexual liberation in Germany become the second era in North America. The translation of the German phrase that appeared on the masthead of the Toronto gay rights activist magazine, *The Body Politic*, recalled a significant moment of transfer and an attempt to transfer the recollection of a history that had been suppressed. In "1986: Interpreting Effects: From Legislative Framework to End Users," Andrew Clifford discloses the potential for tragic outcomes that can occur with mistranslations in medical interpreting where cultural identities are not taken into account, and where "community interpreting" is abandoned to the volunteer efforts of often disadvantaged groups. Sophie McCall points to a significant shift in legal precedent with a profound influence on translation effects. Her contribution, "1997: The Supreme Court of Canada Rules that the Laws of Evidence Must Be Adapted to Accommodate Aboriginal Oral Histories," on the legal status of First Nations stories in land claims trials, while sharing many of the concerns brought up by Philippe Cardinal, points to the possibility of new forms of translatability across narrative traditions and legal systems. In 1997, Judge Lamer rendered a crucial legal decision now referred to as the *Delgamuukw* case. Overturning a previous refusal, it gave legal weight to the testimonies of First Nations people based on oral tradition, thus allowing oral narratives to be considered as evidence in land claims trials. For McCall, the judge's decision introduced a new possibility of equivalence between First Nations oral forms and "hard evidence." At the same time, however, she is, like Cardinal, wary of the conditions under which previously neglected cultural materials are fashioned as originals to be placed on an equal footing with written, historical documents. As McCall asks, what is involved in "adapting" the "laws of evidence" to "accommodate" oral history? The oral materials continue to be considered exceptional, and the rules must be bent to allow their translatability. Thus the *Delgamuukw* ruling continuously attempts to efface or downplay the role of mediating layers of translation while buttressing the stability of evidence. In a sense, McCall suggests, the judge has minimized the difficulties of translation and the struggle implicated in ongoing disputes over land, resources, jurisdiction, and autonomy, making the assumption that translatability is possible when it is so decreed.

David Gaertner's discussion of Canada's Truth and Reconciliation Commission and its model of reconciliation, "20 October 2008: Translating Reconciliation," continues the discussion initiated by McCall, addressing issues of equivalence in another proto-legal forum. His analysis of one particular episode in the life of the Commission, the resignation of Judge Laforme, sheds light on the continuing struggles of the Commission and its attempts to reach consensus. What is successful reconciliation, and how can it be successfully translated – literally and figuratively – into the hundreds of Canadian Indigenous languages? Gaertner explores the question by introducing the term "witnessing," bringing into play a plurality of modes and definitions. Gaertner suggests that successful reconciliation is a paradigm open to a multitude of translations that continually shift and alter its very structure. Contrary to the view put forward by Judge Laforme, translation, according to Gaertner, is part of the very meaning of the project of the Commission and cannot be reduced to a single rule.

Beginning a long overdue discussion, these case studies demonstrate the variety and vitality as well as the significance and pervasiveness of translation events throughout Canada. The effect, we hope, of *Translation Effects* is to expose the strikingly diverse and profound ways in which interactions among many languages and cultures have contributed to the making of modern Canadian culture. By using translations as the lens through which to study these interactions, and by using the tools of "event" and "effect" to place translations into their specific moments in history and measure and describe their impacts, this volume locates translation at the very centre of Canadian cultural history.

Notes

1 See also Godard; Whitfield, *Le métier du double* and *Writing Between the Lines*; Simon; Merkle et al.; Forsyth and Koustas.

2 The student demonstrations of the *printemps érable* (or Maple Spring) in

Quebec in 2012 were largely seen as a specifically Quebec and francophone phenomenon whose meanings were not understood by English Canada. And so translation websites run by volunteer translators were part of the effort to communicate the broader struggle for social justice which fuelled the protest against the increase in student fees.

3 See, e.g., Simon; Flotow; Godard 501–11.

Works Cited

Bassnett, Susan. *Translation Studies*. London: Routledge, 1988.

Bednarski, Betty. *Autour de Ferron, littérature, traduction, alterité*. Toronto: GREF, 1989, 2011.

Brisset, Annie. *Sociocritique de la traduction: théâtre et alterité au Québec (1968–1988)* [1989] / *A Sociocritique of Translation: Theatre and Alterity in Quebec, 1968–1988*. Trans. Rosalind Gill and Roger Gannon. Toronto: University of Toronto Press, 1996.

Casanova, Pascale. *The World Republic of Letters*. Cambridge, MA: Harvard University Press, 2004.

Chesterman, Andrew. "Causes, Translations, Effects." *Target* 10: 2 (1998): 201–23.

De Lotbinière-Harwood, Susanne. *Re-belle et infidèle: La traduction comme pratique de réécriture au féminin / The Body Bilingual: Translation as a Rewriting in the Feminine*. Montréal/Toronto: Les éditions du remue-ménage / Women's Press, 1991.

Delisle, Jean. *La Traduction au Canada / Translation in Canada: 1534–1984*. Ottawa: Les Presses de l'Université d'Ottawa, 1987.

Flotow, Luise Von. *Translation and Gender: Translating in the "Era of Feminisim."* Manchester: St Jerome, 1991.

Forsyth, Louise H., and Jane M. Koustas, eds. "The Politics and Poetics of Translation in Quebec and Canada." *Quebec Studies* 50 Fall–Winter (2010–11).

Godard, Barbara. "Gender and Gender Politics in Translation." *Encyclopedia of Literary Translation into English*, vol. 1, *A–L*. Ed. Olive Classe. London: Fitzroy Dearborn, 2000, 501–11.

– *Gender and Translation: A Bibliography*. Ottawa: CRIAW, 2001.

Godbout, Patricia. *Traduction littéraire et sociabilité interculturelle au Canada (1950–1960)*. Ottawa: University of Ottawa Press, 2004.

Grossman, Edith. *Why Translation Matters*. New Haven: Yale University Press, 2010.

Hollier, Denis, ed. *A New History of French Literature*. Cambridge, MA: Harvard University Press, 1989.

Jay, Martin. "Historicism and the Event." *Against the Grain: Jewish Intellectuals in Hard Times*. Eds. Ezra Mendelsohn, Stefani Hoffman, and Richard I. Cohen. New York: Berghan, 2013, 16–145.

Ladouceur, Louise. *Dramatic Licence: Translating Theatre from One Official Language to the Other in Canada*. Edmonton: University of Alberta Press, 2012.

Merkle, Denise, Jane Koustas, Glen Nichols, et/and Sherry Simon, eds. *Traduire depuis les marges / Translating from the Margins*. Montréal: Nota bene, 2008.

Simon, Sherry. *Gender in Translation: Cultural Identity and the Politics of Transmission*. London: Routledge, 1996.

– *Translating Montreal: Episodes in the Life of a Divided City*. Montreal and Kingston: McGill-Queen's University Press, 2006.

Whitfield, Agnes, ed. *Le métier du double: Portraits de traductrices et traducteurs littéraires*. Montréal: Fides, 2005.

– ed. *Writing Between the Lines: Portraits of Canadian Anglophone Translators*. Waterloo: Wilfrid Laurier University Press, 2006.

Translating Media and the Arts

1885, 1998: Translating Big Bear in Film

Ray Ellenwood

In 1998, the Canadian Broadcasting Corporation presented a four-hour television mini-series devoted to the great Cree Chief Big Bear, who had been notoriously reluctant to sign Treaty Six (and thus consign his people to a reservation) in 1876.[1] After some years of wandering, finding it more and more difficult to feed themselves in the traditional ways, yet aware that others on reservations were often no better off, Big Bear and his considerable band of followers ended up, demoralized and starving, in the vicinity of Frog Lake, not far from what is now Cold Lake, Alberta. There, they learned of attempts by Louis Riel to bring about an alliance among the Métis and Indian peoples of the North West, in what was later called the Riel Rebellion or the North-West Rebellion of 1885. This was seen as a very serious threat by Prime Minister John A. Macdonald, who quickly arranged to send armies from Upper and Lower Canada, using the recently built railroad, to back up the North-West Mounted Police. Some of the younger men around Big Bear, excited by news that Riel's military strategist, Gabriel Dumont, had repulsed a force of police at Duck Lake, rampaged through the village of Frog Lake, killing white settlers and taking prisoners, before moving on to sack Fort Pitt. Unable to stop the carnage, Big Bear watched as his people, along with their prisoners, were soon fleeing before the advancing armies. He was eventually arrested and tried for treason, along with a number of his followers, some of whom were hanged.[2] This was all part of a tumultuous moment of Canadian history, in a time and place where the English and French languages had almost equal weight along with various dialects mainly of Cree and Sioux, when communication was difficult between government agents (most speaking only English) and the people they were supposed to serve, when translation was not just an amusement or convenience but a matter of survival. Treaty negotiations, trade, and legal proceedings, along with reporting on them in the burgeoning print media, obviously depended heavily on translation.

Based on a novel by Rudy Wiebe entitled *The Temptations of Big Bear*, the television film was directed by Gil Cardinal, who collaborated with Wiebe in writing the script. The cast included a number of Native actors well known in Canadian film and television, including Gordon Tootoosis (Big Bear), Tantoo Cardinal (Running Second), Lorne Cardinal (Little Bad Man), and Michael Greyeyes (Wandering Spirit). An ambitious undertaking, the film attempted to show the impact, over ten years, of massive changes affecting Big Bear's people as waves of settlers moved into the region, as the railroad pushed west, as the Cree's main source of food was extinguished with the buffalo, as starvation threatened, and as subservience to an invading army of government officers seemed the only means of survival. With relatively modest means, and certainly no Hollywood cast of thousands, Gil Cardinal was able to suggest large-scale ceremonies and skirmishes and a whole people on the run, providing some very telling dramatic and emotional focus on Big Bear's family as well, carried forcefully by Gordon Tootoosis, all done with a camera that evokes an enormous sense of space and connection to a mystical land.

But from my specific point of view, the most remarkable quality of this production sprang from a decision made by Gil Cardinal and Rudy Wiebe to turn the linguistic tables on their television audience. When the situation in the film calls for Aboriginal characters to speak Cree, they communicate in English, often eloquently; when it calls for white characters who know some Cree to speak that language, they often babble in pidgin English; and when the white characters speak among themselves, or when the context assumes they are speaking English to the Cree, they communicate in a totally incomprehensible, harsh-sounding, guttural language, reminiscent of Anglo-Saxon. The effect is very disorienting. It takes a few minutes to figure out what's going on. The audience is, for the duration of the film, placed in the position of a Cree-speaker of 1885, trying to make sense not only of a confusing political situation, but also of streams of incomprehensible words desperately needing translation. Before discussing in more detail how and why this effect was achieved, we need to consider some more context.

In researching and writing *The Temptations of Big Bear* and his later book on Big Bear (*Big Bear*) for the Extraordinary Canadians series, Rudy

Wiebe was certainly aware of communication difficulties in the Canadian North West at the end of the nineteenth century.[3] In fact, communication problems became a major theme in his novel. The opening two sections of the book depict a treaty signing at Fort Pitt in 1876, and show Peter Erasmus, the famous Métis translator, struggling to find suitable words in an exchange between Governor Alexander Morris, Sweet Grass, and Big Bear. Translating words, translating culture, and translating widely different life experiences are central themes of these opening pages, and before long, Wiebe establishes Kitty McLean as a major character in the novel whose function is to mediate, culturally and linguistically, between Big Bear and her father, W.J. McLean, Factor at the Hudson's Bay trading post, Fort Pitt. The actual, historical McLean children did know Cree from playing with other children in and around the fort, but Wiebe gives them quite an elevated consciousness and status. He actually has Kitty sit beside her father (historically, not very likely), interpreting for him during council meetings in Big Bear's camp. In one passage, she muses, "But there was no way I could get through to him; even Papa would never understand Big Bear's comprehension" (Wiebe, *Temptations* 286). "Translate what?" she asks herself, as she realizes that there are things to be conveyed that go beyond words (288). Wiebe's Kitty, in a way, appropriates the role of the interpreter/translator from the more usual practitioners (Métis such as Peter Erasmus and Gerry Potts) perhaps representing Wiebe himself as Kitty seeks to bridge Aboriginal and white cultures.

Near the end of *The Temptations of Big Bear*, in a trial scene particularly important for the theme of translation and cross-cultural ignorance, Wiebe imagines a dialogue between Big Bear and the court translator, Peter Houri, in which they share an awareness of the impossibility of communicating with Magistrate Hugh Richardson. Big Bear says:

> "My friend, I have seen this Whitehair and I remember him," and he told him at length, gently; Peter's head tilted a little, his right hand on his heart the way he always stood, struggling to fight clear some meaning between them. Big Bear concluded, "I understand what he wants to tell me, and you understand, but we haven't been given words or signs for it, so just let him say his white things." Houri stared gloomily at him, and translated finally [here Wiebe goes to official government transcripts]:

Prisoner: "No, I don't recollect it, nor did I understand what was the charge laid against me. I do not understand that."

Court: "Then you are charged this Friday, the eleventh day of September, 1885, that you, not regarding the duty of your allegiance to the Queen, with other evil-disposed persons, compassed to levy war against the Queen in Canada, against her Crown and dignity." (355)

This climactic section of the book ends in Big Bear's famous speech,[4] to which Wiebe provides a kind of interpolating commentary directed through the consciousness of Peter Houri, the government interpreter, who has particular difficulty finding words to convey Big Bear's humour (395).

Between the writing of these passages in the early 1970s, and the television script in 1997, Rudy Wiebe would have been aware of the kind of research done by Blair Stonechild and Bill Waiser. Recounting the negotiations preceding Treaty Six, they wrote, "The government had already secured the services of two official interpreters: the Reverend John McKay, who spoke a Swampy Cree dialect rarely used on the plains, and the mixed-blood Peter Ballandine, who knew Assiniboine well but whose Cree was questionable" (Stonechild and Waiser 12). The Indians succeeded in naming Peter Erasmus as their interpreter. Stonechild and Waiser suggest it was the later absence of Erasmus (replaced by McKay), and consequently a bad translation, that led to a misunderstanding between Big Bear and Alexander Morris that, in turn, eventually led to the government branding Big Bear as a troublemaker (25–6).[5] With this kind of information in mind, then, one can understand why Wiebe and Cardinal might want to convey not only a set of historical events, but a complicated linguistic experience to their audience.

I recently contacted Wiebe and Cardinal to ask them about the writing and shooting of the script. Wiebe explained the situation in an e-mail response I will quote at length, rather than paraphrase, because of its appealing spontaneity:

I'd been working, with many others, on scripts for some 12 years at least, when the CBC finally came on board and the language question had to be faced. Subtitles, an act of reading [with many viewers in

Can. functionally illiterate] and making strange every time BB spoke. Really stupid. So I insisted that the Cree speak English (since theirs was the key talk anyway) and the English something else. What? Jim Burt, the CBC head of drama asked. A language I'll concoct – and I gave him an example. And he agreed with me! Argued it out with all his people and made sure it happened. Gil and I wrote the script that way (I wrote all the Jabberwocky, as we called it after Lewis Carroll and Alice), and sadly, Jim died of cancer before the whole film was shot – but he was on the first few days of shooting.

I must tell you – the English [characters in the film] do not speak gibberish. It is a completely organized language, with rules like English NVO structure,[6] and the vocabulary is consistent throughout. I made lists and lists of vocabulary. It's hard to make up a whole language! Everything the English say, even in the background, the long speeches not heard on screen, I had to transform into Jabberwocky just in case the editor used them. What a labour of imagination – it would have been simpler to write it in my oral language, Low German, but then every Russian Mennonite seeing the TV show would have died laughing. Once, when I was on the set in front of Fort Pitt where Kitty is translating for her father talking to Big Bear, Gil suddenly called me over and said that one whole turn of conversation had to be written to explain better – than the script on hand – what was going on. So, while the entire company waited – 60–70 people – I wrote a complete conversation in English and Jabberwocky on the spot. Talk about a writer deadline! (E-mail to author, Feb. 2009)

Gil Cardinal, in a telephone conversation on 19 February 2009, agreed with Wiebe's comments that there had been considerable thought and conversation about representing Cree-speakers in the film. One possibility, as already mentioned, was to have them actually speak Cree, with English subtitles or voice-over. But that notion was quickly dropped, as Wiebe explains. And they definitely wanted the audience to feel what the Cree would have felt, faced with these incomprehensible newcomers. The imposition of a language specifically for the whites in the film was a real challenge for the actors who had to use it, especially for Blaine Hart, who played Peter Erasmus. The "Jabberwocky" Rudy Wiebe constructed had to make sense to the actors, and be at once alien and credible to the audience. Public re-action, according to Gil Cardinal, was very positive. People understood what was going on, and what was intended.

The Rudy Wiebe Papers in the archives of the University of Calgary Library include one file labelled "Jabberwocky," containing seventeen pages of the *Big Bear* film script. From them, we can get a sense of the lan-guage Wiebe invented, and the way it was used.[7] There is, for example, the scene of the 1876 treaty signing, mentioned above, as being an important part of both *The Temptations of Big Bear* and of Wiebe's 2008 biography. In the script, Governor Morris' Jabberwocky "English" looks like this: "Me humpret glee, grotle klings, du a wilmming depforth. O a scriple lagu-ranteum Big Bear, du autom gratulayome."

Peter Erasmus then translates this into "Cree": "He says, 'My heart is glad for you, great Chiefs, that you have behaved in the right way. And Big Bear has come, so I can tell him that the Treaty we have made is for him too, as if he were here.'" Big Bear replies in "Cree": "I find it hard to speak." Erasmus translates into "English": "Wah fink el sweare grotle."

And so it goes, with a statement from Big Bear in "Cree" to his fellow chiefs: "It is no small matter we have to consult about, and already I see you dressed in these red coats, these shiny things." This is translated by Erasmus for the benefit of Morris: "El fit cleane sack er consortium, e nuschte wah lum dew draggen disse route hamd, disse glotze stuff."

When Big Bear protests that he knows Police Chief Crozier and Peter Erasmus, but not this "Gov-ern-nor" standing in front of him, Morris replies:

Ma bleve hamd bregit wah lemmel ou de Quanto, dewer Fruh. Was grotle dew, "Wah leve ma routle makede e ma wite." Was kenne el fit sweare ulb wasel wallow, be was lange rumes, was vetestet dew, nemmel oversiggert.

Erasmus translates:

He says, "My blue coat shows I speak for your Great Grandmother, the Queen." She tells you, "I love my Red Children as well as my

White." She knows it is hard for you to live in some parts of her lands, but she has long arms, to help you, so you need never go hungry.

The linguistic system of the film not only emphasizes the absurdity of the Ottawa official's rhetoric by juxtaposing it with Big Bear's eloquence, it also allows the Cree chief to make an in-joke for the benefit of his Aboriginal (and television) audience. Morris looks puzzled as those around him laugh, because Erasmus discretely does not translate: "She may have long arms, but are her *breasts* big enough to feed us all." Big Bear goes on to address the other chiefs, particularly Sweetgrass:

> Yes, you wear her red coats, and you have given away your hand. You are Sweetgrass, our great elder, and you have been touched by the water of that priest, and he named you "Ab-ra-ham." I was never a Company Chief, nor missionary Chief, and I need no new name!

Erasmus translates this for Morris as:

> Few, dew dragge wasel route hamd. E dew havve crump dewer haunde. Dew cham Sweetgrass, uns massa owla, e dew beruhmt de wota disse "priest," e wa lorte dew "Ab-ra-ham." Wah cham nemmel company kling, priest kling, e wah nemmel freshe lort!

It is not unusual in "western" films, of course, to have scenes involving interpreters (usually Native) translating the words of Native spokesmen for the benefit of soldiers or officials of some kind. But I don't ever remember such scenes being so prominent, and taking on so much thematic importance, as they do here.

In a later episode, Big Bear visits McLean, in the Factor's rather elegant house at Fort Pitt, to plead for help for his people, who are starving. This is a moment that precedes the so-called Frog Lake Massacre. Kitty McLean translates for her father in a barely audible voice. The scene goes on, they take tea, Big Bear explains why he has not chosen a reserve, and McLean is moved enough to forego his interpreter and cry out in "Cree": "I kill three animals. You take. Your people." As linguistic difference is highlighted in these scenes, and the attempt is made to force English-speaking viewers to feel for a moment like "the other," those with a knowledge of Canadian history would also be aware that, for approximately eighty years following Big Bear's death, government and church residential schools tried to wipe out Aboriginal languages.

The *Big Bear* production was a fascinating experiment, unique in Canadian television as far as I know. Perhaps not surprisingly, the distributors of the film, on their website, show a selection of clips, but none that give any hint of the "translation" games involved.[8] Surprisingly, and unfortunately, the film in its entirety is very difficult to see. The distributors, Cine-Tele Action Inc. explained to me:

> The Mini Series of *Big Bear* is not available. The screening format it's in is only for broadcasts, we do not have it in any format (such as DVDs or VHS) for screening purposes. Broadcasters that have acquired the Mini Series do not have the right to reproduce copies and distribute them. We will keep your e-mail address and if ever the demand is high enough for us to consider making screening copies for DVD sales we will contact you. (E-mail to author)

Even more surprisingly, the CBC, when asked for a copy by the University of Calgary Archives, replied:

> Any material that we send off site to be placed in an archive is sent to the National Archives in Ottawa. Unfortunately, we don't make copies for private collections or other archives. The problem lies in the fact that there would be no long term control over who would have access to this material; and we are obligated by our contracts with various unions and guilds to maintain control of distribution. (E-mail to Chevrefils)

Thus, a perfectly understandable attempt to control copyright may lead to a situation in which a unique and very worthy cultural document is simply not available to anyone but bureaucrats and archivists. *Neveurmagne* (to use one of Jacques Ferron's untranslated Englishisms), if I was able to get a copy, eventually, and see the whole film without commercials, so may other people. Worthy experiments have a tendency to find an audience, somehow, and we can only hope that will be the case with *Big Bear*.

Notes

1 With two episodes (1 X 91.30 and 1 X 93.30), the film won a number of awards in 1998 and 1999, including "Best Story" at the American Indian Film Festival in California, a Canadian Producers Award, two Gemini for Best Costume Design and Best Achievement in Make-up, as well as Gemini nominations for Best Direction in a Dramatic Program and Best Original Music Score. Rudy Wiebe and Gil Cardinal won a 2000 Writers Guild of Canada Award for the screenplay. More details about the film may be obtained from the distributor's website: http://www.cineteleaction.com or at http://www.imdb.com/title/tt 0159851/fullcredits. *Big Bear* became readily available on DVD in 2011.

2 Louis Riel was also arrested and hanged, in a trial that remains contentious to this day. Big Bear served three years in prison and died shortly after being released.

3 For an account of some of these problems, see Ellenwood, "Translation and the North-West Rebellion of 1885."

4 "There is no official record of what Big Bear said at his sentencing in his own defence. If it was recorded, it has disappeared, unfindable in archives. The only record is one Toronto newspaper summary and several oral accounts – nothing official" (e-mail, Wiebe to author May 2009).

5 Rudy Wiebe picks up on this whole question again, with considerable detail and in a more linear fashion than in *Temptations*, in chapter 5 of his *Big Bear*.

6 Presumably noun/verb/object structure.

7 With thanks to Marlys Chevrefils and the Special Collections Unit, Archives and Special Collections, University of Calgary.

8 To see these, go to http://www.cineteleaction.com click on "Our Productions" and then on "Big Bear."

Works Cited

CBC. E-mail message to Marlys Chevrefils. 11 Feb. 2009.
Cine-Tele Action Inc. E-mail message to the author. 6 March 2009.

Ellenwood, Ray. "Translation and the North-West Rebellion of 1885." *Traduire depuis les marges / Translating from the Margins*. Eds. Denise Merkle, Jane Koustas, Glen Nichols, and Sherry Simon. Québec: Nota bene, 2008, 47–58.

Stonechild, Blair, and Bill Waiser. *Loyal till Death: Indians and the North-West Rebellion*. Calgary: Fifth House, 1997.

Wiebe, Rudy. *The Temptations of Big Bear*. Toronto: McClelland and Stewart, 1973.

– *Big Bear*. Toronto: Penguin, 2008.

– E-mail messages to author. 10 Feb. 2009 and 6 May 2009.

1950–1956: An Interventionist Approach to Versioning at the National Film Board of Canada

Christine York

In 1953, as part of a low-budget series of documentary shorts called *Faces of Canada* that showed individual Canadians of various backgrounds going about their occupations, Roman Kroitor made a film that is now considered a classic of the NFB's "golden years" (Hancox 13). Set in the dead of a winter's night in Winnipeg, it portrays a Polish Canadian street-railway switchman who, in voice-over, speaks contentedly about his life in Canada while recalling the massacre of family members back in his homeland. The producer of the film's French version, Jacques Bobet, would make the surprising decision to expunge all references not only to wartime Europe but also to Winnipeg, shifting the film's focus to a narrow concern with French-Canadian identity.

A new National Film Act came into effect on 14 October 1950, superseding the 1939 act that had created the National Film Board of Canada. Not only did it modify the Board's administrative and legal structure, but the 1950 act articulated a new mandate. "The Board is established," stated section 9, "to initiate and promote the production and distribution of films in the national interest and in particular, (a) to produce and distribute and to promote the production and distribution of films designed to interpret Canada to Canadians and to other nations." This would signal a turning point in the struggle of French Canadians to carve out a space within the NFB for an autonomous francophone unit that not only would make its own hiring and organizational decisions, but could focus on subject matter that reflected Quebec reality (Véronneau, "Early Activities of the Francophone Group at the National Film Board" 169) – and it was through translation that key elements of that struggle were carried out.

The NFB was created in 1939, just months before Canada entered the Second World War, when British documentary filmmaker John Grierson, who had been invited to advise the Canadian government on film production in 1938, became its first commissioner. In its first decade, the NFB had few French Canadians on staff and there was little original French production. As a result of internal and external pressure, the situation gradually changed during the 1950s. The changes were sparked by the revision of the Film Act, strengthened by the move of the NFB's head office from Ottawa to Montreal in 1956, and culminated in the creation of an autonomous French production unit in 1964. In the meantime, one way for francophones to gain a voice within the NFB – given the scarcity of original French productions – was through French-language versions of English-language productions. Those produced in the 1950s, many under the supervision of Jacques Bobet, reveal an underlying attitude to translation that saw it as an active force contributing to a body of film work – in this case, the total French-language output at the NFB. Yet while these versions testify to the role translation can play in affirming an emerging identity, they also reflect a lack of consideration for the author's intent and the cultural specificity of the original productions.

During its first half-decade, the NFB made films that supported the war effort by informing citizens of the battles waged by Canadian soldiers overseas and encouraging those on the home front to do their patriotic duty. Non-theatrical circuits were organized in rural and urban areas so that films could be screened at factories, trade unions, community halls, libraries, and church basements. Short films produced for monthly series – *Canada Carries On* and *The World in Action* in English and *Actualités canadiennes* in French – were shown before feature films in commercial cinemas. By 1945, these series were reaching audiences numbering in the millions and the NFB was one of the world's largest film studios, with a staff of nearly eight hundred. The English-language series were composed mainly of compilation films – stock footage shot by foreign news correspondents as well as captured enemy footage shot by German, Italian, and Japanese crews, edited together, and commented in voice-over narration (Goetz 63).

By contrast, many of the original productions in *Actualités canadiennes* (renamed *Les reportages* in 1943) were shot in Quebec and presented local subject matter – a first step in original French production. After Vincent Paquette and several other French Canadians were hired in 1942 and 1943, it increased to a peak in 1945, when 40 per cent of films produced at the NFB were in French (Véronneau, *Résistance et affirmation* 16). However, this level of representation did not last long. In the postwar period, virtually no francophones were hired and the number of original French productions dropped from thirty films in 1945 down to two films in 1950: the brink of extinction, according to Quebec film historian Pierre Véronneau (*Résistance et affirmation* 19). Correspondingly, the production of French versions increased in importance. The NFB administration was not particularly concerned about whether its French-language production was original or took the form of versions, as long as films in both languages could be listed in its annual report and Parliament was satisfied with its efforts towards bilingualism. Indeed, Commissioner Ross McLean considered that originals and versions amounted to the same thing, with versions having the advantage of being cheaper to produce (*Résistance et affirmation* 19).

The postwar period was challenging for the NFB on several fronts, not only bilingualism. In the transition to a peacetime agency, staff was cut by almost a third. Grierson resigned in 1945 amidst allegations of involvement in a Soviet spy ring; his successor, Ross McLean, was fired after five turbulent years. NFB employees were suspected of being communist sympathizers and obliged to pass security clearance in what amounted to a "witch hunt" (Druick 90–1). At the same time, private film producers, disappointed that the NFB had not been closed after the war, complained of unfair competition, while politicians attacked the films as a waste of taxpayers' money (Evans 6).

Against this backdrop of Cold War tensions and domestic questioning of the NFB's purpose, the 1950 National Film Act, written by newly appointed Commissioner Arthur Irwin, ushered in a period of renewal. The NFB became more autonomous, with more powers vested in the film commissioner, and was given greater separation from the government and its own working capital fund (Evans 16–17). The revised wording of the mandate expanded its audience to include not only Canadians, but also people of other nations. Previously, Grierson had considered that local or regional reality was not appropriate subject matter; films should deal with national subjects and be of interest to Canadians across the country. He envisioned film as an educational tool and a public duty within a centralized, unified state (Véronneau, *Résistance et affirmation* 12). But with the new mandate and change in commissioners, films could move away from Griersonian didacticism and, like other art forms, make a contribution to Canadian culture (Morris 191). Here were the seeds for a new flowering of documentary that would lead by the late 1950s to the innovative Candid Eye films of Unit B and the acclaimed *cinéma direct* of French-Canadian filmmakers.

An Influential Figure: Jacques Bobet

One of the few francophones hired to the NFB during the second half of the 1940s was Jacques Bobet. A young Frenchman studying audiovisual education at Columbia University in New York, he arrived in 1947 as a potential replacement for the retiring music composer, but immediately busied himself working on French versions (Bobet, "Aux innocents les mains libres" 7–8). Within a few years, he was given full responsibility for "French versions, revisions and adaptations."[1] By 1956, when the NFB's head office moved from Ottawa to Montreal, he had been involved in the production of more than five hundred French versions. When the NFB was restructured along linguistic lines in 1964, Bobet became one of four executive producers of French Production. There, he took on the role for which he is most remembered today, as a mentor and inspiration to numerous young Quebec filmmakers. An insightful, open-minded producer, he groomed the talents of such directors as Jean-Claude Labrecque, Gilles Carle, Denys Arcand, Pierre Perrault, and Anne Claire Poirier, producing a total of 233 films. He directed several films himself, often about sports, such as *Game in 21 Points* (1968), which reflected his passion for table tennis. One of his most significant accomplishments was producing the official film of the 1976 Summer Olympics in Montreal. Bobet retired in 1984 to teach music, his first love; he was made a member of the Order of Canada in 1992 and died four years later (McIntosh; National Film Board of Canada).

Given the sheer number of versions on which he worked throughout the 1950s, Bobet is surely an important figure in translation in Canada, and his views must have had repercussions that radiated beyond the confines of the National Film Board. What can be gleaned – through his infrequent writings and interviews as well as the films themselves – about his approach to translation? In his comments introducing an interview he conducted with Bobet, documentary filmmaker and writer Jean-Daniel Lafond describes him as a *bricoleur* — someone who improvises and adapts his methods to the circumstances and materials at hand ("Aux innocents les mains libres" 6). During the early years of Bobet's tenure at the NFB, there was plenty of work, no shortage of money, and little oversight by the administration ("No one was given a freer hand than me," claims Bobet (9, author's translation). Narrators like Roger Baulu, Jacques Desbaillets, and René Lecavalier drove to Ottawa from Montreal after their day's work as television or radio hosts to record the narration texts that Bobet and his colleagues had written the previous day or even that morning ("Les racines cachées" 14). Bobet's biggest challenge, in his view, was to establish a stable team at the French Unit, as staff members rarely stayed longer than a year and new people constantly had to be hired and trained. His other challenge was to improve the quality of versions by installing what he calls "the notion of equal dignity between the two versions of a film" ("Aux innocents les mains libres" 9, author's translation). In fact, he goes farther – and it is here that he comes closest to setting out his approach to translation: "The version is always better than the original" (ibid.). This claim sheds light on the shifts that can be observed between the English original and French version of the films produced at the NFB during the 1950s.

At the time, most documentaries were shot on black-and-white 35mm film and lasted under 20 minutes. The Griersonian approach, which held documentary to be primarily didactic and imbued with a social purpose, was heavily dependent on voice-over narration to make its argument. Because these films used narration rather than synchronized dialogue, making versions was essentially a matter of removing the original voice track, recording a translated narration, and remixing the soundtrack with the new narration. This practice offered considerable freedom to version directors, as they were faced with neither the constraints of lip synchronism that characterize dubbing nor the need for accuracy that stems from the presence in subtitling of both the original soundtrack and the translation. Like dubbing, voice-over is characterized by the effacement of the source text and, thus, the inability of the viewer to detect shifts that may have occurred during the translation process. As noted by film critic Antje Ascheid, this changes the status of the original film "from that of a finished and culturally specific text to that of a transcultural denationalized raw material, which is to be reinscribed into a new cultural context via the dubbing process" (33). The potential for recontextualization found in dubbing is even greater in the voice-over version because the translated narration is unconstrained by the need to match characters' lip movements.

The voice-over method of producing versions prevailed at the NFB for several decades and, indeed, is still the most common way to translate the narration track in documentaries and animated films. As synchronized speech recording became more common in 16mm film starting in the 1960s, subtitling gradually took over as the standard way to produce versions of documentary films. The NFB has always versioned many of its films – but not all. It was up to each studio in the English and French programs to decide whether or not to produce a language version, depending on the film's distribution potential. This meant that some versions were not produced at all or only made when a film was re-released as part of a compilation. It was not until in 2007 that the NFB decided to formulate a policy on versioning, when Torill Kove's animated film *The Danish Poet* (2006, 14 min.) was nominated for an Academy Award, and it emerged that no French version had been produced.[2] The policy, released on 30 May 2008, states that all audiovisual works produced or co-produced by the NFB after 1 April 2005 must be made available in both official languages: a voice-over version in the case of animated films, a subtitled version at minimum in the case of documentary films, and one or the other in the case of other audiovisual genres.

Versioning as Intervention

One of the major series produced by the NFB was *Canada Carries On*, created by John Grierson and Stuart Legg, which ran from 1940 to 1959. The films, 10 to 20 minutes long, were shown in theatres prior to the main feature. In French, the series was known as *En avant Canada* and was composed mostly of versions along with a few original French-language productions. One film in the series is *Toronto Boom Town (Toronto: Ville champignon)* (1951, 10 min.). Produced by Sydney Newman and directed by Leslie McFarlane, it showed how Toronto had become a bustling metropolis with soaring skyscrapers, ambitious construction projects, and a busy stock exchange. It is difficult to determine the authorship of the French version, as the opening credits attribute it to Jean Sarrazin, whereas the NFB website lists Roger Baulu as responsible for "voice and narration," which is the usual credit for the person who both wrote and recorded the narration. Nonetheless, the film falls within the period when Jacques Bobet was directing French versions.

The film looks at Toronto through the eyes of two visitors – presumably actors – who are assigned a name and hometown: Mr Chester Vanderwick of Cleveland, Ohio, and "young Albert McConniky" from Pine Tree Rapids, a place name that seems intended to conjure up small-town Canada. In the French version, however, the young man is identified as a French Canadian, Joseph Dumouchel. When the two visitors meet in a bar at the end of the day to give their impressions of the city, Mr Vanderwick claims he feels right at home, but Mr McConniky has another opinion: "Toronto's a great place for a visit but it's too big for me. I wouldn't live here if you gave me the place!" In the French version, Mr Dumouchel, like his English counterpart, finds Toronto too big for his taste, but concludes, "J'aimerais mieux rester chez moi!" Was this intended to be a subtle message to French Canadians, implying that they need not be envious of Toronto? Earlier in the film, the English version describes the city as one that "reflects the dynamic growth of all Canada. The Toronto of today is vastly different from the Toronto of half a century ago. Back in those far-away times, when you could buy a good suit for ten dollars and a half [over an image of a man in the street wearing a suit], Toronto became known as the Queen City." The French version, however, makes no reference to Canada and adds a comment on Toronto's puritanism: "Aujourd'hui, la grande cité des bords du lac Ontario n'a plus la taille ni la mentalité du Toronto d'il y a cinquante ans. À cette époque, Toronto se vantait d'être un des piliers de l'empire, et Toronto la puritaine s'est toujours réjouie d'être appelée la Ville Reine." Was this a veiled way of telling French Canadians they're just as well off not living in Toronto? These asides constitute an intervention on the part of the translator that circumvents the director's message and sets up direct lines of communication with the target audience.

Another film in the *Canada Carries On / En avant Canada* series, produced two years later, is *Farewell Oak Street (Adieu rue des chênes)* (1953, 17 min.), which had a relatively high budget and used dramatization. It showed the squalid conditions in the Regent Park slum neighbourhood of Toronto, which was razed and replaced with modern low-income housing. The film generated some controversy for its forthright portrayal of poverty

(Evans 37). The French version was done by Jacques Bobet with an unnamed narrator. Again, we find an unexpected aside to French Canadians, but this time it is not contained in the narration: it is inserted into the written text on screen. Part way through the film, a father – identified as "Jim Brown" in the original version but as "Gilles Blais" in the French – shows his family a newspaper with a headline that reads "City to rebuild slums." We can make out part of the subheading: "Total demolition planned for area [...] Oak St." In the French version, the film has been re-edited, as was the usual practice: any English text visible on the screen – such as the opening and closing credits – was replaced by French text. Accordingly, the newspaper headline reads "Des taudis vont disparaître," with the subheadline "La ville commencera bientôt à démolir rue des Chênes." However, under that headline is a smaller one, positioned in the middle column so it is centred on the screen. It reads, "Le bilinguisme sur tous les chèques fédéraux est réclamé." A little farther down and to the left but still clearly visible is another headline, which says, "La question des écoles séparées inopinément soulevée à Ottawa" (the reference is to the publicly funded separate-school system that provides religious education in certain provinces and was supported by Quebec's Catholic Church). The message is almost subliminal, allowing viewers to absorb the information while barely realizing they are reading it. Again, the translation process has opened a window for intervention, through which the translator – specifically the version director – has shaped the original work in pursuit of his own agenda.

A similar strategy was used in a previous film in the same series, *Careers and Cradles*, and its French version *Carrières et berceaux*. Produced in 1947, the year Jacques Bobet was hired to the NFB, it credits Roger Baulu as narrator. The film looks at the changing role of women in Canada since the early twentieth century. The original film starts with a title card on which is written, "Let's go back to the days when the hand that rocks the cradle was shaking the world." It then evokes the actions of the suffragettes in the United States and Great Britain. The French version, however, opens with a very different title card: "Des femmes qui s'en vont à la besogne aussi capablement et d'une si belle humeur [...] il n'y en a pas beaucoup, Maria." This quote from *Maria Chapdelaine*, a novel by Louis Hémon published in 1916, may have resonated with French-Canadian viewers, but it has little connection to the subsequent images of suffragettes, and the reference to "berceaux" (cradles) in the title is no longer connected to anything specific in the film.

In these three instances, the translator's intervention served to establish and strengthen communication with French-Canadian viewers – as much as it was possible to even reach these viewers, given that Premier Maurice Duplessis prohibited the showing of NFB documentaries in Quebec schools and instructed the censor board to limit distribution of what he considered the NFB's "Communist" films during most of the 1950s (Lever 141–2). The French versions contributed to the struggle of francophones at the National Film Board to affirm their identity and autonomy and, as such, can be seen as part of the larger social context that would grow into Quebec nationalism. The shifts in the translation process generally fall within the bounds of accepted translation practice: the replacement of characters' names with ones from the target culture is a fairly common strategy; the substitution of one on-screen text for another, such as an image of a newspaper with French headlines for the original image, is an effective way to avoid the awkward situation in which subtitles are present at the same time as text. At the same time, it is clear from these films and others for which Bobet produced the French version that he was not constrained by notions of accuracy and fidelity to the original.

After proposing the notion of bricolage to characterize Jacques Bobet's inventiveness in the face of an indifferent yet tolerant NFB administration, Jean-Daniel Lafond comments, "Jacques Bobet sets out a morality based on *détournement,* a freedom that draws on ruse" (7, author's translation). This concept of détournement may provide another clue to understanding Bobet's approach. The term originated with the Situationist International, an influential European artistic and political movement that developed a critique of capitalism and consumer society in the 1960s. It refers to the re-use of existing artistic elements in a new work to alter the message and critique or subvert the original. In cinema, détournement was put into practice by René Viénet, who in 1972 released *La dialectique peut-elle casser des briques?* – the "French version" of a Hong Kong martial-arts film remixed with humorous new dialogue that celebrated the revolt of the proletarian masses against an oppressive bourgeoisie (Chollet 90–1). While Bobet did not go as far as to claim to be creating new work, his assertion of "equal dignity" between version and original seemed to allow a creative approach to translation that considered the resulting work not as derivative but as a product in its own right.

If the first three instances of translator's intervention can be considered to fall within the bounds of common practice, this was not always the case in Bobet's versions. Following the passage of the National Film Act in 1950, Arthur Irwin, the new NFB commissioner, developed a low-budget series called *Faces of Canada / Silhouettes canadiennes* that showed individuals from various walks of life and different regions of Canada. The fourteen Canadians portrayed included a blacksmith, a charwoman, a sexton, a lock-keeper, and a taxi driver. Some of the films were made in English and versioned into French, while others were originally in French and versioned into English. One film in the series, *Paul Tomkowicz: Street-railway Switchman* (*Paul Tomkowicz: Nettoyeur d'aiguillages*), directed by Roman Kroitor in 1954, has achieved considerable success and remains in distribution today. It follows Polish immigrant Paul Tomkowicz through a night of work in the winter cold of Winnipeg, where his job for the past twenty-three years has been to keep the streetcar rail-switches clear of ice and snow. Carrying a bucket of salt, a lamp, and a broom, he spends the night going from one switch to the next, sweeping and salting. In the morning, he heads to a lunch counter for a well-deserved breakfast of coffee, bread, sausages, and boiled eggs.

The narration is based on Tomkowicz's own words and read by actor Tom Tweed in a heavy Polish accent: "Winnipeg's all right. In Winnipeg you can go in the streets – daytime, nighttime. Nobody is bother you [*sic*]. My sister wrote me from my village in Poland: the soldiers came in the night. They got 29 people. My brother, my brother's wife. Why they do that? I don't know." The film is clearly situated in time and place, with its reference to Winnipeg and wartime Europe. However, the French version of the narration, written by Jacques Bobet and voiced by Jean Duceppe, refers to Tomkowicz solely in the third person and turns him into an entirely mythical figure, disconnected from the world around: "Cet homme, bâti comme Hercule, transporte un fanal, comme Diogène, et un balai comme les sorcières. Ce sont aussi les attributs du nettoyeur d'aiguillages."

More surprisingly, the French version moves the action from Winnipeg to Ottawa: "Un tramway qui doit tourner à gauche ne doit pas tourner à droite. À gauche, c'est Ottawa, l'Ontario, la langue anglaise. À droite, ce sont les ponts, la ville de Hull, la province du Québec. On va à droite ou on va à gauche." What can explain this out-of-the-blue reference to the dividing line between Ontario and Quebec – with the implication that no French is spoken west of Hull – in a film about an immigrant Canadian that is explicitly set in Winnipeg? Director Roman Kroitor was not informed of the change and, in fact, only found out about it forty-six years later, when Richard Hancox interviewed him in 2000 while researching an article on the film (16). Hancox points out that Winnipeg is significant in Canadian discourse because it represents the linking of eastern and western Canada through the "space-binding technology of the railroad" (22). The French version, by contrast, "reassigned the street-railway switchman to the role of *uncoupling* at a divisional point – the Ottawa River border of Quebec and Ontario – rather than letting him continue *connecting* the rest of Canada at its western 'gateway'" (23, original emphasis).

This "reassignment" of Tomkowicz's location was no doubt rationalized by the producers of the French version by the need to call attention to the reality of Quebec. However valid that objective might have been in a general sense, the elimination of the Polish immigrant's own words, his memories of the horrors of war in Europe, and his reflections on his lonely life in Winnipeg results in a distortion of the film's meaning. Furthermore, the altered narration strips the central character – who, unlike those in other *Faces of Canada* films like *The Sexton* and *The Village Notary*, is identified by name as well as by trade – of his individuality. Instead, it emphasizes the routine and banality of his life: "Toutes les nuits, depuis 23 ans, il songe à la Pologne. C'est une nostalgie sans tristesse. Il a pris l'habitude de songer à la Pologne, entre deux aiguillages, et voilà tout." Indeed, the narrator seems to have little to say and resorts to repeating the obvious, as when, over a shot of Tomkowicz wiping his nose, the narrator comments, "Il en profite aussi pour se moucher" – going against one of the basic tenets of narration writing that says it should complement and add to the image rather than duplicate it (Rabiger 241).

This is a case where the translator's interventionist strategy deliberately alters an essential element of the original work. The struggle to redress the imbalance between versions and original French production led to a détournement of English films, which became – like the archival footage used in the English-language compilation films – raw material to be adapted at will in order to express Québécois reality and appeal to local audiences.

After supervising versions for a decade, Jacques Bobet moved on to a role as producer of original French-language films, where he continued to take advantage of the "hands-off" attitude of the NFB administration. The influence he had acquired through some of the translation effects detailed above no doubt encouraged him to nurture the groundbreaking work of a generation of Quebec filmmakers: the French Unit directors had gained confidence through their work on versions and this helped them get projects approved for original productions (Bobet, "Aux innocents les mains libres" 9). Yet these accomplishments came at a price, one that only becomes evident when we examine the shifts in meaning that occur in certain versions supervised by Bobet: the original English-language works were stripped of their cultural specificity and recontextualized for a Quebec audience.

Notes

1 The annual reports and internal documents indicate that the term "version" refers specifically to language versions; "revision" refers to re-edits of films for other modes of distribution, as when a theatrically released film is revised for television broadcast; and "adaptation" refers to more extensively adapted language versions, such as when a script is re-shot with new actors.

2 Personal communication, Christian Ruel, assistant director, Technical Innovations and Resources, National Film Board of Canada, 15 June 2009.

Works Cited

Ascheid, Antje. "Speaking Tongues: Voice Dubbing in the Cinema as Cultural Ventriloquism." *Velvet Light Trap* 40 (Fall 1997): 32–42.

Bobet, Jacques. "Les racines cachées." Ed. Carol Faucher. *La production française à l'ONF: 25 ans en perspective.* Montréal: Cinémathèque québécoise, 1984, 13–19.

– "Aux innocents les mains libres." *Lumières* 19 (été 1989): 7–10.

Canada. *An Act Respecting the National Film Board. Statutes of Canada.* Ottawa: Queen's Printer and Controller of Stationery, 1950.

Careers and Cradles (Carrières et berceaux). Dir. Jack Olsen. 11 min. 1947.

Chollet, Laurent. *Les situationnistes: L'utopie incarnée.* Paris: Gallimard, 2004.

Druick, Zoë. *Projecting Canada: Government Policy and Documentary Film at the National Film Board.* Montreal and Kingston: McGill-Queen's University Press, 2007.

Evans, Gary. *In the National Interest: A Chronicle of the National Film Board of Canada from 1949 to 1989*. Toronto: University of Toronto Press, 1991.

Farewell Oak Street (Adieu, rue des Chênes). Dir. Grant McLean. 17 min. 1953.

Goetz, William. "The Canadian Wartime Documentary: *Canada Carries On* and *The World in Action*." *Cinema Journal* 16: 2 (1977): 59–80.

Hancox, Richard. "Geography and Myth in *Paul Tomkowicz*: Coordinates of National Identity." Ed. Jim Leach and Jeannette Sloniowski. *Candid Eyes: Essays on Canadian Documentaries*. Toronto: University of Toronto Press, 2003, 13–30.

Lafond, Jean-Daniel. "L'O.N.F. et la naissance du cinéma direct: pour mémoire … Petit éloge du producteur en bricoleur intelligent." *Lumières* 19 (été 1989): 6–7.

Lever, Yves. *Anastasie ou la censure du cinéma au Québec*. Québec: Septentrion, 2008.

Mcintosh, Andrew. "Jacques Bobet." *The Canadian Film Encyclopedia*. The Film Reference Library, Toronto International Film Festival Group. 2004. Accessed 25 May 2009. http://www.filmreferencelibrary.ca

Morris, Peter. "After Grierson: The National Film Board, 1945–1953." Ed. Seth Feldman. *Take Two*. Toronto: Irwin, 1984, 182–94.

National Film Board of Canada. "Politique sur les versions de l'ONF." Accessed 30 May 2008. http://www.nfb.ca

– Accessed 25 May 2009. http://www.nfb.ca

Paul Tomkowicz: Street-railway Switchman (Paul Tomkowicz: Nettoyeur d'aiguillages). Dir. Roman Kroitor. 9 min. 1953.

Rabiger, Michael. *Directing the Documentary*. 2nd ed. Boston: Focal Press, 1992.

Toronto Boom Town (Toronto: Ville champignon). Dir. Leslie McFarlane. 10 min. 1951.

Véronneau, Pierre. *Résistance et affirmation: La production Francophone à l'ONF 1939–1964*. Montréal: Cinémathèque québécoise, 1987.

– "Early Activities of the Francophone Group at the National Film Board." *A Celebration of Canada's Arts, 1930–1970*. Ed. Glen Carruthers and Gordana Lazarevich. Toronto: Canadian Scholars' Press, 1996.

3

October 2006: *Territoires et trajectoires* Is Launched in Montreal and "Cultural Race Politics" Are Introduced to Quebec

Sherry Simon

Territoires et trajectoires is the title of the French translation of *13 Conversations about Art and Cultural Race Politics*, a book of interviews on the topic of art and race politics in Canada from the 1980s onwards. These slim volumes were both published by Artextes Editions (or Éditions Artextes) in Montreal, the English version in 2002 and the French version in 2006 – when it was launched at a well-attended event at the Galerie la Centrale in Montreal. Monika Kin Gagnon, writer, critic, curator, and professor at Concordia University, and Richard Fung, prominent Toronto video artist and professor at the Ontario College of Art and Design, the book's editors, were present at the launch and participated in a panel discussion. The debate, like the book itself, focused on the way that questions of cultural identity within minority groups such as Asian Canadians, First Nations, and African Canadians had influenced the art that had been produced and exhibited by these groups. In their book, Gagnon and Fung asked artists, critics, and curators to reflect on their experiences at the intersection between race and art, and to look back at a decade of heady activism and debate. Conversations between the two editors are interspersed with the interviews. The discussions evoke a set of ideals, strategies, and actions that take on a shape and a retrospective coherence.

What makes the French version of this book significant and unusual is the aim and mode of its translation. The same firm published both the English and French versions – a singular event in itself. Artextes Editions specializes in contemporary art theory. Its website defined the "Prendre parole" collection as "Critically engaged and at times polemical [...] The collection was introduced to provide artists and intellectuals with a forum for discussing topical ideas related to the arts," and most of the publications (a modest 15 or so in all since 1982) are produced in both English and French. The translation/adaptation of this volume is by Colette Tougas, who has been active in the art world over the past twenty-five years as a curator, translator, editor, production coordinator, and publisher, particularly in visual arts, media arts, and dance. She was managing editor of the influential arts journal *Parachute* and has translated many articles and catalogues. And so it can be inferred that Tougas' participation in the translation might well be that of a participant, fully aware of the issues of the art world and the particular scene being discussed. And, indeed, as Gagnon explained during the discussion, conversation between editor and translator did influence some of the translation choices.

As a critic of the visual arts, Gagnon demonstrates a rare sensitivity to language issues. In her expanded preface to the French edition, she explains that her own background in both Quebec and English-speaking Canada, her own displacements across Canada and abroad, made her attentive to the zones of non-equivalence between the two languages and between the two artistic milieux. Part of the aim of the translation was to draw attention to the very process of translation – and to the way it would reveal the distinctive characteristics of the two artistic cultures. Language disturbances were not to be neutralized or flattened out. In order to create a resonance for the conversations within the Quebec context, she chose to add two new interviews to those already in the book, with Sylvie Paré and Gaetane Verna – curators who work in Quebec and who have special insights into the work of First Nations artists and artists of colour, respectively. Rather than simply conveying to a francophone audience the content of debates that had preoccupied the artistic communities of English Canada, rather than simply *reporting* on issues that had been in the forefront there, Gagnon notes that her desire was to create a "cultural translation" of the original work. By this she means that her intent is to extend these debates into the Quebec context. Therefore, the conversation begun by Gagnon and Fung now aimed to include Montreal and the cultural politics of Quebec. If the ferment within the art world in English-speaking Canada over race politics had taken place mainly in Toronto and Vancouver, if it had not been replicated within Quebec, if there was in fact as yet no similar movement of ideas in Quebec, no equivalent for the "cultural race politics" that have been invented in English Canada, then such equivalence could perhaps be imagined – and stimulated into existence through the work of translation.

Territoires et trajectoires can, therefore, be understood as a work of "activist translation." This is a term whose parameters can be very broad. All translations to some extent carry the imprint of the translator, but these are often subtle turns of tone or vocabulary. What turns a translation into a form of activism? More than subjective interventions, activism refers to work by translators that is shaped by a pattern of social or political beliefs. Over the course of the twentieth century, cultural politics has involved the struggle for the recognition of collective identities, based on nation, language, social class, or gender. Translation has become an ally in representing, reinscribing, or reinforcing these identities, such as those promoted by feminism, First Nations, and national minority groups. Translated texts contribute to these struggles by reanimating a neglected past, by valorizing marginalized languages or text-types (such as oral literature), and by introducing innovative forms of writing or vocabulary into the new language system. Translations are a form of engagement when the necessary partiality of translation becomes *partisan*, when translators adopt advocacy roles in order to promote progressive social agendas.

Unlike books that are translated into another language with a purely informational intention ("this book will inform you of the ideas and debates taking place elsewhere"), activist translations have a more proactive intention. They wish to open a discussion with a new public. The process of achieving equivalence becomes complex. Because the equivalent sensibilities and institutions do not yet exist in the receiving culture, the terms must be invented. An "as if" situation is created through neologisms or through unusual uses of syntax or rhetorical effects. Translation in this sense can be considered performative: it creates its own reality through the stating of it.

Among areas of activist translation in Canada (translation of First Nations literature and community interpretation and advocacy in the areas of fragile subjects such as refugees, hospital patients, members of minority groups involved with institutions of state authority like the police and the courts), the area of activist translation most theorized has been feminist literary translation of the 1980s and 1990s (see Alessandra Capperdoni's contribution to this volume). Because activist translation is animated by explicit social, aesthetic, and ideological goals, it carries an agenda of desired effects. These effects can be the immediate solution to a crisis situation (in the case of community interpreting) or more long-term goals of justice for fragile and suffering people. In the case of texts that argue for or demonstrate a new social position through art (literature or visual art), the effect would be a change in attitudes, in the conceptualization of agency, in writing styles, in sensibilities. For feminist translation, one could point to effects in the form of translations that stimulate similar production in the new language, for instance, the writing of Daphne Marlatt as influenced by conversations with the work of Nicole Brossard.

In her remarks during the panel presentation, Gagnon made frequent mention of the discussions she had had with Tougas, the translator. What were the words that stopped the flow of conversation? How did these obstacles turn out to be the seeds of new conversations? Some of the problematic words mentioned were "white supremacy," "politically correct" (terms that are not translated but reproduced in the French text, in italics; see *13 Conversations about Art and Cultural Race Politics* 175), "Black power," "cultural studies" – realities that were powerfully articulated within the English-speaking world at a specific historical moment. The most problematic term for the translator, however, was the central issue in the book: the question of "race" and particularly "cultural race politics." This term is used by Gagnon in *Other Conundrums* to replace "identity politics," a term that Gagnon considers problematic in its automatic assumptions about the easy relation of an individual to a pre-identified community. "Cultural race politics" insists, rather, on the interdependence of the separate words, on the way each of these terms informs the other culture, race, politics. What expression in French could convey the same insistence on the interdependence of these ideas; what term could account for the mix of theoretical critique and activism that has vivified the visual arts scene in English-speaking Canada? The solution devised by Tougas and Gagnon is to invent a phrase "la politique racio-culturelle" – a pure invention that signals the absence of any more "natural" or already existing equivalent. Although it appears artificial, because it *is* a neologism, the term effectively highlights a zone of non-equivalence in the relation between English Canada and Quebec. Since the 1980s, the politics of race has been a powerful stimulant in the production and exhibition of the visual arts in cities like Toronto and Vancouver. The extent of this ferment is detailed in the contributions by Fung, for instance, who explains the changes that cultural race politics have brought about at all levels of artistic production and diffusion. The activism of the late 1980s was produced by a particular confluence of energies, which included British-inspired cultural studies, progressive organizations and journals, festivals, government programs, etc.

By contrast, "cultural race politics" in Quebec has not been taken up to the same degree or within the same type of debate. One could argue, in fact, that the question of "cultural race politics" clearly traces the separate contours of social discourse in the two language communities. In the writing world, for instance, while the "Women and Words" conference of 1983 had brought together and stimulated collaboration between Quebec and English-speaking Canada, the controversial "Writing thru Race" conference organized by Roy Miki in 1994 did not have its equivalent in Quebec, nor did it have a similar resonance. Used liberally in artistic debate in English, the term "race" rarely appears in similar discourse communities in Quebec. The recently published report of the Bouchard-Taylor Commission on "Reasonable Accommodation" in Quebec – the fruits of a lengthy consultation process during which the topic of race (as well as racist outbursts) were made public – interestingly, adopts a neologism, "groupes racisés" (no doubt a translation of "racialized"), to designate groups previously referred to as visible minorities.[1] This is an indication of the rapidly evolving vocabulary of cultural relations, but also of the relative absence of public discussion on questions of race politics in Quebec.

One of the effects that translation can have is to draw attention to the historical evolution of structures of discourse and thought across language systems.[2] Such an investigation would show how the use of "race" in English and French in Canada has diverged in the context of their respective discourse communities during the past twenty years. Both Gagnon and Fung speculate in the original text on the different reasons that may have caused this divergence. Gagnon suggests the most obvious of these explanations when she says, "I also think that the language issue within Quebec has displaced more complex discussions around race, ethnicity and cultural difference" (*13 Conversations* 81). She explains that powerful tropes, like the east-west division in Montreal impose a certain geography of immigration which has excluded certain communities, like the Chinese who lived below Sherbrooke Street on a lesser-explored section of Boulevard Saint-Laurent – and who therefore have been absent from the narrative that sees Saint-Laurent as the historic home of immigrant communities like the Jewish, Portuguese, and Italian communities. Fung acknowledges that while certain strains of Quebec nationalism have been progressive (83) and Quebec cultural protectionism is important, other strains of nationalism have been less inclusive. He is no doubt referring here to the entrenched expressions of "ethnic nationalism," which have found mouthpieces at various times in right-wing political parties (or fractions of parties), journals (*Action nationale*), and organizations (la Société Saint-Jean-Baptiste). In the French version, Gagnon has added a paragraph to acknowledge that the cultural situation in Quebec has changed remarkably over the last decades and, in particular, since the defeat of the 1995 referendum. Referring to the increasingly mixed populations of post–Law 101 francophones, she notes that this generation now composes a crucial political force to be reckoned with (*Territoires et trajectoires* 105).

It would be appropriate here to introduce additional elements that might further clarify the reasons for the absence of an equivalent for "cultural race politics" in Quebec. These elements can be drawn from the discursive history of the cluster of terms: "race," "ethnicity," and "people." "Race" in Quebec was long associated with "la race canadienne-française," sometimes a neutral word, sometimes used with its unsavoury associations of ethnic purity, moral-cultural superiority, and economic inferiority (as epitomized in the work of Lionel Groulx). Discredited in favour of new definitions of territorial citizenship, the term "race" has been neglected and marginalized rather than redefined. In the recently published and authoritative *Histoire de la littérature québécoise*, written by Michel Biron, Elisabeth Nardout-Lafarge, and François Dumont (2007), the only entry for "race" is a historical reference to the earlier French-Canadian meaning and no updated meaning. This does not go to say, however, that Quebec literature has not been attentive to the contributions of Black writers. In fact, the real presence and influence of Haitian writers has occurred to a large extent without the intervention of the notion of race despite Dany Laferrière's notorious focus on race issues in his book *How to Make Love to a Negro* and Gérard Etienne's scholarly study of race in Quebec literature (*La question raciale et raciste dans le roman québécois*). Significant entries in the *Histoire de la literature québécoise* for Emile Ollivier and Dany Laferrière duly note the extensive influence that writers of Haitian origin have had in Quebec. Nevertheless, these entries are not cross-listed with any reference to race (or to ethnicity) but rather subsumed under the category of "écriture migrante" – the term that gained immediate currency in the 1990s and that encompasses writers of diverse origins who write in French in Quebec. In the *Bibliography of Comparative Studies in Canadian, Québec and Foreign Literatures* (www.compcanlit.ca), a search for the category of "race" yielded 144 results, with the overwhelming majority of entries (all save three or four) in English. This is to say that the notion of "race" has not yet emerged as a crucial element of the vocabulary of francophone literary critics.

That the terms for cultural identities do not align between French-language Quebec and English-language Canada can be further contextualized through reference to the term "ethnic." The debates around cultural identity in Quebec crystallized from the 1960s to the 1980s around the term "ethnie." The notion of "classe-ethnie" or "peuple-ethnie" was developed in the 1960s and 1970s by Quebec thinkers to refer to French-Canadian inferiorization as economic and cultural (Marcel Rioux). Theories of decolonization saw French Canadians become the "Nègres blancs d'Amérique," in the wildly successful term invented by Pierre Vallières (see Julia McDonagh's contribution in this volume). Quebecers identified with Blacks, especially the Blacks of French colonies and, in particular, the Algerians of Frantz Fanon's *Wretched of the Earth*. Comparisons between Québécois and militant Black groups were frequent, and Gérald Godin, for instance, compares *joual* to the "jive-talk" of American Blacks, noting that Québécois writers are simply imitating a tactic successfully used first by Blacks (Siemerling 128). A major discursive transformation occurred in the early 1980s when "ethnique" was applied no longer to the situation of French Canadians within Canada, but to the public emergence of immigrant communities as players on the Quebec political and cultural scene. By the 1980s, "groupes ethniques" or "communautés culturelles" were used to refer to the non-French and non-Anglo minorities in Quebec. Central to this transformation was a sea-change in the self-perception of Quebec, which, with the victory of the Parti québécois in 1976 and cultural measures implemented to ensure the primacy of the French language (Law 101 and other policies such as Godin's "Autant de manières d'être québécois" in 1983), adopted the position of the majority culture and acknowledged the existence of minority cultures within the province.

As a relatively recent import into Quebec cultural debates, the notion of ethnicity did not receive the same confirmation in Quebec social science and literary terminology as it did in the Anglo-Saxon world (Simon, *L'in-*

scription sociale de la traduction au Québec 26–48; Simon and Leahy, "La recherche au Québec portant sur l'écriture ethnique"). The prominence of theoretical models, such as those of Lyotard, Deleuze, Derrida, and Scarpetta, promoted a language of anti-essentialism. The journal *Vice versa* was influential in turning discussion away from political issues of representation (related to both ethnicity and race) and concentrating, instead, on undermining all categories of cultural identity including that of the white Québecois (see Siemerling 120–33). "Métissage" and "transculturalism" had extensive currency in Quebec during the 1990s well before they migrated into the English language. "Transculture," in particular, deflected questions of ethnicity to broader critiques of identity. The importance of the Haitian community within these debates must be underlined. As an exile community in Quebec since the 1970s, Haitian writers enjoyed real prominence. Neither Emile Ollivier nor Dany Laferrière, for example, engaged in confrontational language on race (the less prominent writer Gérard Etienne was perhaps a notable exception).

It has been argued that the rapid and successful entry of terms like "métissage" and "transculturalism" had the effect of blunting social critique. Monika Kin Gagnon wonders whether "métissage" had the effect of "softening" a history that "in particular in relation to native peoples in their relation to the French" has often been violent (*13 Conversations* 131). Indeed, cultural critic Simon Harel claims that the swift acceptance of "métissage" and "transculture" into the debate on culture difference in Quebec promoted a too-consensual and euphoric idea of social harmony (*Les passages obligés de l'écriture migrante*).

These elements of discourse on cultural identity in Quebec help to explain how the concept of race politics was marginalized in Quebec – and questions of racialization collapsed into the general category of métissage. These are factors that help delineate the differing structures of discourse around cultural identity that developed in English-speaking Canada and in Quebec – and the fact that social movements do not necessarily occur in a temporal or spatial alignment, in particular, in terms of the visual arts. This non-alignment is not necessarily related to the more general question of racism. Both cultures must be recognized as racist, and there is no gain to be made in determining which milieu is more racist than another.

Paradoxically, although the translation of *13 Conversations* adopts an activist strategy in the text, the choice of title is somewhat discordant.

Territoires et trajectoires illustrates the ways in which cultural difference has been pulled in the direction of abstraction within the Quebec milieu. Rather than using the term "race," rather than creating a list in which race is linked to a nexus of terms (art, culture, race, politics) suggesting the powerful imbrication of art within inescapable constraints, the French presents plurals of possibility. *Territoires et trajectoires* well reflects the Quebec discursive context, where the fortune of such similar terms as "traversées" and "transculture" sustain both an elegant rhetoric of form and militate against such confrontational terms as politics and race. The translation of the title, by conforming to the rhetorical norms of French-language discourse, therefore, seems to contradict the approach taken in the text. Here the cultural and linguistic norms of Quebec have prevailed, erasing the confrontational intentions of the original title. The choice of a new cover illustration (a montage by Ramona Ramlochand bringing together a territory and a trajectory: an image juxtaposing the open spaces of the desert, a Land Rover in motion, and an urban streetlight) and the trimmer more mellifluous title acknowledges the new readership.

The significance of the translation of these conversations is enhanced by the fact that few literary works have yet appeared in French by English-Canadian writers who problematize issues of race politics. A similar gap exists in the other direction, as many of Quebec's writers of minority origin have yet to be translated into English. This means that, inevitably, there will be a skewing in the image of alterity that each group presents to the other.

This modest book and its translation have important implications for the transmission of cultural debates within a framework of conflictual sites of meaning-creation. Encouraging the reader to take note of the gap between two sociopolitical contexts, translation pushes towards change. The activist translator argues for a new consciousness of the way art is produced and displayed in societies marked by intractable differences.

Notes

1 The official web page of the Bouchard-Taylor Commission defines the mandate of the commission as follows:

On 8 February 2007, Quebec Premier Jean Charest announced the establishment of the Consultation Commission on Accommodation Practices

Related to Cultural Differences in response to public discontent over reasonable accommodation. The Order in Council establishing the Commission stipulates that it has a mandate to:

- take stock of accommodation practices in Québec;
- analyse the attendant issues bearing in mind the experience of other societies;
- conduct an extensive consultation on this topic; and
- formulate recommendations to the government to ensure that accommodation practices conform to the values of Québec society as a pluralistic, democratic, egalitarian society.

The Commission's mandate, as defined, could be broached in two ways, in a broad sense or in a narrower sense. The narrower sense would consist in confining the Commission's deliberations to the strictly legal dimension of reasonable accommodation. This notion, which stems from labour-related jurisprudence, designates a form of arrangement or relaxation aimed at combatitng the discrimination that a seemingly neutral norm can bring about in its effect, usually an infringement of an individual's right to equality. In general language, the meaning of the concept has gone beyond this legal definition and encompasses all forms of arrangements allowed by managers in public or private institutions in respect of students, patients, customers, employees, and so on.

The second approach to the Commission's mandate would be to perceive the debate on reasonable accommodation as the symptom of a more basic problem concerning the sociocultural integration model established in Quebec since the 1970s. This perspective calls for a review of interculturalism, immigration, secularism, and the theme of Quebec identity. The Commission has decided to follow the second course with a view to grasping the problem at its sources and examining it from every angle.

2 One of the most compelling efforts to mobilize the importance of translation to this end is the dictionary of European thought edited by Barbara Cassin. This *Vocabulaire européen des philosophies: Dictionnaire des intraduisibles* shows how the aporia of translation can be windows into the history of concepts, and how the difficulties of translation can be productive in revealing the differential histories of thought within a linguistic community. Taking as entries philosophical terms from a dozen languages, Cassin uses these "intraduisibles" as the basis of a contrastive history of European philosophy. Under the entry "peuple," for instance, there is a discussion of the differences and similarities among the

Greek, Latin, German, English, and French variants of the terms "people,"
"race," "nation" – with the warning that the notion of race is ineluctably
linked to theories that make the war among races the principal driving force
of history (918).

Works Cited

Biron, Michel, Elisabeth Nardout-Lafarge, and François Dumont. *Histoire de la
littérature québécoise*. Montréal: Boréal, 2007.

Bouchard-Taylor Commission. Commission de consultation sur les pratiques d'ac-
commodement reliées aux différences culturelles. Government of Quebec 2008.
Accessed 26 Dec. 2009. http://www.accommodements.qc.ca/index-en.html. Path:
Commission; Mandate.

Cassin, Barbara, ed. *Vocabulaire européen des philosophies: Dictionnaire des intraduisibles*. Paris: Seuil/Le Robert, 2004.

Etienne, Gérard. *La question raciale et raciste dans le roman québécois*. Montreal:
Balzac, 1995.

Gagnon, Monika Kin, and Richard Fung, eds. With contributions by Cameron
Bailey, Dana Claxton, Karma Clarke-Davis, Andrea Fatona, Sharon Fernandez,
Gaylene Gould, Richard William Hill, Ken Lum, Scott Toguri McFarlane, Alanis
Obomsawin, and Kerri Sakamoto. *13 Conversations about Art and Cultural
Race Politics*. Montréal: Artextes Editions–Prendre parole, 2002.

– Trans. and adapt. Colette Tougas. With contributions by Karma Clarke-Davis,
Dana Claxton, Andrea Fatona, Sharon Fernandez, Gaylene Gould, Richard
William Hill, Ken Lum, Scott Toguri McFarlane, Alanis Obomsawin, Sylvia Paré,
Kerri Sakamoto, and Gaetane Verna. *Territoires et trajectoires: 14 dialogues sur
l'art et les constructions raciales, culturelles et identitaires*. Montréal: Éditions
Artextes–Prendre parole, 2006.

Harel, Simon. *Les passages obligés de l'écriture migrante*. Montréal: XYZ, 2005.

Laferrière, Dany. *How to Make Love to a Negro*. Trans. David Homel. Toronto:
Coach House, 1987.

Siemerling, Winfried. *The New North American Studies*. London: Routledge,
2005.

Simon, Sherry. "Espaces incertains de la culture." *Fictions de l'identitaire au
Québec*. Eds. Pierre L'Hérault, Robert Schwartzwald, Sherry Simon, and Alexis
Nouss. Montréal: XYZ, 1991, 13–52.

– *L'inscription sociale de la traduction au Québec*. Montréal: Office de la Langue française, 1989.

– and David Leahy. "La recherche au Québec portant sur l'écriture ethnique." *Ethnicity and Culture in Canada: The Research Landscape*. Eds. J.W. Berry and J.A. Laponce. Toronto: University of Toronto Press, 1994, 387–409.

4

June 2007: Quebec Politicians Debate a Bill to Impose Strict Controls on Audiovisual Translation, and Fail to Pass It

Luise von Flotow

In June 2007, a noisy scandal erupted in Quebec on the topic of film dubbing. It was set off by a politician's reaction to the synchronization (or dubbing) "made in France" of an animated Hollywood film for children: *Shrek the Third*. A rather strange topic for such an outcry, this was the third in a series of children's movies constructed around a green ogre who sets out with a noisy donkey at his side to free his swamp of various fairy tale creatures, and meets love in the process. Due to the distribution policies of Dreamworks/Paramount studios, these English-language Hollywood movies are dubbed in France, and then distributed in Quebec. And the version of French used to dub the film is what raised the ire of local conservative Quebec politician Mario Dumont (Action démocratique), to such an extent that he mobilized the media and sought to address the problem with legislative solutions. Claiming that the French (which he described as Parisian slang) used in the dubbing was incomprehensible for his and other children in Quebec, he tabled a bill that would require all movies distributed in Quebec to be dubbed in Quebec, or not shown at all (CTVM.info).

While Dumont objected, in particular, to the "incomprehensible" French slang used in *Shrek the Third*, many other aspects of French dubbing annoy Quebec audiences: regional French expressions, French syntax, French pronunciation, and the pitch of the actors' voices which is much higher and more "pointu," more hectic. Dumont's bill did not go far in the Assemblée nationale in Quebec City, since it did not have the support of Christine St-Pierre, the minister of culture who, instead, dispatched a representative to Hollywood to try to broker a deal with the major studios that would encourage them to dub their work specifically for Quebec audiences.

Still, the controversy served to once again heat up opinions in Quebec on the French versions of contemporary English-language audiovisual materials (largely feature films and TV series). It allowed journalists to give once again their favourite examples of unacceptable Franco-French language and to call for dubbing "made in Quebec."

Yet, dubbing "made in Quebec" is not always the best solution either, as the following uproar attests. In 1999, an American TV series, *Ally McBeal*, about the lives and times of young lawyers in Boston, was bought by Quebec's TVA, dubbed into Québécois, and scheduled to run at 8 p.m. in the evenings, at the same time as the National Hockey League playoffs. The acquisition and airing of this "délicieuse série américaine" was considered a good idea by local TV reporters. According to many, however, it was less of a good idea to present this program dubbed into Quebec French. Louise Cousineau, a journalist specialized in TV explains:

> Je n'ai rien contre les séries québécoises qui parlent notre langue. Elles expriment notre identité et si elles parlaient un français trop pointu, elles n'auraient aucune crédibilité. Mais quand j'entends un personnage étranger dire, "J'me suis encore mis les pieds din plats," ça ne passe pas. Depuis le temps que nous voyons des séries doublées nous nous sommes fait l'oreille à un français international. (D2)

This reaction is not untypical of those expressed in countless letters to the editor on the topic of audiovisual work dubbed into any form of Québécois. The tolerance level is low. Quebec French is reserved for local productions, where it provides a credible reflection of local "identity" in that very specific space of TV series or feature films set in Quebec.[1] In any other audiovisual texts, it is not deemed appropriate for "strangers" to use Québécois French.[2] Indeed, the discourse around French-language dubbing in Quebec often gets highly charged and laced with issues of identity, cultural politics, and aesthetics that can coagulate around a thematic of "them and us," "foreigners and locals," and "our language." The *Ally McBeal* controversy grew quite heated, with journalists, television viewers, and representatives of the TV and dubbing industries weighing in, until the Québécois version was withdrawn and replaced three years later with the version dubbed in France.

Neither Franco-French nor Québécois seem to work well as a dubbing language in Quebec. The required norm on screen is, in fact, "international French," as every dubbing studio in Montreal will confirm.[3] This is the most neutral, and least irritating, form of the language. But this option, too, is subject to virulent criticism, mainly by Quebec film buffs who find it so drab and colourless and weak that it cannot do justice to emotions, expressive outbursts of any kind, or any constructed film dialogue. They claim it destroys the filmic experience.[4] The industry, on the other hand, imposes it, and even furnishes dubbing translators with lists of expressions and terms that are prohibited in the dubbing process in order to ensure the bland neutrality of the dialogue.[5]

The discourses around audiovisual translation, specifically dubbing, in Quebec have a forty-year history and regularly erupt into scandals and parliamentary debates, never moving completely out of the media. They serve for regular political uproars, amendments to laws and regulations, and numerous letters to the editors, websites, and blogs. The question is which French to use. At least three versions of French are deployed for the purposes of dubbing for Quebec audiences. The controversies around them, and their histories and outcomes reflect Quebec society's extremely complex relationship with language. And the dominant policy – of dubbing into "neutral" international French – is doubtless implemented for a very specific effect.

Dubbing in Quebec

Film dubbing has a short history in Quebec. It dates from the late 1960s when the call for "le français sur nos écrans" began to bear fruit. This was a response to a no longer acceptable situation, namely, the distribution during the 1940s, 1950s, and 1960s of increasing numbers of popular American film products throughout the province, with only a rare French (dubbed-in-France) version appearing as late as a year afterward (Gill and Longpré 9). In other words, film became one of the most important public entertainments but French versions were scarce, foreign-sounding, and poorly distributed. Foreign film (largely Hollywood film that still makes up over 90 per cent of Quebec imports – see the report by Gill and Longpré on *L'industrie du doublage au Québec,* published by SODEC[6]) was first and foremost shown in English. Further, even the French films that came to Quebec were often dubbed into English, and distributed only in English. French-language films, made in Canada, were rare, and National Film Board productions were largely prohibited by the Duplessis government as "Communist" materials (see the contribution by Christine York to this volume). Small wonder that dubbing made-in-Quebec became an issue, and that Quebec's Loi sur le cinéma (1975) included a (now much reviewed) clause on film synchronization, which calls for all dubbing to be done in the province, a condition Dumont's failed 2007 bill also demanded, and a feature of the law that has never been enforced. But neither did the Loi sur le cinéma ever address the question of which French should be used in film translation, an issue that bundles a whole raft of questions about whether and how to control the quality of language with questions about cultural history, identity, and political power.

An important problem that affects the dubbing industry in Quebec is the stance assumed by France. It maintains a protectionist decree dating from 1949 (and reissued in 1961) that ensures that all foreign materials shown on French screens are dubbed in France.[7] While this position has had to soften in regard to the European Union, permitting dubbing done in Belgium, for example, it continues to exclude all work from Quebec, except English-Canadian film products which are the only Quebec dubbing allowed to circulate in France. This severe restriction doubtless has a negative effect on the dubbing industry in Quebec; however, it could be turned to good use and lead to a more localized form of dubbing that uses the local idiom and complies with research findings that audiences prefer "la langue de proximité" (Lampron). However, while this French decree limits distribution of Quebec-dubbed film, it also has provided useful arguments for substantial tax credits to support the industry in Quebec. These were established after repeated industry crises in the late 1980s and early 1990s, and now cover over 30 per cent of costs.

Cultural, Economic, and Linguistic Stakes

As early as 1969, a "Mémoire du comité de culture cinématographique," prepared for the Gendron Commission,[8] clearly connects the government's responsibilities for language and culture with the audiovisual. It casts film dubbing into French as an activity that will "safeguard" the local culture and argues that French-dubbed films will "donner un visage français dans les cinémas du Québec." Henceforth, French shall not only be the "langue de travail" of the province, but also it will become the "langue des loisirs." Such sentiments come up in many subsequent publications on dubbing – see, for example, the studies by the Institut québécois du cinéma (IQC), *Enquête sur la sortie des films dont la version originale est en langue anglaise* (1988); *Le français à l'écran* (1989); *La situation du français à l'écran et l'avenir de l'article 83* (1990); *Le français au grand écran en 1991* (1993). These documents take this cultural argument as their very foundation, reiterate the opening remarks in the Loi sur le cinéma – "Attendu que le cinéma constitue l'un des moyens les plus puissants d'expression et de diffusion de la culture; Attendu que le Québec se doit d'affirmer sa souveraineté dans ce domaine" (IQC, *La situation du français*, 10) – and conclude that the government's recognition of the power of cinema as a "véhicule d'un imaginaire collectif et de valeurs culturelles" must also accord importance to the language of cinema (ibid.).

Opinions on dubbing "made in France" often make this link between culture, language, and cinema. The IQC writes, "Le décret français crée chez nous une situation de 'colonialisme culturel,'" forcing "argot français" onto Quebec viewers, and imbibing "our" North American culture with a language and culture "qui ne nous ressemblent pas" (ibid., 13, 15). A further addition to this cultural strand comes from Quebec's Union des artistes (UDA) which argues that French-language cinema in Quebec is a must in order for immigrants to better acclimatize to the French-speaking culture of Quebec (*Mémoire de l'UDA*).

Analyses of the logistics and economics of film dubbing and distribution enter into many of the reports and studies produced over the past thirty years in Quebec. In the early years, they centred on the delay between the arrival of the English version of a film and that of the French-dubbed film from France, as well as on serious distribution problems (see CEGIR). In the 1970s, the Commission d'étude sur le cinéma et l'audiovisuel noted that, in fact, the French versions of films were not shown until the English version had run its course, which had the effect of privileging the English version, since audiences were in a hurry to see the new films and did not wait for the (poor) dubbed version. In the early 1980s, when VHS technology brought with it a sharp reduction in the number of cinemas, with many small-town movie houses closing down, the proportion of films shown in

French dropped dramatically – from 71.7 per cent to 53.5 per cent (IQC, *La situation du français*, 12). This had the effect of further reducing the variety of the films available in French, with only those expected to make more than $300,000 – "les films porteurs" – being considered to warrant the expense of dubbing in Quebec. In fact, much is made of the finances for dubbing and film distribution. Given the small francophone population, Hollywood distributors (with few exceptions) are loath to invest the tens of thousands of dollars required for dubbing, although they invest liberally in marketing. Quebec lobbyists and institutes have continued to insist that only government subsidies will improve the situation and meet the objective of "le français sur nos écrans" within a realistic time frame, and with an appropriate number of copies of each film available to reach out into the countryside and small towns in the language of the local population.

Throughout the reports and analyses around dubbing in Quebec, questions of language, economics, and government funding converge to bolster arguments that all foreign language films be dubbed in Quebec: to provide work and continued high-tech training and expertise for local artists and technicians, to support the local industry, and to ensure that a good, local version of French is circulated, not only in the cities but throughout the province, in turn, ensuring that the resident population as well as immigrants have access in good French to the foreign audiovisual products that are increasingly international events. This has yet to be made law and be fully funded.

Which French?

The question of which language to use in dubbing, the question that regularly sets off controversies such as those around *Ally McBeal* and *Shrek the Third*, was formally addressed for the first time in the Lampron Report (*L'industrie du doublage*) which argued that in all countries that share a language with another country (e.g., Argentina with Spain, Belgium with France) the population prefers the local language for film dubbing: "la population accepte mal une version dans laquelle elle ne se reconnaît pas" (23). Lampron concludes that the Quebec populace should hear good French for pedagogical reasons ("acquisition de compétences linguistiques de base"), and it should hear its own French ("la langue de proximité") in order to truly enjoy the films. When these two requirements are fulfilled, it will not only be satisfied with its access to international culture, but also will have acquired added educational value along the way. The question that arises is the extent to which "international French" fulfils these requirements.

International French and le synchronien

"International French," a standardized but rather abstract version of French, became an alternative to "Parisian French" in the 1960s, playing an important role in Quebec as a counterbalance to *joual* or "patois canadien."[9] It provided a version of French that would not only "redonner du prestige au français au Québec" (Bouchard, *La langue et le nombril* 250) and garner respect and status for it within Canada, but also foster international francophone contacts and exchanges, coinciding with the French used in the capitals and other large cities of the entire francophone world. Not surprisingly, perhaps, this has come to mean that as a dubbing actor in Quebec:

> vous devez maîtriser le français dit "international." La diction doit être irréprochable. À l'exception de TRÈS rares cas (la série *Les Simpson*, par exemple), les productions doublées au Québec se font dans un français qui doit être exempt d'accent local. ("Questions Réponses" 1.1)

In other words, "la langue de proximité" has become "international French." This means the absence of any trace of Quebec French: anglicisms, regionalisms, blasphemes, jokes, proverbs, sayings, Quebec pronunciations, and so on. The term "le synchronien" (synchronian) is often used in the industry for such constructed language.

A number of problems surface with "le synchronien" made in Quebec: recent studies of Quebec-dubbed film have shown that the "international French" used by the industry neutralizes and standardizes French to a degree where it could well be described as a "langue de nulle part."[10] In its efforts to use safe neutral language, Quebec-dubbed film tends towards drab, vague, and desperately "correct" translations of the English source dialogue. Contrary to dubbing "made in France" (which has its own problems), the effort to provide proper French to the film-going public in Quebec often produces a strangely literary language or garbled texts that make little sense when analysed. Worse, Quebec-dubbed products often forego the creative, lively, and natural language normally expected in the translation and, especially, the interpretation of oral dialogue, namely, creativity and naturalness.[11] They do so in the face of the ongoing "obsession with language" in this minority culture (Bouchard, *Obsessed with Language*). One brief comparative example will illustrate this.[12]

Bridget Jones' Diary is a romantic comedy that follows the life and rather virtual love life of Bridget Jones, a young British woman in her thirties, who is seeking a partner. While she is also a young professional, although not particularly successful, her main focus is on finding a man, and making that fit with her career aspirations. Part of a genre now called "chick-lit," Helen Fielding's *Bridget Jones' Diary* was published as a book in 1996, and successfully adapted into a "chick-flick" film in 2001, starring Renée Zellweger and Hugh Grant.

It has been argued that creativity and naturalness in language are vital in the translation/rendering of oral dialogue – for interest and meaningfulness, as much as for character identification. But these qualities are generally absent from Quebec dubbing. In the scene described below, Bridget is set to report on the events around Guy Fawkes Day, a British holiday that celebrates with bonfires, fireworks, and other public festivities the foiling of the attempt to blow up the Houses of Parliament in the seventeenth century. She is reporting on the preparations from a fire hall, and the TV anchor, Richard Finch, is giving excited, energetic instructions for filming, and urging his media team into action. Bridget is instructed in what she should be wearing and in how the camera shots will be organized, but things go awry, and the scene leads to the comic revelation not only of Bridget's incompetence and awkwardness but also of her backside.

Fire Hall Scene from *Bridget Jones' Diary*

In comparing the two French versions with the original English text, we find that, in general, the Quebec version is considerably weaker (certainly in terms of the creativity factor noted above); nevertheless, it is free of regionalisms and enunciated with international French sounds. Two brief examples must suffice here: in a crucial segment of this scene, Finch (the TV anchor) is giving clear instructions to Bridget, standing below him and about to enter the scene. She is told what to wear, what to do, and then asked to go straight to her interview with the fire chief. Finch is, in fact, directing the arrival of the interviewer. The Franco-French version deals with the text in straightforward, clear language, and, perhaps just as importantly, with balanced syntax: "je veux que tu prennes la lance d'incendie, je veux que tu glisses le long de la perche, que tu enchaines tout d'suite sur l'interview." The Quebec version, on the other hand, presents garbled, vaguely literary language, and a change in syntax that turns Bridget into the interviewee: "je veux te voir qui pointes une lance, qui descends le long d'un mât et puis, tu vas droit à cette entrevue." The construction "te voir qui" is heavy and reminiscent of the poetic style of the mid-nineteenth century. It seems quite inappropriate for excited last minute instructions as cameras are about to roll – but very proper. The last part sends Bridget to be interviewed by the station chief, while the English clearly has her interviewing him (as does the French).

In another segment, Finch is irritated at Bridget Jones' premature descent down the fire pole and expresses this with a very usual English formulation, "Neville, what the fuck is going on?" The Franco-French does not shy away from this emphatic sexualized slangy vulgarity, "Qu'est-ce qu'elle fout là? Qu'est-ce que c'est que ce bordel?" – incorporating both the verb "foutre" (fuck) and the term "bordel" (bordello/mess). The Quebec version, however, opts for the safer, much less expressive, "Mais, tu veux me dire ce qui se passe?" adding the unnecessary "mais" in order to fill the actor's open mouth. In a similar penchant for linguistic correctness of sorts, the Quebec version produces a picture perfect "chassé-croisé" in order to render "she's supposed to be sliding down the pole" as "Elle doit descendre en glissant le long du mât, pas y grimper, je pense!" adding further filler with "je pense." In terms of oral style, this Quebec rendering is unwieldy and unnatural. The present participle construction "en glissant" slows down the oral rhythm, an effect enhanced by the unnecessary "je pense." In contrast, the rhythm of the Franco-French version is much quicker: "Elle doit glisser du haut d'la perche, pas y r'monter!" The words are short and sharp, and contractions are used. The structure is simple: subject + verb + complement, which corresponds to the action, where everyone is under stress, under pressure, and short of time.

Research results have shown such tendencies repeatedly in Quebec dubbing; the work is proper, and presumably pedagogical: dubbing becomes a tool for teaching or reinforcing correct French.

The Proper French of Quebec Dubbing

The three language options for audiovisual materials made in Quebec were described at the outset, along with the kinds of criticisms they elicit: Franco-French (too "pointu," with inappropriate vocabulary for a society that wishes to "hear itself"), Quebec French (reserved for Quebec-made productions that represent "us"), and "international French." Of these three, "international French" with its neutralized tone, has won out on the dubbing scene in Quebec. The industry produces it, the general public accepts it. It is the acceptable in-between non-language solution, where "le synchronien" (or in English "synchronian") – the special wooden language of dubbing prevails. While French from France is often the rule in TV series (which are largely bought already-dubbed in France) Quebec French/ Québécois has lost out for dubbed materials.[13] And yet, given the arguments for dubbing in the local vernacular, and given the fact that Quebec-dubbed film is made for the local market and hardly circulated abroad (because of France's restrictive decree), and finally, given the fact that there are funds and political will available in Quebec, it would be possible to dub into a standard version of Québécois, especially given the often "local" North American source situations. Why is this not being done?

One explanation may be gleaned from *The Simpsons*, one of the rare TV series dubbed in Quebec that uses a certain amount of Quebec French. Eric Plourde ("Le doublage de *The Simpsons*") has shown that in this version only the relatively uneducated working-class, or downright stupid characters (Homer, Marge, Bart, Lisa, and Grampa Simpson, Chief Wiggum, Lenny, Agnes Skinner) speak a rough, vulgar version of Quebec French; "standard" French is reserved for the "intelligentsia" of Springfield (Principal Skinner, Reverend Lovejoy, Kent Brockman, Sideshow Bob, Doctor Hibbert). Plourde's study seems to reveal what sociolinguists have been couching in circumspect and descriptive academic terms: although francophone Quebecers view the French language as the most important identity marker, the prevalent vernacular in use is somewhat compromising. It is not always "international," and sometimes it cannot be described as "standard" French. In the mouths of strangers it is an inappropriate embarrassment. Its use is, in fact, internal: it establishes and maintains community, a sense of belonging, a certain clannishness in a hostile world. It has to do with the socially relevant and acceptable and not the proper uses of language, and its use expresses and affirms solidarity, closeness, togetherness (Laforest). The local vernacular serves to create and confirm the community, and is reserved for this community. Yet, and this is important for the language of dubbing as well as other language use in public, the speakers of this vernacular may well devalue, or even despise it: they experience what linguist Labov has termed "linguistic insecurity." And herein lies at least a part of the intended effect of dubbing into "le synchronien" or international French. There is a pedagogical intention, although not always well informed. Further, it spares the viewers the embarrassment of listening to this private idiom in the mouths of international stars. In Quebec, the conflict between the drive to speak standard French, on the one hand, and the failure or refusal to do so, on the other, is at the heart of the scandals, arguments, conflicts, and parliamentary debates around film dubbing, a conflict that is assuaged by recourse to the neutrality of "international French" and its synchronian applications.

Notes

1 The success of homemade local TV productions that reflect this "reality" has been documented and commented upon by Murray et al., 5–6 and 15–18.

2 Clearly stated by interviewees at Technicolor, a Montreal dubbing studio (Personal interview).

3 This was confirmed by a series of interviews conducted by the author at Montreal dubbing studios Cinélume, Technicolor, and Audio Postproduction conducted in July 2007.

4 A good example of such criticism is found in the publications, letters to the editor, and other documents produced by Sylvio Le Blanc, including "Le doublage québécois."

5 Prohibited expressions include: faire la peau (tuer), faire une faveur (anglicisme/rendre un service), faux-cul, flemmard, flingue, flinguer (revolver, fusil, arme), fourguer (rendre, donner, se débarrasser), foutre une trempe, fric (argent, magot, butin), gonflé (du culot), graillons (graisse), grue – dans le sens de pute, prostituée, je t'emmerde (va te faire voir/foutre), job (travail), lardons (enfants), mec (type, gars, amis, vieux), mettre une dégelée (flanquer une raclée), nana, nénette (fille, femme). For additional examples, see Flotow, "Frenching the Feature Film, Twice."

6 SODEC: Société de développement des entreprises culturelles incorporates the Institut Québécois du cinéma (IQC), which was created on 19 June 1975 by the adoption of the Loi sur le cinéma to meet long-standing demands from Quebec cinematic groups. Its mandate was to promote and support the creation, production, distribution, and showing of high-quality films in Quebec. The law also defined certain requirements in dubbing, subtitling, children's films, and film research that were designed to strengthen the Québécois presence in the industry. The members of the IQC represented all sectors of the industry and its clientele (*Canadian Encyclopedia*, online).

7 This decree was reinforced by at least two strikes by French industry workers who feared a softening of the ruling as a result of pressure from Quebec: in 1978 and 1987.

8 The Gendron Commission, also known as "La Commission d'enquête sur la situation du français et des droits linguistiques au Québec," published its report in 1972. This report was used by the Bourassa government to devise Bill 22, the forerunner of Bill 101 (Bouchard, *La langue et le nombril* 262–4).

9 These are two terms for dialectal versions of French spoken in Quebec, with *joual* dating from the 1960s and "patois canadien" from the nineteenth century.

10 This is a term often used by local film buffs such as Sylvio Le Blanc to criticize the local output.

11 "Creative translation/interpretation has to do with unpredictable non-institutionalised use of language … A creative product must be novel and must contain an element of surprise, it must be singular or at least unusual" (Marianne Lederer quoted in Kussmaul 39).

12 For more examples, see Flotow, "Frenching the Feature Film, Twice" 86–102; "When Hollywood Speaks 'International French'" 27–45.

13 Certain cartoons/animations are dubbed into Quebec French including *The Flintstones* and *The Simpsons*. Eric Plourde has discussed *The Simpsons* dubbing in some detail in his MA thesis ("Le doublage de *The Simpsons*").

Works Cited

Audio-Postproduction. Dubbing studio. Personal interview. July 2007.

Bouchard, Chantal. *La langue et le nombril: une histoire sociolinguistique du Québec*. Montréal: Fides, 2002.

– *Obsessed with Language*. Trans. Luise von Flotow. Toronto: Guernica, 2008.

Canadian Encyclopedia. "Société de développement des entreprises culturelles." Pierre Vérronneau. 2009. Accessed 26 Dec. 2009. http://www.thecanadianency-clopedia.com/index.cfm?PgNm=TCE&Params=A1ARTA0004018

CEGIR Inc. *Délais de distribution des films américains en version française.* Submitted to Institut québécois du cinéma. Montréal: CEGIR, 1983.

Cinélume. Dubbing studio. Personal interview. July 2007.

Commission Gendron. Commission d'enquête sur la situation de la langue française et des droits linguistiques au Québec. *Mémoire du comité de culture cinématographique de l'Office des communications sociales à la Commission d'enquête sur la situation de la langue française et sur les droits linguistiques au Québec.* Montréal: Le comité, 1969.

Cousineau, Louise. *La Presse* – Arts et spectacles, 24 avril 1999: D2.

CTVM.info. "Dépôt du projet de Loi 193: L'ADQ veut assurer l'avenir de l'industrie du doublage au Québec." 7 juin 2007. Accessed 26 Dec. 2009. http://www.ctvm.info/article.php3?id_article=625

Flotow, Luise von. "Frenching the Feature Film, Twice – Or le synchronien au débat." *New Trends in Audiovisual Translation.* Ed. Jorge Díaz Cintas. Buffalo, NY: Multilingual Matters, 2009, 86–102.

– "When Hollywood Speaks 'International French': The Sociopolitics of Dubbing for Francophone Quebec." *Quebec Studies*, special issue on Translation in Quebec (2011): 27–45.

Gill, Anne-Marie, and Mélina Longpré. *L'industrie du doublage au Québec: État des lieux (1998–2006).* Cahiers de la SODEC. May 2008. Accessed 26 Dec. 2009. http://www.sodec.gouv.qc.ca/documents/publications/doublageetatdeslieux2008.pdf

Kussmaul, Paul. *Training the Translator.* Amsterdam: John Benjamins, 1995.

Laforest, Marty. "Attitudes, préjugés et opinions sur la langue." *Le français: Une langue à apprivoiser.* Eds. Claude Verreault, Louis Mercier, and Thomas Lavoie. Sainte-Foy, QC: Les Presses de l'Université Laval, 2002, 81–91.

Le Blanc, Sylvio. "Le doublage québécois: Le gouvernement doit mettre fin aux credits d'impôt." Submitted to the Consultation publique sur l'actualisation de la politique québécoise du cinéma et de la production audiovisuelle, 19 sept. 2002.

Lederer, Marianne. *La traduction aujourd'hui: Le modèle interprétatif.* Paris: Hachette, 1994.

Hart, Sylvie, A.I. Laursen, and D. Orengo. "Le conflit du doublage cinéma et télévision: 1987." Discussion paper for the seminar on conflict with Professor Jean

Daniel Reynaud. Paris: Institut d'études politiques de Paris, Cycle supérieur de sociologie, 1988.

Institut québécois du cinéma (IQC). *Enquête sur la sortie des films dont la version originale est en langue anglaise, de mai à octobre 1988.* Muriel Kearney and Bernard Boucher. Montréal: IQC, 1988. Accessed 26 Dec. 2009. http://amicus.collectionscanada.ca/aaweb-bin/aamain/itemdisp?sessionKey= 999999999_142&l=1&d=2&v=0&lvl=1&itm=25005771

– *Le français à l'écran: De mai 1988 à 1989.* Muriel Kearney. Montréal: IQC, 1989.

– *La situation du français à l'écran et l'avenir de l'article 83.* Montréal: IQC, 1990.

– *Le français au grand écran en 1991.* Andrée Letendre. Montréal: IQC, 1993.

Lampron, Pierre. *L'industrie du doublage: Consolidation et nouveaux marchés.* Québec: Ministère de la culture et des communications, 1997. Rpt. by Société de développement des entreprises culturelles (SODEC), 1998. http://www.sodec.gouv.qc.ca/documents/publications/cinema_doublage.pdf

Murray Catherine, Roger de la Garde, and Claude Martin. "Star Wars: Canadian TV Drama." *EuroCanadian Fiction 2000.* Burnaby, BC: Simon Fraser University, School of Communication, 2001, 1–24. Accessed 26 Dec. 2009. http://www.sfu.ca/cmns/faculty/murray_c/assets/EuroCanadianFiction.pdf

Plourde, Éric. "Le doublage de *The Simpsons*: Divergences, appropriation culturelle et manipulation du discours." MA thesis. Université de Montréal, 1999.

"Questions Réponses." www.doublage.qc.ca: Le site officiel du doublage au Québec. Question 1.1. Accessed 26 Dec. 2009. http://www.doublage.qc.ca

Technicolor. Dubbing studio. Personal interview. July 2007.

Union des Artistes (UDA), and l'Association québécoise des industries techniques du cinéma et de la télévision. *Mémoire de l'Union des artistes et de l'Association québécoise des industries techniques, du cinéma et de la télévision présenté à la Commission de la culture dans le cadre de l'étude du projet de loi 117: "Loi modifiant la Loi sur le cinéma."* Submitted to the Commission permanente de la culture. UDA and l'Association, 1991.

5

Summer 2008: *Pays de la Sagouine*:
Cultural Translation at an Acadian Theme Park

Glen Nichols

Just thirty minutes northeast of Moncton, New Brunswick, on the picturesque Northumberland Strait sits the village of Bouctouche (population 2,476), birthplace and summer residence of Acadian writer, Antonine Maillet. Nestled on the edge of a large bay and intersected by the scenic Bouctouche River, nearly half a kilometre wide as it empties into the sea at the Bouctouche Marina, the village has also been home to a unique summer attraction since 1992: Pays de la Sagouine, a theme park dedicated to the plays and fiction of Antonine Maillet, to the particular vision of Acadie that is constructed through her writing. Ironically, however, the site is marketed as "All you want to know about the Acadian culture!" (Pays de la Sagouine, *Season program* 33). In fact, the well-known tourist destination performs a spatial translation of Acadian culture, transforming Acadian culture, as constructed through the writing of Antonine Maillet, into temporal and spatial simulacra for the pleasure and edification of visiting crowds.

The theme park effects a spatial and temporal reiteration of the plays and characters, a dynamic performance of Acadian culture for tourist consumption. This is achieved by means of the theme park's geography, layout, context, marketing, and history, but in particular, through the presentations themselves which have a pre-theme-park resonance. Although all of the plays are performed in their original Acadian French language, the park simulates a kind of cultural translation as the visitors come with a sense of Acadie already in place. This view is consumed both within Acadie and by outsiders through the wide popularity and renown of Maillet's books, and is translated into spatial and temporal systems in the theme park that not only reinforce the preconceived notions of Acadie, but also extend and reify them. Although none of the performance texts done on site are translations, and although Sherry Simon is explicitly speaking of linguistic transfer when she postulates translation as "the materialization of our relationship to otherness, to the experience […] of what is different" (161), the reconstitution and transformation of the literary into the spatial and temporal modes at Pays de la Sagouine effects precisely this "materialization."

The Pays de la Sagouine site is structured around three distinct sections or phases that lead the visitor out of the "real" world and into the land of La Sagouine. The countrified but tidy admissions and gift shop building greet visitors on the shore of the inner Bouctouche Bay. Here also are located the restaurant and dinner theatre, the mega-spectacle outdoor venue, and a smaller indoor studio theatre.[1] The heart of the "Pays," though, is located on the small Île aux puces linked to the mainland by a winding 300-metre boardwalk that creates a panoramic transitional phase to the visitor's experience. The island itself is laid out to suggest a miniature village, a self-contained and highly encoded enclosed space (Edensor 64) featuring buildings that are human-scaled, brightly coloured, and cleverly situated to control the flow of foot traffic to the two theatres at the centre of the island.

A number of issues in studies of translation find echoes in contemporary tourism studies and offer useful ways of extending the analyses developed in the literary field to the spatial and temporal aspects of this tourist site and performance venue. Of particular relevance are the tensions between source versus target text orientations and the resulting effect of translations on source and target cultures, the impact of translator self-inscription into new texts, and the effect of spatial embodiment to reinforce the cultural translation on the performance of source and target cultures. For example, in his argument concerning the performativity of cultural tourism,[2] Tim Edensor observes how tour operators on the island of Mauritius "translate" local dances and dramas for tourist consumption by "selecting which cultural aspects are accessible and which should be edited out, charting a course between 'exoticism' and comprehensibility. Performances are typically devised to titillate tourists without alienating them by sticking too closely to complicated cultural meanings" (70). Just as a literary translator may negotiate between foreignizing and domesticating strategies (Eco 23), the tour operator makes choices in constructing the local "source" experience to meet anticipated expectations of the target tourist. Edensor then goes on to examine how a set of Mauritian dances has been adapted for

Western tourist consumption to the degree that, according to locals, "the meaning of the dance has become cheapened and diluted […] so that Mauritians are now sexualized objects rather than convivial participants in their own dance" (70–1). Just as literary translations construct how target readers understand the source culture of the work, so too do tourist sites construct meaning of the Other for visitors.

Overall, the Pays de la Sagouine site negotiates its way between, on the one hand, creating an Acadie that is familiarized for visitors, matching their expectations and, on the other hand, exhibiting an "exoticized" time and place that translates Acadie as an historical fantasy, both nostalgic and epic.[3] The past is carefully packaged as clean, amusing, heart-warming, self-contained, and innocent. The site's buildings emphasize the use of wood and traditional domestic architecture. To get to the Pays, visitors turn off the main highway and are led down a long paved lane through thick woods, as if going back in time. Separated from their "real" world, visitors are engulfed in a nostalgically encoded "village," the perfect setting to absorb a mythology embodied in a variety of theatre performances.

After crossing the winding bridge to Île aux puces, visitors encounter a small oblong public square formed by the fronts of three houses: La tchuisine des Mathilda, La maison de la Sainte, and La maison de la Sagouine.[4] In the first, visitors can listen to interactive demonstrations about traditional Acadian cooking in a warm, rustic room decorated with domestic antiques placed around the public area. The other two houses are of more theatrical interest.

Visitors to "La Sainte's" and "La Sagouine's" houses are treated to monologues by the respective housekeepers: Zélica and Séraphine, each woman gossiping about her neighbour and their squabbles.[5] The houses are decorated in a style suggesting the 1930s: La Sainte's house is a bit more modernized with an electric stove and fine mirrors, whereas La Sagouine's house has a wood-burning stove and more basic ornaments. The spaces are not immense; indeed, people have to crowd into the houses in order to hear the actors, as if they were "really" visiting a "real" home. The feeling of both spaces is akin to visiting a fantasy "grandma's house": quaint, friendly, clean, but slightly out of date.

On the other extreme from this domestic simulation is the past depicted as heroic struggle in the aptly described "mega-spectacle" *Pélagie*. Adapted from Maillet's novel, *Pélagie-la-charette*, which won the 1979 Prix Goncourt, this spectacle is the second epic to be featured at the Pays.[6] In "15 scenes, on a backdrop of inspiring music, songs, special effects, lasers and fireworks" (Pays de la Sagouine, *Season program* 7), the show portrays the odyssey-like post-deportation return of Pélagie and her family as a metaphor for the Acadian people defying and defeating "History." "History," allegorized as a flouncing, effeminate fop, decrees that the Acadians "are finished," their page in the book of the world has been turned, and they should accept their fate. However, the Acadian refugees outsmart and out-manoeuvre "History," proving themselves more resilient and more heroic by overcoming even these greatest of odds. The mythologization of the long struggle and return of the Acadians concludes with a hymn to even further endurance, for although "la Déportation est bel et bien finie [...] c'est la dispersion qui commence," and they'll have to work away quietly out of sight for another hundred years, waiting for their opportunity to "come back out of the woods."[7]

When we consider the "legends and tales" told at Gapi's lighthouse, and the traditional music provided by the two house bands, Borlico and Les Cotchineux, it becomes clear that the emphasis of the site's performances is historical. Indeed, the only theatre piece in the summer of 2008 that depicted a contemporary Acadie was Robert Gauvin's new romantic comedy, *La peau de l'autre*, performed twice weekly in a small barnlike studio theatre situated off the main pathway to Île aux puces and partly concealed in a clearing in the woods. However, the sense of "history" must be considered very carefully as the site translates a very particular view for the tourist gaze.

Just as "translation strategy must negotiate between the ideological demands of social discourse and the exigencies of literary language" (Simon 160), in tourism "individual managers, developers, researchers [...] engage in small and large games of cultural, social, environmental and historical cleansing, as they promote and project some socio-political universes and chastise or omit other possible contending worldviews" (Voase 285). Just as literary translations can be said to write the translator and are a performance of the translator's time, place, and ideology, so too, the tour sites perform an inscription of site creators and operators, implementing their interpretation of the local culture (ibid.).

In the case of Pays de la Sagouine, history is constructed as a very simple thing, pleasantly nostalgic or heart-warmingly heroic; Acadie is presented as a unified entity, its history a singular familial fairy tale. Tensions within the society are erased, avoiding any complications of Acadie's past or present, such as those between the elite and poorer parts of society, or between the various regions, or even acknowledging the complexity of the Church's role in the development of Acadie.

Just as literary translation choices may be conditioned as much by perceived expectations in the target readership as by the particularities of the source text, so too, must tourist sites "resonate with the expectations of the cultures of the tourist and the expectations of those tourists" (Clarke 28). Pays de la Sagouine's unified vision of Acadie somehow matches "a fixed version of the culture," a vision that precedes the Pays in the literary works of Maillet. This vision, translated, embodied, and "experienced," replaces "an authentic feel for the living cultures of the places visited" (ibid.), and the modern, complex, and dynamic Acadie is invisible behind the screen of this more "acceptable" Acadie.

The vast majority of visitors to the Pays are, of course, French-speaking, or at least bilingual, because, although the theme park is very welcoming to English-speaking visitors, providing a fully bilingual guidebook and offering English-language tours, monolingual anglophones would find the performances in Acadian French fairly inaccessible. On the other hand, the lively atmosphere, food, music, colourful buildings, and delightful location in the midst of Bouctouche Bay make an impression on visitors, regardless of language, that might not in the end be all that different from the one constructed by and for francophone visitors: more simplified no doubt and less nuanced than that available to someone comprehending the language of the texts being performed, but on a continuum with that consumer version of Acadie rather than something completely different.

The separation between the physical features of the "park" and the plays presented there is intentionally ambiguous: everything about the park, from its buildings, their layout, names, and appearance to the costumed "animateurs," musicians, and even those serving food (and the food itself!) are all designed to bring to life the characters and locations, the stories, and atmosphere of Maillet's plays and fiction, and by implication, to bring to life a version of "real Acadian culture" as suggested in the park publicity. Although the anglophone visitor might not understand the spoken language of the performances, there is a clear sense of "Acadie" translated into and by the space itself through visual and tactile languages. For francophone visitors the spaces reinforce the images of the pays; for anglophone visitors the spaces become and replace the images of the plays. And for both groups the Acadie that is constructed is a simplified, countrified, historicized, and safely contained, non-threatening space of idyllic escape. This construction meets the expectations of visitors who have already had their impressions of Acadie, literary Acadie at least, shaped by their memory of reading or seeing Maillet's work on stage.

For the tour operator the language of translation is not literary, however, but spatial and temporal, creating places for visitors to explore and spend time (and money), in places and times that simulate an "experience" of the translated source culture. Cultural tourism, however, magnifies the effects of translation through these spatial and temporal interactions of the target visitor and source culture. While the literary product also performs culture, of course, the "embodiment" remains abstract: the imaginary of place, while undeniably powerful, remains interiorized and linguistically mediated. The tourist site, on the other hand, becomes a full-body, "lived" experience, and the mediation effects are closer to those of theatre performance than those of literary translation. Kevin Meethan's measure of performance and embodiment in the geographical and identity narratives of cultural tourism links translation concepts to tourism studies in the analysis of theatre production because this Acadian theme park is "more than just a passive container within which activities occur" (7): not only is the culture "translated," but through the creation of embodied experience the site also "translates" visitors from passive consumers of culture to interactive performers.

One of the most obvious ways Pays de la Sagouine is structured to translate visitors from passive consumers to interactive performers is through the encouragement of audience participation. Theatre performances take place not only in the theatres, but also in the "houses" and on the "street," and these have an impact on how the interactions are perceived. The basic monologues for Zélica and Séraphine are scripted, retelling a variety of misadventures the women have experienced with each other. But the proximity of audience and actor, the performance of a "relaxed" homey context, and the desire to construct visitors as participants encourage extensive improvised interactions. Keeping within the scope of the "scripted" moment, the actors have considerable latitude to play with the audience. For example, by asking the audience where they are from, the actor may learn someone has driven a long ways (say from Montreal), so Séraphine may ask that person to take Zélica back with him or her, and an exchange with the audience member on how this could be done, where she could be picked up, dropped off, etc., ensues. Clearly adaptable in many situations, with variations depending on how the audience member reacts, such inter-changes give the performances a sense of immediacy and reinforce the transformation of the tourist visitors into "real" visitors, dropping into a home and taking a role in the village. In addition, the two actors also do a show in the "village square" between their houses, bickering, haranguing the audience to vote for one or the other, even using them as shields in the occasional scuffle, again reinforcing the participation of the visitors in a "real" confrontation with social implications.

The visitors are able to wander about the site "at will," joining or leaving a performance as the mood strikes. Even the formal shows in the large Île aux puces theatre in the middle of the village use monologue as the form of choice, which frames a relatively flexible, episodic performance that is more conducive to listeners arriving late or leaving early.[8] Here visitors can listen to characters like Noume, Gapi, Citrouille, Mariaagelas (characters from Maillet's plays and fiction but in texts written specifically for the Pays), and even La Sagouine herself played by Violet Léger, who created La Sagouine and has played the character for a generation of Acadian the-atregoers. The theatre building itself is a large open structure with backless benches arranged in rows between two stages, one at each end. The theatre has a roof but no sidewalls, allowing audience members to come and go easily, and the "village" context is never forgotten. People can observe the onstage action as they stroll by the theatre, and the audience can watch the passers-by. The actors walk through the audience to get to the stage and often improvise exchanges with audience members. The visitors to the Pays become, literally, part of the show. They do not simply watch the spectacles from a distance, protected by an illusionistic fourth wall; the entire island becomes the stage, and the visitors wander into and through it. While the mega-spectacle and studio theatre productions in the on-shore productions treat the audience in a more traditional, passive role, the emphasis in the island theatres is on constructing a participatory audience. The boundaries between staged and apparently random improvised encounters is not clearly demarcated, but rather, the improvisation crosses out of the textual and aesthetic limits of the scripted monologues and staged presentations, and even, literally, out of the physical precincts of "theatres" and into the "street." The effect is lively and interactive, with a sense that the audience is seeing and shaping the characters, just as they are being shaped by the performances, effecting the construction of "community," or at least the simulation of one.

Another aspect is the opportunity for visitors to re-acquaint themselves with well-known actors in a space constructed as more personal, more "shared" than what one normally experiences in a theatre. Although all the actors on site are professional and often seen on the stages of Théâtre l'Escaouette or Théâtre Populaire d'Acadie, among other venues in the region and beyond, the primary example of this is the iconic Viola Léger. The reception of Léger is starlike: audiences in the theatre doubled in number for her monologues when I was there, and there was spontaneous applause as she walked into the theatre. After her performance she gave a ten-minute photo-op, allowing people to have their picture taken with La Sagouine outside "her" house. The parade to the house from the theatre drew a large number of spectators, and she was (politely!) mobbed by the crowd.

One day I was there in 2008, Antonine Maillet was also at the site and she accompanied Léger to the photo-op, with Maillet herself recognized and equally mobbed by the crowd who wanted to have their picture taken with the iconic famous author. The performance of community was palpable as an effect of the informal, interactive embodiment of character and persona.

With a name like *Pays* de la Sagouine, one is reminded of that other famous theme park: Disney*land*. Both sites translate the diegetic world of fictional characters into a four-dimensional "real" "land" tourists can visit, explore, and "experience" not only in space but also in time, creating performative effects on both the "target" and "source" elements of this translation.[9] Spatialization of the diegetic worlds for an expectant audience is "not the simple consumption of a spectacle, but [...] a form of interaction between people and place [...] an acknowledgement that tourism is about, among other things, processes of transformation" (Meethan 9). And this "transformation" becomes the reinforcement of preconceived truths about the "source": in the case of Disney, the fun, safe, child-friendly world of the cartoons, on the one hand, and the wholesome, heroic grand narrative of the "American" adventure, on the other. Visitors to Pays de la Sagouine, who have enjoyed Maillet's fictional characters through reading or on stage, come to experience them in a "real" situation.[10] It is the chance to see and hear characters such as those from the novel, *Pélagie-la-charrette*, "come to life," to see the novel illustrated. Visitors may also know the characters from the theatre, so a visit to the Pays is a chance to hear "new" monologues by familiar characters, imagine them in lives beyond those familiar from the original stage versions.

Other touristic sights along the Acadian shore, like Village Historique Acadien in Caraquet, use reconstructions of actual historical buildings to tell the story of Acadian history, but without explicit fictional reconstitution, other than, of course, the implicit narrativizing of history itself. However, the Village Historique, along with the artisanal "soapery" at Sainte-Anne-de Kent and the Bouctouche Dunes nature park, both just up the road from the "Pays," as well as Kouchibouguac National Park, all form a string of tourist sites that reinforce the "natural," homey, safely historicized, and quaintly rural images of Pays de la Sagouine. These tourist sites have a strong resemblance to that other famous Maritime creation, the Anne of Green Gables "industry" on nearby Prince Edward Island. Like Pays de la Sagouine, the house that tourists visit at Cavendish reflects literary constructions of the famous redheaded character.[11] However, distinctly unlike "Green Gables" and even the other Acadian tourist sites, Pays de la Sagouine goes beyond the simple rural idyll to perform a translation of a much grander narrative of Acadian history: the performance of a more nationalistic and patriotic sense of community through the mega-spectacle that mythologizes a simplified Acadian past, elevating events to the status of "epic." Tourists come to revel in the stars of Acadie: actors, Maillet's characters, La Sagouine, even Maillet herself, but they are also invited to come to "learn about Acadian culture through its history, past and present" (Pays de la Sagouine, *Season program* 33). The site provides a spatial translation of that culture and history with important implications for the symbolic understanding of Acadie. As Edensor notes, "tourist space is also (re)produced by tourists, who perform diverse meanings about symbolic places, dramatizing their allegiance to places and kinds of action. For tourist performance maps out individual and group identities, and alludes to imagined geographies of which the stage may be part" (71). Through its spatial and temporal translation of Maillet's diegetic worlds, Pays de la Sagouine performs easily consumed and homogeneous impressions of

Acadie, reinforcing the clichés of Acadie as a simple, old-fashioned, and non-threatening myth that more sophisticated "come-from-aways" can safely indulge in.

Notes

1 In October of 2008, the 250-seat "L'Ordre de bon temps" restaurant and theatre was destroyed by fire, along with much of the site's technical equipment and stock of props and costumes stored there – one of a series of arson attacks in the area. However, the theatre was rebuilt and reopened in 2009.

2 Cultural tourism acknowledges "both the cultural nature of, and the role of, tourism as a process and set of practices that revolve around the behavioural pragmatics of societies, and the learning and transmission of meanings through symbols and embodied through objects [...] Tourism, as an expression and experience of culture, fits within this form of historical contextualisation and also assists in generating nuanced forms of culture as well as new cultural forms" (Robinson and Smith 1). Tourism studies today are careful to separate cultural tourism from simply the production and consumption of "high" art and heritage with which it is often associated and suggest, instead, that cultural tourism "reaches into some deep conceptual territories relating to how we construct and understand ourselves, the world, and the multi-layered relationships between them" (2).

3 See, for example, Eco's discussion of how literary translators negotiate between foreignizing and domesticating strategies (23), the literary parallel to what happens in spatial and temporal terms at Pays de la Sagouine. See also Edensor on how tourist sites construct meanings of the Other for visitors (70).

4 These characters, especially La Sagouine, are quintessential Maillet creations and extremely popular among her readers.

5 "La maison de la Sagouine" is described as La Sagouine's "dream house" because, after all, "Sa vraie maison n'avait pas de planchers, rien que de la terre" (Pays de la Sagouine, *Site Map*).

6 *Odysée 1604–2004: La marche d'un people*, originally created to celebrate the 400th anniversary of Acadie, ran from 2004 to 2006. Due to the 2008 fire, the mega-spectacle did not run in the summer of 2009.

7 Starting in the fall of 1755, British soldiers deported several thousand French Acadians from what would become the Canadian provinces of Nova Scotia,

New Brunswick, and Prince Edward Island. Although many would eventually return, the complete destruction of their villages and the expropriation of their lands by New Englander "Planters" meant the returning Acadians were "dispersed" across the Maritimes and only in the late nineteenth century were they able to begin to reconstitute a collective national identity.

8 David Lonergan also makes the connection between Maillet's use of monologue in so much of her work and the importance of orality in Acadian culture.

9 Jean Baudrillard, of course, cites Disneyland as the "perfect model of all the entangled orders of simulation" (174). The comparison to Pays de la Sagouine, although beyond the scope of this essay, is intriguing. Just as Disneyland's "imaginary world [of illusions and phantasms] is supposed to be what makes the operation successful [...] what draws the crowds is undoubtedly much more the social microcosm, the miniaturized and religious revelling in real America, in its delights and drawbacks" (ibid.). Given the Pays marketing nod to "all you want to know about Acadian culture," one is more than tempted to read "real Acadie" for Baudrillard's "real America."

10 One is reminded of the appeal of studio tours such as those in the Disney chain or the Granada Studio tours to the "Coronation Street" back lot in the UK where people are thrilled to walk the "real" street where the show is "actually" filmed (see Couldry 96f).

11 But it is, in fact, a conflation: the house was not "Anne's" house, nor even that of the author, L.M. Montgomery (although both of these impressions are left open), but belonged to the author's relatives and may have been the inspiration for the "Green Gables" of the novels.

Works Cited

Baudrillard, Jean. "Simulacra and Simulations." *Jean Baudrillard: Selected Writings.* Ed. Mark Poster. Stanford: Stanford University Press, 1988, 166–84.

Clarke, Alan. "The Power to Define: Meanings and Values in Cultural Tourism." *Expressions of Culture, Identity and Meaning in Tourism.* Ed. Mike Robinson et al. Sunderland, UK: Centre for Travel and Tourism, 2000, 23–36.

Couldry, Nick. "The View from Inside the 'Simulacrum': Visitors' Tales from the Set of *Coronation Street.*" *Leisure Studies* 17: 2 (1998): 94–107.

Eco, Umberto. *Experiences in Translation.* Toronto: University of Toronto Press, 2001.

Edensor, Tim. "Performing Tourism, Staging Tourism: (Re)Producing Tourist Space and Practice." *Tourist Studies* 1: 1 (2001): 59–81.

Lonergan, David. "Quand le littéraire devient populaire." Colloque International Antonine Maillet: 50 Ans de Carrière Littéraire. Université de Moncton, 28–31 Aug. 2008.

Meethan, Kevin. "Introduction: Narratives of Place and Self." *Tourism, Consumption and Representation: Narratives of Place and Self*. Ed. Kevin Meethan, Alison Anderson, and Steve Miles. Wallingford, UK: CABI, 2006, 1–23.

Pays de la Sagouine. *Season program*. Bouctouche: Pays de la Sagouine, 2008.

– *Site Map and Day Program*. Bouctouche: Pays de la Sagouine, 2008.

"Le Pays de la Sagouine Will Reopen Next June." CBC *News*. 13 Nov. 2008. Accessed 27 Dec. 2009. http://www.cbc.ca/canada/new-brunswick/story/2008/11/13/nb-sagouine-rebuild.html#socialcomments

Robinson, Mike, and Melanie K Smith. "Politics, Power and Play: The Shifting Contexts of Cultural Tourism." *Cultural Tourism in a Changing World: Politics, Participation and (Re)presentation*. Ed. Mike Robinson and Melanie K Smith. Buffalo, NY: Channel View, 2006, 1–17.

Simon, Sherry. "The Language of Cultural Difference: Figures of Alterity in Canadian Translation." *Rethinking Translation: Discourse, Subjectivity, Ideology*. Ed. Lawrence Venuti. London: Routledge, 1992, 159–76.

Voase, Richard. "Creating the Tourist Destination: Narrating the 'Undiscovered' and the Paradox of Consumption." *Tourism, Consumption and Representation: Narratives of Place and Self*. Ed. Kevin Meethan, Alison Anderson, and Steve Miles. Wallingford, UK: CABI, 2006, 284–99.

6

February 1968: Acadian Activism and the Discontents of Translation

Denise Merkle

> Moncton. Un lieu exact, une erreur monumentale sur la carte de notre destin, le nom de notre bourreau commun graffiti sur la planète. Moncton […] Et pourtant, c'est de cet espace que jaillit notre conscience, vécu dans les méandres de la diaspora et articulée dans un faisceau rutilant de colère et d'ironie.
> – Herménégilde Chiasson[1]

> Moncton. A specific place, a monumental error on the map of our destiny, the name of our common hangman graffiti on the planet. Moncton […] And yet, it is from this space, lived in the meanderings of the diaspora, that our consciousness, articulated in a gleaming bundle of anger and irony, surges forth. (Translation by the author)

New Brunswick, February 1968: Charges for "public mischief" were laid against two Université de Moncton students from Quebec in the New Brunswick Superior Court before Justice J. Hughes. Like Justice Henry Murphy of the lower court, Justice Hughes refused to hear their case in French. Their offence was to have offered Moncton Mayor Leonard C. Jones the gift of a "tête de cochon" ("a pig's head").[2] The case in which translation, or rather non-translation, played a central role raised national interest around the equality of Canada's two charter languages, when the students insisted their case be heard in French. This event also highlights the surge of nationalist feeling at the time in Acadie, which focused on language and culture, and resulted in literary works referred to now as the Second Acadian Renaissance.[3] Many of these literary works were subsequently translated into English both inside and outside New Brunswick in well-meaning attempts to understand and communicate interculturally.

On 7 February 1968, more than a thousand striking Université de Moncton students and members of the Acadian community marched from the Université de Moncton campus to Moncton City Hall to demonstrate their opposition to Mayor Jones' rejection of official bilingualism and their support for a more visible francophone presence in greater Moncton.[4] Acadian students were, in fact, participating in the transnational 1960s movements of student activism, in this case, fighting for greater equality between New Brunswick's anglophone and francophone populations. They were demonstrating to defend their linguistic and cultural rights and to turn back the tide of assimilation. Quebec's Quiet Revolution had spread to Acadie, and thanks to filmmakers Michel Brault and Pierre Perrault the events were documented in the film, *L'Acadie, l'Acadie?!?*, completed in 1971.[5]

The conflict centred on translation: two of the students who met with city council, Bernard Gauvin, a co-organizer of the demonstration, and Irène Doiron, were forced to plead their case to the mayor in English; in *L'Acadie, l'Acadie?!?* Dorion states clearly that this prevented her from expressing her thoughts. Some of the documents that the Université de Moncton delegation had wished to submit to council were written in French, but the mayor accepted only documents submitted in English, stating that translation services were not available since translation doubles the cost of doing business. A week later he received the special gift that would bring national attention to Moncton.[6]

Despite Mayor Jones' intolerance and refusal to offer translation services to francophones, Acadians did not submit quietly to the labour of self-translation into English that life in 1960s New Brunswick seemed to demand. Instead, they saw that the path to surmounting assimilation lay in Acadian unilingualism and a more intimate connection with Acadian culture. They understood that Jones' obstinate position on translation was grounded in his desire to see Acadians quietly fade into the dominant English culture through self-translation. They also wagered that the key to improved communication between the two language groups was increased bilingualism on the part of anglophones, for bilingual anglophones would then assume the task of translating Acadie into English.

"A Cry to Fend Off Death" through Poetry

The turn to nationalist poetry written by Acadians during the 1960s and especially the 1970s stemmed from and echoed the concerns that the students shared with city councillors in 1968.[7] Important collections, such as *Cri de terre* by Raymond Guy LeBlanc (1972), the first publication by the newly founded Les Éditions d'Acadie, *Acadie Rock* by Guy Arsenault (1973), and *Mourir à Scoudouc* by Herménégilde Chiasson (1974), exemplify the Acadian nationalism of this period,[8] and contributed actively to the Second Acadian Renaissance. Like their Quebec counterparts, they decried one-sided bilingualism that more often than not resulted in identity disintegration and, eventually, assimilation. In the following passage from LeBlanc's "Je suis Acadien," the first two lines vehemently denounce the insinuation of English into the most emotional areas of personal expression: "Je jure en anglais tous mes goddams de bâtard / Et souvent les fuck it me remontent à la gorge" (65). He concludes in anguish:

> Je suis acadien
> Ce qui signifie
> Multiplié fourré dispersé acheté aliéné vendu révolté
> Homme déchiré vers l'avenir. (65)

The anxiety expressed by Acadian poets in and through their bilingual verse results in linguistically hybrid poetry that combines the dominated and dominant languages in such a way that the verse can hardly be translated into English without sacrificing the expression of sociolinguistic angst that is at its centre (Mboudjeke). Exploring the alarming and demoralizing impact of assimilation on the Acadian psyche in the 1970s and the perceived danger of a hybrid language despite its aesthetic qualities, Mboudjeke takes as a case in point Jean Fraterne's poem, "Voilà mon pays,"[9] which describes the sociolinguistic reality that confronted Acadians on a daily basis. While, at the outset, the poet refers optimistically to the spirit of bilingualism that was intended to unite Canada's two charter language groups and put them on an equal sociolinguistic footing, hard reality quickly rids him of his idealistic illusions. In fact, only francophones are bilingual. At work and in social settings, they speak in English to the anglophone majority. French is very rarely used.

> Deux langues, un cœur,
> Two languages, one heart,
> Voilà mon pays
> Bilinguisme et biculturalisme
> Bilingualism and biculturalism.
> (Fraterne, in Mboudjeke 89)

Similarly, the prose poem "Jaune" (1974) by Herménégilde Chiasson explores the source of the problem,[10] and lays it squarely on the shoulders of patronizing anglophones and bilingual Acadians who submit body prostrate to unilingualism:

> PLEASE PLEASE PLEASE please kill us [...] please treat us like shit please, le premier mot que nous apprenons à leur dire et le dernier que nous leur dirons please. Please, make us a beautiful ghetto, not in a territory, no, no, right in us, [...] Nous fondons comme une roche à la chaleur de l'indifférence de la tolérance de la diplomatie du bilinguisme [...] de l'aplatventrisme chronique. (Chiasson, in Mboudjeke 91)

Writers who wish to address the anglophone public with such verse are faced with the daunting challenge of transferring not only the words but also the emotionally charged message that the choice of a hybrid language articulates. In other words, Fraterne's, Chiasson's, and LeBlanc's poetry is hardly translatable into English without serious loss of the fragments of English that are in the French text and that exemplify the poet's sociolinguistic distress. The dominant English-language group that represents the cultural threat would thus find it hard to hear the minority culture's unique voice. Nevertheless, translations were done: by New Brunswick's Fred Cogswell – whose mother was an assimilated Acadian[11] – from the 1970s,[12] and jointly by Cogswell and Jo-Anne Elder (subsequent to her move to Fredericton) in 1990: *Unfinished Dreams*, an anthology of Acadian poetry that was followed the same year by the publication of *Rêves inachêvés*, the French "original."[13]

From Unfinished Dreams to "Side-by-Side/Côte-à-côte"

In *Unfinished Dreams*, Cogswell and Elder translated a broad selection of modern Acadian literature into the dominant language, thereby helping Acadian poets free themselves from self-translation into English.[14] However, only one of the poems examined in the previous section was included in the Cogswell and Elder collection, LeBlanc's "Je suis Acadien." It is possible that Cogswell and Elder interpreted the bilingual poems of Fraterne and Chiasson as a deliberate attempt on the part of the poets to undermine the possibility of translation. And, in a show of intercultural respect, the translators deferred to the poets' wishes. In other words, they understood that the translation of Fraterne's and Chiasson's hybrid poems into English would incur the loss of the fragments of English that exemplify the Acadian poets' sociolinguistic distress. Anglophones who wished to read their poems would have to be bilingual. Raoul Boudreau, professor of Acadian literature at the Université de Moncton, gave his stamp of approval to this anthology by penning the introduction.

In 2002, Canada's only journal of literary translation, *Revue Ellipse mag*, moved from Sherbrooke to Fredericton to be edited by Elder. In addition, Elder founded a small literary translation festival, Side by Side Festival Côte à côte, the only festival of its kind in Canada. It is held annually starting on International Translation Day (30 September) in Fredericton and Moncton. Since the beginning of the new millennium, the translation of Acadian writing in New Brunswick has not been limited to poetry. Fiction has been added to the list thanks to translations of Gérald Leblanc's *Moncton Mantra* (1997/2001)[15] and Françoise Enguehard's *Les litanies de l'Île aux Chiens* (*Tales from Dog Island: St Pierre and Miquelon*) (1999 /2002),[16] both of which were written primarily in "standard" French and translated by Jo-Anne Elder.[17]

Further, the dissemination of Acadian theatre to the anglophone majority is also taking place through translation: *Angels and Anger: Five Acadian Plays*, translated by Glen Nichols,[18] was published in 2003 by Toronto's Playwrights Canada Press after the plays were performed in English in New Brunswick and elsewhere. One of the plays, Laval Goupil's *Dark Owl*, was put on by the National Theatre School (Montreal) and then toured to the Magnetic North Festival in Ottawa (2003) (Nichols, e-mail exchange).

Acadian drama critic David Lonergan lauds the translations and assesses the use of both English and French in the texts as interesting (6). He also notes with surprise that two of the works, Chiasson's *Cap Enragé* and Vanhecke's *Le tapis de Grand-Pré*, had not yet been published in French. Bruce Barton calls Nichols' achievement "a particularly impressive landmark in Canadian dramatic publishing" that opens "French-language Acadian drama to a broader audience of spectators and readers" (276). Gillian Lane-Mercier adds that this collection offers:

> an overview not only of [each play's] thematic, social, and political content but also of the translation difficulties encountered. These range from questions of word-play and imagery to problems related to dialect and voice. Nichols has been successful in [...] maintaining their "acadianness." Extremely readable, his translations will undoubtedly evoke for non-Maritime Anglophone readers a subtle sense of otherness, especially in the case of Goupil's and Couturier's plays. (292)

In other words, there have been some noteworthy production and reception of English translations of Acadian work produced by bilingual New Brunswickers, and in several different genres. In fact, both Elder's *Tales of Dog Island* and Nichols' *Angels and Anger* were shortlisted for the 2003 Governor General's Award for literary translation into English. Yet, in his essay "When the Same Isn't Similar: Herménégilde Chiasson in English," Nichols is not in the least self-congratulatory, expressing regret that Chiasson's plays in translation "are read as more sociological than artistic, as a kind of examination of this 'other' culture" (81). In the introduction to his anthology of theatre translation, he notes that his translations are rarely staged and may, in fact, have inadvertently been transformed into ethnographic "museum pieces" (Nichols, "Angels," iii).[19] Indeed, readability may, ironically, be the most important drawback of his theatre translation work.

Unfinished Dreams, the poetry anthology, is also highly readable, in some instances thanks to the erasure of uncomfortable linguistic hybridity: the English version of LeBlanc's "I Am Acadian" is a clear example (see Table 6.1).

While Fred Cogswell and Jo-Anne Elder produce an accurate translation of LeBlanc's heart-wrenching poem from a linguistic point of view, they

Table 6.1 LeBlanc's "I Am Acadian"

Je suis Acadien	I Am Acadian
Je jure en anglais tous mes goddams de bâtard	I curse in English every mongrel *goddamn* in the book
Et souvent les fuck it me remontent à la gorge	And *fuck-its* often stick in my throat
Avec des Jesus Christ projetés contre le windshield	Along with *christs* flung against the *windshield*
Saignant medium-rare	Bleeding *medium-rare*
Si au moins j'avais quelques tabernacles à douze étages	Had I at least a few twelve-storey *tabernacles*
Et des hosties toastées	And toasted *hosties*
Je saurais que je suis québécois	I'd know myself to be a Québécois
Et que je sais me moquer des cathédrales de la peur	Know I could blaspheme cathedrals of fear
Je suis Acadien, je me contente d'imiter le parvenu	But I am Acadian and content with aping Johnny-come-lately
Avec son Chrysler shiné et sa photo dans les journaux	With his shiny *Chrysler* and his picture in the papers
Combien de jours me faudra-t-il encore	How much longer will it take
Avant que c'te guy icitte me run over	Before this *guy* here *runs me over*
Quand je cross la street pour me crosser dans la chambre	When I *cross the street* to play with myself in a room
Et qu'on m'enterre enfin dans un cimetière	And they put me at last in a graveyard
Comme tous les autres	Like all the others
Au chant de "Tu retourneras en poussière"	To the tune of "You will return to dust"
Et puis Marde	And then Shit
Qui dit qu'on ne l'est pas déjà	Who says we're not that already

Table 6.1 LeBlanc's "I Am Acadian"   *Continued*

"Je suis Acadien	I am Acadian
Ce qui signifie	Which means
Multiplié fourré dispersé acheté aliéné vendu révolté	Stuffed dispersed bought alienated sold out rebellious
Homme déchiré vers l'avenir"	A here there and everywhere
	Man torn open towards the future

Source: Raymond LeBlanc, *Cri de terre: Poèmes* [1972] 1992: 65.

Source: Fred Cogswell and Jo-Anne Elder, eds. and trans., *Unfinished Dreams*, 1990: 121.

seem unable – despite their best efforts – to reproduce the sociopolitical tensions that underpin the source text, conveyed through the use of English swear words in the French poem (goddams/goddamn, fuck it/fuck-its) in addition to Chiac ("windshield," "medium-rare," "guy," "me run over," "cross la street").[20] This is not to say that they do not make a valiant attempt at reproducing linguistic hybridity, the manifestation of Acadian sociolinguistic angst. Their solution is to make certain English words stand out in the English text by italicizing them. Unfortunately, English readers may simply wonder why the italics are there. It will likely not occur to them that the italicized words are drawing attention to vestiges of English in the French source text or to culturally bound French words (hosties, tabernacles).[21] Translation is one labour of communication among many that can work towards intercultural understanding. In this case, however, it has had the effect of largely erasing the issue of identity disintegration that LeBlanc highlighted in his poem, and muting his unique voice.

One is left to ponder the circumstances under which members of a dominant culture might be able to develop a translation strategy that successfully reproduces the sociopolitical underpinnings and effects of source texts produced by a dominated culture.[22] It must be acknowledged that members of the dominant culture are – at times despite themselves and often unconsciously – in a vertical (power) relationship with respect to the dominated culture.[23] Some well-intentioned attempts at translating, representing, and valorizing Otherness in the New Brunswick, not to mention the Canadian, context may thus have unexpected and unplanned effects. Translators can successfully transfer words and produce ethnographic documents; however, doing so may be at the expense of the emotionally charged message that the original text articulates, that is, the author's sociolinguistic distress or political discontent. As a result, the minority culture's unique voice may inadvertently be silenced in translation. It is perhaps more ethical in such instances to opt for non-translation, which amounts to acknowledging with due humility the limits of translation and recognizing that to understand the experiences of the "other" one must share those experiences. The solution, then, would be for anglophones to learn French. This would enable them to read the hybrid originals, which is perhaps, when all is said and done, the intention of the poets.

Some progress has been made in New Brunswick to correct the one-sided bilingualism decried in the 1960s and 1970s. French immersion programs are popular, and the proportion of bilingual anglophones has increased from 14 per cent to 16 per cent during the ten years spanning 1996 to 2006. During the same period, bilingualism in French and English among New Brunswick allophones increased to 16.9 per cent from 15.7 per cent.[24] Apparently understanding that translations cannot always meet the challenge of transferring the emotionally charged message that a hybrid language articulates, many New Brunswick anglophones and allophones have chosen to read and listen to the unique voice of the franco-Acadian culture. Although progress has been made in making the province of New Brunswick both bicultural and bilingual, the dream of linguistic and cultural parity between the charter languages has yet to be achieved. And assimilation is still a problem.[25] Yet relations in the public arena between the two language groups have improved dramatically since those tense years of the late 1960s and 1970s. Even if fewer anglophones learn French than francophones learn English, the former are more tolerant of the French minority and generally support the principle of equal language rights. Literary translators such as Cogswell, Elder, and Nichols have sought to contribute to this progress through their sincere efforts to make Acadian otherness comprehensible to the dominant language group and to promote intercultural understanding.

In 2008, the Université de Moncton celebrated the fortieth anniversary of the student unrest that was the catalyst of social change and that culminated in Moncton city council's decision of 7 August 2002 to make both languages official, the first city in Canada to do so. Where the refusal to translate in the 1970s was a measure of the confrontational relationship between the anglophone and francophone populations of New Brunswick, the subsequent years and the subsequent translations and translation events bear witness to considerable improvements. The challenging and painful texts of the Acadian Renaissance spoke of sociopolitical dysfunction; the translators provided versions whose effects underline the necessary ongoing processes of communication.

Notes

1 The book from which this quotation is taken is Gérald Leblanc 1988 (Chiasson signed the preface).

2 Mayor of Moncton from 1963 to 1973.

3 For a television broadcast that provides detailed information about the "first" nineteenth-century Acadian Renaissance, we refer readers to a Radio-Canada interview (in French) with Anselme Chiasson, "La première renaissance acadienne."

4 The Université de Moncton, founded in 1963 during the tenure of Louis J. Robichaud, the first elected Acadian premier of New Brunswick, is the largest francophone university outside Quebec; its primary mandate is to serve the French-speaking Acadian community.

5 The film was not viewed by the Acadian community until 1972.

6 Not only Moncton students found the mayor to be reactionary. In a speech to the Alliance for the Preservation of English in Canada made by Jones in Toronto on 20 November 1978, Jones admits he was "thrown out of the Conservative Party" before he was elected to the House of Commons as an independent Member of Parliament for Moncton.

7 The phrase cited in the heading of this section is taken from Raoul Boudreau's, "Poetry as Action" (xix).

8 The Parti acadien existed from 1972 to 1982 and was founded in northeastern New Brunswick, a region that was noticeably poorer than the "golden triangle" of southern New Brunswick (Fredericton, St John, Moncton). Its first leader was Euclide Chiasson. The party's goal was to create an autonomous Acadian province.

9 The poem was first published in Runte, Chiasson, and LeVert, *Plumes d'icitte: La première Acadie s'exprime*, 111.

10 The poem was first published in Chiasson, *Mourir à Scoudouc*, 44.

11 For a detailed and revealing biography of Fred W. Cogswell, see the *New Brunswick Literary Encyclopedia* which can be consulted online.

12 The following is a partial list of Acadian poetry first translated by Fred Cogswell in the 1970s and published in *Canadian Literature*, sometimes under different names: Guy Arsenault: "To Celebrate September," "The Wharf"; Herménégilde Chiasson: "Between the Season of Extravagant Love and the Season of Raspberries," "All the King's Horses"; Ronald Després: "Hymn to Spring," "I Loved You," "I Thought of You All Day"; Léonard Forest: "And I Dreamed of a Great Black Sun"; Raymond Guy LeBlanc: "Winter," "Land-cry."

13 Fred Cogswell and Jo-Anne Elder, *Unfinished Dreams* and *Rêves inachêvés*.

14 The phrase in the heading alludes to the title of Jo-Anne Elder's "Côte-à-côte: Traduction et diffusion de la littérature acadienne." See White, "La traduction littéraire en Acadie"; and White, Blanchard, and Noël, *Bibliographie de l'Acadie traduite*, for references to Acadian literature translated by Acadians, among others.

15 Gérald Leblanc's French original *Moncton Mantra* was published in 1997 by Moncton's Perce-Neige. Elder's English translation that bears the same title was published in 2001.

16 The French original was published by Moncton's Édition d'Acadie and the English translation by Creative Book Publishing of St John's, Newfoundland.

17 See, in particular, Chantal Richard's article, "La problématique de la langue dans la forme et le contenu de deux romans plurilingues acadiens: *Bloupe* de Jean Babineau et *Moncton Mantra* de Gérald Leblanc," in which the author notes Leblanc's choice of "standard French" timidly peppered with *Chiac*, despite his calls for a *Chiac* literature.

18 The five plays translated by Glen Nichols – formerly a professor of English and head of the Department of English at the Université de Moncton, now director of Drama at Mount Alison University – are Herménégilde Chiasson's *Alienor* (*Aliénor*) and *Cape Enrage* (*Cap Enragé*), Gracia Couturier's *My Husband's an Angel* (*Mon mari est un ange*), Laval Goupil's *Dark Owl, or The Renegade Angel* (*Le Djibou, ou l'Ange déserteur*), and Ivan Vanhecke's *Twelve Strands of Wool* (*Le Tapis de Grand-pré*).

19 For a detailed discussion of the relationship between ethnography and translation, see Kate Sturge's *Representing Others*.

20 In "Aspects fondamentaux du metissage français/anglais dans le chiac de Moncton (Nouveau-Brunswick)," Marie-Ève Perrot explains that *Chiac* has a

French matrix and a vocabulary that is peppered with English. However, the degree of anglicization is variable, and often depends on the communication situation of the speaker.

21 For an examination of the Cogswell/Elder translation of this poem's hybridity, see Merkle, 79–81.

22 In this essay, we set out to study translations produced in New Brunswick of the works of Acadian writers. It is thus, unfortunately, beyond the scope here to present examples of minoritizing translation such as Majzels' *Life's Little Difficulties*, his translation of France Daigle's *Les petites difficultés d'existence*. In his translation, Majzels attempts to create an English equivalent of Moncton *Chiac* (see Leclerc, "Between French and English, Between Ethnography and Assimilation," for an analysis of the translation).

23 For an exploration of vertical and horizontal translation strategies, see the in-augural issue of *Alternative francophone,* "La traduction verticale ou horizon-tale?"

24 For additional information, see Statistique Canada, "Tableau 17."

25 In 1996, 242,410 New Brunswickers declared their mother tongue to be French (33.2 per cent); in the 2006 census, the number dropped to 235,270, or 32.7 per cent of the province's population; see Statistique Canada, "Tableau A5." In addition, consider the popularity of *Chiac* spoken in large part, but not exclusively, by Acadian youth in southeastern New Brunswick. Considerable debate surrounds the language that some consider a sign of assimilation and others a sign of resistance. For an extensive bibliography, see Chevalier, "Les français du Canada: Faits linguistiques, faits de langue"; and Leclerc, "Between French and English."

Works Cited

Alternative francophone. "La traduction verticale ou horizontale? Entre langues et cultures en 'mode mineur.'" *Alternative francophone* 1: 1 (2008). http://ejournals.library.ualberta.ca/index.php/af/issue/view/346

Arsenault, Guy. "Les Éditions d'Acadie." *Acadie Rock,* 1973.

Barton, Bruce. "Letters in Canada 2003: Drama." *University of Toronto Quarterly* 74: 1 (2004–05): 250–77.

Boudreau, Raoul. "Poetry as Action." *Unfinished Dreams*. Fredericton: Goose Lane Books, 1990, xvii–xxvii.

Brault, Michel, and Pierre Perrault. *L'Acadie, l'Acadie?!?* Ottawa: Office national du film, 1971. http://www.onf.ca/film/Acadie_Acadie/

Chevalier, Gisèle. "Les français du Canada: faits linguistiques, faits de langue." *Alternative Francophone* 1: 1 (2008). https://ejournals.library.ualberta.ca/index.php/af/article/view/4139/3381

Chiasson, Anselme. "La première renaissance acadienne." *Reflets d'un pays.* Radio-Canada. 31 aug. 1984. http://archives.radio-canada.ca/politique/langue_culture/clips/2396/

Chiasson, Herménégilde. *Mourir à Scoudouc.* Moncton: Éditions d'Acadie, 1974.

– Préface. *L'Extrême frontière: Poèmes 1972–1988.* Gérald Leblanc. Moncton: Les Éditions d'Acadie, 1988.

Cogswell, Fred. *New Brunswick Literary Encyclopedia.* http://w3.stu.ca/stu/sites/nble/c/cogswell_frederick_william.html

– *Rêves inachêvés.* Moncton: Les Éditions d'Acadie, 1990.

– and Jo-Anne Elder, eds. and trans. *Unfinished Dreams.* Fredericton: Goose Lane Books, 1990.

Daigle, France. *Les petites difficultés d'existence.* Montréal: Boréal, 2002.

Elder, Jo-Anne. "Côte-à-côte: traduction et diffusion de la littérature acadienne." *L'émergence et la reconnaissance des études acadiennes: À la rencontre de Soi et de l'Autre.* Ed. Marie-Linda Lord. Moncton: Université de Moncton and Association internationale des études acadiennes, 2005, 158–78.

– trans. *Moncton Mantra.* Toronto: Guernica, 2001.

Enguehard, Françoise. Trans. Jo-Anne Elder. *Les litanies de l'Île aux Chiens / Tales from Dog Island: St Pierre and Miquelon.* St John's: Killick Press, 2002.

Jones, Leonard. "The Bigot: Speech to the Alliance for the Preservation of English in Canada." Toronto. 20 Nov. 1978. http://www.languagefairness.ca/docs/news_bigot.htm

Lane-Mercier, Gillian. "Letters in Canada 2003: Traductions/Translations, Trends in English-Language Translation." *University of Toronto Quarterly* 74: 1 (2004–05): 283–93.

Leblanc, Gérald. *Moncton Mantra.* Moncton: Perce-Neige, 1997.

LeBlanc, Raymond. *Cri de terre: Poèmes* [1972]. Pref. Pierre l'Hérault. Crit. anal. Murielle Belliveau. Moncton: Les Éditions d'Acadie, 1992.

Leclerc, Catherine. "Between French and English, Between Ethnography and Assimilation: Strategies for Translating Moncton's Acadian Vernacular." *TTR: Traduction, traductologie, rédaction* 18: 2 (2005): 161–92.

Lonergan, David. "Un événement maintenant incontournable." *L'Acadie Nouvelle,* 2 mai (2003): 6.

Majzels, Robert. *Life's Little Difficulties.* Toronto: House of Anansi, 2004.

Mboudjeke, Jean-Guy. "La poésie acadienne: Entre esthétique de l'hybridité et intraduisibilité." *Traduire depuis les marges / Translating from the Margins*. Eds. Denise Merkle, Jane Koustas, Glen Nichols, and Sherry Simon. Québec: Nota bene, 2008, 75–92.

Merkle, Denise. "Francophone Dynamics in a Translated Canada: From the Margins to the Centre and Back." *Translation Today* 7: 1–2 (2010): 69–95.

Nichols, Glen, ed. and trans. *Angels and Anger: Five Acadian Plays*. Toronto: Playwrights Canada Press, 2003.

– E-mail exchange with D. Merkle. 23 March 2009.

– "When the Same Isn't Similar: Herménégilde Chiasson in English." *TTR: Traduction, traductologie, rédaction* 22: 2 (2009): 63–92.

Perrot, Marie-Ève. "Aspects fondamentaux du metissage français/anglais dans le chiac de Moncton (Nouveau-Brunswick)." Doctoral dissertation. Paris: Université de la Sorbonne nouvelle, 1995.

Richard, Chantal. "La problématique de la langue dans la forme et le contenu de deux romans plurilingues acadiens: *Bloupe* de Jean Babineau et *Moncton Mantra* de Gérald Leblanc." *Studies in Canadian Literature / Études en littérature canadienne* 23: 2 (1998): 19–35.

Runte, Hans R., Jules Chiasson, and Nicole LeVert, eds. *Plumes d'icitte:la première Acadie s'exprime*. Yarmouth: Imprimerie Lescarbot, 1979.

Statistique Canada. "Tableau A-5, Population de langue maternelle française, Canada, provinces, territoires et Canada moins le Québec, 1996 à 2006." http://www12.statcan.ca/census-recensement/2006/as-sa/97-555/table/A5-fra.cfm

– "Tableau 17, Taux de bilinguisme français/anglais chez les anglophones et les allophones, (langue maternelle unique), Canada, provinces, territoires et Canada moins le Québec, 1996 à 2006." http://www12.statcan.ca/census-recensement/2006/as-sa/97-555/table/t17-fra.cfm

Sturge, Kate. *Representing Others: Translation, Ethnography and the Museum*. Manchester: St Jerome Publishing, 2007.

White, Mylène. *La traduction littéraire en Acadie: sources premières et sources secondes*. Moncton: Université de Moncton Institut d'études acadiennes, 2008. http://www0.umoncton.ca/iea/Documents/4.B.1-Biblio._000.pdf

– Christian Blanchard, and Julie-Anne Noël. *Bibliographie de l'Acadie traduite*. 2nd ed. Moncton: Institut d'études acadiennes *forthcoming*.

7

1970: The October Crisis and the FLQ Manifesto

Robert Schwartzwald

The 1970 October Crisis forced Canadians to think hard about the nature of their federation and the place of Quebec within it. It also tested their willingness to defend, or yield, civil liberties in the face of political violence exercised by a small, terrorist organization. Throughout, only those relatively few English-speakers in Quebec and across the country who possessed sufficient knowledge of French were able to follow "the biggest domestic news story Canada had ever experienced" (Wainstein xx) in the *version originale*.[1] For the majority of Canadians, key moments of this unprecedented drama took place in a language they did not understand and through the filter of French-to-English translation.

Before October 1970, most English-speaking Canadians knew the Front de Libération du Quebec (FLQ) by its *acts*, especially the successive bombing campaigns it unleashed beginning in 1963. By placing bombs in mailboxes in wealthy, anglophone Westmount, the FLQ not only symbolically, but literally addressed its anti-colonial, pro-independence message to English-speaking Canadians.[2] With the kidnapping of British Trade Commissioner James Cross, on 5 October 1970, *words* became of paramount importance as the FLQ issued a string of communiqués listing the conditions for the diplomat's safe release.[3] On 8 October, in compliance with one of the group's seven demands for Cross's release, the FLQ Manifesto was read in prime time on Radio-Canada, the French-language counterpart of the Canadian Broadcasting Corporation.[4] The document went beyond the limited, conjunctural content of the communiqués to provide the most complete account of the group's vision of Quebec as an oppressed nation poised for independence and anti-capitalist revolution. Yet, for this important event, English-speaking Canadians were faced with a significant *translation gap*, as the CBC did not offer a simultaneous telecast.

As the crisis deepened, events followed quickly upon each other: on 10 October, Quebec Deputy Premier and Labour Minister Pierre Laporte was kidnapped by another FLQ cell;[5] on 16 October, a state of "apprehended insurrection" was declared, leading to the first peace-time imposition of the War Measures Act in Canadian history.[6] The Act allowed police to search without warrant and detain individuals indefinitely without charges. Hundreds of trade union leaders, social movement activists, and artists were rounded up and imprisoned while the military patrolled the streets of Montreal. On 17 October, Laporte was murdered. What information and whose voices were translated – and when – not only reveal much about the fears and assumptions that prevailed at the time, but also shaped the assessments made of the long-term impact of the October Crisis on relations between Quebec and the rest of Canada. Indeed, differences in French and English media coverage of the events have been the subject of much debate and even polemic, both at the time and in subsequent scholarly reflection. Raphael Cohen-Almagor offers the following assessment:

> The French-language papers stressed the search for a peaceful solution and the negotiation aspect of the situation; they were interested in the international reaction to the crisis, especially from Europe and *la Francophonie.* They also focused more on personalities and civil rights issues. The English-language press, in contrast, focused attention on the manhunt for the terrorists, largely dealing with police activities connected with apprehending the kidnappers and freeing the hostages. They also reported on political institutions and on the economic cost of the crisis, and showed a greater interest in the national and American reaction to the crisis." ("The Terrorists' Best Ally")

Given the FLQ's politics, the absence of an "official" translation of the Manifesto is hardly surprising. Although the CBC did not provide one at the time, a variety of translations and summaries filled the vacuum in the days that followed. In Montreal, the *Gazette* published the Manifesto in full, on 9 October, while the *Star* preferred to merely summarize it in seven brief paragraphs, choosing particularly inflammatory passages and concluding its report by citing the Manifesto's proclamation that "the day is arriving where [*sic*] the Westmounts of Quebec will disappear from the map."[7] While neither the Toronto *Globe and Mail* nor the *Ottawa Citizen* published a complete translation, the larger-circulation *Toronto Daily Star* did, but in a different version from the *Gazette*'s.[8] In the months following the Crisis, translations of the Manifesto appeared in several special journal issues devoted to the events.[9] The Manifesto began:

> Le Front de libération du Québec n'est pas le Messie, ni un Robin des bois des temps modernes. C'est un regroupement de travailleurs québécois qui sont décidés de tout mettre en œuvre pour que le peuple du Québec prenne définitivement en mains son destin. (Simard 11)

> The Front de libération du Québec is not a messiah, nor a modern-day Robin Hood. It is a group of Quebec workers who have decided to use all means to make sure that the people of Quebec take control of their destiny. ("FLQ Manifesto")

In authorizing the Radio-Canada broadcast of the Manifesto, federal External Affairs Minister Mitchell Sharp undoubtedly shared the confidence of many of his Cabinet colleagues and, in particular, Secretary of State Gérard Pelletier that the document's radical views would discredit its authors. It has also been argued that Sharp wagered the concession might buy more time to track down and free Cross at the same time as it showed him to be fulfilling his ministerial responsibility to protect a foreign diplomat.[10]

It quickly became clear, however, that Sharp had miscalculated. It took only thirteen minutes for Gaëtan Montreuil, a public service announcer (pointedly, *not* a newscaster), to read the Manifesto "for humanitarian reasons," but that was sufficient to confer "stature" to the FLQ, in the words of *Canadian Dimension*. The reading of the Manifesto contributed enormously to what Montreal *Star* reporter Terence Moore regarded as the FLQ's initial success: to the degree that revolutionaries must shatter "the mystique of power and the permanence of the state [...], for a time [the FLQ] made fools of the police and opened a breach in the appearance of power" (Moore).

From radical leftist magazines like *Canadian Dimension* to centre-left ones like *Canadian Forum* and even conservative papers like the *Financial Post*, journalists and commentators seized upon the events to offer analyses of the socio-economic, political, and cultural issues plaguing Quebec. At the outset, however, what a great many in the English-language Canadian media found themselves *translating* for their readers was the broad sympathy the Manifesto had elicited from francophone Quebecers. As Montreal journalist Ann Charney diffidently noted in the *Toronto Daily Star*, the sentiments and goals of the FLQ "did find wider support in the French community than one might have expected" (Charney), a situation that led even the conservative *Financial Post* to admonish its readers that the Manifesto "deserves attention, despite its rhetoric. It is a critique of Quebec's lingering institutional weaknesses. It strikes sympathetic chords when it alludes to slow justice, chronic troubles in labour-management relations and the fact that the French language is not used where it should be used" ("The Challenge" n.p.).

This was not the FLQ's first manifesto – others had been issued in April 1963 and June 1970.[11] The revolutionary *anti-capitalist* rhetoric of the October 1970 text distinguished it from its predecessors. *Canadian Dimension* found the text's effective cataloguing of social injustices to be "devoid of the usual jargon"; accordingly, "many Quebeckers who could not approve the kidnappings could easily associate with the message of the manifesto" ("War Declared" 5).[12] The *New York Times* noted how the Manifesto was "worded to appeal to working people" (Cowan), while in the *Toronto Daily Star* Andrew Salwyn reported that the text's "tough language" hardly shocked workers in an east-end Montreal tavern, who appreciated its explicit support in the many labour conflicts of the day and especially its denunciation of members of the ruling class *by name* ("Jobless"). Sometimes, the translation of these class-struggle sentiments missed the mark for lack of context: when, for example, the FLQ boasts that "100,000 revolutionary workers" will be ready to confront Quebec Premier Robert Bourassa, it is engaging in a rhetorical flourish, mocking Bourassa's campaign promise earlier in the year to create 100,000 new jobs in Quebec. Yet, this phrase was often quoted in English media as proof that a state of "apprehended insurrection" existed in Quebec.

Particularly curious is the variety of ways in which the Manifesto's scathing reference to "Trudeau la tapette" is translated. Anti-colonial, proindependence militants in Quebec had long used homophobic invective against their federalist adversaries. For them, the *homme colonisé québécois* was inauthentic, emasculated, and prone to perform degraded imitations of his colonial master. In the "Portrait du colonisé québécois" issue of *Parti pris*, the journal that best exemplified these views during the 1960s, such *vendus*, or "sell-outs," are infamously referred to as *fédérastes* (*fédéraliste* + *pédéraste*, a French term of opprobrium for homosexuals).[13] While the *Toronto Daily Star* refers to Trudeau "the queer" and the James Boake translation of 1973 to "Trudeau the pansy," the Montreal *Gazette* demurely allows Trudeau to be castigated as a "chatterbox!" Was the paper trying to spare the feelings of the warrior prime minister who, in his various statements at the time, went out of his way to mock the "bleeding hearts" and "weak-kneed people" who weren't able to stomach his strong prescriptions for restoring law and order? Of course, once Trudeau gave his famous "just watch me" interview and imposed the War Measures Act, criticisms of his supposed weakness evaporated.[14] While some commentators in English Canada did question the necessity of the Act, most fell into line.

Coming so soon after the euphoria of Canada's centennial celebrations in 1967, and especially in the afterglow of Montreal's dazzling Expo 67, there is no doubt that the October Crisis came as a bitter shock to English Canada. Yet, in truth, the Expo festivities had provided only temporary relief from the social upheaval in Quebec that had been making Canadians uneasy throughout the decade. If the FLQ attacks that began in 1963 were the work of small cells of terrorists, the same could not be said about the enormous protests at the time of the royal visit in 1964, when thousands lined the streets to turn their backs on *La Queen*. Many thousands more cheered French President Charles de Gaulle when, three years later, he exclaimed, "*Vive le Québec libre!*" from the balcony of Montreal's City Hall. Then, there was the 1969 campaign to demand that Montreal's prestigious, English-language McGill University become *McGill français*, and the raucous demonstrations the same year against Bill 63, which was seen as a direct threat to the survival of the French language in Quebec because it allowed all parents – but most importantly immigrants – to choose French or English as the language of education for their children. There were seemingly innumerable labour disputes, with many turning violent, as had the annual Saint-Jean-Baptiste Day parade in 1968 when, the night before the federal election, Pierre Elliott Trudeau stood stonily on a reviewing stand in Montreal as protesters pelted him with eggs and the police launched assaults on the crowd.

By the time of the October Crisis, it was not so uncommon for English Canadian journalists to present Quebec's turbulent social and political reality as essentially foreign. In the *Maclean's* issue of January 1971, Peter Desbarats quoted early twentieth century Prime Minister Wilfrid Laurier's contention that "Quebec does not have opinions, but only sentiments" to claim that democracy is an inherently alien, or untranslatable, concept there. He reassures English Canadians that they should not worry themselves about "applying political principles that don't conform to real conditions" (7–8).[15] To do so would be "folly," Desbarats argues, noting that "Quebec society remains essentially the most conservative in Canada." He insists that only the profound alienation of Quebec intellectuals from the deep conservatism of the masses leads them to take such desperate measures as supporting or joining the FLQ. Published in a large-circulation magazine like *Maclean*'s, Desbarrat's article comforts English Canada and absolves it of any responsibility for what is transpiring in Quebec (he does, however, reserve a few words of blame for the English minority in Quebec).[16] Similarly, in the generally anti–War Measures Act *Canadian Forum*, a dissenting contribution by J.W. Daly heaps scorn on critical intellectuals in English Canada, arguing that "in nothing have our intellectuals shown themselves more isolated from the country than in their total failure to *feel* with it." In other words, English-Canadian intellectuals had failed to grasp that the "unity of feeling" to which the October events gave rise among ordinary Canadians "was not anti-Quebec at all [but] was built on an instinctive sympathy for Quebecers" (22–3). Daly, it should be noted, was writing in the wake of Laporte's murder, when polls consistently showed an overwhelming majority of people in Quebec, as in the rest of Canada, supporting the imposition of the War Measures Act.

Robin Spry's documentary film *Reaction* (1973) records the response to the October events by diverse groups of English-speaking Montrealers, many of them immigrants.[17] Each translates the October events through the prism of life experience, whether they be Hungarian émigrés who fled after 1956, corporate executives, or students. The traumatic impact of the events is obvious, but not always in the ways one would expect. It is the well-off immigrant guest in a stately Westmount home who responds to Trudeau's speech justifying the War Measures Act by protesting, "That's how it all started in Germany in 1932 and '33!" Conversely, it is a mother in the poor district of Saint-Henri who, braving the scepticism of others around the table, expresses relief at seeing troops in the streets of Montreal, insisting that she now felt safer herself and for her children.

The translation of the FLQ's aims and methods through the filter of international terrorism also became de rigueur in the media, especially after the kidnapping and murder of Laporte. In its retrospective issue on the crisis, *Canadian Dimension* notes how "to give the whole affair the flavour of an international conspiracy, many newspapers included on their front pages a series of articles about guerilla training in Algeria and Cuba" ("War Declared" 16), and cites an article in *Weekend* magazine (a supplement to many Saturday editions of Canadian newspapers) in which journalist Patricia Welbourn "interviewed two young Québécois training with Arab commandos in Jordan. They were learning the art of 'selective assassination'" ("War Declared" 33); a Radio-Canada reportage featured the same story.

The international press, in particular, associated the FLQ's acts with those of revolutionary groups abroad. The *Times* of London compared the initiative held by the FLQ in the early days of the Crisis to the one enjoyed by the Popular Front for the Liberation of Palestine (PFLP) after it hijacked a BOAC jet on 9 September 1970. It explained how the FLQ was ideologically aligned with similar groups in the Middle East and Latin America and saw in its revolutionary platform an objective well beyond *le Québec libre*. The new nation, claimed the *Times*, would be "a base from which to attack the United States and the West" ("Dangerous Days").[18] A companion article maintained that the preservation of French language and culture in Quebec are, for the FLQ, "secondary issues, a convenient base from which to work for their own ideals," namely, global revolution (Brigstocke 8). In perhaps the most original linkage of the FLQ to international events, Marshall McLuhan discusses the "resemblance" between hijacking jets and kidnapping dignitaries in the *Toronto Daily Star*. McLuhan maintains that "as long as the FLQ can get coverage, it can win," and the possibilities for coverage are ever greater in the new age of "media decentralization." He observes that "the entire public rallies to the cause of activist minorities [because] the passive and unorganized public always *feels* like a helpless minority" (8).[19]

Another important question for English-language media was the extent to which all oppositional movements in Quebec were to be tarnished by the October events and the FLQ. *Canadian Dimension* lamented that "all too many Canadians [...] were too willing to believe that the FLQ was a symbol of all the dissenting voices. So they cheered the War Emergencies Act [*sic*]" ("War Declared" 4). The magazine's concerns were not exaggerated: when federal Cabinet Minister Jean Marchand claimed that Montreal's Front d'action politique (FRAP) opposition slate was actually a "front" for the FLQ, he effectively wiped it off the map in the November 1970 municipal elections (Marchand would subsequently blame his "bad English" for this "misunderstanding"). As Evelyn Dumas, associate editor of the Montreal *Star*, put it: "Nothing Mr Marchand will say now can repair the damage in time for the election. It would have been just as well if our governments, as an extension of the War Measures Act, had declared [Mayor] Drapeau and his 52 candidates to council elected by decree" (13).

Canadian Dimension went even further, arguing that Trudeau had seized upon the kidnappings as an opportunity to deliver what he hoped would be a lethal blow to the independence movement as a whole. Walter Gordon, the former minister of finance in the Lester Pearson government, essentially concurred, writing in the *Canadian Forum* that "in the public mind, the bomb-throwers, the terrorists, the kidnappers and the murderers of Pierre Laporte have been identified, at least to an extent, with René Lévesque and his Parti Québécois" (27). The *New York Times* found it hard to see how Lévesque would keep his coalition together, given his own revulsion at the FLQ's tactics, on the one hand, and the ambivalent responses of many of the party's members, on the other ("Terrorists Dismay"). Political philosopher Charles Taylor, however, took a different, and prescient view: "In the short run terrorism has set back the cause of peaceful independentism [and] is disastrous for the Parti Québécois; in the long run it may make the PQ appear as the only way out of the impasse" (Taylor 29). Indeed, the Quebec Liberals were re-elected with a large majority in the 1973 provincial elections, and the Parti Québécois celebrated its first electoral victory on 15 November 1976.[20]

By spring 1971, the Crisis had receded.[21] Special journal issues aside, there was reason to suspect that English Canada was still reticent to "comprehend the frustrations that allowed the FLQ to flourish in the first place" (Newman 68). Exemplary in this regard was the response to the publication, in early 1971, of the English translation of *félquiste* Pierre Vallière's autobiography, *Nègres blancs d'Amérique*. The autobiography is precisely a compelling account of growing up poor on Montreal's south shore and of a political apprenticeship that led Vallières to embrace radical social change and Quebec independence. In a review of the book in *Maclean's*, Donald Cameron deplores the lack of critical attention given to it in Canada. Cameron quotes a representative of McClelland and Stewart, the publisher of *White Niggers of America*, who complains that while many thoughtful reviews of the book were appearing abroad (the translation was first published in the US by Monthly Review Press), "most Canadian papers are taking the ostrich approach." He adds: "Let's be honest. Vallières scares us. He makes English Canada feel guilty and defensive. If Quebec is oppressed, we might be the oppressors" (Cameron 72; see also the next chapter herein, by Julie McDonough Dolmaya).

Questions of translation also haunted the discussion of Quebec that took place at the New Democratic Party's convention shortly after the crisis wound down. When the Quebec wing of the party sought to introduce a resolution supporting Quebec's right to self-determination, it chose to distribute campaign buttons bearing the French term *autodétermination*. Michael Cross, reporting on the convention for the *Canadian Forum*, explains how many delegates regarded this as a "shibboleth," or code word for separation. Charles Taylor intervened to deride "ping pong words" and to urge the party to take an unambiguous stand in favour of federalism. In the end, the committee's resolution would be "a federalist document with only minor concessions to Quebec that the NDP would not support maintaining confederation by force" (Cross 6).[22]

Was the sequel to the October Crisis destined to be nothing more than a chilling debate over maintaining Quebec's place in the Canadian federation through brute force? Most of those who sought to translate the events to English-speaking Canadians tried to imagine other ways forward. In his post-Crisis dialogue with Claude Ryan, the editor of Montreal's *Le Devoir*, the daily French "newspaper of record,"[23] Peter C. Newman argued for bridge building, or the effective translation of reciprocal needs, as the alternative: "Perhaps the choices have been reduced to keeping Quebec in Canada by force or working out some arrangement that would cause English Canada to recognize once and for all the special character of your society, while at the same time proving to Quebec that a united Canada is your best guarantee for the long-term survival of the French presence on the continent" ("What Does Quebec Want?" 68). This, of course, has been the challenge at the heart of Canadian politics for the past forty years.

Notes

1 Why would Wainstein's report be produced seven long years after the events?
   The timing can probably be explained by the electoral victory of the pro-
   independence Parti Québécois in November 1976.

2 On 17 May 1963, bombs were placed in ten residential mailboxes in Westmount. Federal buildings and installations were frequent targets in the early
   attacks. A night guard was killed by an FLQ bomb at a Canadian Forces Re-
   cruiting Centre, in April 1963. Towards the end of the 1960s, Eaton's department store, the Montreal Board of Trade, and the Montreal Stock Exchange
   were also targeted.

3 The FLQ selected radio stations CKAC and CKLM as their principal conduits.
   For the most part, the communiqués were treated as news items in the press
   and promptly published in translation, sometimes with a facsimile of the original French version alongside or in the background.

4 The FLQ also demanded that the Manifesto be published in newspapers in
   every region of Quebec.

5 Cross had been kidnapped by the Libération cell of the FLQ; Laporte's kidnapping was carried out by the Chénier cell.

6 The War Measures Act was approved on 19 October in the House of Commons by a vote of 190 to 16. The opposed were all members of the social-
   democratic New Democratic Party, whose leader T.C. Douglas spoke out
   vociferously against the legislation.

7 Only later in the year, when it published an 84-page book on the Crisis, would
   the *Star* publish the full text of the Manifesto (*The FLQ* 80).

8 Neither is signed, and it must be assumed that each newspaper used its own in-
   house or freelance services. The first signed translation of the Manifesto is by
   James Boake. It appears as an appendix in *Quebec in Question* – the translation of Marcel Rioux's *La question du Québec* – first published in 1969 and
   revised in subsequent editions. This translation is also available on Wikipedia.
   The Marianopolis College (Montreal) website contains a different translation,
   by Claude Bélanger.

9 In addition to the Montreal *Star* book (*The FLQ*), the most comprehensive
   treatment is to be found in *Canadian Dimension* (the special issue "War Declared on Quebec," 1970); *Canadian Forum* (issue of Jan. 1971, with responses
   in the issue of April–May 1971); and *Maclean's* ("Quebec: What Now?" Jan.
   1971; "War Measures: Ottawa in Crisis and the Plot that Never Was," Feb.
   1971). This latter issue also featured interviews with prominent Montrealers

detained under the War Measures Act; and "What Does Quebec Want to Be?" (May 1971) featured a dialogue between editor Peter C. Newman and *Le Devoir* editor Claude Ryan.

10 See Cohen-Almagor for a well-documented account of discussions in and around Cabinet.

11 The manifestos are all available in *Le Manuel de la parole: Manifestes québécois* by Daniel Latouche and Diane Poliquin-Bourassa. *Canadian Dimension* published an English translation of the 1963 and the October 1970 manifestos in its special issue "War Declared on Quebec." The *Georgia Straight* in Vancouver published an English translation of the June 1970 Manifesto – which it claims was written in May 1970 – on 14 October 1970, apparently believing it to be the one the FLQ wanted to be broadcast and published.

12 In a *Maclean's* interview, Normand Caron, a 25-year-old Parti Québécois activist, admits that while the FLQ's clandestine structure and terrorist tactics undermined his own, mass-based political action, he regards the televised reading of the Manifesto as an "achievement" that will cause people to think and reflect, in all probability accelerating the process of social change ("Quebec: What Now?").

13 For a fuller discussion, see my "Fear of Federasty: Quebec's Inverted Fictions."

14 After the Manifesto was telecast on Radio-Canada, much of the press, especially in western Canada, attacked Trudeau. "It feels he is pandering to separatism and feeding rather than dousing the flames," remarked the *Times* of London in an editorial entitled "Dangerous Days for Canada." On 16 October, the *Toronto Daily Star* published a summary of what the press across Canada had to say under the headline "Hard Line Advocated on FLQ Demands." Actually, the prime minister was furious with Mitchell Sharp for authorizing the broadcast of the Manifesto. In fact, Trudeau felt the media were giving far too much attention to the events. Speaking in the House of Commons, Trudeau "rebuked the news media for giving extensive publicity" to the kidnappings. For the occasion, he adopted a decorous tone: "I do sometimes wish the media would exercise a bit more restraint in talking about these topics" ("PM Criticizes Press Coverage of Kidnaps" n.p.).

15 In a Letter to the Editor responding to Desbarat's article, one reader wonders where he is writing from: "Pretoria, South Africa?" *Maclean's*, Mar. 1971.

16 So, too, does Ann Charney when she regrets the "smugness and false euphoria" of Quebec anglophones after the Liberal victory in the April 1970 provincial election ("Kidnappers Won Emotional Support"). In the election, the Parti

Québécois received 24 per cent of the popular vote but only seven seats out of 108 in the Quebec National Assembly. The FLQ cites this result in the Manifesto as a reason for rejecting electoral politics.

17 Spry's better-known companion documentary, *Action: The October Crisis of 1970*, was also released in 1973.

18 Two days earlier, the PFLP had hijacked three other jets. One was destroyed in Cairo after the passengers were released, while the other two, like the BOAC jet, were flown to Jordan and destroyed there. In response to the hijackings, the Israeli army arrested some 450 Palestinians in the Occupied Territories, effectively using them as hostages. The *Guardian*, in supporting Prime Minister Trudeau's imposition of the War Measures Act, drew parallels: "The Government has started to play the Front's own game. Even the stupidest French-Canadian terrorist ought to now realize that Mr Trudeau is in effect taking hostages too." The article continues with a lengthy comparison of the FLQ and the PFLP ("Mr Trudeau Counter-Attacks").

19 McLuhan, of course, is writing in the pre-Internet, pre-interactive media age. The FLQ's communiqués still had to be published and disseminated *by someone else*. His observations are further radicalized and superseded by new interactive media, with their direct links to willing and "empowered" consumers and participants.

20 The election of the Parti Québécois did not, of course, signify majority support for Quebec independence. When the government held its referendum on a mandate to negotiate "sovereignty-association" with Ottawa, in May 1980, it lost by a 60–40 margin.

21 One of Pierre Laporte's kidnappers was arrested on 6 November; the other three were found and arrested on 28 December. On 2 December, James Cross was released and his kidnappers flown to Cuba.

22 In his article, Cross makes it clear that he would have preferred the NDP to explore the viability of a strategic alliance with the Parti Québécois around a shared social-democratic orientation, but this is not what came to the floor of the convention.

23 During the Crisis, *Le Devoir* organized Quebec intellectuals and political figures in an appeal to the Canadian government to negotiate for James Cross's release. Ryan was accused of trying to set up an alternative provincial government to replace Robert Bourassa's, a charge that was widely disseminated but shown to be completely false.

Works Cited

Bélanger, Claude. "Manifesto of the FLQ." Marianopolis College Library. 23 Aug. 2000. Accessed 14 Nov. 2009. http://faculty.marianopolis.edu/c.belanger/ quebechistory/docs/october/manifest.htm

Boake, James. *Quebec in Question*. Trans. of *La question du Québec*, by Marcel Rioux. Toronto: James Lorimer, 1971.

Brigstocke, Hilary. "Revolution? It Just Couldn't Happen Here, Said the Parliamentarians in Ottawa: Danger Signals that Canada Ignored." *Times* [London], 14 Oct. 1970, 8.

Cameron, Donald. Rev. of *White Niggers of America*, by Pierre Vallières. *Maclean's*, June 1971, 72.

"The Challenge." *Financial Post*, 17 Oct. 1970 (CPCS).

Charney, Ann. "Kidnappers Won Emotional Support." *Toronto Daily Star*, 17 Oct. 1970, 9.

Cohen-Almagor, Raphael. "The Terrorists' Best Ally: The Quebec Media Coverage of the FLQ Crisis in October 1970." *Canadian Journal of Communication* 25: 2 (2000). Accessed 14 Nov. 2009. http://www.cjc-online.ca/index.php/journal/issue/ view/92

Cowan, Edward. "Kidnappers Set 'Final' Deadline in Quebec and Threaten Briton." *New York Times*, 10 Oct. 1970, 7.

"Crisis in Quebec." *Canadian Forum* 50 (Jan. 1971): 320–58.

Cross, Michael. "Third Class on the Titanic: The NDP Convention." *Canadian Forum* 51 (April– May 1971): 6.

Daly, J.W. "Responses to the Quebec Crisis." *Canadian Forum* 51 (April–May 1971): 22–32.

"Dangerous Days for Canada." Editorial. *Times* [London], 13 Oct. 1970, 11.

Desbarats, Peter. "Quebec: What Now?" *Maclean's*, Jan. 1971, 1–8.

Dumas, Evelyn. Quoted in *Canadian Dimension* (Dec. 1970): 13.

"The FLQ Manifesto." *Gazette*, 9 Oct. 1970, 10.

"FLQ Manifesto." *Georgia Straight*, 14 Oct. 1970 (CPSC).

The FLQ: Seven Years of Terrorism: A Special Report by the Montreal Star. Montreal: Montreal Star and Simon and Schuster of Canada, 1970, 80.

Gordon, Walter. "Responses to the Quebec Crisis." *Canadian Forum* (April–May 1971): 27.

Haggart, Ron. "War Measures: Pauline and Gerald and Henri and Michel and the Night Canada Threw Them in Jail." *Maclean's*, Feb. 1971, 21–5.

– and Aubrey Golden. "War Measures: Ottawa in Crisis and the Plot That Never Was." *Maclean's*, Feb. 1971, 26–7.

"Hard Line Advocated on FLQ Demands." *Toronto Daily Star*, 16 Oct. 1970 (CPCS).

Latouche, Daniel, and Diane Poliquin-Bourassa, eds. *Le manuel de la parole: Manifestes québécois*, vol. 3, *1960–1976*. Montréal: Boréal Express, 1979.

McLuhan, Marshall. "How Radio and TV Help the Cause of Groups Like the FLQ." *Toronto Daily Star*, 17 Oct. 1970 (CPCS).

Moore, Terence. "Kidnap Crisis Has Hidden Dimensions." *Montreal Star*, 9 Dec. 1970.

"Mr Trudeau Counter-Attacks." Editorial. *Guardian*, 17 Oct. 1970.

Newman, Peter C. "What Does Quebec Want to Be?" A Dialogue Between Peter C. Newman and Claude Ryan." *Maclean's*, May 1971, 68.

"PM Criticizes Press Coverage of Kidnaps." *Toronto Daily Star*, 13 Oct. 1970 (CPCS).

Salwyn, Andrew. "Jobless Quebecker Says Manifesto Has 'Lots of Truth.'" *Toronto Daily Star*, 8 Oct. 1970, 1.

Schwartzwald, Robert. "Fear of Federasty: Quebec's Inverted Fictions." *Comparative American Identities: Race, Sex, and Nationality in the Modern Text (Essays from the English Institute)*. Ed. Hortense J. Spillers. New York: Routledge, 1991, 175–95.

Simard. Francis. *Pour en finir avec octobre*. Montréal: Stanké, 1982, 11–15. Accessed 14 Nov. 2009. http://pages.infinit.net/histoire/manifst_flq.html

Spry, Robin, dir. *Action: The October Crisis of 1970*. 1973.

– *Reaction*. 1973.

Taylor, Charles. "Behind the Kidnappings: Alienation Too Profound for the System to Contain." *Canadian Dimension* 7: 5/6 (1970): 29.

"Terrorists Dismay the Other Separatists in Quebec." *New York Times*, 18 Oct. 1970, 2.

Vallières. Pierre. *Nègres blancs d'Amérique: autobiographie précoce d'un "terroriste" québécois*. Montréal: Parti pris, 1968.

"Vulgarités." *Parti pris* 9, 10, 11 (Portrait du colonisé québécois) (1964): 174.

Wainstein, Eleanor S. "The Cross and Laporte Kidnappings, Montreal, October 1970." Report Prepared for Department of State and Defense Advanced Research Projects Agency. Santa Monica, CA: RAND Corporation 1977.

"War Declared on Quebec." *Canadian Dimension* 7: 5/6 (1970): 4–7, 9, 12.

8

1971: Pierre Vallières Comes to English Canada via the United States

Julie McDonough Dolmaya

27 September 1966: While protesting in front of the United Nations in an effort to "sensibiliser certains pays – que l'on disait révolutionnaires – à la cause d'un Québec libre et socialiste" (Vallières, *Nègres blancs* 30),[1] Pierre Vallières was arrested by agents from the United States Department of Immigration acting on behalf of the Canadian government. He and his colleague, Charles Gagnon, were taken to the Manhattan House of Detention for Men, where they awaited deportation to Canada. After a twenty-nine-day hunger strike, Vallières spent the next two months writing *Nègres blancs d'Amérique*, an autobiographical and revolutionary text that would eventually be used to support the sedition charges laid against him by the Canadian government. Because his New York guards spoke no French, Vallières was able to smuggle the manuscript out of prison in chapters by writing "Notes for my lawyers" at the top of each sheet (*Nègres blancs* 35). The manuscript was finished a few days before Vallières and Gagnon were deported to Montreal on 13 January 1967. The final chapters of his book were given to Vallières' lawyers by agents from the US Department of Immigration shortly after Vallières was deported.[2]

Once in Canada, Vallières awaited trial for more than a year; on 5 April 1968, he was sentenced to life imprisonment for involuntary manslaughter in the death of Thérèse Morin, who was killed when an FLQ bomb exploded in the LaGrenade shoe factory. Vallières notes that during his trial, "il fut très peu question de l'accusation de meurtre levée contre moi. On ne fit pas le procès d'un présumé assassin, mais celui du Front de libération du Québec et de la révolution québécoise en général" (*Nègres blancs* 1968, 375). One of the judges who ordered a second trial made a remark to this effect as well, as noted in Sypnowich (21), and Vallières was later acquitted of the manslaughter charges, on 1 March 1973.

Nègres blancs d'Amérique was published in 1968 by Éditions Parti pris, the publishing house associated with the socialist, pro-independence review of the same name. Controversial when first released, since it was used as evidence to support the federal government's charges of sedition against Vallières and was briefly banned around the time of the October Crisis, *Nègres blancs d'Amérique* has arguably had a lasting effect in Canada and internationally. When revised French editions were published in Quebec in 1979 and 1994, the book was positioned as an important historical and sociological document.[3] And when Pierre Vallières died in 1998, *White Niggers of America* was mentioned in nearly every obituary published in the French- and English-Canadian press, illustrating how important this work was considered to Vallières' life (see Downey; Gatehouse; Myles; Vennat). For decades after its original publication, the book was discussed in scholarly and popular texts about the FLQ/October Crisis (see Reid, "The Adventures"; Fournier), and in 2005 and 2007, the *Literary Review of Canada* listed *Nègres blancs / White Niggers* as number 50 of Canada's 100 most important books.[4]

Shortly after its publication in Quebec, *Nègres blancs d'Amérique* reached new audiences through translation and international publication. A Paris edition was published in 1969 by left-leaning house Maspero, and translations into German, English, and Spanish appeared in 1969, 1971, and 1972, respectively. One year after its initial publication in Canada, the English edition had gone into its fourth printing. The translation was fairly widely reviewed in English-language Canadian periodicals (particularly in Quebec)[5] – not just in newspapers and magazines for the general public (Desbarats, "*White Niggers* – A Revelation"; Richmond), but also in academic journals and specialized reviews (Bebout; Brown). It was, moreover, the subject of essays in various scholarly or popular periodicals (Desbarats, "Quebec's Imprisoned Revolutionary"; Stock) and excerpts from the translation were printed in *Saturday Night*, among other sources (e.g., "From Working Class Slum," in *Canadian Dimenson*).

Understandably, then, the English translation of *Nègres blancs* had several effects on Canada – particularly in the years immediately following its publication. *Nègres blancs d'Amérique* was Pierre Vallières' first book, his autobiography, and the translation made his views available to English-speaking Canadians for the first time. Until this point, Vallières had been discussed in the English-Canadian press, particularly during his trial and the October Crisis, but *White Niggers* made Vallières' own version of events available for the first time, and the English-Canadian left, at the very least, had awaited the translation impatiently.[6] Moreover, the translation had the effect of highlighting a gulf between English- and French-speaking Canadians, as *White Niggers* was published when the Public Order Temporary Measures Act, which banned membership in, association with, and communication on behalf of the FLQ, was still in effect. At this time, French copies of the book were banned and being seized in bookstores and libraries in Quebec,[7] and yet the English translation was being made available to Canadians who spoke little or no French.

These effects are directly tied to how the English version of *Nègres blancs* came to be published in Canada. This is because, even though *White Niggers of America* appeared in English in Canada in 1971, it was not prepared by a Canadian publisher, nor was the translator from Canada. The English rights to *Nègres blancs* were acquired by Monthly Review Press, a socialist publishing house based in New York, and the editors approached translator Joan Pinkham with the project. An American who had already worked for the publisher on the translation of several articles and a book – Paul Nizan's *Aden, Arabie* – Pinkham initially knew very little about Vallières and the political situation in Canada in the early 1970s, although this changed considerably as she prepared her translation. When I corresponded with her in the summer of 2008, she explained:

> my admiration and affection for the editors [at Monthly Review Press], and for the circle of friends who were more or less associated with them, was the basic reason for my eager acceptance of the translation. Then, when I read the book, I was delighted with the author. I particularly liked the early autobiographical chapters. I do remember thinking that a large portion of the book – a section on politics and philosophy – was tedious, heavy-handed, and ill-fitting; fortunately, Vallières himself suggested that it be omitted in the English version.
>
> Since you ask, the political atmosphere in Canada at the time scarcely affected my decision, because I knew nothing much about it. (Of course, I was well aware of the repressive atmosphere in my own country.) I learned of [Pierre Vallières'] hunger strike, arrest, and trial [...] only from the book itself. His courage and commitment

were evident from the rest, and in any event, I would have wanted
to be his English voice. (Correspondence with the author)

Thus, the translation was initially undertaken outside Canada, where
the Public Order Temporary Measures Act did not apply, and where the
publisher and translator could not be prosecuted for communicating on
behalf of an FLQ member. As Pinkham indicated, the manuscript she was
given to translate was not identical to the version Parti pris published in
1968. Instead, it matched the revised French edition first published in Paris
in 1969, and then republished by Parti pris in Quebec that same year.[8]
This abridged text is also the same version that appeared in the 1979 and
1994 Quebec re-editions of *Nègres blancs*. As one might expect, then, the
cuts to the original manuscript were made by Vallières himself rather than
Monthly Review Press, and Pinkham confirmed this hypothesis during our
correspondence:

> It seems that the question of cutting the original 1968 text had come
> up even before MR Press sent me a copy of it in September of that
> year. Their Reader's Report had made the suggestion, describing cer-
> tain sections as "tedious," "wandering," "repetitious," and, indeed,
> "unreadable." I agreed. But it emerges from the correspondence that
> the cuts – about 165 pages' worth – were made a couple of months
> later, by the author himself, not at [Monthly Review]'s request but
> at the request of the publisher of a French edition in Paris (Maspero).
>
> Apparently Vallières suggested (or agreed) that we should use the
> same cuts for the English. Early in January of 1969 Parti pris sent us
> another copy of the 1968 edition modified in the author's own hand.
> That amended version became my "source text," and I think it is
> identical to the one that appeared later in 1969 as Parti pris's "nou-
> velle édition revue et corrigée." (Correspondence with the author)

So the version published by Monthly Review Press in the United States
was abridged – although only in the same way in which all future French-
language versions were also abridged revisions of the original 1968 edition.
What about the Canadian version, then? If the translation was prepared
and published in the United States, how did it come to Canada, and when
it did, were both editions the same? The answers to these questions help
explain the effect of the translation in Canada.

While Monthly Review Press had acquired the English rights to *Nègres blancs*, largely due to its sympathetic view of Vallières and his cause,[9] the publisher sold the Canadian rights for Joan Pinkham's translation to McClelland and Stewart, who were obligated to reproduce the target text exactly as it appeared in the United States. Monthly Review Press editor Harry Braverman elaborated on the agreement between the publishers in the March 1971 edition of *Monthly Review*:

> The translation will be published as is, without cuts or changes, or it will not be published at all. We have been assured by McClelland and Stewart, both contractually and orally, that they will use exactly what we give them, and in fact may even photo our pages [...] McClelland and Stewart will only be a few weeks behind us, since they intend to produce and publish as fast as possible after they have our negatives. (357)

This detail is important, because the fact that a shorter version of *Nègres blancs* was being translated into English was raised in several English-language Canadian newspapers. In an article published in January 1971, the left-wing paper *New Canada* asserted that English-speaking Canadians would be getting a "censored" version of the book and criticized Monthly Review Press for selling the rights to "a traitor capitalist enterprise like McClelland and Stewart" (*New Canada* 5). While *New Canada*'s version of events was later contradicted by Monthly Review Press – and, indeed, contained numerous errors of fact regarding the Canadian publication of *White Niggers of America* – the cuts were also discussed in other, more widely distributed periodicals. For instance, John Richmond, writing for the *Montreal Star*, noted that "the 1968 edition [carried] two lengthy chapters [...] both [of which are] omitted from the 1969 edition on which *White Niggers of America* is based" and hypothesized that these omissions were "no doubt undertaken for excellent legal reasons" (15). However, he considered these cuts "frustrating" because Vallières used the missing chapters to provide "a 'philosophical' apologia for global revolution while describing the means required if the FLQ revolutionary movement is to succeed" (15).

Here, then, is the first effect of translation on Canada with respect to *Nègres blancs d'Amérique*: the October Crisis led many Canadians to worry that documents by (suspected) FLQ members were being censored due to legislation in effect at this time, and *Nègres blancs / White Niggers* was used as an example of how anglophones, unlike francophones, could not get the full story about the people involved in the Quebec independence movement. English-speaking Canadians were not able to read the full, first edition of Vallières' book in their native tongue, while French-speaking Canadians were. Whether they would have wanted to read these deleted chapters is a moot point: the cuts to the original 1968 edition had enough of an effect on English-speaking readers that the omissions were cited in book reviews or articles. Further, the "censored" English translation led *New Canada* to become "the exclusive distributors in English Canada of the uncensored [French] version of Vallières' book" ("*White Niggers of America*: Canadians to Get Censored Version" 5) so that anglophones able to read French could see the missing chapters for themselves. Moreover, McClelland and Stewart must have been aware of the remarks about the omissions, because the back cover to the paperback version of *White Niggers* notes that "this is a complete and unexpurgated edition," despite the fact that the translation – although a complete edition of the 1969 manuscript, is not a complete translation of the edition Vallières originally prepared while in prison in New York. Clearly, this is a strategy designed to assuage potential concerns that English-speaking Canadians were being offered a censored or otherwise abridged version of *Nègres blancs*, demonstrating the effect that fear of censorship of FLQ documents had in Canada in the early 1970s (see Robert Schwartzwald in this volume).

Because the translation was published in the United States, it also had the effect of removing – to a certain extent – English-Canadian ties to the book.[10] As indicated earlier, McClelland and Stewart simply copied the translation page for page, including explanatory footnotes for American readers about parties and organizations such as the NDP and Progressive Conservatives. Although M&S intended to add a preface to the English-Canadian edition (indeed, one was prepared by McGill history professor Laurier LaPierre), Vallières himself refused to have it included in the translation (Richmond 15; Desbarats, "*White Niggers* – A Revelation" 42).[11] Moreover, an acknowledgment to Joan Pinkham's Canadian consultant, journalist Malcolm Reid, was not included in either the US or Canadian edition, because Reid himself asked to remain anonymous.[12] When I corresponded with him in the summer of 2008, Reid noted that he declined to be acknowledged because of the recent October Crisis, explaining that "fear was in the air. (All gone now)." So it is not surprising that several reviewers remarked on the fact that the translation was, in fact, American in origin, or quoted from the American reviews that compared Vallières favourably with Malcolm X and Frantz Fanon. The October Crisis, War Measures Act, and Public Order Temporary Measures Act made Canadians reluctant to associate themselves with FLQ-related documents like *Nègres blancs / White Niggers*, and this, in turn, led to lack of acknowledgment of the Canadian who had participated in its publication. Moreover, the translation lacked the overt support it was given by the US publishers, because it did not contain sympathetic paratexts. In the Monthly Review Press edition, the back cover contains excerpts from several book reviews, which compare Vallières and *White Niggers of America* favourably with such activists as Che Guevara, Malcolm X, Eldridge Cleaver, and Frantz Fanon. In addition, the American edition contains a publisher's afterword that highlights the harassment, unjust imprisonment, and unfair trial Vallières was subjected to by Canadian authorities. By contrast, the McClelland and Stewart edition does not contain this afterword – or, indeed, any new prefatory text – and the covers lack the favourable quotes that are found on the Monthly Review Press edition. *White Niggers*, then, is an important example of how the translation of FLQ-related documents was viewed as a potentially dangerous activity around the time of the October Crisis.

Perhaps the most important effects of the *Nègres blancs d'Amérique* translation in Canada, then, are the ways in which it highlighted differences between francophones and anglophones during a time of political tension between Quebec and the federal government. The French edition was being seized, and yet the English edition was being published, despite the fact that the Public Order Temporary Measures Act applied to all Canadians. Additionally, the fact that the *White Niggers* translation was based on the revised 1969 source text and not on the original 1968 edition led an English-language Canadian left-wing publisher to distribute the original French text outside Quebec (Sypnowich 21; "*White Niggers of America*: Canadians to Get Censored Version" 5), which meant that English-speaking Canadians were able to purchase French and English copies of a book being seized in French within Quebec (cf. Sypnowich 21; Desbarats, "*White Niggers* – A Revelation" 42; "*White Niggers of America*: Canadians to Get Censored Version" 5).[13] Thus, the translation made Pierre

Vallières' own views known to English-speaking Canadians for the first time, but as an "important social document,"[14] rather than the revolutionary, activist autobiography it was originally published as in French.[15] Moreover, because many reviewers commented on the fact that the translation would be a resource for understanding various Quebec issues,[16] they clearly considered the book a source of insight into the Other and were passing this assessment on to review readers. The emphasis on *White Niggers* as an important social document was also heightened by the fact that several Canadian newspaper reviews and articles commented on the American origin of the translation or mentioned the book reviews from various US newspapers,[17] demonstrating to English-speaking Canadians that Vallières was making an impact outside Canada: not only was his book deemed of enough importance to non-Canadian readers that translations were required, but also it was of such significance that, outside Canada, Vallières was being compared to well-known activists like Eldridge Cleaver and Malcolm X.

The translation of *Nègres blancs d'Amérique* into English via the United States, therefore, affected the way Vallières was portrayed in Canada: he came back into the country after having won the approval of reviewers and publishers there. Then-current legislation led Vallières to receive less overt support from the Canadian publishers, and it led another English Canadian – Pinkham's consultant Malcolm Reid – to refuse to be acknowledged for his role in the translation, even though he hoped the English version of *Nègres blancs* would lead the English-speaking Canadian left to "draw inspiration from Quebec culture. [To] get in on the fun" and help "put Quebec on the world map of lefts" (Personal correspondence, 5 Aug. 2008). Ultimately, the lack of supportive paratexts and acknowledgment of the English Canadian who had helped with the translation resulted in a less sympathetic presentation of *White Niggers of America* – and by extension, of Pierre Vallières himself – to English-speaking Canadians than to Americans or French-speaking Canadians.

Notes

1 Unless otherwise indicated, all French citations of *Nègres blancs d'Amérique* are taken from the 1994 Typo edition.

2 Vallières points out that had these agents not kept their word to forward the

chapters to Vallières' lawyers, *Nègres blancs* might never have been published. See n7 on p 44 of the 1994 edition. As this essay will show, this is the first – although not the only – instance of Americans helping *Nègres blancs* and *White Niggers* to be published in Canada.

3 The back cover to the 1979 edition, for instance, describes the book as "une réédition […] d'un ouvrage qui demeurera un événement capital dans l'histoire politique et culturelle du Québec," while the back cover to the 1994 re-edition notes that *Nègres blancs* "a été salué, dès sa parution, en février 1968, comme un ouvrage capital, une introduction indispensable à l'effervescence révolutionnaire des années soixante et soixante dix."

4 See the 2007 full list online at http://lrc.reviewcanada.ca/uploads/The_LRC_ 100_2007.pdf and the 2005 list is always available (Goerzen A4).

5 The English edition was also reviewed in newspapers and magazines outside Canada, including the *New York Times, Nation*, and *Library Journal*, but such reviews are less important to this essay, which discusses the effect of this translation on Canada, not on the US or the UK.

6 See the *New Canada* article ("*White Niggers of America*: Canadians to Get Censored Version") for one example of how important some English-speaking Canadians on the left considered the book and its translation.

7 This Act, which replaced the War Measures Act, did not expire until 30 April 1971. Despite the ban, however, copies of *Nègres blancs* continued to circulate in Quebec. One example can be found in Reynolds ("Les bibliothèques de McGill"), who includes an account by a McGill librarian who denied being able to locate the library's copy of *Nègres blancs* when the police came to seize it. Moreover, Vallières himself claims that the ban served only to increase the number of copies of his book that were sold in secret (*Nègres blancs* 9).

8 This republication occurred before the October Crisis and the implementation of the War Measures Act, so no law prohibited its dissemination at this time.

9 Both Pinkham and her Canadian consultant Malcolm Reid commented on the fact that Vallières accepted Monthly Review Press's bid to translate *Nègres blancs* because of the publisher's socialist stance. During our correspondence, Pinkham explained, "I have since learned that Pierre Vallières and the people at Parti pris read the magazine, or at least were aware of it. Apparently, MR Press's early bid to translate the book was quickly accepted because of their sympathetic outlook."

Likewise, during my correspondence with Reid, he argued, "Other things might be cited in the story of how the *Nègres blancs* came to be translated in the United States, but I feel this was the basic one. Pierre must have had the say on to whom his book was to be sold for English translation [...] and Monthly Review had won his approval. There was, I'd say, an MR mystique."

The publishers themselves expressed their support for Vallières in their response to *New Canada*'s 1971 article accusing Monthly Review Press of censoring *Nègres blancs*. In it, MR editor Harry Braverman asserted, "Certainly Pierre Vallières, his extraordinary book, and his cause will not be helped by surrounding the Canadian publication of the English edition of his book with such a cloud of falsehood and misinformation" (357).

10 Although some reviews did not specifically acknowledge the translation's American origin, many quoted from American reviews of *White Niggers*, demonstrating that Canadians were not the only readers of the translation. In addition, other articles published prior to the translation mentioned that *Nègres blancs* was being published in English by Monthly Review Press (e.g., Stock 23; Desbarats, "Quebec's Imprisoned Revolutionary" 15; "Toronto Firm Will Publish" 8).

11 As the *Montreal Star* reported, Vallières "objected to the inclusion on the grounds that the book must speak for itself" (Richmond 15). However, this may not be the real reason, as Vallières did not object to the afterword included in the Monthly Review Press edition.

12 Reid became involved with the translation project because Pinkham asked Monthly Review Press for a Canadian consultant who could help her with the cultural references, allusions, etc. in *Nègres blancs*. At that time, Reid was preparing *The Shouting Signpainters*, a book about the *Parti pris*, for Monthly Review Press.

13 Desbarats hypothesized in his review of *White Niggers of America* that the book would have more impact on anglophones because francophones in Quebec were unlikely to learn anything from the book that they did not already know, while "most English-speaking Canadians will find it a revelation" ("*White Niggers* – A Revelation" 42).

14 This is how publisher Jack McClelland described the book to the English-Canadian press ("Vallières' Book" 8). He also expressed his lack of sympathy for the FLQ but noted that Canadians had a right to know what Vallières had to say ("Toronto Firm Will Publish" 8).

15 The original 1968 edition, subtitled *autobiographie précoce d'un "terroriste" québécois*, contained telegrams of support for Vallières from various activist

groups – most notably Black activist Stokeley Carmichael – and appeals for donations to support the Comité d'aide au groupe "Vallières-Gagnon." These appendices do not appear in subsequent versions of *Nègres blancs*. In addition, the subtitle, which is included in the US edition, has been dropped from the English-language Canadian version.

16 For instance, one *Books in Canada* review argued that *White Niggers* would help English-speaking Canadians understand what Quebec wants (Brown 19), another that it would allow anglophones to see what sent Vallières to jail, "presumably without having to worry about going ourselves" (Bebout 18). Likewise, the Montreal *Gazette* noted that the translation would reveal to English-speaking Canadians much that they didn't know (Desbarats, "*White Niggers* – A Revelation" 42) and *Maclean's* that it would allow English-speaking readers to understand Quebec, provided they came to terms with Vallières (Cameron 72). Further, Cameron remarked that "to dismiss or ignore *White Niggers* is irresponsible and dangerous" (72).

17 For example, Syponowich 21; "White Niggers of America: Canadians to Get Censored Version" 5; "From Working Class Slum" 37; Desbarats, "Quebec's Imprisoned Revolutionary," 15; "Toronto Firm Will Publish" 8; Cameron 72; Brown 20.

Works Cited

Bebout, Ricard. "Brothers under the Skin." Rev. of *White Niggers of America*, by Pierre Vallières. *Books in Canada* (May 1971): 18–19.

Braverman, Harry. Notes from the Editors. *Monthly Review* 22: 10 (1971): 1, 357.

Brown, C. Alexander. (1971). "Brothers under the Skin." Rev. of *White Niggers of America*, by Pierre Vallières. *Books in Canada* (May 1971): 19–20.

Cameron, Donald. Rev. of *White Niggers of America*, by Pierre Vallières. *Maclean's*, June 1971, 72.

Desbarats, Peter. "Quebec's Imprisoned Revolutionary." *Saturday Night* 85 (1970): 15–17.

– "*White Niggers* – A Revelation for the English … But If You Think about It – It's Actually Illegal." Rev. of *White Niggers of America*, by Pierre Vallières. *Gazette*, 27 Mar. 1971, 42.

Downey, Donn. "Intellectual Ex-leader of FLQ Worked Hard for the Disadvantaged." *Globe and Mail*, 24 Dec. 1998, A8.

Fournier, Louis. *FLQ: Histoire d'un mouvement clandestin*. Montréal: Lanctôt, 1998.

"From Working-Class Slum to the FLQ: The Life Story of Pierre Vallières." *Canadian Dimension* 7 (1970): 37–41.

Gatehouse, Jonathan. "FLQ Leader Rallied Separatists: Pierre Vallières, 60, Dies in Montreal Hospital." *National Post*, 24 Dec. 1998, A6.

Myles, Brian, "Pierre Vallières (1938–1998)." *Le Devoir*, 24 Dec. 1998, A6.

Pinkham, Joan. Correspondence with the author. Summer 2008.

Reid, Malcolm. "The Adventures of Vallières and Gagnon." *Canadian Dimension* 29: 2 (1995): 14–20.

– Correspondence with the author. 5 Aug. 2008.

Reynolds, Mark. "Les bibliothèques de McGill: Les livres, c'est leur rayon." *McGill News* 2002–03. http://www.mcgill.ca/news/2002/winter/bibliotheques/

Richmond, John. "Overture to October." Rev. of *White Niggers of America*, by Pierre Vallières. *Montreal Star*, 27 March 1971, 15.

Stock, Brian. "Reflections on Pierre Vallières." *Tamarack Review* 56 (1971): 20–9.

Sypnowich, Peter. "The English-French Irony over a Separatist Book." *Toronto Star*, 8 Jan. 1971, 21.

"Toronto Firm Will Publish Book by Jailed FLQ Writer." *Toronto Star*, 29 Dec. 1970, 8.

"Vallières' Book *White Negroes* [sic] to Be Brought Out by McClelland." *Globe and Mail*, 29 Dec. 1970, 8.

Vallières, Pierre. *Nègres blancs d'Amérique*. Montréal: Typo, 1994.

– *Nègres blancs d'Amérique: Autobiographie précoce d'un "terroriste" québécois.* Montréal: Parti pris, 1968.

– *Nègres blancs d'Amérique: Autobiographie précoce d'un "terroriste" québécois.* Montréal: Parti pris, 1969.

– *White Niggers of America: Autobiography of a Quebec "Terrorist."* Trans. Joan Pinkham. New York: Monthly Review Press, 1971.

– *White Niggers of America*. Trans. Joan Pinkham. Toronto: McClelland and Stewart, 1971.

Vennat, Pierre. "Malgré ses virages et ses contradictions, Pierre Vallières a toujours haï l'injustice." *La Presse*, 24 déc. 1998, A8.

"*White Niggers of America*: Canadians to Get Censored Version." *New Canada* (Jan. 1971): 5.

9

January/February 1977: Independence, Secession, Political Duels or Lévesque and Trudeau in the United States[1]

Chantal Gagnon   Translated by Trish Van Bolderen

> Pierre Elliott Trudeau and René Lévesque have become like an old married couple whose bickerings are a kind of performance. These two men, hailed by Quebeckers as national saviours, have deployed great bravado to lead us through hopelessly personal battles to the deadest of dead ends of our history.
> – Lise Payette, *Le pouvoir? Connais pas!*
> (Translated by Trish Van Bolderen)

When Two Enemy Brothers Face Off

In Quebec and Canada, the months of January and February 1977 were marked by a historic duel between two great political rivals. In one corner, René Lévesque and his 25 January 1977 speech to the Economic Club of New York; in the other, Pierre Elliott Trudeau with his 22 February 1977 response in Washington, to the United States House of Representatives. Each politician's speech was translated at that time, and excerpts were published in newspapers in Quebec, anglophone Canada, and the United States. Both Quebec natives of the same generation, Lévesque and Trudeau were symbols par excellence of the political antagonism between Quebec sovereignism and Canadian federalism. Consequently, Trudeau and Lévesque were known as "frères ennemis," or enemy brothers. Throughout their careers, these men engaged in bitter battles, and their January and February 1977 speeches are striking examples of these.

The speeches they delivered on US soil are historic in that they relate to contemporary history and reflect the sociopolitical ties between Quebec and Canada in the 1970s. Moreover, this event is often described in the biographies of these politicians. Comparing Lévesque and Trudeau's speeches allows us to make certain observations about how the translations affected the speeches' respective audiences. The following discussion will focus on these effects by contextualizing each speech and its translation, as well as presenting a snapshot of the political vocabulary and ideologies used in the translations.

Contextualizing the Political Speeches and Their Translations

The two political speeches discussed here share several characteristics: both were delivered in 1977, roughly one month apart, by eloquent political opponents, and both were concerned with the same subject matter, namely, the US reaction to the first ever election of the Parti Québécois, a political party that explicitly sought Quebec independence. While Premier René Lévesque attempted to convince US citizens that the aim of the Parti Québécois was well founded, Canada's Prime Minister Pierre Elliott Trudeau wanted to persuade them of the exact opposite.

The premier's speech was originally written in French, by Lévesque and a team of his chief advisers. Not only was Lévesque involved in writing the original speech but he also translated it himself into English for the US public – a very rare instance of self-translation. In the second half of the twentieth century, few Canadian political figures invested so much in the creation or translation of their own speeches.

Trudeau's speech was probably written first in English and then translated into French, seeing as, in the Prime Minister's Office, speeches are typically written in the language of the primary target audience (Gagnon, "Language Plurality as Power Struggle"), in this case, the US public. One or more of his collaborators would prepare the speech, and Trudeau would give feedback either in writing or in person. Other collaborators then translated the speech into French, often at the last minute, sometimes even the night before the speech was to be delivered. In the Prime Minister's Archives, many memoranda indicate that those working closely with Trudeau were very concerned with the way the various target audiences would respond to these speeches: they tried, for example, to anticipate how the speech (either the original or the translation) would affect the Canadian public.

René Lévesque's Speech: Its Impact and Target Audience

René Lévesque's speech was delivered abroad, during a state visit to the United States. In Quebec, great media hype surrounded the event (Cousineau A6). Yet René Lévesque was not as successful as he had hoped he would be. The following comment made by the vice president of the Manufacturers Hanover Trust Bank exemplifies the US reaction: "We thought we were going to get assurances that our investments in Quebec are safe. Instead, he threw us a quote from our own Declaration of Independence. We don't see the analogy between separation of Quebec from Canada and our Declaration of Independence. We see it more akin to our civil war" (Unger 1). This failure on US soil prompted a lot of writing on the topic in the United States, Quebec, and Canada. In an interview, Claude Ryan, then editor of Montreal's *Le Devoir* newspaper, and Claude Morin, one of Lévesque's cabinet ministers, explained that Lévesque's message was partisan: the person delivering the speech to the US public was not the premier of Quebec; rather, he was the leader of the Parti Québécois (Lisée 225). Therefore, the nation René Lévesque was representing was that of separatist, francophone Quebecers. His focus on this community is demonstrated in the following excerpt from his New York speech:

> Le Québec est né en même temps que les premières colonies américaines.

> French Quebec was born at the same time as the first American colonies. (Quebec, 1)

Lévesque is, of course, referring to New France, but the term he uses in the English version evokes both the past and the present. This double reference was intended to make US citizens understand that the origins of Lévesque's Quebec – both old and contemporary – were strictly French and drew attention to the values and ideologies of the Parti Québécois, the institution he had founded and was leading.

In his translation, Lévesque seemed to be addressing the US public as though he were speaking to Quebecers. In fact, Lévesque believed that the citizens of Quebec and the United States shared strong similarities, even assigning himself the title "Yankee-bécois" in his memoirs (*Attendez* 166).

This rather fanciful notion of commonality likely explains why his speech was unable to convince the US public. Because Lévesque did not convey his message in a manner appropriate for his audience, the speech lost its intended effect.

Pierre Elliott Trudeau's Speech: Its Impact and Target Audience

In contrast, the speech Trudeau delivered in Washington aimed to reassure US leaders about the political situation in Canada and encourage them to play a key role in establishing a new world order. The Canadian prime minister's message was very well received in the United States (Bergeron 174).

It is reasonable to assert that the primary target audience of Pierre Elliott Trudeau's speech was the United States House of Representatives, since Trudeau delivered the speech to this body. However, it is important to note that the Canadian people were a further, albeit external, key target audience, as suggested by *La Presse* journalist Marcel Pépin: "Mr Trudeau hasn't for one moment stopped thinking about his Canadian audience, which desperately seeks leadership in this debate that threatens to turn the country upside down" (A6, trans. by Van Bolderen). This Canadian audience could be divided into three groups: English-speaking Canadians, federalist Quebecers, and sovereignist Quebecers. According to Pépin, Pierre Elliott Trudeau delivered a message to each of these groups (A6). For example, Trudeau took a firm position against the independence schemes of the Parti Québécois, a stance that pleased English Canadians. Also, by showing his determination to help French Quebecers feel at home across Canada, Trudeau appealed to federalist Quebecers, giving them ammunition to fight the sovereignist enemy. Finally, although it is unlikely that Trudeau convinced any sovereignist Quebecers to abandon their cause, by publicly stating that Canada had not created conditions in which French-speaking Canadians felt fully equal to English-speaking Canadians, he at least managed to avoid offending them.

Was Trudeau's message, which reached a wide audience, less partisan than Lévesque's speech, delivered one month earlier? Not according to Pépin, who wrote that, by trying to please all members of his target audience, Trudeau was mainly interested in scoring points. Therefore, even when Trudeau was speaking as prime minister of Canada, the Liberal Party leader was not far away (Pépin A6). Perhaps Trudeau's partisanship did not affect the reception of his speech because it was crafted more skilfully than Lévesque's.

All aspects of the French translation of Trudeau's speech suggest that it was produced with the Quebec audience in mind. Although the speech revolved around two themes – Quebec nationalism and Canada-US relations – only the portion on Quebec nationalism reveals discrepancies between the French translation and the English original. The second half of the translation is more faithful (in the traditional sense of the term) to the original than the first half, as illustrated in the following example:

> That is why a small minority of the people of Quebec feel they should leave Canada and strike out in a country of their own. The newly elected government of that province asserts a policy that reflects that minority view despite the fact that during the election campaign it sought a mandate for good government, and not a mandate for the separation from Canada.

> Voila [*sic*] pourquoi certains Québécois pensent qu'ils devraient se séparer du Canada et fonder leur propre pays. Le nouveau gouvernement du Québec a adopté une politique conforme aux vues de cette minorité, bien qu'au cours de la campagne électorale le Parti québécois ait sollicité un mandat pour former un bon gouvernement et non pour faire la sécession. (Canada 2)

This translation choice indicates that, compared with the English original, the translated version of the speech was aimed at a narrower audience: it exclusively targeted francophones living in Quebec, whereas the original version was directed at US citizens and English-speaking Canadians. Consequently, when translated, Pierre Elliott Trudeau's political text loses its attempted "universality" and thereby proves itself to be more "localized." The distance created in the English version is quite suitable, since the state leader was addressing a foreign audience. In French, this distance disappears: that part of the speech loses its statelike characteristics but gains a proximity that allows the prime minister to address domestic issues at home, even with a speech delivered in another country.

Translating the Political Vocabulary of the Speeches

Given the close relationship between politics and language, it is important to analyse the semantic elements found in political speeches. The translation choices made for this type of discourse are generally informed by the text's intended audience, which is identified by either the translator or the institution paying for the translation.

From US Independence to the Independence of Quebec

In his speech, René Lévesque used the political vocabulary belonging to his party's ideology: nationalism. Jean-François Lisée summarizes it well:

> Lévesque certainly could have sung his separatist anthem less emphatically. He used the terms "independence" and "sovereignty" 13 times – and uttered the evil word "separation," which is used in the Declaration of Independence – without once connecting them to the word "association." A new record. (trans. by Van Bolderen)

Lisée's calculation applies to the English text only: in the French, the terms "indépendance" (independence) and "souveraineté" (sovereignty) appear ten times. What accounts for this difference? The word "independence" appears so frequently in the English version of Lévesque's speech because the main goal of the speech was to encourage the US public to connect their Declaration of Independence to Quebec's independence project. The following example, taken from Lévesque's speech, supports this assertion:

> Et comme base de cet engagement, nous avons donné à nos concitoyens l'assurance de tenir, sur la question de l'indépendance, un référendum qui permettra a tous les Québécois en âge de voter, sans distinction d'origine, de se prononcer sur l'avenir du Québec. (Québec 9)

> As you probably know, we have solemnly assured our fellow citizens that a referendum will be held on the question, so that all Quebecers of voting age, without distinction as to their origins, will share equally in this historic decision on independence. (Quebec 8–9)

By reworking the translated text and emphasizing the idea of independence in English, Lévesque hoped he could convince US citizens of the validity of his statement – that is, that the independence proposed by his government was similar to the United States Declaration of Independence. In other words, he wanted to make it clear to his audience that the Parti Québécois government wanted the kind of independence achieved by Americans two centuries earlier. However, the Americans did not understand independence the same way the Péquistes did: they completely rejected Lévesque's bold comparison between the political situations in Quebec and the United States. The francophone audience of the speech was equally unimpressed by Lévesque's strategy: emotionally and politically loaded, the word "indépendance" (independence) was off-putting for many Quebecers, hence the reason Lévesque generally used it sparingly, preferring the more ambiguous and less threatening term "souveraineté" (sovereignty).

From the US War of Secession to the Secession of Quebec

Table 9.1 presents four occurrences in Trudeau's speech of political terms related to independence, and the translation for each.

The word most frequently chosen in Trudeau's English speech – "separation" – was used by the federal government throughout the first term of the Parti Québécois. During this period the government never used the word "sécession" (secession). So, what does this translation choice suggest? The answer lies in the communicative context of the original speech: the speech was delivered in the United States, which had known its own war of secession, the Civil War (1861–65). According to political scientist Louis Balthazar, the US associated the Quebec independence project with their war of secession (Bouchard, "La victoire"). The term "sécession" in the translation prepared for francophones reminded all sovereignist and federalist Quebecers that the United States saw Quebec independence in a negative light. It is important also to remember that Trudeau's speech was a response to the address Lévesque had delivered. Lévesque had been unsuccessful in his attempt to convince the US businessmen of the connection between the independence of Quebec and that of the United States. More skilful than Lévesque, Trudeau wanted to avoid being criticized by the United States for associating Quebec's secession and the US war of secession. However, nothing prevented him from drawing this parallel when he

Table 9.1 Four Occurrences in Trudeau's Speech of Political Terms
Related to Independence, and the Translation for Each

English version of the speech	French version of the speech
Separation (p. 2)	Sécession (p. 2)
Separation (p. 3)	Sécession (p. 3)
Separation (p. 3)	Séparation (p. 3)
Sudden departure of Quebec (p. 3)	Sécession (p. 3)

delivered his speech in French, since the Americans would read or hear only
the English version.

Conclusion

The episode of Lévesque and Trudeau in the United States reveals certain
features that are characteristic of political speech translations in general.
Specifically, it points to two phenomena that directly affect all audiences
of translated speeches, namely, power relations and the textual treatment
of ideological terms.

The issue of "partisan" translation is at the heart of these power relations since this type of translation risks excluding a portion of the audience.
In the original, French version of Lévesque's speech, the Quebec premier
in large part addressed the Péquiste voters who had elected him. When the
speech was translated for the so-called primary audience – that is, the US
citizens at the Economic Club – the partisan aspects of the speech were not
properly adapted: rather than giving US citizens the speech of a head of
state, Lévesque delivered a party leader speech, the results of which have
already been discussed. That being stated, partisan translations are merely
an example of power struggles. In Canada, for example, tensions between
linguistic communities sometimes lead the prime minister to neglect certain
minority groups. This was the case with the speech Jean Chrétien gave during the 1995 referendum campaign: even though Chrétien professed that
his message to the nation addressed all Canadians, the French version of
the speech excluded francophones living outside of Quebec (Gagnon, "Language Plurality"). At the European Union, minority groups have been
equally poorly served by translation. The case of Finnish institutional doc-

umentation has been well recorded: the syntax and terminology imposed on Finnish translators at the EU seem to complicate the readability of texts, consequently making these kinds of speeches very difficult if not impossible for the general public to access (Gambier; Pym; and Koskinen).

The implications of political speeches are generally significant, which is why each ideological term (in both the original and the translated texts) is carefully considered and selected by the translating institution. Yet the examples discussed above demonstrate that a term's effect on the audience is not always the one anticipated. In French, as much as in English, the use of "indépendance/independence" did not appeal to the audience. Given that the English version of Lévesque's speech was particularly poorly received by the US public, it seems clear that the cultural and political dimensions of the speech were not adequately considered during the translation process. The mission of Quebec in the United States was an abysmal failure, even though Lévesque's government had counted on support from the United States in order to legitimize its sovereignty project in the eyes of Canadians and the international community. Perhaps because he had learned from the mistakes made by his Quebec counterpart, the prime minister of Canada was relatively successful in Washington. Moreover, the changes reflected in the French translation reached a public Trudeau knew intimately, since he belonged to the same cultural community as that of the target audience. Therefore, by understanding the culture of the target audience, Trudeau's translator could more accurately predict the effects of the translation on that public and translate accordingly. This assertion joins Schäffner's work ("Third Ways and New Centres"), which deals with another case where translating ideological terms led to a lukewarm response, namely, the document "Europe: The Third Way/Die Neue Mitte," co-produced in 1999 by the British Labour Party and the Social Democratic Party of Germany. Schäffner explains that textual choices made in translations of political speeches have notable consequences for political parties and society. She also believes that terms rooted in the history of a language or culture must be translated carefully, for fear of being received poorly. Hitler's autobiography (*Mein Kampf*) also illustrates the problems associated with translating words that are ideologically loaded. In his study, *Translating Hitler's* Mein Kampf, Baumgarten uses the concept of "semantic instability" (Sornig) to discuss the textual treatment of certain delicate expressions in *Mein Kampf*. A term is considered semantically unstable when, context permitting, it generates strong feelings within the reader. According to Baumgarten, some translators of *Mein Kampf* exploited the instability of certain words in order to establish Hitler's political credibility. Whether concerned with narrowing an emotional gap or narrowing a political-cultural gap, the process of translating ideological terms requires sensitivity, given that the results can have either a positive or a negative impact on the way in which the text is received.

Generally, history offers few examples of translated political speeches. Yet the power of these political texts and the impact they have on their audiences deserve to be highlighted and analysed. When the important effects of these texts are overlooked so, too, is the possibility of better understanding society – its politics, culture, and history.

Note

1 The research that contributed to this essay was made possible by grants for studies at the master's and doctoral levels from the Fonds de recherche sur la société et la culture and from Concordia University. Finally, this material was originally presented at a colloquium held at Cambridge University (see Gagnon, *Institution*, for an abridged version of this chapter).

Works Cited

Baumgarten, Stefan. *Translating Hitler's* Mein Kampf. Saarbr cken: VDM Verlag, 2009.

Bergeron, Gérard. *Notre miroir à deux faces*. Montréal: Québec/Amérique, 1985.

Bouchard, Jacques, dir. "Épisode 7: La victoire." Point de mire sur René Lévesque. Radio-Canada, Montreal 2002. Accessed 14 Dec. 2009. http://www.radio-canada.ca/radio/profondeur/renelevesque/episode7.html

Canada, Prime Minister Pierre Elliott Trudeau. Address. Réunion conjointe de la Chambre des représentants et du Sénat des États-Unis/Joint Meeting of the House of Representatives and the Senate of the United States. Canadian Embassy. Washington, DC, 22 Feb. 1977.

Cousineau, Louise. "Pour Lévesque, on sabre dans le hockey." *La Presse*, 25 jan. 1977, A6.

Gagnon, Chantal. "Institution in Translated Political Speeches: A Canadian Example." *CamLing 2003: Proceedings of The University of Cambridge First Postgraduate Conference in Language Research in Association with the Cambridge*

Institute of Language Research, 26 April 2003. Ed. Damien Hall et al. Cambridge: Cambridge Institute of Language Research, 2003, 433–9.

– "Language Plurality as Power Struggle, Or Translating Politics in Canada." Literary Heteroglossia in/and Translation: How Legitimate Is the Other and Its Language? Spec. issue of Target: *International Journal of Translation Studies* 18: 1 (2006): 69–90.

Gambier, Yves. "Mouvances eurolinguistiques: Cas de la Finlande." *Europe et traduction*. Ed. Michel Ballard. Arras: Artois Presses Université, 1988, 295–304.

Koskinen, Kaisa. "Institutional Illusions, Translating in the EU Commission: A Finnish Perspective." *The Translator* 6 (2000): 49–66.

Lévesque, René. Attendez que je me rappelle … Montréal: Québec/Amérique, 1986.

– "Québec: Good Neighbour in Transition." Economic Club of New York. Hilton Hotel, New York, 25 Jan. 1977. Original French text. Accessed 14 Dec. 2009. http://www.mri.gouv.qc.ca/document/SPDI/FondDoc/FDOC_alloc_1574_19770125_levesque-rene.htm

Lisée, Jean-François. *Dans l'oeil de l'aigle: Washington face au Québec*. Montréal: Boréal, 1990.

Payette, Lise. *Le pouvoir? Connais pas!* Montréal: Québec/Amérique, 1982.

Pépin, Marcel. "Un discours qui aura eu le don de plaire à tous." *La Presse*, 23 fév. 1977, A1.

Pym, Anthony. "The European Union and Its Future Languages: Questions for Language Policies and Translation Theories." *Across Languages and Cultures* 1: 1 (2000): 1–17.

Québec, Premier Lévesque, René. "Quebec: Good Neighbour in Transition." Translated by René Lévesque. Economic Club of New York. Hilton Hotel, New York, 25 Jan. 1977.

Schäffner, Christina. "Third Ways and New Centres, Ideological Unity or Difference?" *Apropos of Ideology, Translation Studies on Ideology: Ideologies in Translation Studies*. Ed. María Calzada Pérez. Manchester: St Jerome Publishing 2003, 23–41.

Sornig, Karl. "Some Remarks on Linguistic Strategies of Persuasion." *Language, Power and Ideology*. Ed. Ruth Wodak. Amsterdam: John Benjamins, 1989, 95–114.

Unger, Harlow. "Bankers dubious; Speech may boost interest on bonds." *Gazette*, 26 Jan. 1977, 1–2.

10

2007: Translating Culture during the Bouchard-Taylor Commission

Renée Desjardins

Quebec City, 29 October 2007: As they arrive to participate in one of the regional citizens' forums of the Consultation Commission on Accommodation Practices Related to Cultural Differences, the citizens of Quebec City are asked to fill out a small survey pertaining to their values and beliefs. They are then ushered into the conference room, where camera crews are setting up for what will surely be another night of colourful commentary, heated debates, and insightful exchanges between groups and individuals that may never have been in contact with each other prior to the forum. The gathering is diverse: men, women, young adults, teenagers, seniors; some are veiled, some in jeans, some in formal business attire; some anxiously hold their notes while others look around the room quietly. The Commission's co-chairs, Mr Bouchard and Mr Taylor, enter. There is whispering and last-minute adjusting of the microphones and sound equipment. Cameras flash. Cultural translation in action is about to take place.[1]

The Consultation Commission on Accommodation Practices Related to Cultural Differences (CCAPRCD) officially started its mandate in 2007 in the province of Quebec. This was not only a unique and singular event in Canada:[2] it was novel within an international context as well. The Commission sought to address some of the manifold challenges brought forth by globalization, specifically in this case, immigration to Quebec, that pertain to national identity, multicultural policy, human rights, intercultural communication, and so on. Most Canadians tend to express an open attitude towards cultural difference and would generally cite the "multicultural mosaic" as one of the cornerstones of *Canadiana*.[3] However, in spite of this laudable reputation, the Canadian multicultural mosaic has been garnering more criticism lately because of racism, xenophobia, gender inequality, and fear of cultural difference continue to be at the forefront not only in press headlines but also in everyday interactions between citizens of differing and even similar micro-cultures.[4]

Thus, in essence, for Canada and most other host countries, globalization has created spaces of constant cultural negotiation. Evidently, the role citizens can play in these negotiations largely depends on the prevailing ideologies and the political climate of the host countries. In Quebec, it was this particular characteristic of citizen involvement that set the CCAPRCD apart. It engaged a whole province to candidly discuss not only the positive aspects of multiculturalism, but also the negative aspects, in public and transparent settings. The Commission thus acted not only as a grassroots-style strategy for discussing multiculturalism in general, but also as a space of cultural negotiation, of cultural translation, and even more specifically, *cultural translation in action*.

Translation is generally understood as a form of interlinguistic transfer, but many different disciplines, from ethnography to cultural studies, have relied on the concept and framework of translation to explain a diverse and broader set of transformative practices. Very broadly, translation has been described as the "reframing of meanings from one set of cultural categories to another" (Sturge 7), particularly in the context of intercultural contact. Cultural translation then means "more than a transfer between [languages or linguistic systems]"; it is a "form of intercultural and social interaction" (Wolf 190). In short, cultural translation is a space of negotiation between cultures (cf. Bhabha; Buden; Sturge). The concept of intercultural contact as cultural translation is particularly pertinent in the context of a multicultural and plurivocal country like Canada because it suitably circumscribes the constant negotiation between Canada's micro-cultures, where harmonious "understanding" between cultures is not always possible, but where, at the very least, the contact can open up a space for *potential* transformation. As Buden states, "[Cultural translation] brings around social change and opens new spaces of emancipation. It [changes] everyday social relations." From the perspective of these conceptualizations of translation, the CCAPRCD is a particularly evocative example of cultural translation precisely because it is a tangible, real-world example of the conceptual process described above.

Sources of the Debate

The debate pertaining to cultural difference in Quebec began to take shape in mid-2006 (Potvin), when the collocation "accommodement raisonnable"[5] began to permeate Québécois mainstream media in the context of an upcoming provincial election to be held in 2007.[6] Although the term "reasonable accommodation" had been used in English in a legal context since 1985, it took on new, non-legal connotations in French; connotations at times even inconsistent with the legal definition.[7] In short, the term "reasonable accommodation" was originally a legal concept in the Canadian Charter of Rights and Freedoms meant to ensure that institutions and employers (a) would not discriminate on the basis of an individual's personal circumstances (e.g., marital status, pregnancy), permanent traits (e.g., disabilities, skin colour), or sociocultural background (e.g., religion, language) (cf. Bouchard and Taylor, *Fonder l'avenir* 64–6); and (b) would "accommodate," whenever possible, these practices and traits. But, eventually, "reasonable accommodation" became a term most Canadians used to designate any form of cultural "accommodation" in the public sphere (Geadah 16–18), for instance, in classrooms, restaurants, and community centres (i.e., agreements between private parties).[8] Adelman states that "reasonable accommodation [accommodements raisonnables] has an ordinary informal cultural, as well as a formal legal meaning" (113), and it was confusion between the two uses of the term that often sparked debates in the media and created tension between citizens as it was not always clear which cases had legal ramifications and which did not.

In January 2007, following a series of events that stereotyped "accommodements raisonnables" as being negative and usually requested by immigrants (Bouchard and Taylor, *Fonder l'avenir* 67–73), the "accommodation" wildfire, or more aptly in a Canadian context, the "accommodation snowball," hit a small rural town in Quebec named Hérouxville. Having followed the media frenzy surrounding the debate on accommodation, the municipal counsellor of the town, André Drouin, with the general support of his township, decided to draft a code of conduct for newcomers wanting to move to the small community. Based on a survey in which the townspeople had answered a number of questions relating to their daily activities, cultural practices, and religious beliefs (named "current norms" in the survey), Drouin drafted a code entitled *Mode de vie* (Way of Life) that stated a set of norms by which newcomers (with an emphasis on foreign immigrants) to Hérouxville would henceforth have to abide. Drouin argued that the code would avoid some of the problems encountered in Canada's metropolitan areas because immigrants would have a clearly defined set of rules before they arrived, thus enabling them to make "an informed decision prior to moving to Hérouxville."[9] Drouin also argued that he was simply acting on behalf of the electorate, listening to their input, and taking into consideration what they deemed tolerable and acceptable in terms of accommodating cultural differences. It could be argued that Drouin *translated* Hérouxville's norms and beliefs into clear, jargonless terms so that they could be easily conveyed to newcomers with differing belief systems. Evidently, the goal of this instance of cultural translation, that is, the publication of the code, was not necessarily to encourage the coexistence of two or more varying cultural and belief systems but, rather, to impose one set as the established norm. This would be an example of cultural translation *in action* that does not necessarily try to act as a positive transformative process.

The "effects" of this particular document of cultural translation were multiple. On the one hand, Drouin was seen as a hero, standing up for the "Nous" ("Us") Québécois as well as this group's traditional beliefs and values;[10] on the other hand, he was ridiculed and shunned for being simple-minded, xenophobic, and closed-minded.[11] In fact, Drouin's document played a key role in instigating the creation of an official commission on cultural diversity, in February 2007.

The Mandate and Its Implementation

The CCAPRCD was called for by provincial Premier Jean Charest "to take stock of accommodation practices in Quebec (legal and civic); analyze the attendant issues bearing in mind the experiences of other societies; conduct an extensive consultation on this topic; and, formulate recommendations to the government to ensure that accommodation practices conform to the values of Quebec society as a pluralistic, democratic, egalitarian society" (Bouchard and Taylor, "Mandate"). The mandate was carried out in three stages: (1) the organization of the consultation and other activities (March to August 2007); (2) the public consultation (September to December 2007); and (3) the drafting of the final report (January to March 2008).

Stage 2, the public consultations were the venues of cultural translation in action, where effective "negotiation between cultures" was to take place. This stage involved hearings (or "citizen forums") in seventeen cities throughout the province of Quebec;[12] the study of perceptions of harmonization practices; meetings of other focus groups; and provincial forums held in collaboration with the Institut du Nouveau Monde in Montreal. The overarching goals of the forums were to "inform the Commission of the viewpoints of Quebecers of different generations, backgrounds and regions of Quebec on the management of diversity and Quebecers' shared values; [to] create a spirit and a forum conducive to dialogue between Quebecers of different origins; [to] encourage reflection in the main communities concerned" (Bouchard and Taylor, "Purpose of the Consultation").

Each of the citizens' forums followed a three-step procedure: the Commission co-chairs presented the forums' themes and discussion topics to the participants; this was followed by an open discussion with the participants, and then concluding remarks about the exchange were given by the co-chairs. The key themes largely revolved around notions of assimilation, tolerance, accommodation, stereotyping, and misconceptions about cultural differences, gender equality, human rights, and other correlative issues. Citizens who chose voluntarily to contribute their experiences, opinions, and observations were given two to three minutes of "air time" and were allowed to express themselves on any topic relating to accommodation and cultural differences provided that they were "tempered and civil" (Bouchard and Taylor, "Purpose of the Consultation"). The forums received bad press for being a soapbox opportunity in some rare and unfortunate cases for the voices of xenophobia, racism, sexism, and intolerance, a fact Adelman ("Conclusion: Religion, Culture, and the State") discusses in his analysis of the Commission, post-report.[13] Although these examples reveal the more negative side of cultural translation in action, it is still important to note that the forums were remarkable in that they gave nearly all citizens the opportunity to *have* a voice, to translate/represent themselves, and to translate their value and belief systems for others.[14] Undeniably, the opportunity to self-translate to and for others was a positive factor for smaller micro-cultures that do not generally have a "voice" in the larger mass media institutions responsible for so many of the detrimental stereotypes of "Otherness" disseminated over the course of the debate.

It is interesting to note that the translation strategies used to frame cultural practices by participants generally followed the same age-old trends found in interlingual translation: either there appeared to be a very conscious and concerted effort on behalf of many citizens, Quebecers and newcomers alike, to discuss diverging cultural practices and beliefs in ways that would be intelligible for all parties, thus demonstrating a desire to encourage and foster understanding, akin to a sort of "domestication" or "common ground," or there was a refusal to try and "mediate" one's beliefs, opting instead for a more uncompromising stance, which to some extent corresponds to a sort of resistance, "foreignization," or refusal to find "common ground." The former trend may be the preferable version of cultural translation in action in which the intentional re-framing of certain cultural assumptions seeks to promote points of convergence within spaces of divergence. Drouin's original Hérouxville document is an example of the latter more resistant version.

Cultural translation can thus act as a form of alternative dispute resolution, with the cultural mediators (cultural translators) incessantly translating the needs, feelings, and emotions of one party for another in the hope not necessarily of finding some utopian middle ground, but rather, of determining a sufficient number of commonalities with shared cultural relevance to enable the parties to go beyond the conflict or reassess prevailing stereotypes – or, at the very least, to turn seemingly incomprehensible cultural practices into more comprehensible ones. This does not imply neutrality on behalf of the cultural mediator/translator, as neutrality is a myth that has been disproven in both the disciplines of translation studies and conflict studies (see Venuti; Baker). Rather, more in line with the concept of *civic translation* proposed by Basalamah ("La traduction citoyenne n'est pas une métaphore"), this type of cultural translation requires that the cultural citizen-translator be fully invested in wanting to transform divergent cultural perspectives and representations, not because the citizen-translator is by nature more virtuous than, say, the media, but because, by definition, citizen-translators are just that: citizens who have every reason to participate in "the identity conflict which [they] also mediate" (Simon 12). Moreover, these citizen-translators took on the responsibility for the translations they produced of their communities, values, beliefs, and cultural practices. This was especially so not only because the forums were public, televised, and recorded, but also because they formed the foundational data for the drafting of the Commission's recommendations that may eventually influence policy making.

Effects

In the context of the Bouchard-Taylor Commission, cultural translation, particularly as it occurred during the provincial public forums, had four major effects. Two of these effects can be construed as "positive," while the other two effects may provide further insight into the construction and understanding of Québécois national identity, as well as how micro-cultures are represented in Québécois political and media discourse.

First, the CCAPRCD public forums gave voice to a succession of citizen-translators,[15] as opposed to an exclusive institutional, authoritative "translator" (e.g., the Canadian government or the provincial government). By giving a translational voice to everyday citizens, the Commission gave agency to all members of society, not just the educated elite or politically invested.[16] The concept of citizen "agency" is crucial: in the context of everyday social interaction, vulnerable micro-cultures do not always have the means, tangible or symbolic, to speak for or represent themselves. The Commission's concerted effort to offer "translational" agency to all citizens may have curtailed an extreme asymmetrical distribution of representational power. Moreover, the agency to translate oneself and one's experience with managing cultural diversity was not given exclusively to the dominant micro-culture de facto; rather, peripheral or minority communities were greatly encouraged to participate and counter many of the prevailing stereotypes that were wrongly attributed to them (e.g., Muslim women countering the notion that the *hijab* is a form of submission, or individuals from rural communities countering the notion that they were automatically against cultural differences). Additionally, what cultural translation in this type of setting can reveal is that what appear to be conflicts over differences are, in fact, conflicts involving similarities (e.g., in their quest for rights and recognition, cultural, linguistic, or religious groups may initially seem to have antagonistic goals and desires; however, upon closer inspection, it is possible to find that what may initially seem like points of divergence are actually similar plights). Bernard Gagnon (23) further stresses the singularity of this type of citizen-centric, collective cultural translation:

> la Commission Bouchard-Taylor fut l'un des rares lieux de mobili-
> sation et de délibération à l'échelle de la nation. La possibilité de dé-
> battre ouvertement et démocratiquement est un héritage et un
> privilège; nous n'en reconnaissons pas suffisamment les acquis […]
> nous pouvons statuer que la [Commission], malgré les critiques for-
> mulées à son endroit, a fait la démonstration que le Québec dispose
> d'une capacité collective à débattre avec sérénité et respect d'enjeux
> aussi cruciaux pour sa destinée collective.

Increased agency through cultural translation also has a number of smaller, subsequent effects. For instance, greater opportunities to translate oneself and one's needs generally lessen political and social apathy, which presumably would encourage more citizens to participate in the debates that inform public policy. Proof of this assertion can be found in the attendance data for the public forums (see n2 below). Moreover, cultural translation of this sort sets up the possibility for exchange between groups that may have otherwise never had a chance to communicate directly with one another.

The second "effect" is that the Commission has now set a precedent for the types of viable methodologies (cultural translation included) useful for talking about and dealing with multicultural discourse and policy in a culturally and linguistically heterogeneous social space.[17] While it may be possible to question whether or not the Commission was successful in providing and implementing concrete strategies post-Commission,[18] the fact remains that up until this point, such a large-scale democratic and civic "census" pertaining to the issues of tolerance, equality, and diversity was unheard of.[19] For host countries trying to find ways to encourage and foster collective democratic debate, the Bouchard-Taylor Commission and its activities could provide a template. A number of the Commission's activities seem to have successfully resonated with the public, which was attested by high public turnout and desire to *actively* participate. Moreover, many of these activities were, indeed, manifestations of various forms of cultural translation; the public forums, described earlier, are one example, but the same could be said of the written briefs and research papers submitted by cultural groups, community-based organizations, religious groups, etc – they, too, "translated" the needs, aspirations, and perceptions of their authors' cultural and group affiliations.

An additional effect was the "re-translation" of the Québécois "Nous." Be it a literary or cultural text (Geertz), the translation of any source "text" opens up the possibility for new/revised (and even controversial) interpretations to come to the fore in the translated version. In the context of the Commission, the participants/contributors shared their versions of the "Nous" narrative (ontological narratives), in turn shaping a collection of new target texts, or perhaps more accurately, a collection of *fragments* that, combined, would create the overarching "Nous" target text. For some participants, the "Nous" narrative could not and should not be disassociated from its historical underpinnings, which is in direct reference to the Québécois minority's ongoing struggle to gain and maintain recognition in an Anglo-Saxon/English-Canadian majority. In other words, some "old-stock" Québécois felt that any threat leading to a dilution of Québécois identity should be countered – which, at times, could be read as disdain for or fear of the cultural "Other" (e.g., Hérouxville's code of conduct). In other versions of the translated "Nous" narrative, participants felt a need to reassert the importance of shared "Québécois" values: equality between the sexes, separation of Church and State, and the use of a shared language (in this case, Québécois French) (Laforest 131). Incidentally, these "Québécois" values largely echo Western liberal values (Thériault 153), a fact that seems to have been periodically forgotten by some of the participants and politicians during the debate, as though newcomers, even those hailing from the "West" needed to be reminded of these Western liberal values. Finally, another version of the "Nous" that emerged was that of a generally welcoming and open-minded "Nous"; a "Nous" that continues to see the influx of newcomers an asset to Québécois culture as opposed to a threat (Toledo Freiwald 83); participants cited, among other things, diasporic and cultural activities (theatre, dance companies, literary circles), enriched business opportunities, and fusion cuisine as positive consequences of immigration. Evidently, within these three broader categories, nuanced and hybrid versions of these narratives also surfaced, which would indicate that Québécois identity and culture are not "static" texts, but rather texts that are in the process of being translated and re-translated as the provincial demographic changes. This parallels Adelman's assertion that "[societies] are living organisms subjected to a continuous interaction of competing moral and cultural forces" (116).

The final effect is unfortunately less salutary. Pre- and post-Commission media coverage, largely blamed for "igniting" and "fuelling" the debate (Bouchard and Taylor, *Fonder l'avenir*), did indeed, create a number of cultural stereotypes through the systematic pairing of the verbal collocations "accommodements raisonnables" and "reasonable accommodations" (or other, similar collocations referring to the debate) and visual representations of cultural "Others." These "inter-semiotic" (visual verbal) cultural translations, published in most Québécois dailies over the course of 2006–08 and televised on various regional stations, regrettably, played into the insecurities and fears of some Québécois (Adelman 111), subsequently feeding into the rhetoric that the "Other" inevitably posed a significant threat. And while some the previous effects and events were generally contained within the borders of Quebec, the negative visual/verbal stereotypes were not. For instance, the national publication *Maclean's* ran a cover that depicted a veiled Muslim woman with the headline: "Do Immigrants Need Rules?" (see Figure 10.1.) The effect of this particular "translation" was that it further disseminated three negative stereotypes: first, that immigrants need to be taught or given "rules"; second, that the "face" of immigration is synonymous with that of the veiled Muslim woman; and third, that the Québécois (especially rural townspeople) are the only ones "brash" enough to ignite such a controversial debate. Moreover, while this is but one example, it was not a singular occurrence: veiled Muslim women; angry Caucasians; neo-Canadians with apparent culturally distinctive features (e.g., traditional dress, religious symbols); these media "translations" further cemented the associations made between "accommodements raisonnables" (in its larger, non-legal, informal sense) and specific cultural groups.

Conclusion

The work of the Commission used forms of cultural translation unique to Canada (and unique in shaping Canadian discourse on the management of cultural diversity). This parallels and highlights translation's potential more generally as an intercultural mediation paradigm and as a means to face intercultural encounters in other contexts. Finally, the Bouchard-Taylor Commission promoted ideas of civic responsibility and self-representation/self-translation as well as agency in the shaping of policy on cultural diversity.

Figure 10.1

Cover of *Maclean's*, 5 March 2007.

Notes

1 This description is a personal account of the Quebec City public forum, which
   I attended on 29 October 2007.

2 Quelques statistiques de base suffiront pour établir, à tout le moins quantitati-
   vement, l'importance de l'opération: plus de 3000 personnes ont assisté aux
   20 forums régionaux organisés par elle; son site Internet a reçu 500 000 visites;
   901 personnes ont rédigé des mémoires et la Commission a accueilli plus de
   300 de ses auteurs, auxquels il faut ajouter plus de 250 témoignages person-
   nels. Les exercices de démocratie participative interactive proposés par la
   Commission sur son site Internet ont suscité quelque 120 000 réponses. La
   Commission a aussi organisé quatre forums nationaux, mis sur pied plusieurs
   groupes d'experts et piloté un nombre important de projets de recherche. Son
   coût global s'élève à quelque 3,7 millions de dollars (Laforest 125).

3 "According to a SOM survey conducted in September and October 2007 on behalf of *La Presse*, 71.7 percent of Quebecers whose mother tongue is French
   surveyed found Canadian society overly tolerant of accommodation, compared
   with 35.2 percent of Quebecers whose mother tongue is a language other than
   French. This finding is obviously somewhat imprecise because English-speakers
   are not separated from allophones" (Bouchard and Taylor, *Fonder l'avenir*
   [English version] 67). However, this is not to say that French Quebecers were
   the *only* Canadians who expressed dissatisfaction with cultural accommodation.

4 Ulf Hannerz (*Cultural Complexity*) suggests that "micro-culture" is a more
   suitable way of describing smaller cultural groupings within a larger context.

5 It should be noted that although the term "accommodation raisonnable" has
   recently garnered more attention from the media, it is not a new term nor is it a
   new phenomenon in Canada. In the Canadian context, the term "reasonable
   accommodation" was first used in its legal sense in 1985 in *Ontario Human
   Rights Commission (O'Malley)* v. *Simpson-Sears* (Geadah 16) and was also
   used in the terminology of work policy to "describe the integration of the men-
   tally and physically handicapped into the workplace" (Patriquin, "Not particularly accommodating").

6 For example, as part of his political platform and rhetoric, Mario Dumont, then
   head of the ADQ, would often use the term "accommodation raisonnable" to
   refer to agreements held between private parties. Acknowledging that this did,
   indeed, blur the understanding of the term for the general public, he demanded
   that the term be revised by means of a commission. While Fall and Vignaux (28)

state, "Ce que Mario Dumont [...] a réussi c'est d'avoir posé les termes d'un débat qui ose affronter des questions de fond, des questions qui dérangent," some critics have observed that Dumont was likely being opportunistic. Anctil states, "[Dumont's] campaign was widely seen by commentators as having the potential of successfully boosting the political profile of the young leader and positioning him favourably for the following provincial elections" (6).

7 For instance, in its *legal* definition, groups or collective entities cannot demand a "accommodement raisonnable," only individuals can request said accommodations from their employers/institutions. Despite this proviso, on multiple occasions, groups were portrayed by the Quebec-based media as requesting "accommodements raisonnables" (i.e., term being used to designate a non-legally binding agreement between two parties) (Bouchard and Taylor, *Fonder l'avenir* 66).

8 Indeed, the media played a paramount role in the skewing and distortion of 15 key events (Bouchard and Taylor, *Fonder l'avenir* 67–73) pertaining to accommodation (in the broad sense of the term) in Quebec. A chronology of these events, along with their stereotyped and factual renditions, is provided in the final report of the Commission.

9 My translation of a section of the document *Municipalité d'Hérouxville: Publication des normes en place* excerpted in Thompson (*Le syndrome Hérouxville* 49–50).

10 The narrative of the "Nous Québécois" ("Us") is a recurrent theme in social discourse in Quebec. Brisset (120–3) argues that the narrative of collective identity in this particular context can actually be viewed from a number of different perspectives. The idea of a "Nous" ("Us") implicitly connotes a threatening "Eux" ("Them" or "Other/Others") that generally takes the form of either English-speaking Canada or neo-Canadians (immigrants). Interestingly, First Nations people are rarely portrayed as being much of a threat per se; if anything, they are ignored by this discourse or framed as being part of a larger set of social "problems" which involve unemployment, education rights, substance abuse, and land ownership. Thus, the "Nous" discourse has a dual purpose: on the one hand, it is empowering for Quebecers because it frames them as a cohesive, homogeneous, and distinct group (which promotes a refusal of letting "Others" into the in-group); but on the other hand, it also constructs the "Nous" as being fearful of being persecuted by "Others" (even if these "Others" are effectively smaller micro-cultures within the framework of the

province or country). Quebecers thus find themselves in a double bind, torn between self-promotion and assertion, and self-doubt and victimization. In a section titled "Anxiety over Identity," Bouchard and Taylor summarize the issue of collective identity in relation to the debate on accommodation as follows: "the so-called wave of accommodation clearly touched a number of emotional chords among French-Canadian Quebecers in such a way that requests for religious adjustments have spawned fears about the most valuable heritage of the Quiet Revolution, in particular gender equality and secularism. The result has been an identity counter-reaction movement that has expressed itself through the rejection of harmonization practices [...] We can conclude that Quebecers of French-Canadian ancestry are still not at ease with their twofold status as a majority in Québec and a minority in Canada and North America" (*Fonder l'avenir* 18).

11 The public's reaction to Drouin and his actions falls in line with the dichotomous discourse mentioned earlier; those who chose to be open to cultural differences opposed him, suggesting that he was limiting the possibility of change and transition in Quebec, while others lauded him for wanting to preserve Quebec's inherent identity.

12 The 17 cities are: Montreal, Montreal Côte-des-Neiges, Sherbrooke, Laval, Drummondville, Saint-Georges, Quebec City, Trois-Rivières, Longueuil, Saint-Hyacinthe, Bonaventure, Rimouski, Joliette, St-Jérôme, Saguenay, Sept-Îles, Rouyn-Noranda, and Gatineau (some of the cities hosted the citizen forums twice).

13 "In Canada, the process gave voice to xenophobia and the maligning of other communities, though [...] there were a significant number of articulate and well-thought-out briefs" (Adelman 113).

14 Bernard Gagnon (12) asserts, "Si elle fut parfois un objet de risée, dû aux propos malhabiles ou disgracieux de certains citoyens participant aux audiences, la Commission a néanmoins reçu une attention soutenue dans les médias et fut loin de laisser la population indifférente. Son rapport de plus de 300 pages ne fait pas l'unanimité, mais il constitue un ouvrage essentiel et porteur de balises dans la poursuite du débat public sur les différences culturelles."

15 Such citizen-translators hailed from all parts of society and ranged from community leaders (e.g., Cardinal Marc Ouellet, Max Gros-Louis), scholars (e.g., les Professeures et chercheuses de l'Université Laval, la Faculté de théologie et de sciences des religions de l'Université de Montréal), individuals, spiritual

leaders (e.g., Assemblée des évêques catholiques du Québec, B'nai Brith Canada), politicians or representatives of political parties (e.g., Bloc Québécois, Liberal Party, NDP), and representatives from a wide range of social organizations (e.g., Conseil québécois des gais et des lesbiennes, Fédération des femmes du Québec, Muslim Women of Québec, Association québécoise des professeurs de français).

16 Whereas philosopher John Rawls ("The Idea of Public Reason Revisited") suggests such debates should be restricted only to society's political and legal elite, this essay tends to echo the work of philosophers Habermas (see Calhoun) and Charles Taylor (*Multiculturalism*), as well as the observations made by Adelman and Anctil (*Religion, Culture, and the State*). Adelman sums up this line of thought as follows: "One can fall back on the comforting position that although public discourse is extremely fragile, there is no better alternative if we are to understand how we operate as political animals in the public sphere [...] The debate cannot be restricted, neither in its content nor to certain participants" (115). Anctil also stresses the importance of the civic dimension: "[The Bouchard-Taylor Commission] gave citizens from all walks of life and on a wide regional basis the occasion to express themselves on a theme crucial to the future of their society. This in a sense was a major innovation presented by the Commission, even though it led at times to racist and xenophobic pronouncements, which, sadly, the co-chairs did not always see fit to contradict on the spot" (15).

17 Pierre Anctil shares a similar observation: "There is no doubt in my mind that the Bouchard-Taylor Commission was a watershed in the debate on cultural diversity in Québec" (14).

18 Two recent publications tend to suggest that while the Commission was generally successful in providing quantitative and qualitative data for policy recommendations, little has been done on the politicians' end in terms of implementing said recommendations since the publication of the Commission's official report in May 2008 (cf. Fall and Vignaux; Gagnon).

19 "Tenir une consultation publique sur un sujet aussi délicat que les accommodements culturels et religieux exigeait un certain courage de la part du gouvernement" (Fall and Vignaux 78).

Works Cited

Adelman, Howard. "Conclusion." *Religion, Culture, and the State: Reflections on the Bouchard-Taylor Report*. Ed. Howard Adelman and Pierre Anctil. Toronto: University of Toronto Press, 2011, 100–16.

– and Pierre Anctil, eds. *Religion, Culture, and the State: Reflections on the Bouchard-Taylor Report*. Toronto: University of Toronto Press, 2011.

Anctil, Pierre. "Introduction." *Religion, Culture, and the State: Reflections on the Bouchard-Taylor Report*. Ed. Howard Adelman and Pierre Anctil. Toronto: University of Toronto Press, 2011, 3–15.

– "Reasonable Accommodation in the Canadian Legal Context: A Mechanism for Handling Diversity or a Source of Tension?" *Religion, Culture, and the State: Reflections on the Bouchard-Taylor Report*. Ed. Howard Adelman and Pierre Anctil. Toronto: University of Toronto Press, 201l, 16–36.

Aubin, Benoit, and Jonathan Gatehouse. "Do Immigrants Need Rules? The Debate Rages On." *Maclean's*, 5 March 2007. Accessed 5 June 2011. http://www.macleans.ca/homepage/magazine/article.jsp?content=20070305_1030 84_103084

Basalamah, Salah. "La traduction citoyenne n'est pas une métaphore." Traduction engage / Translation and Social Activism. Special issue of *TTR: Traduction, traductologie, rédaction* 18: 2 (2005): 49–69.

Bhabha, Homi. *The Location of Culture*. London: Routledge, 1994.

Bouchard, Gérard, and Charles Taylor. Commission de consultation sur les pratiques d'accommodement reliées aux différences culturelles. *Fonder l'avenir: Le temps de la reconciliation*. Québec: Gouvernement du Québec, 2008. Rapport final. Gouvernement du Québec. Accessed 28 Dec. 2009. http://www.accommo dements.qc.ca/

– "Mandate." Accessed 28 Dec. 2009. http://www.accommodements.qc.ca/ commission/mandat-en.html

– "Purpose of the Consultation." Accessed 28 Dec. 2009. http://www.accommode ments.qc.ca/consultation-publique/finalite-en.html

Brisset, Annie. *Sociocritique de la traduction: Théâtre et altérité au Québec (1968– 1988)*. Longueuil: Préambule, 1990.

Buden, Boris. "Cultural Translation: Why It Is Important and Where to Start with It." *Translate.eipcp.net*. European Institute for Progressive Cultural Policies, June 2006. Accessed 28 Dec. 2009. http://translate.eipcp.net/transversal/0606/buden/en

Calhoun, C., ed. *Habermas and the Public Sphere*. Cambridge, MA: MIT Press, 1992.

Fall, Khadiyatoulah, and Georges Vignaux. *Images de l'autre et de soi: Les accommodements raisonnables entre préjugés et réalité*. Québec: Les Presses de l'Université Laval, 2008.

Gagnon, Bernard, ed. *La Diversité québécoise en débat: Bouchard, Taylor et les autres*. Montréal: Québec/Amérique, 2010.

Geadah, Yolande. *Accommodements raisonnables: Droit à la différence et non différence des droits*. Montréal: VLB, 2007.

Geertz, Clifford. *The Interpretation of Cultures*. New York: Basic Books, 2000 [1973].

Hannerz, Ulf. *Cultural Complexity: Studies in the Social Organization of Meaning*. New York: Columbia University Press, 1992.

Laforest, Guy. "La Commission Bouchard-Taylor et la place du Québec dans la trajectoire de l'état-nation modern." *La Diversité québécoise en débat: Bouchard, Taylor et les autres*. Ed. Bernard Gagnon. Montréal: Québec/Amérique, 2010.

Ontario Human Rights Commission (O'Malley) v. Simpson-Sears [1985] 2 S.C.R. 536. *CanLII*. Canadian Legal Information Institute. Accessed 28 Dec. 2009. http://www.iijcan.org/en/ca/scc/doc/1985/1985canlii18/1985canlii18.html

Patriquin, Martin. "Not Particularly Accommodating: Quebec Voters Are Making Fear of Visible Minorities a Hot Issue." *Maclean's*, 24 Sept. 2007. Accessed 20 Jan. 2009. http://www.macleans.ca/article.jsp?content=20070924_109270_109270

Potvin, Maryse. *Crise des accommodements raisonnables: une fiction médiatique?* Outremont, QC: Athena, 2008.

Rawls, John. "The Idea of Public Reason Revisited." *Chicago Law Review* 64: 3 (1997): 765–807.

Simon, Sherry. "Presentation." Translation and Social Activism. Special issue of *TTR: Traduction, traductologie, redaction* 18: 2 (2005): 9–16.

Sturge, Kate. *Representing Others: Translation, Ethnography and the Museum*. Manchester: St Jerome, 2007.

Taylor, Charles. *Multiculturalism: Examining the Politics of Recognition*. Princeton, NJ: Princeton University Press, 1994.

Thériault, Joseph Yvon. "Entre républicanisme et multiculturalisme: La Commission Bouchard-Taylor, une synthèse ratée." *La Diversité québécoise en débat:*

Bouchard, Taylor et les autres. Ed. Bernard Gagnon. Montréal: Québec/Amérique, 2010.

Thompson, Bernard. *Le syndrome Hérouxville, ou, les accommodements raisonnables*. Boisbriand, QC: Momentum, 2007.

Toledo Freiwald, Bina. "'Qui est nous?' Some Answers from the Bouchard-Taylor Commission's Archive." *Religion, Culture, and the State*. Ed. Howard Adelman and Pierre Anctil. Toronto: University of Toronto Press, 2011, 69–85.

Venuti, Lawrence. *The Scandals of Translation: Towards an Ethics of Difference*. London: Routledge, 1998.

Wolf, Michaela. "Culture as Translation – And beyond Ethnographic Models of Representation in Translation Sudies." *Crosscultural Transgressions*. Ed. Theo Hermans. Manchester: St Jerome, 2002, 180–92.

PART THREE

Translating Poetry, Fiction, Essays

11

1923: "Foreign" Immigrants Write Back:
The Publication of Laura Goodman Salverson's
The Viking Heart

Daisy Neijmann

During the 1920s and 1930s, "foreign" immigrant writers begin to make themselves heard in Canadian literature for the first time. From various backgrounds, these writers translate their own experiences, and those of their cultural groups, into a Canadian literary idiom – experimenting with language and form to accommodate them. Canadian multiculturalism, although not an official policy until 1971, has of course been a fact of life in Canada since the earliest days of immigration, not least in the Canadian West, where many of the non–Anglo-Celtic immigrants initially settled. Culturally, however, Canada had been virtually exclusively defined and expressed in Anglo-Celtic terms, even in the few instances that included the presence of cultural "others." It is only when the immigrants themselves embark on the long and difficult process of cultural translation, writing themselves and their experiences into Canadian literature and making themselves heard, that the definition of Canada and Canadian culture gradually becomes more inclusive. The Icelandic-Canadian author Laura Goodman Salverson was the first to publish a Canadian immigrant novel from a non–Anglo-Celtic perspective, and to do so to great contemporary acclaim. Her achievement and success in translating her own cultural background and her vision for a multicultural Canada inspired many others who soon followed in her wake.

Laura Goodman Salverson's debut novel *The Viking Heart* was published by McClelland and Stewart in 1923, a time when Canada enjoyed a great surge of nationalist feeling. Its contribution to the First World War had launched Canada onto the international scene and had created a sense of national awareness. One of the areas where this wave of Canadian nationalism exercised a profound influence was that of literature. No longer were writers in Canada to model their works on British or American literature; instead, everyone now eagerly awaited the arrival of "the great Canadian novel" (Pacey 665–6). This feeling was particularly strong in western Canada, which had been developing a staunch sense of distinct regional pride and identity. The early decades of the twentieth century were a time of rapid expansion and economic boom on the Canadian prairies, which were regarded, by many western Canadians, at least, as the symbol of Canada's potential and future, rather than the colonial east, which had always looked to Britain and the past.

Canadian writers, and indeed Canadian publishers, had always faced great obstacles, including copyright issues and a general lack of interest in Canadian literature by a readership that either believed that literature and culture came from Europe, or was content with cheap, sensational American formula writing (popularly known as "dime" novels). Writers usually worked in isolation, as a national or local infrastructure to support authorship was virtually non-existent. In 1921, however, the Canadian Authors Association (CAA) was founded by a small but active group of Canadians who were concerned with the development of a Canadian writing and reading culture. Among its objectives were the encouragement and protection of Canadian authors, the creation of a national literary forum, and the promotion of Canadian writing among readers and publishers through the organization of annual conventions and events to introduce the Canadian public to its literature, and through its publications in the *Canadian Bookman* (founded in 1919).

At this time, it was still a generally acknowledged fact that when people spoke of a "Canadian" culture and literature, what they meant was something New World, yes, but nevertheless solidly Anglo-Celtic. The majority of the initial settlers in the west were from Ontario, and their Anglo-Canadian heritage recreated any definition of (western) Canadian culture in its image. Those Canadians who took an active interest in literature were generally from the Anglo-Canadian conservative, genteel middle class. The face of western Canada, however, was changing rapidly, as immigrants from other European countries arrived and contributed to its development in every way that was open to them. And while the prevalent view among the Anglo-Canadian establishment was inherently chauvinistic and strongly favoured a rapid assimilation of these suspect masses of "foreigners," it is clear that, at the same time, a fascination existed with the nation-building process that was taking place in the west, which now accommodated people from every corner of the world.[1]

Laura Goodman Salverson was the daughter of two such "foreigners." She was born in Winnipeg in 1890 to Icelandic parents who had immigrated to Canada three years previously. She had a peripatetic childhood, living in many places in the Canadian and American West, and mostly in poverty – an experience that gave her an acute, first-hand knowledge of immigrant life on the homesteads and in the cities of this fast-expanding area of the continent. The Icelanders were among the first "foreign" immigrants to western Canada, from 1875 onwards, and they brought with them a cherished and widely practised literary tradition. Despite poverty and hardships, the Icelandic immigrants started to write down their experiences in the new country almost immediately, first in documentary form, later in poetry and fiction. Literature was never the sole domain of an exclusive social class in Iceland, and inimical circumstances notwithstanding, Salverson was brought up with a great love and respect for literature. Both her parents were avid readers, and her father was also a regular contributor to the Icelandic immigrant newspapers. In her autobiography, *Confessions of an Immigrant's Daughter*, Salverson relates how she had a vision in a public library when she was ten years old and had just started learning English: "I, too, will write a book, to stand on the shelves of a place like this – and I will write it in English, for that is the greatest language in the whole world!" (238).

She describes how she had almost given up on the possibility of ever becoming a writer, but, while living in western Canadian cities with local CAA branches, she received invaluable encouragement from enthusiastic Canadian literary nationalists and authors, notably Austin Bothwell and Nellie McClung. Salverson knew exactly what she wanted: to translate the experiences, tribulations, and trials of the poor and simple, the downtrodden and marginalized, into literature. More specifically, she wanted to show that the "foreigners" living among "respectable" Canadians were not a mass of uncultured and unsavoury brutes by portraying the price they paid for their place in Canadian life. So far, the western immigrant experience had only found its way into Canadian literature from an Anglo-Celtic point of view, in homesteading novels and works such as Ralph Connor's notorious novel *The Foreigner* (1909), which espoused a strong assimilationist ideology and patronizing and chauvinistic portrayals of anyone not of Anglo-Celtic stock.

The Viking Heart, whose original title was, significantly, *The Price of Country*, was intended to change the nature of the immigrant novel in Canada. And in one respect, at least, Salverson was in an excellent position to do so. The Icelandic immigrant experience in Canada was exceptionally well documented at this point, and Icelandic immigrant literature flourished: Stephan G. Stephansson had firmly established his reputation as an exceptional poet by then, and had just launched a bombshell with the publication of his anti-war poems in *Vígslóði* (*Trail of War*, 1920); Jóhann Magnús Bjarnason's last instalments of the serial *Í Rauðárdalnum* (*In the Red River Valley*), later to be published as a novel (1942), had appeared in the magazine *Syrpa* (1914–1918); Guðrún H. Finnsdóttir had newly made her début as a short story writer with "Landskuld" ("Land Debt"), published in 1920 (reprinted in *Hillingalönd*, 1938), the same year in which Guttormur J. Guttormsson's second volume of poetry, *Bóndadóttir* (*Farmer's Daughter*), came out. In addition to providing Salverson with the obvious advantage of writing about a group of people whose experiences she shared and knew better than anyone, the Icelanders exemplified a group that had become well established in Canada yet had succeeded in preserving its cultural heritage despite pressures to assimilate. Her main challenge was how to translate this culture and experience, not just into English, but into a literary language and form that would imbue it with meaning for a Canadian readership, and inscribe it into Canadian literature.

The Viking Heart set out to challenge facile Anglo-Canadian assumptions of foreigners who either persisted in their barbarity or could hardly wait to shed it to assume a blameless Canadian skin. But it also challenges the very definition of "Canada" and "Canadian" as an Anglo-Canadian preserve, advocating instead a much more revolutionary ideal of Canada as a truly new world governed by freedom, egalitarianism, and social justice. It is, like many western Canadian novels of the day, a nation-building novel, but the nation it envisions is one informed by the best of the various peoples that make it, their cultures, their ideals, and their sacrifices. It was, in other words, an early vision of a multicultural Canada. Finally, Salverson intended for her novel to carry a strong message of social reform. As she explains in *Confessions*, for Icelanders, literature was never just entertainment, but a forum for ideas and ideals, to expand the mental horizon.

Salverson needed to find a literary form that could contain her various aims. Her deepest wish, throughout her career, was to write a saga; the sagas were Iceland's greatest literary treasure. Writing a Canadian saga would allow her to translate the most precious part of her cultural heritage into Canadian literature. At the same time, it would powerfully highlight the theme of cultural continuity in her novel, while the saga form also provided her with the epic historical scope she envisioned, as well as the rather loose structure allowing for a focus on specific important events in the lives of several generations. And last but not least, the much lauded realism of the sagas was well suited to social critique.

However, her readership had not grown up on a literary diet of sagas, as Salverson had; on the contrary, it was a completely unknown genre to the average Canadian. To get her message across, she needed something more Canadian. At the time, the romance was the prevalent form in Canadian fiction. Having its basis in myth, romance is particularly suited to the immigrant and nation-building novel, which, after all, deals with death and rebirth, the start of a new life (Kroetsch 84–94). Many western Canadian writers, in particular, had been making prolific use of the garden myth, depicting "the West as a new Eden." The most popular authors of the day, Ralph Connor, Robert Stead, and Nellie McClung, "glamourized the adventures of White Anglo-Saxon Protestants, innocents burning with zeal, who see the West as a new Eden and who are determined to build a Christian society there" (Thompson 239). In *The Viking Heart*, it is through death, the ultimate sacrifice, that the Icelandic pioneers finally embrace Canada and are reborn as Canadians. This was a message her readership could understand, and, considering the novel's popularity, was willing to accept. Borga and her family are driven from their native Iceland by a volcanic eruption, in which her brother Carl loses his life. The family immigrates to Canada, where Borga meets Bjorn Lindal, another Icelandic immigrant. They get married, start a homestead, and bring up three children. The family's hopes to "make good" are bound with Thor, the talented son who is to become a doctor. His death at Passchendaele marks the end of the Lindals as immigrants, and their birth as Canadians proper, as their debt to their adopted country has now been paid. This is symbolized through the birth of the first grandchild shortly after, who is christened Thor the Second, and the successful careers of Elizabeth, the remaining daughter, and her husband Balder, underlining the family's final integration into Canadian society.

The Viking Heart is not a translation of the cultural heritage of the old country. In many ways, it can be seen as bringing together and translating into English the large corpus of immigrant literature written in Icelandic in Canada. Since 1890, Icelandic immigrant writers had been experimenting with the theme of immigration in literature in the safety of their own language, and gradually, a distinctive form and vision had developed that came to characterize this writing. The overarching vision is one where immigrants successfully embrace two worlds, the old and the new, and where the cultures and contributions of all the various peoples that make up Canadian society are equally respected. The dominant structure of these works is cyclical, following a pattern of exodus from the old country, arrival in the new world, hardships leading to a (symbolic) death, followed by a (re)birth and (the promise of) success in the new country. Characteristic themes are cultural continuity, and the solidarity of all cultural groups in the face of Anglo-Canadian chauvinism. Heroes are successful and gain general recognition by contributing something of their cultural heritage to Canadian society, while villains turn their back on the old ways for material gain and advancement (see Bjarnason, *Eiríkur*; Finnsdóttir, *Hillingalönd* and *Dagshríðar Spor*). Any reader of *The Viking Heart* will easily recognize all of these characteristics.

Interestingly, the translation of these themes into English found a difficult reception, not among Canadian readers, but in the Icelandic immigrant community itself, where objections were raised to the way in which Salverson had appropriated community narratives and exposed them to a Canadian readership. Similar objections were raised regarding Salverson's translation of Icelandic culture in the novel. How to represent a culture in the language and literature of another is, of course, riddled with questions of cultural politics and power. From the novel it is clear that Salverson tries to explain her people's ways to an audience unfamiliar with Iceland and what she calls "the Norse soul," in an attempt to dispel the idea of all "foreigners" as barbarians. Cultural translation of the "other" inevitably runs the risk of overcompensation, and simply replacing negative stereotypes with positive ones, as the Canadian literary establishment several decades later accused *The Viking Heart* of doing (see Craig 81–93). Contemporary reviewers, however, make no mention of any "excessive nationalism." On the contrary, one reviewer refers to it not as a novel specifically about Iceland and Icelanders, but as a work about "the European in Canada" (Altair 6). At the time, Salverson probably needed to shout as loudly as she did on behalf of her people, just in order to be heard by the dominant majority.

Salverson finds different ways of translating her culture for a general Canadian readership. Most obviously, she uses sweeping, generalizing statements to explain Icelandic ways: "The Icelander loves a holiday"; "Then, in the way of the Icelander the world over, once his reserve is down, they sobbed on each other's necks" (*Viking Heart* 72 and 225).[2] In many instances, similar statements are made with regard to a quintessential Icelandic or Norse "soul," not infrequently with reference to Old Icelandic literature, which not only gives meaning to actions and events and provides a code of behaviour in a new context, but also serves to highlight, again, the theme of cultural continuity. Thus, Bjorn reminds Borga, "Remember how Hermond sang with the arrow in his breast. It is the way of our fathers" (*Viking Heart* 48), while their Canadian-born children, Thor and Elizabeth, have "some of that wanderlust which never quits the Scandinavian heart" (250). The Canadian reader is given an idea of what to expect Icelanders and their descendents to contribute to the country. This, of course, finds its epitome in Balder's international success as a Canadian musician.

The idea of contribution to Canadian society is crucial to an understanding of the main theme of the novel as it translates this dominant theme in Icelandic immigrant literature. The main protagonist of *The Viking Heart* is called Borga, which means "to pay." Gudsteins's "Rediscovering Icelandic Canadian Pacifism" explains that Icelandic immigrants invariably used the term *skuld* ("debt") to indicate their indebtedness and allegiance to Canada, not least in relation to participation in the First World War. When Bjorn, Borga's husband, complains about the superior attitude assumed by many Anglo-Canadians and the difficulties "foreigners" experience in Canada, the Icelandic minister, Sjera Bjarni, counters, "Remember, that we must expect to pay for the right to claim a part in this country" (108). Having lost her parents and siblings and experienced hardships during the early years of emigration and settlement, Borga never sees Canada as more than "a farm." It is only when she pays the ultimate price, the death of their son Thor, on whom they had pinned all their hopes, that she comes to see Canada as "a dear and precious possession" (305). As the minister points out in his memorial speech, Thor will live on "in the life of our country" (321). His "last sacrifice" ties her inextricably to the new land: "This Canada which had demanded so much of them – it was her country" (325).

One of the most salient aspects of the immigrant experience is that of being caught between languages. It is here that we experience *The Viking Heart* as a translation. Although the novel was conceived and written in English, the Icelandic language is everywhere. It resounds in the names of its characters, their cultural and mythological overtones (Thor, Loki, Balder), the cultural references (Sigurd the Volsung, Heimskringla, the "Deces," the eyes of Thiassi). On several occasions, the author provides an English translation of an Icelandic poem or proverb, and even the first line of an Icelandic song, which is, notably, introduced as "the Icelander's 'Auld Lang Syne'" (80). While English translations often hide the original language, the text is nevertheless peppered with Icelandic words and phrases. These are generally introduced in quotation marks, followed by an English translation in parentheses, but will often, upon later recurrence, stand unmarked and untranslated, equal to the English rather than just as colourful illustration. The Icelandic terms mostly cover areas such as food and housing, as well as greetings and exclamations, recreating the daily environment of the immigrants. Significantly, the English schoolteacher, Miss Wake, who finds she has to discard all her prejudices about these "foreigners," is quickly made to learn the Icelandic essentials, hellos, goodbyes, and thankyous – an important message that cultural traffic should flow two ways, and that English has no right to claim precedence here. In many instances, the Icelandic spelling has been adapted, not just to English orthography but to English pronunciation, so that the words, when pronounced by an English speaker, approximate the Icelandic (Guðsteinsdóttir 9).

Perhaps the most groundbreaking feature as far as language is concerned is Salverson's attempt to render the Icelandic way of speaking English in the text. The reader is reminded at the beginning of the novel that the main characters do not speak English, which to their ears is a "strange-sounding speech" (*Viking Heart* 47). They are eager to learn, though, viewing it as the "key to all manner of excellent things" (ibid.). Although the immigrants have little time to spare during their difficult homesteading years and lives among other Icelanders, Miss Wake finds to her surprise that Bjorn and Borga both speak English quite fluently "with but very slight dialect" (137). However, as readers we are not allowed to forget that these people speak their native language among each other. In their mouths, English takes on a very different, more formal quality, and different cadences and turns of phrase: "Please to help yourselves" (79), Bjorn tells his guests, while Borga says to her little son, "So shall we be good to others!" (83). Finna, the kindly neighbour, provides the most colourful examples:

> "[…] might be big enough for the poor thing – him with a mother like that, gone half crazy, God pity her! And it would be a good rest to sit and mend a little for the wee man, and me a strong woman with a good husband, God bless him!" (71)

> "It's a visit you'll have to make us, Borga dear [...]. Now that the children are so big, and it's my little Thor you mustn't leave behind either." (144)

In the chapter on Katrine Hafstein, who has had no opportunity to learn the language of her adopted country, there is a poignant scene where a shop assistant indulges in "misconstruing what foreigners try to say," which has become "a popular sport": although Katrine has the money to pay for the toy she would like to buy for her child, he pretends not to understand that she would like to see it before buying it, and takes pleasure in her confusion (131).

Salverson's representation of Icelandic speech in the novel, on the other hand, turns "what foreigners try to say" into literature: in *The Viking Heart*, it is the foreigners who get a voice, and are allowed their own way of speaking.

The children, meanwhile, all speak in a recognizably Canadian idiom, indicating their roots in the new country. Although they respect their cultural heritage and the old ways of their parents, Canada is their home, and it is through them that Salverson celebrates its promise and ideals. Thor, in particular, is a New World child, enraptured by the land that is his:

> "No one place can ever be as dear. This is a great land [...] These prairies are enthralling [...] Sun-bathed and free and rolling unhindered to the sky [...] They are so wide, so vast – there is room for us all and all our opinions. They are like a broad mind unprejudiced and open to all improvement." (294)

When Borga replies that she would not like him to forget his Norse blood, Thor responds by saying he can best prove his Norse blood "by honouring this country which is mine" (294). The land is vast and full of promise, and belongs to all who work and honour it.

The effect of the publication of *The Viking Heart* and its widespread popularity was that new cultural material was introduced to Canadian readers. Canadian immigrant history was presented here from a completely new perspective and in completely new ways, involving the incorporation of Icelandic language and culture. The treatment of immigrants, native peoples, and the poor is subject to sharp criticism in the novel, as is the position of women. It was a source of great frustration to Salverson that she was curtailed in this respect by her publishers, who feared the reaction of a small, conservative readership used to genteel literature.[3] Despite these curtailments, *The Viking Heart* sounded a new note in Canadian literature: although nowadays it reads like a romance, at the time it was hailed as "one of the first and strongest of the novels of the 'new realism' in Canadian fiction" (Bothwell 13).

The Viking Heart pioneered the multicultural immigrant novel, what we might now call ethnic or minority literature. Two years later, in 1925, Martha Ostenso and Frederick Philip Grove followed suit with *Wild Geese* and *Settlers of the Marsh*, and even a popular Anglo-Canadian author like Nellie McClung found herself inspired to write about the foreign immigrant experience that same year in *Painted Fires*. Ostenso and Grove also continued Salverson's initial experiments with realism and form, while literature of social reform finally came into its own during the 1930s. Although since eclipsed in reputation by these later works, *The Viking Heart*'s most important long-lasting achievement remains that it paved the way for other writers to translate the "foreign" immigrant experience into Canadian literature, thereby establishing a new literary genre: Canadian multicultural literature was born.

Notes

1 See, e.g., Ralph Connor's preface and first chapter in *The Foreigner: A Tale of Saskatchewan*.

2 Originally published in 1923, *The Viking Heart* was reprinted in 1975 by McClelland and Stewart in volume 116 of the New Canadian Library. All references are to this edition.

3 Salverson complained to Morley Callaghan that an entire chapter from *The*

Viking Heart was cut because it contained references that might offend people who were still alive, and she also mentions the deletion of references "which might have offended Mrs Prue" ("Letter to Morley Callaghan").

Works Cited

Altair. "Icelandic Canada in Fiction." *Lethbridge Daily*, 3 Apr. 1926. 6.

Bjarnason, Jóhann Magnús. *Eiríkur Hansson: Skáldsaga frá Nýja Skotlandi* [Eiríkur Hansson: A Novel from Nova Scotia] 1899–1903. *Ritsafn* IV. Akureyri: Bókaútgáfan Edda, 1973.

Bothwell, J.R. "*The Viking Heart*: A Classic." *Regina Leader Post*, 28 May 1947, 13.

Connor, Ralph. *The Foreigner: A Tale of Saskatchewan*. Toronto: Westminster, 1909.

Craig, Terrence L. "The Confessional Revisited: Laura Salverson's Canadian Work." *Studies in Canadian Literature* 10: 1/2 (1985): 81–93.

Finnsdóttir, Guðrún. *Hillingalönd* [Land of Mirages]. Reykjavík: Félagsprentsmiðjan, 1938.

– *Dagshríðar Spor* [Tracks of Day's Struggle]. Akureyri: Árni Bjarnarson, 1946.

Gudsteins, Gudrun Björk. "Rediscovering Icelandic Canadian Pacifism." *Rediscovering Canadian Difference*. Ed. Gudrun Björk Gudsteins. Reykjavík: Nordic Association for Canadian Studies, 2001, 50–60.

Guðsteinsdóttir, Guðrún Björk. "'Kalda stríðið' í þýðingum á íslensk-kanadískum bókmenntum 1923–1994." *Jón á Bægisá* 3 (1997): 5–19.

Kroetsch, Robert. "The Grammar of Silence." *The Lovely Treachery of Words*. Oxford: Oxford University Press, 1989, 84–94.

Pacey, Desmond. "Fiction 1920–1940." *Literary History of Canada*. Ed. Carl F. Klinck. Toronto: University of Toronto Press, 1970.

Salverson, Laura Goodman. *The Viking Heart*. Toronto: McClelland and Stewart, 1975 [1923].

– *Confessions of an Immigrant's Daughter*. Toronto: University of Toronto Press, 1982 [1939].

– Letter to Morley Callaghan. [n.d.] Morley Callaghan Papers. Ottawa: Library and Archives of Canada. MG 30 D 365, accession 95/0023.

Thompson, Eric. "Prairie Mosaic: The Immigrant Novel in the Canadian West." *Studies in Canadian Literature* 5: 2 (1980): 239.

12

September 1970: Publication of a "Monologue" on Translation

Patricia Godbout

On 22 September 1970, a few days before the beginning of the October Crisis, Anne Hébert and F.R. Scott's *Dialogue sur la traduction*, published by Hurtubise HMH, was launched in Montreal. Earlier that month, on 4 September, Hébert who was then living in Paris, had sent the publisher Claude Hurtubise a telegram apologizing for her absence: "REGRETTE NE POUVOIR ASSISTER LANCEMENT TRADUCTION STOP AUTORISE LANCEMENT AVEC SCOTT 17 SEPTEMBRE STOP SERAI MONTREAL DÉBUT NOVEMBRE AMITIÉS ANNE."[1] Thus, Scott was left to pursue on his own what had already become a monologue on translation over his numerous English versions of Hébert's poem "Le Tombeau des rois"; his "conversation" with the author on these translations had, in fact, taken place and ended many years before.

F.R. Scott published his first translations of two Hébert poems, "La fille maigre" and "En guise de fête," in 1952, in *Northern Review*. His first letters to the poet also date from the same period, something that is worthwhile mentioning here in view of the fact that the *Dialogue* takes the form of an exchange of letters between Hébert and her translator. Scott probably met the author in person for the first time in 1954 in Ottawa, where she was working for the National Film Board (see Godbout 79; and also Watteyne et al. 24–7).

The *Dialogue* first appeared in the Montreal literary periodical, *Écrits du Canada français*, ten years before Claude Hurtubise decided to publish it in book form. When the *Écrits* version of the "dialogue" came out in 1960, its editorial board comprised not only significant writers and critics like Robert Élie, Gilles Marcotte, and Marcel Dubé, but public intellectuals such as the future prime minister of Canada, Pierre Elliott Trudeau, who knew both F.R. Scott and Anne Hébert very well. On the cover of the journal, the exchange between writer and translator is, indeed, titled "Dialogue sur la traduction," although the piece itself inside the issue bears the title "La traduction. Dialogue entre le traducteur et l'auteur." In any case, it is evident here that the idea is to present this correspondence as a model and source of inspiration (Hébert and Scott, "La traduction").

Jeanne Lapointe (1915–2006) is the real "matchmaker" in this instance, and the main force behind the first publication of the "Dialogue" in *Écrits* in 1960. In her "Note explicative," she explains what led to this innovative concept. "On the eve of her departure for Paris last fall [1959]," Anne Hébert sat down with her – in all likelihood in Quebec City – to look at an English version of her poem produced by Scott. Jeanne Lapointe soon realized that this conversation concerning the translation of Hébert's poetry would be well worth publishing. She then orchestrated an exchange of letters between writer and translator. Using the notes taken during her working session with Lapointe, Anne Hébert was to write to Scott from Paris, conveying her various remarks on his rendering of "Le tombeau des rois," to which she would add a missive on the art of translation. As Lapointe – who was a professor at Laval University and a literary critic contributing to magazines like *Cité libre* – wrote, this was clearly "a professor's" and a "critic's idea." In her "Note," she delivers astute comments on what she dubs a "little literary experiment." Her contribution is, indeed, a pioneering effort in a research field that, years later, was called "translation studies" by Antoine Berman and others. On the heels of the 1958 publication of Vinay and Darbelnet's *Stylistique comparée du français et de l'anglais*, Lapointe refers, for example, to this field of study to make pertinent observations on the "impossibility of translating" (Hébert 2013, 597) certain terms due to the lack of a cultural equivalent in the other language. When broaching the question of the sound patterns of Hébert's verses, she offers daring reflections on the phonetic characteristics of Quebec French in relation to Anne Hébert's "accent canadien cultivé" at the time of the original publication of "Le Tombeau des rois" in 1953.

Using an image that was bound to please her friend Anne Hébert, whose love of theatre was well known to her, Jeanne Lapointe presents the exchange between poet and translator as a short two-act play featuring translation. Needless to say, that interlinguistic activity doesn't often get such centre-stage attention, the place devoted to it usually being much more discreet, to the point of becoming nearly, even entirely invisible. In this case, however, the Translator isn't left completely unseen in the towering shadow of the Author. On the contrary, the translation process is at the very heart of the publication of the "Dialogue." Furthermore, in *Écrits*, the translator is favourably and prominently presented as "a law professor at McGill, a political thinker, a writer and an excellent English-language poet," as well as the "best translator of French-Canadian poets."

While Act 1 of this "play" had seen Lapointe review Scott's translation with the author in 1959, Act 2 took place on 5 January 1960, that is – as Lapointe purposefully points out – "en la veille des Rois" (599), at Frank Scott's home, at 451 Clarke Avenue, in Westmount. On that occasion, Jeanne Lapointe and Frank Scott pored over the commissioned letter dutifully sent from Paris by Hébert, while at the same time pouring themselves glasses of a brand of whisky bearing the very relevant name of "Teacher's." In her letter, Anne Hébert scrutinizes every verse of the first English translation of "The Tomb of the Kings" sent to her by Scott. Her reading is very attentive and her remarks are received with extreme reverence by her translator. This "dialogue," in the course of which, up until now, the two main protagonists never actually spoke with one another, takes up eighteen pages in *Écrits*. As Hébert explains in the "Dialogue," it is only through Jeanne Lapointe's staging that this "play" was ever made possible (600).

This staged correspondence was reprinted in Toronto during the summer of 1962 in the influential *Tamarack Review*. One can assume that it was on Scott's suggestion that its editor, Robert Weaver, agreed to this second publication of what is called "an unusual dialogue" (Hébert and Scott 1962, 65). The exemplary nature of this exchange between Hébert and Scott is underlined in the title it bears in this new English venue: "The Art of Translation." Scott needs no introduction to the readers of the *Tamarack Review* since he is, "of course well known as a writer and poet" (65). In recent years, the magazine goes on to explain, "he has also made many sensitive translations from the work of the modern poets in French Canada." As for "Miss Hébert," she "is one of the most admired of these poets, and she has also written fiction and drama" (65).

In *The Tamarack Review*, the "second" version of "The Tombs of the Kings," which was published in *Écrits*, was replaced with what Scott refers to in a "Note" as a *nouvelle version*," which he considers to be "final." From that "Note," we learn that after the publication of the "Dialogue" in *Écrits*, Scott "had the rare pleasure of going over with [Hébert] personally the wording of this revision." This meeting took place in November of 1960. Scott admits that they "had not previously enjoyed a dialogue *tête-à-tête*" (88). Hébert and Scott then agreed to ten more changes in his translation. But in the absence of Lapointe, who wasn't there to take notes of the exchange and underline its pedagogical value, "the reasons for the changes," says Scott, "have disappeared with our conversation" (88).

The *Dialogue* was to have a prolonged effect on translators and Translation Studies scholars. In *Meta*, in 1975, Jean Delisle wrote that through such a dialogue the reader attained the heart of poetic creation and was made "to grasp the high level of linguistic skills required of the translator of poetry" (229). The following year, in the same journal, Pierre Marchand underlined the perilous, even impossible task of the translator of poetry: "the different phonic traits of each language can only produce poems that are radically and indomitably different" (160).

While some critics underline the perils and pitfalls of poetic translation, Scott doesn't seem to have been unduly daunted by the task. In fact, he was more concerned with the task of bringing closer together the two main cultural traditions of Canada, as he testifies in the *Dialogue* (Hébert 2013, 62). He dwelled on the same idea when he wrote in his introduction to *Poems of French Canada*: "Translation is not only an art in itself, it is also an essential ingredient in Canada's political entity" (vi). From that perspective, the *Dialogue* became the model for a mutually beneficial intercultural relation between English and French Canada, or a bridge between the two cultures, an image that was to be frequently used during the 1960s and 1970s (as Kathy Mezei aptly showed in her text "A Bridge of Sorts: The Translation of Quebec Literature into English"). Later on, E.D. Blodgett used the *Dialogue* as a starting point for his analysis of literary translation in Canada in an important article titled "Towards a Model of Literary Translation in Canada." More recently, in *Translating Montreal*, Sherry Simon re-examines Scott's efforts to bring English- and French-speaking Montreal writers together in the 1950s and 1960s. Although she acknowledges the limits of his intervention on the ground, Simon writes that Scott nevertheless exerted a crucial influence on the next generation of English-Canadian translators (53). In her doctoral thesis centred on the English translations of Anne Hébert's poetry, Lee Skallerup sums up the thoughts of many translators and scholars when she writes: "Anne Hébert, the poet, in English would not be the same if not for F.R. Scott" (56).

One cannot underestimate, conversely, the influence that Hébert had on Scott. As his biographer Sandra Djwa has shown, F.R. Scott was wrong when he wrote in the *Tamarack Review* in 1962 that it was "not likely that any more revisions" would be made to "The Tomb of the Kings"; in fact, that poem was to exert power on his imagination for years to come:

> Scott persisted in his attempts to find precise equivalents for the French text; in 1978 for the second edition of the book he had further "corrections" to make. Later, just before his final illness in 1984, he was still making changes. This desire for accuracy reflected, in part, his legal training, but Scott may have felt also that in penetrating to the precise meaning of the poem he was penetrating to the heart of the society it symbolized. (376)

Indeed, the publication in book form of *Dialogue sur la traduction* in 1970 by Hurtubise HMH gave Scott an opportunity to keep going down on his own to "The Tomb of the Kings." In a short introductory note to his third version of the poem, he writes: "I have taken this opportunity of having a fresh look at the dialogue between Anne Hébert and myself, and I am now persuaded that there are further changes I should make. This is done entirely on my own initiative and without further correspondence between us." Immersed in a *tête-à-tête* with the poem rather than the poet, Scott now firmly believes that a translation "can thus never be said to be finally completed" (Hébert 2013, 632).

Claude Hurtubise's decision to print the *Dialogue* in book form did not have anything to do with the pursuit of the dialogue between Hébert and Scott up until 1970. It had more to do with Hébert's ascending literary career in the 1960s, notwithstanding the fact that Scott himself was at that point a renowned man of letters and constitutionalist. The 1970 edition comes with an imposing strong peritext: one notes, in particular, Northrop Frye's foreword (in English as well as in Jean Simard's French translation). Frye was a highly respected literary critic who had published important books such as *Anatomy of Criticism*. It is interesting to note that in this short piece Frye talks more about poetry than about translation. Using a distinction, made by Gerard Manley Hopkins, between a poet's "overthought," or explicit meaning, and his "underthought," or the meaning given by the progression of images and metaphors, Frye states that the latter is the "real poetic meaning" and that Scott went directly to this "meaning" when he translated Hébert's poem (Hébert 2013, 590).

In a letter of 12 January 1970, Claude Hurtubise wrote to Anne Hébert that Frye read the *Dialogue* when he was in his office on the occasion of the *lancement*, the year before, of the French version of *The Educated Imagination* (*Pouvoirs de l'imagination*), and found it to be "extremely interesting." Two weeks later, on 26 January 1970, Hurtubise officially asked Frye in a letter if he would accept to write a foreword: "This would make a very interesting book both in English and French Canada, and also in France." Hurtubise thus had in mind a very wide and diversified readership for this book. Ironically, though, what was supposed to be presented as a perfect example of a genuine and fulfilling literary and artistic *rapprochement* between the "two solitudes" came out shortly before the political turmoil of the October Crisis and at a time when the "dialogue" between author and translator was becoming more and more a monologue on translation carried on by Scott on his own.

In fact, a close reading of the second and third versions of "The Tomb of the Kings" shows that after having taken into account Anne Hébert's comments to produce his second version, Scott often reverts to his original phrasing in the third version, as well as in subsequent publications – such as *Poetry of French Canada in Translation* (1977) and his *Collected Poems* (1981). To give but one example, at one point in the course of the *Dialogue*, Anne Hébert had underlined the significance of the inversion she had reverted to in a line such as "Et viennent les pas nus," indicating that this stylistic device marked a presence that was only gradually being felt. In his second version, Scott had obediently "introduced the same inversion as in French," as he explains himself in the *Dialogue*, "to give the effect of an action that starts imprecise and becomes steadily clearer" (Hébert 2013, 618). However, in the third version of the poem, the translator cancels the inversion to go back to his original version, perhaps because he didn't feel that this rhetorical device produced the same effect in English. More generally, he probably decided that he could settle the matter for himself now that the exchange with the author was behind him.

When studied closely, both Hébert's and Scott's comments in the *Dialogue* underscore each in their own way the separateness and utter difference between the original and the translation. Hébert remarks in many instances on the tendency of Scott's English-language versions to be more precise and concrete than her French original wishes to be. Although Scott professes to be a literalist, the very fact that he included poetic translations in his *Collected Poems* (1981) signals that he believed they were part and parcel of his own oeuvre. As for Hébert's original poem at the centre of the *Dialogue*, it is, as Scott himself notes, "left standing alone" (Hébert 2013, 613).

Note

1 Anne Hébert mistakenly gives the 17th as the date of the book launch. I am thankful to publisher Hervé Foulon, from Hurtubise HMH, for having granted me permission to use material from their *Dialogue* file. *Dialogue sur la traduction* was reprinted in 2000 (Montréal: Bibliothèque québécoise). A critical edition of Anne Hébert's poetry, including the *Dialogue*, was recently published by les Presses de l'Université de Montréal (2013), under the supervision of Nathalie Watteyne. I worked on the critical edition of the *Dialogue* with the collaboration of Shirley Fortier.

Works Cited

Blodgett, E.D. "Toward a Model of Literary Translation in Canada." *TTR: Traduction, traductologie, redaction* 4: 2 (1991): 189–206.

Delisle, Jean. "*Dialogue sur la traduction* (A. Hébert et F. Scott)." *Meta* 20: 3 (1975): 228–9.

Djwa, Sandra. *A Life of F.R. Scott: The Politics of the Imagination.* Toronto: McClelland and Stewart, 1987.

Frye, Northrop. *Pouvoirs de l'imagination.* Trans. Jean Simard. Montréal: Hurtubise HMH, 1969.

Godbout, Patricia. *Traduction littéraire et sociabilité interculturelle au Canada: 1950–1960.* Ottawa: Les Presses de l'Université d'Ottawa, 2004.

Hébert, Anne. *Oeuvres complètes d'Anne Hébert.* vol. 1: *Poésie suivi du Dialogue sur la traduction.* Eds. Nathalie Watteyne and Patricia Godbout. Collection Bibliothèque du Nouveau Monde. Montréal: Les Presses de l'Université de Montréal, 2013.

Hébert, Anne, and F.R. Scott. "La traduction: Dialogue entre le traducteur et l'auteur." *Écrits du Canada français* 7 (1960): 193–233.

– "The Art of Translation." *Tamarack Review* 24 (1962): 65–100.

– *Dialogue sur la traduction, à propos du Tombeau des rois*. Pres. Jeanne Lapointe. Preface Northrop Frye. Montreal: Hurtubise HMH [1970]. Montréal: Bibliothèque québécoise, 2000.

Marchand, Pierre. "À propos de la traduction du *Tombeau des rois*." *Meta* 21: 2 (1976): 155–60.

Mezei, Kathy. "A Bridge of Sorts: The Translation of Quebec Literature into English." *Yearbook of English Studies* 15 (1985): 201–26.

Scott, F.R. *Poems of French Canada*. Vancouver: Blackfish Press, 1977.

Simon, Sherry. *Translating Montreal*. Montreal and Kingston: McGill-Queen's University Press, 2006.

Skallerup, Lee. "Found in Translation: The Journey of Anne Hébert's Poetry in(to) English." Ph.D. dissertation, Edmonton, University of Alberta, 2007.

Vinay, Jean-Paul, and Jean Darbelnet. *Stylistique comparée du français et de l'anglais*. Paris: Didier, 1958.

Watteyne, Nathalie. et al., eds. *Anne Hébert: Chronologie et bibliographie des livres, parties de livres, articles et autres travaux consacrés à son œuvre*. Montréal: Les Presses de l'Université de Montréal, 2008.

13

11 September 1973: Latin America Comes to Canada[1]

Hugh Hazelton

On the morning of 11 September 1973, Chilean fighter planes began to strafe and bomb the Moneda, the presidential palace of their country, acting on orders from a military junta headed by General Augusto Pinochet. By that afternoon, after a valiant defence, the president of the country, Salvador Allende, and a number of his staff were dead, and Chile, which had an almost uninterrupted history of democratic governance, was under military dictatorship. This coup d'état was part of a series of similar military takeovers inspired by the United States that began in Brazil in 1964, continued on to Uruguay in 1973, and befell Argentina in 1976. By the end of the 1970s, most of southern South America was under military rule, a trend that was to continue in Central America during the 1980s. These were not palace coups, simply in favour of an opposing party or group of officers: they were vast, traumatic, meticulously planned projects aimed at eliminating the entire liberal and left-leaning population of the country, abolishing social programs, and transforming the economy along monetarist principles. The Chilean coup, in particular, marked a change so profound that over a million people, most of them in their twenties and thirties, left the country, initiating the first large-scale migration of Latin Americans to Canada.[2]

The effect on Canada was of major importance for two principal reasons. First, as the country began to take in thousands of refugees and exiles from the Southern Cone, Canadians started to realize that they were not simply denizens of an isolated country of French and British descent in the northernmost latitudes of the Western Hemisphere. Instead, they were interconnected with the peoples of over twenty-five other nations, all of which were part of the Americas, that shared a single land mass stretching from Ellesmere Island to Tierra del Fuego. In numerous ways, Canadian patterns of historical, cultural, and literary development had more in common with those of their fellow nations of the Americas than they did with the old countries of Europe. Canada had an increasing commercial, political, and cultural role to play in the Americas; as new generations of Latin Americans settled in Canada, all the while maintaining their connections with their homelands, the struggles of Latin America were now becoming part of Canada's own national sphere of experience. Second, as an outgrowth of this new wave of immigration, Canada came into increasing contact with the Spanish and Portuguese languages, along with the cultures and literatures in which they flourished. Translation between the two official languages of the country, French and English, had just been established as an essential element of national unity and identity; there was a heightened mutual interest between English-language Canadian and Quebec literatures, and Canada was already considered a pioneering country in the field of translation and Translation Studies.[3] Third languages, however, had been largely left out of these new developments. Now, with the arrival of the Chileans, followed by wave after wave of immigration from other Latin American countries, new cultural and literary ties would be made between English and French and Spanish and Portuguese. Moreover, the emergence of Latin American writing on the world stage during the boom period of Latin American literature – with writers such as Jorge Luis Borges, Mario Vargas Llosa, Gabriel García Márquez, and Carlos Fuentes becoming popular in English translation – coincided with the arrival of many talented and well-known writers among the refugees and exiles who settled in Canada, thus ensuring that Latin American writing would occupy a powerful new space in Canadian culture. A number of early works published by these authors, whether Chileans during the 1970s or Salvadorans during the 1980s, were brought out in bilingual Spanish-English or Spanish-French editions by small Spanish-language presses within the community. The most important of these publishers, Ediciones Cordillera, founded in Ottawa by Leandro Urbina, Jorge Etcheverry, and other Chilean compatriots, brought out the first bilingual anthology of Chilean-Canadian writing, *Chilean Literature in Canada / Literatura chilena en Canadá*, edited by the distinguished poet and critic Naín Nómez, in 1982. This groundbreaking work, largely (and outstandingly) translated by Christina Schantz, set a high literary standard and was a milestone in Spanish translation in Canada. Innumerable other translations of Hispanic-Canadian writing would follow its lead over the next thirty years; just as the Chilean coup d'état brought Latin America to Canada's attention, the publication of *Chilean Literature in Canada / Literatura chilena en Canadá* firmly established Spanish translation in the North. When Canadian publishers finally moved into the translation and publication of works from outside Canada in the early twenty-first century, the breakthrough would largely be in Spanish, due to the momentum that had been gathering from the translation of Latino-Canadian literature.

Canada and Latin America have a long and complex literary relationship that includes parallel historic, artistic, and cultural currents, as well as a remarkable number of authors who have written about each other's regions. The Iberian and Latin American presence in Canada, of course, dates back to the very first visits to the country by Basque fishermen and whalers in the sixteenth century (and possibly earlier), followed by explorers sailing under the Portuguese flag on the east coast, as place names such as Labrador, Baccalieu, Fogo, and Bonavista attest. Later, towards the end of the eighteenth century, the cartographical and scientific expeditions of the Peruvian Juan Francisco Bodega y Quadra, the Spaniard Alejandro Malaspina, and others explored the west coast as far north as Kodiak Island in Alaska, naming many islands, straits, mountains, and glaciers.[4] There was also an influx of Spaniards (including many academics) into Canada after the Spanish Civil War and through the 1940s and 1950s, as well as of Ecuadorians in the 1960s. The Spanish novelist and poet Jesús López Pacheco – author of the acclaimed novel *Central eléctrica*, which was shortlisted for the Nadal Award in Spain in 1956 – continued his intense literary activity while teaching at the University of Western Ontario. Manuel Betanzos Santos, a Galician poet, critic, and journalist who settled in Montreal in 1959, founded the trilingual literary review *Boreal*, which would appear intermittently for the next quarter-century and which circulated in both Canada and the Americas. Betanzos also read at cafés in the city, appearing together with English- and French-speaking writers, and published a selection of English-Canadian and Quebec poetry in the Argentine literary review *Cormorán y Delfín* in 1969 and a short anthology of Canadian writers in Mexico a few years later, as well as a key article giving an overview of contemporary Quebec and English-Canadian poetry in the *Revista de la Universidad Complutense* in Madrid in 1974.

Major interest in the Spanish-speaking world in Canada, and vice versa, began with the large numbers of Latin Americans who started to arrive in the country in the 1970s, eventually numbering over 300,000, making Spanish the fifth-most spoken immigrant language (after Chinese, Italian, German, and Punjabi), followed closely by Portuguese. Most of the immigrants came for economic reasons, often due to the restructuring of the economies of their home countries, but many were also exiles and refugees from military regimes that hunted down, tortured, disappeared, and eliminated sectors of the population that opposed them. In some cases, the choice of coming to Canada or another country was simply a matter of which embassy was accepting refugees on a given day. A large proportion of Latin American immigrants were artists, musicians, and writers from the most progressive sectors of their society: some had already begun to publish or produce their work before they left their home country, while others, often younger, began to write or work in other artistic endeavours once they arrived in Canada. These authors eventually created a parallel Spanish-speaking literature that included all genres of writing, from novels, poetry, essays, and journalism to children's books, history, and political science. Most wrote in Spanish, although a few preferred to work directly in English or French as well. As they became more acclimatized to the Canadian milieu, many of them wanted to reach out to a larger English-speaking Canadian and Quebec audience and realized that the only way to do so was through translation.

Translations from Spanish into English and French increased exponentially: many people who began translating works by Latino-Canadian writers – often the friends, lovers, wives, or husbands of their authors – went on to become professional translators and would ultimately constitute the first wave of Spanish-language literary translators in Canada. The vanguard publication of *Chilean Literature in Canada / Literatura chilena en Canadá* was followed in 1984 by a trilingual (Spanish/English/French) anthology of fiction, poetry, and theatre, *Literatura hispano-canadiense / Hispano-Canadian Literature / Littérature hispano-canadienne*, the most all-inclusive collection till that time. This anthology included works by Peninsular authors as well as Latin Americans and was edited by the Spaniard Diego Marín, who taught at the University of Toronto; given its unique scope, it was published by the Alianza Cultural Hispano-Canadiense rather than a commercial or trade press. In the meantime, in Montreal, a variety of bilingual editions of individual books of poetry began to appear regularly and, by the 1980s, included works by the Colombian poet Yvonne América Truque, translated by Jean Gauthier; the illustrated *livre d'artiste, Juglario*

/ *Jongleries*, by Chilean poet and filmmaker Jorge Cancino, translated by Pierre Demers and Gloria Clunes; and the illustrated Zen children's book *Cuentos de la cabeza y la cola / Contes de la tête et de la queue*, by the Chilean playwright Rodrigo González, translated by Micheline Bail.

In tandem with the trend towards bilingual books produced within the community, several literary reviews also began to publish in multilingual form. In Toronto, Margarita Feliciano, a professor of Spanish at York University and a key literary figure, brought out several issues of *Indigo*, a trilingual review dedicated to the Spanish-Canadian presence in the arts that included poetry, prose, literary and cultural articles, interviews, translations, and photographs. In the early 1990s, following in the footsteps of Manuel Betanzos Santos, another Montreal publication, *Ruptures:La revue des Trois Amériques*, under the direction of Edgard Gousse, a Haitian Canadian who had studied in Buenos Aires, reached a type of apotheosis of multilingualism, publishing work from the Americas and other parts of the world in the four principal languages of the Western Hemisphere: French, English, Spanish, and Portuguese. This attractively produced review, which included drawings with its texts and full-colour paintings on its covers, published fourteen issues between 1993 and 1998, enriching and cross-fertilizing cultures through a flood of translated work, much of it done by other writers. It also included five thematic issues, dedicated to the literatures of Mexico, Quebec, the Caribbean, the Southern Cone (some 600 pages), and Venezuela, which constituted, in effect, quatrilingual anthologies of contemporary work from each country or region. *Ruptures* served as an exchange between translators and authors from different languages and countries and was enthusiastically received abroad. The fact that it published writers from outside Canada, however, made it largely ineligible for grants, and virtually all translation and revision was done on a volunteer basis.

As Spanish-speaking authors began to receive heightened recognition in the English- and French-speaking literary worlds, small trade presses started to take increasing interest in their work. In the 1980s a number of both French- and English-language publishers in the Montreal area brought out bilingual and unilingual French and English editions of work by Latino-Canadian authors. Humanitas published *Dieuseries et odieuseries / Dioserías y odioserías*, by the Salvadoran poet Salvador Torres, translated by Laure Palin, and awarded it their annual prize in 1989. André Goulet, of

Les Éditions d'Orphée, which had published early works by many of Quebec's most noted authors – including Nicole Brossard, Jacques Ferron, and Claude Gauvreau in the 1950s and 1960s, as well as those of Anglo-Canadian writers such as Irving Layton – brought out ten books of poetry by the Chilean author Alfredo Lavergne, many of them translated by Sylvie Perron, four of them in bilingual editions in back-to-back format. On the English side, Cormorant Editions, founded by Gary Geddes, took the lead, publishing translations of works by Chilean authors Leandro Urbina and Naín Nómez and the distinguished Salvadoran writer Alfonso Quijada Urías. In 1990 Cormorant also brought out *Compañeros: An Anthology of Writings about Latin America*, edited by Gary Geddes and myself, which included work by English-language Canadian authors and translations of works by Québécois, Haitian-Canadian, and Latino-Canadian writers. Éditions Fides and Éditions Boréal both published work by the accomplished Mexican novelist and short-story writer Gilberto Flores Patiño, who writes in Spanish but publishes chiefly in French, thanks to the translations by Ginette Hardy. Interestingly, Flores Patiño himself has translated four plays by Quebec playwrights into Spanish for presentation in theatres in Mexico City. Meanwhile, several Toronto publishers, including Mosaic, Exile, and Oasis Editions, published a number of works by the prolific and celebrated Chilean surrealist poet Ludwig Zeller, who immigrated to Canada in the late 1960s, translated for the most part by Beatriz Hausner and A.F. Moritz. One of the most linguistically unique bodies of work of the period was that of the noted Chilean playwright, poet, and singer/songwriter Alberto Kurapel, whose experimental multimedia theatre was well received in Montreal and in English-Canadian literary circles (see Klaus; Gómez). The seven plays that Kurapel wrote and produced in Quebec (he returned to Chile in the late 1990s), in which dialogue and stage instructions are given consecutively in both Spanish and French, are always essentially bilingual, but only two of them are actually translations. The other five plays are, in reality, hybrid texts in which some passages are fully translated and others only partially so or not even at all. In this way, Kurapel fuses the two languages into a single meta-language, writing his plays in Spanish and French simultaneously for what is essentially a bilingual audience.[5]

Since the turn of the millennium, interest in Latin American writers living in Canada has accelerated, as has their rate of translation into both English and French, generally by professional translators working directly for the publisher, and works by well-known authors such as the Argentine-Canadian writers Pablo Urbanyi and Nela Rio have now appeared in both English and French. A number of universities, particularly, York, Ottawa, the University of British Columbia, McGill, the Université de Montréal, and Concordia now have classes and programs dedicated to translation between Spanish and English or French, both on a professional and a literary level, in which new and enthusiastic generations of translators are being trained. The beachhead for Spanish and Portuguese translation that was established by the translators of the first Chilean and other Hispanic-Canadian writers in the 1970s and 1980s is now being pushed forward by this new wave of younger translators whose work increasingly includes the translation of authors from outside the country.

The Canada Council has, of course, been the key financial backer of the translation and publication of Hispanic-Canadian literature. Without its programs of subsidies to translators and publishers of works by Canadian citizens and landed immigrants who write in languages other than English and French, the works of Spanish-speaking authors in Canada would have gone largely unknown. Even so, though, the numbers are relatively low: only four translations from third languages received grants from the Canada Council in 2010. Fortunately, provincial arts programs in Quebec, Ontario, Manitoba, and other provinces also support third-language translation. The essential axis of translation in Canada, however, remains between English and French: virtually all literary translation awards in the country are only for works translated between the two official languages, the sole exception being the John Glassco Award of the Literary Translators' Association of Canada, which is open to works from any language into English or French. Moreover, translation from Spanish is certainly no guarantee of public success: the English- and French-language literary worlds – which Jorge Etcheverry has ironically referred to as "the hegemonic literatures"[6] – are far more receptive to the work of Hispanic- and Luso-Canadian writers who work directly in one of the official languages, without having to pass through the filter of translation, than they are to translated authors, perhaps because publishers and critics feel that translated writers will have more difficulty in promoting and discussing their works. One has only to compare the acceptance in Canada of Argentine-Canadian authors Alberto Manguel and Guillermo Verdecchia, who write directly in English, and Brazilian-born Sergio Kokis and the Catalan-Canadian novelist Jacques Folch-Ribas, who work directly in French, with the difficulty that translated authors such as Pablo Urbanyi and Alfonso Quijada Urías have had in gaining access to the Canadian literary mainstream. The French translation of Leandro Urbina's award-winning novel *Cobro revertido, Longues distances*, by Danièle Rudel-Tessier, received only one mention in Montreal's French-language press. Moreover, an issue of *Lettres québécoises* dedicated to immigrant writing in French (no. 66, summer 1992), was limited only to work written directly in French, thereby excluding almost all of the Latino-Québécois community (see Jonaissant).[7]

Nevertheless, translation has continued to advance, boosted by poetry readings and the increased publication of Hispanic works in literary reviews such as *Arc, Canadian Fiction Magazine, Lèvres urbaines, Canadian Literature / Littérature canadienne*, and *Ellipse*. Latino-Canadian poetry readings have evolved into bilingual or multilingual events attended by a wider public at which either the poets or their translators read their work in both Spanish and English or French. The indomitable Janou St-Denis, for example, always reserved several evenings per year for Latino poets at her Place aux poètes in Montreal, and poets also continue to give bilingual readings at Harbourfront's Ritmo y Color festival and the yearly events of the Semana del Idioma Español (Spanish Language Week) in Toronto, as well as multilingual readings at El Dorado in Ottawa and Noches de Poesía and Lapalabrava in Montreal. Some authors have even begun to write in both Spanish and English or French, creating their work in one language and then translating it – or writing an equivalent version – in the other. The degree of correspondence between the original text and the self-translation or parallel version depends on the author's linguistic interests: the Argentine poet Margarita Feliciano prefers to take greater leeway with the English versions in her bilingual books, which she translates herself; Jorge Etcheverry, who sometimes also writes directly in English and then translates into Spanish, works in tandem with an anglophone adviser (usually his *compañera*); Blanca Espinoza, a Chilean poet who is also a professional translator, prefers seamless translations of the same text; and Carmen Rodríguez, who studied English before leaving Chile, brought out her last book of short stories in parallel versions almost simultaneously, in Vancouver under the title *and a body to remember with* and in Santiago as *De cuerpo entero*. Other writers, often those who left their home country at a relatively early age, prefer to work directly in English or French. The prolific Brazilian author, painter, and psychologist Sergio Kokis, who fled Brazil after the military coup d'état there in 1964, writes exclusively in French; the Brazilian edition of his first book, *Le pavillon des miroirs*, was translated from French into Portuguese.

The first major Canadian novel to have an impact in Latin America was Malcolm Lowry's *Under the Volcano* – originally published in 1947, superbly translated into Spanish by the renowned Mexican translator Raúl Ortiz y Ortiz, and published as *Bajo el volcán* in 1967. It caused a considerable stir in Mexican letters, although it was in the tradition of several other major works about Mexico written by foreigners, such as D.H. Lawrence's *The Plumed Serpent*, the short stories of Katherine Anne Porter, and the novels of B. Traven.[8] As the diffusion of Canadian literature through translation continued, it was sometimes aided by the efforts of Canadians living in Latin America. The Montreal poet Lake Sagaris, for instance, took up permanent residence in Santiago, Chile, in 1981, where she worked as a translator and as a journalist in both English and Spanish. In 1986 she translated and published a lengthy anthology of twelve contemporary Canadian poets, *Un pájaro es un poema*, which was published in Santiago by Pehuén Editores with assistance from Casa Canadá, a cultural arm of the Canadian embassy in Chile. Sagaris' own poetic work includes *Medusa's Children*, a historical and cultural comparison of the islands of Newfoundland and Chiloé, located at the northern end of the Chilean archipelago.

Interest in Canadian literature has grown tremendously in Spain and Latin America over the past several decades, in tandem with the expansion of Centres for Canadian Studies abroad. In Spanish-speaking countries, it is prose authors who have been most frequently translated on the English-Canadian side, reflecting the international appeal of writers such as Margaret Atwood, Michael Ondaatje, and Alice Munro, while poets such as Nicole Brossard, Hélène Dorion, and Claude Beausoleil have been favoured among Quebec writers (see Gunn). In Portuguese, fiction from both English-speaking Canada and Quebec has been the most popular in Brazil and has included an ample although eclectic range of translations of works by authors ranging from Anne Hébert, Gérard Étienne, and Réjean Ducharme to Alberto Manguel, Carol Shields, and Mordecai Richler ("Autores Canadenses com Publicações em Português"). A number of plays, particularly by Quebec writers, have also been translated for presentation in both Spain and Latin America, although the scripts are sometimes for production rather than publication, and include works by Michel Tremblay, Robert Lepage, and Évelyne de la Chenelière. There have also been numerous anthologies of Canadian work published in Latin America, including *Vozes do Quebec: Antologia* (1991), edited by the Brazilian Canadianist Zilá Bernd and Joseph Melançon; *Literatura francófona II: América* (1996), edited and translated by the Mexican scholar Laura López Morales, which includes a large selection of Quebec authors; and *¿Dónde es aquí? 25 cuentos canadienses*, edited by Claudia Lucotti, a selection of contemporary English-Canadian short stories published in Mexico. In a complementary fashion, the Quebec publishing house, L'instant même, brought out an anthology of Mexican short stories, *Nouvelles mexicaines d'aujourd'hui*, edited and translated by Louis Jolicoeur in 1993.

The Canada Council and Heritage Canada have also aided the diffusion of Canadian works by making grants available for their translation abroad. Canadian publishers, however, have been slower to translate the works of Spanish- and Portuguese-speaking authors from outside the country, owing both to the concentration of resources on domestic translation and the long-established dominance of British, American, and French publishing houses in the translation of international literature. Nevertheless, over the past fifteen years, two Quebec firms have established themselves as major publishers of writers from Latin America, thus not only marking the first time that Canadian-based publishing houses have moved decisively into the translation of authors from beyond their borders, but also underscoring the key role that Spanish translation has played in the gradual evolution from domestic to international translation. The first to do so was Les Écrits des Forges, which, under the leadership of Gaston Bellemare, has published more than sixty translations of poetry from Spanish over the past decade. More than fifty of these books are by Mexican authors, ranging from the high-profile (Jaime Sabines, Elsa Cross, Homero Aridjis) to the newly published, but there are also books by Colombian, Venezuelan, Uruguayan, and Argentine authors (including Juan Gelman). The majority of works have been published in bilingual format, and Nicole and Émile Martel have translated over thirty of them. In tandem, Les Écrits des Forges has also brought out some forty bilingual French-Spanish translations of works by Québécois poets, ranging from Saint-Deny-Garneau to Yolande Villemaire.

All of these translations, now totaling over a hundred works, are distributed in Mexico and other parts of Latin America, as well as in Canada and France (Bellemare, personal communication).[9] The size of the exchange, the range of authors involved, and the extensive, unprecedented involvement of a Canadian publisher in Latin American poetry have caused the initiative to have a major literary impact, especially in Mexico. The second publisher to move ahead on her own was Brigitte Bouchard, whose Éditions Les Allusifs specialized in the translation of fiction from other countries to such an extent that three-quarters of the press's titles are translations. Les Allusifs was also prescient in choosing prominent writers at an early stage in their careers, garnering translation rights for a number of works by the Chilean writer Roberto Bolaño and the Salvadoran novelist Horacio Castellanos Moya before they achieved widespread recognition in North America. Leméac Éditeur of Montreal took over Les Allusifs in 2012, and plans to continue publishing translations from abroad in its Allusifs division (see Hélène Buzelin's contribution in this volume).

Canadian Studies programs have grown steadily throughout Latin America over the past quarter-century and have had a major impact not only on cultural and literary exchanges, but also on the development of a comparativist dynamic and framework. Almost forty institutions and universities are members of Canadian Studies programs in Argentina, Brazil, Venezuela, Mexico, and Cuba. The Brazilian association of Canadian Studies, ABECAN, publishes a review, *Interfaces Brasil/Canadá*, which includes comparative articles, as does the Mexican *Revista Mexicana de Estudios Canadienses*. These publications have served as the basis for comparativist research that runs to well over forty books and theses in Brazil alone. *Confluences littéraires Brésil-Québec: Les bases d'une comparaison*, a 1992 collection of essays compiled by Michel Peterson and Zilá Bernd, laid the basis for a theoretical comparativist structure for studying Brazilian and Quebec literatures. At the same time, Canadian literary reviews such as *Dérives*, *Vice Versa*, *Ruptures*, and *Canadian Fiction Magazine* have been highly instrumental in the translation and diffusion of Latin American literature to the English-speaking Canadian and Quebec public. Canada's best-known review of literary translation, *Ellipse: Canadian Writing in Translation / Textes littéraires canadiens en traduction*, founded by Doug Jones and others at the Université de Sherbrooke in 1969, traditionally published bilingual editions dedicated to an English-speaking Canadian and a Quebec poet whose work had a certain affinity, although in 1997 it brought out a special issue (no. 58) on four Latino-Canadian writers who also published in English or French. Just after the turn of the century, Jo-Anne Elder, of Fredericton, took over its editorship and decided to expand its scope to include translations from (and into) other languages, including those of First Nations cultures. In 2004, the review brought out a trilingual edition of contemporary poetry from Argentina (no. 74), which I edited, and the following year published a trilingual collection of English-language Canadian and Quebec prose and poetry edited by Patrick Imbert and translated into Spanish in Buenos Aires. In the spring of 2011, the review launched a trilingual double issue (nos. 84/85) dedicated to present-day Brazilian literature, selected by Sonia Torres of the Universidade Federal Fluminense in Rio de Janeiro and Eloína Prati dos Santos of the Universidade Federal do Rio Grande do Sul, with all works translated from Portuguese into English or French. This is to be followed by a trilingual issue of Canadian writing set in Brazil, which will be translated from French and English into Portuguese.

Perhaps one project that epitomizes the role of both translation and the Spanish language in the interchange between Canada and the Americas is the Banff International Literary Translation Centre, a program within the Banff Centre that was established by Linda Gaboriau in 2003. This residency program is open both to literary translators from the founding countries – Canada, Mexico, and the United States – translating from any language into French, English, or Spanish, and to international translators working on literature from the Americas. The result is a cosmopolitan mix of translators from a wide variety of countries, all with an underlying connection to the Western Hemisphere. Fifteen professional translators and three student translators – one from each of the founding countries – are accepted for the three-week, all-expenses paid residency each June. Over the years, some 150 translators from twenty-six countries have participated, working among thirty-six different languages, including Indigenous languages of the Americas. Six to nine authors are also invited each year, as are three to five translator advisers, and a yearly award is presented on a rotating basis to an eminent translator from Canada, Mexico, or the United States who has made a significant contribution to literature and the art of translation.

As the interchange between writing in Spanish and Portuguese and writing in English and French continues in Canada, a certain maturation is now taking place. New generations of Spanish- and Portuguese-speaking writers will continue to arrive in the country, both as immigrants and as refugees from social and political difficulties in the score of nations in which the languages are spoken. Many will continue to search for translators among friends and lovers, but a number of them will undoubtedly directly approach the experienced literary translators who have honed their skills on the work of an earlier generation of Latino-Canadian writers and are now available in the field. As multilingualism becomes increasingly common, perhaps even the norm in the future, more young authors will also work both in Spanish or Portuguese and in English or French, writing with equal ease in both languages, and translating between them, too, as does Paulo da Costa, an Angolan-born poet and translator now living in Vancouver, one of a new generation of bilingual writers/translators. Some authors now prefer to write books in multiple languages, as Bolivian-born Alejandro Saravia has done in *Lettres de Nootka*, a hybrid book that contains poems composed directly in Spanish, English, and French; others, such as Salvador Torres, will continue to bring a hispanicized, baroque style and sensibility to the poetry they compose in French or English, enriching their texts with the echoing strangeness of the other language. Latin America has come to Canada, bringing with it new linguistic, literary, and cultural relationships that increase English-speaking Canadian and Quebec awareness of the North as being part of the Americas, at the same time as Canada is finally receiving vastly greater interest in the Spanish- and Portuguese-speaking worlds.

Notes

1 Portions of this study have previously appeared in Hazelton, "Traduzir o Latino-Canadá: Translation Strategies of Spanish- and Portuguese-Speaking Authors in Canada," and in "Transculturation and National Identity in the Novel *Rojo, amarillo y verde*, by Alejandro Saravia."

2 As of the 2006 census, some 26,505 Chileans had immigrated to Canada, the third-largest Spanish-speaking nationality in the country, after Mexicans (49,924) and Salvadorans (42,780). Portuguese (150,390) and Spaniards (10,290); Brazilians (15,120). (Statistics Canada "Place of birth, 2006"; see also "Language spoken most often at home, 2006").

3 The French translator, Jean Maillot, a close associate of the founder of transla-

tion studies in Spain, Valentín García Yebra, underscores these advances in his discussion of initiatives in translation in Quebec (*La traducción científica y técnica* 54–5).

4 See *Alejandro Malaspina: Portrait of a Visionary* (Kendrick) for an excellent recounting of the scientific voyages of discovery of one of the three great European circumnavigators of the Age of Enlightenment (along with James Cook and Louis Antoine de Bougainville). Juan Francisco Bodega y Quadra's colourful and insightful account of his voyage up the west coast, *El descubrimiento del fin del mundo* (Alianza) is also of interest.

5 See my essay, "Polylingual Identities: Writing in Multiple Languages," 225–45.

6 "The more optimistic among us believe that a Spanish-speaking literature is now beginning to arise that is increasingly autonomous in relation to the English- and French-speaking hegemonic literatures" ("Notas para situar la literatura chilena en Canadá," my translation).

7 The linguistic parameters had been tightly set: the only Latino-Québécois author included was the Uruguayan-Canadian literary critic Javier García Méndez. Jonaissant, himself a Haitian-Canadian, lauded the work of Latino-Québécois authors in his review of the first French-language anthology of their work, "Des poésies québécoises actuelles," 37–8.

8 For an interesting and thorough analysis of American, Canadian, and British fiction set in Mexico, as well as of the fascination Mexico exerted for certain English-speaking writers, from Langston Hughes to Jack Kerouac, see Gunn, *Escritores norteamericanos y británicos en México*.

9 Conversation with Gaston Bellemare at the Guadalajara Book Fair, 27 Nov. 2004. Les Écrits des Forges has a kiosk every year at the fair, which is the largest in the Spanish-speaking world, and the Quebec publishing house maintains a strong presence in the Mexican literary world.

Works Cited

"Autores Canadenses com Publicações em Português." Associação Brasileira de Estudos Canadenses. http://www.abecan.org.br/ traducoes.htm

Bellemare, Gaston. Personal communication. Guadalajara Book Fair. 27 Nov. 2004.

Canadian Fiction Magazine. "Latin American Writers in Canada." Special issue (1987): 61–2.

Gómez, Mayté. "Infinite Signs: Alberto Kurapel and the Semiotics of Exile." *Canadian Literature / Littérature canadienne* 142–43 (1994): 38–50.

Gunn, D. Wayne. *Escritores norteamericanos y británicos en México*. Trans. Ernestina de Champourcin. Mexico City: Fondo de Cultura Económica, 1977.

Hazelton, Hugh. "Polylingual Identities: Writing in Multiple Languages." *The Canadian Cultural Exchange / Échanges culturels au Canada: Translation and Transculturation / Traduction et transculturation*. Ed. Norman Cheadle and Lucien Pelletier. Waterloo: Wilfrid Laurier University Press, 2007, 225–45.

– "Traduzir o Latino-Canadá: Translation Strategies of Spanish- and Portuguese-Speaking Authors in Canada." *Interfaces Brasil/Canadá: Revista da ABECAN (Associação Brasileira de Estudos Canadenses)* 11 (2010): 29–42.

– "Transculturation and National Identity in the Novel *Rojo, amarillo y verde*, by Alejandro Saravia." *Canada and Its Americas: Transnational Migrations*. Ed. Winfried Siemerling and Sarah Philips Casteel. Montreal and Kingston: McGill-Queen's University Press, 2010, 219–30.

Jolicoeur, Louis, ed. and trans. *Nouvelles mexicaines d'aujourd'hui*. Quebec City: L'instant même, 1993.

Jonaissant, Jean. "Des poésies québécoises actuelles." *Lettres québécoises* 62 (36) (1991): 37–8.

– "De l'autre littérature québécoise, autoportraits." *Lettres québécoises* 66 supplement (1992): 2–16.

Kendrick, John. *Alejandro Malaspina: Portrait of a Visionary*. Seattle: University of Washington Press, 1999.

Klaus, Peter. "Latin American Literature in Canada and Quebec: A Genesis?" *Encounters with Quebec*. Ed. Susan L. Rosenstreic. Binghamton: Global Academic, 1998, 161–78.

Maillot, Jean. *La traducción científica y técnica*. Prologue Valentín García Yebra. Trans. Julia Sevilla Muñoz. Madrid: Gredos, 1997, 54–5.

"Notas para situar la literatura chilena en Canadá." escritores.cl. http://www.escritores.cl/base.php?fi-articulos/texto/congreso.htm

Peterson, Michel, and Zilá Bernd, eds. *Confluences littéraires Brésil-Québec: Les bases d'une comparaison*. Candiac, QC: Balzac, 1992.

Statistics Canada. "Language spoken most often at home by immigrant status and broad age groups, 2006 counts, for Canada, provinces and territories." http://www12.statcan.ca/english/census06/ data/highlights/Immigration/Table405

– "Place of birth for the immigrant population by period of immigration, 2006 counts and percentage distribution, for Canada." http://www12.statcan.ca/english/census06/data/highlights/Immigration/Table404

14

1978: Language Escapes: Italian-Canadian Authors Write in an Official Language and Not in Italiese

Joseph Pivato

The important year for Italian-Canadian literature is 1978–79, the year in which three writers separately and simultaneously made conscious decisions to write in a standard official language of Canada rather than in standard Italian or their immigrant dialect, Italiese. That year in Toronto, Pier Giorgio Di Cicco brought out *Roman Candles*, the first anthology of Italian-Canadian poetry, and it augured the beginning of this new ethnic minority literature. As editor, Di Cicco had deliberately decided that this anthology should include only work in English. In Ottawa in 1978, F.G. Paci published his first novel, *The Italians*, in English, and it soon became a bestseller. In Montreal, in 1979, Marco Micone staged his first play, *Gens du Silence*, in standard French rather than in Italiese.

How do Italian-Canadian writers deal with the immigrant culture that exists in Italiese? While the majority of works are written in English, writers in Quebec like Micone often adopt French, and a number of writers from the older generation still use standard Italian. Sometimes works are translated from one of these languages to another. So, translation for Italian Canadians is not just a single act of transferring an Italian text into English or French, but the constant practice of code switching from one language to another in daily life and in creative work. It is a kind of translation as existence (Pivato, *Echo*).[1]

The effect of the translation and writing practices of many Italian-Canadian writers has been the avoidance of stereotyped immigrant literature and the creation of models for linguistic diversity and minority ethnic writing. Their practice and decisions about language and translation involve questions about the aesthetic values of the work, the social roles of the ethnic minority writer, and voices from the community, immigrant culture, and negative stereotypes. These writers are ever conscious of such questions as they approach each work. When they include Italian words in their English poems, add Italian expressions to their French plays, or reject the use of any Italiese in their writing, they testify to the limitations of translation. While most writers chose to publish in one of the official languages, at the same time, they did not want to limit their work to unilingual perspectives, but to explore the experience of diglossia. Three of these writers, Fulvio Caccia, Lamberto Tassinari, and Antonio D'Alfonso, founded *Vice Versa*, a trilingual magazine that was active in the 1980s and 1990s. Their work brought much-needed linguistic diversity to Canadian writing and served as an example to other ethnic minority writers.

Italiese is a dialect spoken by Italian immigrants that is the result of mixing Italian and English, and in Quebec, Italian and French. Typically, you will find an Italian sentence with English expressions, phrases, and words. Often, the English words are given Italian pronunciation or accent. Examples are: carro for car, fenza for fence, morgheggio for mortgage, fornitura for furniture, pusciare for to push, drivare for to drive, pintare for to paint, segnare for to sign, figurare for to figure out, colletare for to collect, and many other loan words. There are also words from the Italian regional dialect of the speaker. Italiese is the language that the majority of Italian immigrants speak every day. It is the language you will hear in many Italian homes, offices, community centres, food stores, and restaurants in Toronto, Montreal, Vancouver, and other Canadian cities.

Linguists have been studying this phenomenon since the 1970s. The first researcher to use the term "Italiese" in a published study was Gianrenzo Clivio in 1985. Marcel Danesi describes this language as an ethnic *koiné*:

> The distinguishing features of an ethnic *koiné*, such as Canadian Italian (known also as "Italo-Canadian" or "Italiese") are: An ethnic *koiné* is essentially the language of origin which, through protracted contact with the culturally-dominant language (e.g. English), and through isolation from its natural psycho-communicative setting, has altered its lexical repertoire by borrowing and adapting words from the dominant language. ("Ethnic *Koinés*" 115)

Italian immigrants live in an environment of constant translation and code switching. In Italy, many grew up bilingual: speaking a regional dialect at home and standard Italian at school. Some of these dialects such as Friulano, Bergamasco, Abanian, and Sardo are really languages that are quite different from Italian. When these people came to Canada they had to learn another language: French in Quebec and English in the rest of Canada. But there is also the fourth language, Italiese. This makes writers very aware of the sounds and meanings of words and the problems of translation from one language to another. They live in a constant environment of different languages and the ambiguities of words.

Italiese is the language most Italian-Canadian writers grew up hearing and speaking at home, but it is not the language they use in their writing. Not only did Di Cicco, Paci, and Micone reject Italiese, but the other hundred or so active writers of Italian background have done so as well. They include Mary di Michele, Nino Ricci, Darlene Madott, Joe Fiorito, Gianna Patriarca, Pasquale Verdicchio, Marisa De Francheschi, and Mary Melfi. A few Italiese words might appear in a bit of dialogue in a play or in a short story; otherwise, Italiese is the rejected language. The reasons for rejecting the language of the home are many and varied, which I will explore here.

Aesthetic Reasons

Italian-Canadian writers try to bring the beauty of Italian into English with their use of sound, their inclusion of Italian words, and occasionally Italian sentence structure. Italiese may be a useful functional language but it is not beautiful to hear or to write. It is not standard, since there are variations between that spoken in Toronto and Montreal, for example. The vocabulary also varies depending on the Italian dialect in the background of the speaker. Thus, Italiese is the rejected language for writers (Scarola 27–47).

Standard Italian does influence these writers in their style. Written Italian can be very elaborate, using long wordy sentences and figures of speech in contrast to English's plainer style. Italian-Canadian writers tend to follow the plain style of English in a conscious reaction to the decorative style of Italian. The rural background of many Italian immigrants and the experience of translocation make them want to leave behind a communication system that can obscure meaning. Toronto novelist Maria Ardizzi is an example of how English has influenced Italian writing style. She has published four novels in Italian using a plain style that is not common in Italy but is common in Canadian English.

In Quebec, we have the phenomenon of French influencing the Italian writer. Antonio D'Alfonso writes first in French and later produces an English translation; he sees the French bringing his writing closer to an Italian or Latin sensibility. However, the translation from Italiese is not from written texts but from lived experience and daily dialogue.

When Caterina Edwards' English-language play, *Terra Straniera*, was staged at the Edmonton Fringe Theatre Festival in 1986 it was a sold-out success. Nevertheless, one reviewer criticized the play because all the Italian immigrant characters spoke in perfect English, without accents, dialect, Italiese. Edwards explained that these characters would be speaking to each other in Italian and would be quite articulate about their feelings, ideas, and disagreements. She wanted the audience to hear their thoughts, ideas, and conflicts in clear English, and not through the filter of ethnic stereotypes, of inarticulate immigrants using broken English and Italiese. To achieve this clarity, Caterina Edwards had to translate the culture of these Italian immigrants into English. She went so far as to change the play's title into English when it was later published as *Homeground*. One of the goals of writers like Edwards is the creation of articulate and beautiful works rather than stereotyped immigrant writing.

Social Reasons

In the preface to *Roman Candles* Di Cicco explained his focus on English writing:

> I decided to do an anthology, banding together those poets whose work expressed this bicultural sensibility. I decided to limit the work to that written in English, largely to avoid an anthology the title of which would be *The Italian Poets Writing in Canada*; but also to see what, if anything, these poets could bring to Anglo-Canadian poetry. In searching for contributors, I found isolated gestures by isolated poets. (9)

Di Cicco wanted the poems in the anthology to explore bicultural conditions of these ethnic minority writers since he was conscious that a complex dynamic was taking place among these young authors. In a 1976 letter to Joseph Pivato, he tried to explain the changing nature of this process:

The anthology is contemporary if anything, stating the situation, linguistic and sociological-cultural, that exists for the authors now [...] I want poems that speak about the Italian poet in Canada, a man of different cultural substance speaking in English terms of his dilemmas, his insights, his frustrations, his passions, etc.

Di Cicco was aware that one of the linguistic and cultural frustrations that these writers faced was the widespread use of Italiese in the community. How do you translate this language code into standard English? Di Cicco, like other ethnic minority writers, had to use English, but he also tried to express the dual condition of immigrant culture. Also implied in his 1976 letter is the realization that a language like Italiese is not stable. How long would this language last beyond the second or third generation of immigrants? A work written in English, however, would be read for many decades.

The language problem still preoccupied Di Cicco ten years later, and after having published fourteen books of poetry, as evident in this interview with Robert Billings about *Virgin Science* (1986):

Question: In some of the poems here you use English phases and then translate them into Italian ones and say, pointedly, that the Italian phrase is better. Does this demonstrate a lack of ability by the English language to express even the findings of the new science [...] ?
Di Cicco: A language grows with a culture's thought. Its limits reflect that culture. The subject-object split in a language protracts and maintains the subjective-objective myth and the heart-mind split. (4)

In the more abstract language Di Cicco used in the poems included in *Virgin Science*, he moved further away from any Italian dialects; nevertheless, he still used some words from standard Italian. This is a pattern he began in his early poetry where we find many poems with Italian titles such as "La Gente," "Fotografia," and "Primavera." Di Cicco uses Italian words in very personal ways, but also to capture the diglossia of the whole community (Pivato, "Poetry of a Lost Generation," 51–6).

To Speak for the Voiceless

Novelist Frank Paci had many reasons for choosing English as his literary language. It is his language of education in Canada, the language that opened up a whole new society for this Italian immigrant from Sault Ste Marie and is, of course, the language of literature and culture in North America. Yet he realizes that this language makes his novels, *The Italians* and *Black Madonna*, inaccessible to many Italians in Canada, even to his own parents. In a 1981 letter to Joseph Pivato, Paci writes:

> Do you know any Italo-Canadian film-makers? This (a film of *The Italians*) more than anything would get the story to the first-generation Italians whom the book was written for in celebration and thanks. (I don't know about your background, but my parents aren't even able to read the book).

These people speak Italiese and Paci's English novels cannot easily cross over the divide. In a later interview, Paci explains one of his motivations for becoming a writer: "I became a more committed reader [...] My parents didn't read and there were no books whatsoever in the house. I reacted strongly against my family, wanting to be exactly the opposite of what they were" ("The Stone Garden" 231). Paci is not alone in his reaction. Part of the reason for embracing English is in reaction to the limitations of the immigrant family. And one of those limitations is Italiese. Later, in the same interview, Paci explains that, as he understands it, his mission as writer is to create clarity among the languages:

> The language problems in Italian-Canadian writing are not the creation of the writers, but the real condition of miscommunication and silence among immigrants. The revolutionary aspect of the writing here is that the author is giving these people a voice for the first time, and creating a language for them, and with them. (234)

That language in which the author creates is English, but an English that expresses the immigrants' points of view, their ideas, their feelings, and their silence. This involves translating from Italiese into English. In Paci's novel, *Black Madonna*, the character of the mother, Assunta Barone, represents an isolated immigrant woman who becomes a widow and must cope with the inability to communicate to her children. She speaks her regional dialect, some Italiese, and no English. Her husband was her interpreter, now that he is dead she is left voiceless. Paci must give her a voice in the novel, and he does this by giving her an English voice and translating the incommunicable state of Assunta Barone into English:

> "You can't speak to me anymore?" She said in *dialetto*. "You come into my house and you don't eat my food and you can't speak to me, your mother? You go to a big school and read many books and you act like this? An ingrata you are. A stranger you are. How can you be my daughter?" (*Black Madonna* 102)

In Quebec, Marco Micone saw his mission as speaking for the immigrants who do not have the language to speak for themselves. In his play, *Gens di silence*, he has Nancy articulate the social role of the artist:

> Il fault que tu écrives en français pour que tout le monde te comprenne. Il fault que les jeunes puissent se reconnaître dans des texts écrits par quelqu'un qui a vécu comme eux, qui les comprend et veut les aider. (95)

To Escape Italiese Culture

Mary di Michele has spent her life dealing with these language problems, both personally with her parents and professionally with her writing. She expresses her conflict with Italiese:

> When I look at my own experience, however, I see that at some point I wanted to identify myself with the intellectual and public world of English. I took English to be my own and wanted it because it seemed to me to be an escape from the kind of emotional morass of the Italian family. While at home my position was that of a daughter, I wanted more than the emotional life of a daughter, and later of a mother. I wanted an intellectual life too, so I embraced English as my salvation. On the other hand I am aware that Italian represents a side of my life charged with feeling, an emotional dimension. For

this reason Italian words often come out in my work as if they have come from another realm of experience or intensity of feeling. ("Interview" 198–9)

Mary di Michele uses dozens of Italian words in her poems, but they are all from standard Italian. Not one is Italiese. It remains the rejected language. At the 1986 conference of Italian-Canadian writers, di Michele explained her use of Italian words in these terms: "I write my poems in English, clear elegant English. But I also include an Italian word from time to time. It is as if I put a stone on the smooth English highway to remind the reader that there is another reality, another culture, underneath the English" ("Notes"). This is di Michele's way of translating the Italian culture into an English poem. One of the best examples of this is her poem, "Life is Theatre or O to be Italian in Toronto drinking cappuccino on Bloor Street at Bersani & Carlevale's," which has many Italian words and ends with the Italian woman being dismissed with, "Marriage to you would be like living in an Italian opera" (*Stranger in You* 42). An English reader can quickly grasp the sad irony of this rejection.

To Escape the Stereotypes

Italiese, the ubiquitous language, is not mentioned directly by any of these writers. It is as if they have all taken it for granted as part of the environment. Italiese is the language they have all rejected.

There is one more reason why Italiese is rejected: to avoid the negative stereotypes associated with Italians. In the North American media, there are two negative stereotypes that have been applied to Italians for about a hundred years: the dumb wop and the Mafioso.

The unintelligent "cumba" is often portrayed as speaking broken English mixed with Italian expression. He has a loud voice and uses hand gestures as if he were partly deaf-mute. And if he speaks English it is street talk full of slang expressions, generally uneducated. He is the caricature of an Italian immigrant.

There is also the dark side of this Italian cartoon character: the dangerous Mafioso. These members of organized crime, or crime families, are also portrayed as speaking poor English, sprinkled with words from Italian, or a regional dialect. These people may speak loudly or they may speak softly, but their hand gestures can suggest violence. The media image of the crime boss is so prevalent that we have begun to think of all Italians as "connected."

By using Italiese in their works, Italian-Canadian writers would be suggesting links with these negative stereotypes. This would be a great disservice to their communities and to their own literary works. These authors reject not only Italiese, but also the negative stereotypes of Italians. Of the hundred or so active Italian-Canadian writers there is no aspiring Mario Puzo working on a Canadian Godfather novel. Paci explains his own motivation:

> When I wrote my first novel, *The Italians*, I was well aware that Mario Puzo's *The Godfather* (1969) was very popular. I wanted to show readers that there were other types of Italian heroes, that you don't have to be a gangster to be a hero. The vast majority of Italian immigrants lead very quiet lives. I am writing about these quiet heroic people. ("The Stone Garden" 233)

Paci consciously chose a clear English language to represent these ordinary Italian immigrant heroes. And other writers strongly support these artistic choices, as Caterina Edwards maintains in her essay on Paci's style:

> In denying us the distancing effect of irony which would allow us to smile at Mark, and perhaps to place him, Paci instead uses language that is serious, exact and intimate, thus allowing us to both identify with Mark and to judge him harshly. I must conclude that Paci's stylistic choices in *Black Blood* and *Under the Bridge* were deliberate. ("The Confessions of Mark Trecroci" 26–7)

Paradoxically, by using English, Paci is able to both escape the limiting ethnic stereotypes so common in the North American media and to re-embrace an immigrant culture which he can chronicle for readers.

Coda

In his 1992 book of essays, *Le figuier enchanté*, Marco Micone explains his new translated identity, "Ni tout à fait italienne, ni tout à fait québécois, ma culture est hybride" (100). Like Micone, Italian-Canadian writers are using translation in complex ways to share their works with the wider community and to create a new literature based on the hybrid culture of the immigrant experience, a practice that Homi Bhabha calls "acts of cultural translation" (242). The effect of the rejection of Italiese has made Italian-Canadian writers more conscious of their daily experiences of diglossia and translation, and it has helped them to produce a rich body of work that has brought more linguistic diversity to Canadian writing and served as a positive example to other ethnic minority authors.

Note

1 A brief list of books by Italian-Canadian writers translated from Italian to English and from French to English includes Ardizzi, *Made in Italy*, and *Conversations with My Son*, a bilingual Italian-English collection of poems; Caccia, *Acknos*; D'Alfonso, *Avril: ou l'anti-passion* and *L'autre rivage*; Salvatore, *Tufo e Gramigna*; Micone, *Gens du silence*. Micone has also translated classical Italian and English plays into French for Quebec audiences.

Works Cited

Ardizzi, Maria. *Made in Italy: Romanzo* [1982]. Trans. *Made in Italy: A Novel*. Toronto: Toma, 1982.

– *Conversations with My Son*. Toronto: Toma, 1985.

Bhabha, Homi K. *The Location of Culture*. London: Routledge, 2004.

Billings, Robert. "*Virgin Science*: The Hunt for Holistic Paradigms, an Interview with Pier Giorgio Di Cicco." *Poetry Canada Review* 8: 1 (1986): 3–9.

Caccia, Fulvio. *Acknos* [1983]. Trans. *Acknos and Other Poems*. Toronto: Guernica, 1998.

Clivio, Gianrenzo. "Su alcune caratteristiche dell'italiese di Toronto." *Il Veltro* 29: 3/4 (1985): 483–91.

D'Alfonso, Antonio. *L'autre rivage*. Montréal: VLB, 1987. Trans. *The Other Shore*. Montreal: Guernica, 1988.

– *Avril: Ou l'anti-passion*. Outremont: VLB, 1990. Trans. *Fabrizio's Passion*. Toronto: Guernica, 1995.

Danesi, Marcel. "Ethnic Language and Acculturation: The Case of Italo-Canadians." *Canadian Ethnic Studies* 17: 1 (1985): 98–103.

– "Ethnic *Koinés* and the Verbal Structure of Reality: Psycholinguistic Observations on Canadian Italian." *Italian Canadiana* 3: 1 (1987): 113–23.

Di Cicco, Pier Giorgio. Letter to Joseph Pivato, 16 Nov. 1976 (unpublished).

– *Virgin Science.* Toronto: McClelland and Stewart, 1986.

– ed. *Roman Candles: An Anthology of Poems by Seventeen Italo-Canadian Poets.* Toronto: Hounslow Press, 1978.

Di Michele, Mary. "Notes." Vancouver: The First National Conference of Italian-Canadian Writers, 15–19 Sept. 1986 (unpublished).

– *Stranger in You.* Toronto: Oxford University Press, 1995.

– "Interview." *Mary di Michele: Essays on Her Works.* Ed. J. Pivato. Toronto: Guernica, 2007, 189–204.

Edwards, Caterina. *Homeground.* Montreal: Guernica, 1990.

– "The Confessions of Mark Trecroci: Style in Frank Paci's *Black Blood* and *Under the Bridge.*" *F.G. Paci: Essays on His Works.* Ed. J. Pivato. Toronto: Guernica, 2003, 19–27.

Micone, Marco. *Gens du silence.* Montréal: Éditions Québec/Amerique [1982]. Trans. *Voiceless People.* Montreal: Guernica, 1984.

– *Le figuier enchanté.* Montréal: Boréal, 1992.

Paci, F.G. *The Italians.* Ottawa: Oberon Press, 1978.

– Letter to Joseph Pivato, 3 March 1981.

– *Black Madonna.* Ottawa: Oberon Press, 1982.

– "The Stone Garden." *Other Solitudes: Canadian Multicultural Fiction.* Ed. Linda Hutcheon and Marion Richmond. Toronto: Oxford University Press, 1990, 219–34.

Pivato, Joseph. "Translation as Existence." *Echo: Essays on Other Literature.* Toronto: Guernica, 1994.

– "Poetry of a Lost Generation." *Pier Giorgio Di Cicco: Essays on His Works.* Ed. J. Pivato. Toronto: Guernica, 2011, 42–60.

Salvatore, Fillippo. *Tufo e Gramigna* [1977]. Trans. *Suns of Darkness.* Montreal: Guernica, 1980.

Scarola, Giovanni. *L'Italiese in Canada: Considerazoni sul Lessico.* Vaughan, ON: G.F. Graphics, 2007.

15

1984: Disquieting Equivalents: David Homel Retranslates *Le cassé* by Quiet Revolution Novelist Jacques Renaud

Gillian Lane-Mercier

While the shock waves created by Jacques Renaud's unprecedented use of *joual* as a political tool in his 1964 novel *Le cassé* have long since subsided in Quebec, their effects still fuel research and debate in the areas of literary history, criticism, and sociolinguistics. Some commentators continue to uphold the more traditional view, frequently expressed in the 1970s, whereby *joual* is a rather hermetic, monological stylistic device. Others adopt a more positive attitude, stressing the ongoing political and aesthetic relevance of literary *joual*.[1] Thus, in 1991, playwright Michel Tremblay exclaimed: "Mort le *joual*? Pantoute!" (21). Indeed, since the late 1980s, specialists and critics have called attention to the status of *joual* as one of the many registers of spoken French from which Quebec authors may freely choose. More significantly, far from serving as a marker of Québec identity, *joual* has become the universal symbol of the characters' minority status.

Some of political *joual*'s tenacious effects, however, can be found in the areas of literary translation and Translation Studies. From this perspective, the most obvious features of *joual* reside, on the one hand, in its aesthetic, sociocultural, ideological, and ethical untranslatability, and on the other hand, in the fascinating issues this untranslatability has raised – and continues to raise – in the Quebec and English-Canadian context since the publication of Renaud's novel. One of the more complex issues can be summarized as follows: whereas *Le cassé* has been translated twice into English, all of the works in *joual* by the other authors who, like Renaud, were associated with the short-lived literary and political movement Parti pris, founded in 1963 by a group of angry left-wing intellectuals well versed in Marx's theory of alienation and Sartrian existentialism, have yet to be translated. Renaud's novel is thus linked not only to questions of untranslatability, but also to questions of non-translation and retranslation – a challenging combination that David Homel's 1984 retranslation, entitled *Broke City*, brings sharply into focus.

For the question that comes immediately to mind is: why retranslate *Le cassé* twenty years after its publication? While questions pertaining to selection and timeliness are standard fare in translation theory, in this particular case they take on an interesting hue for at least two reasons. The first is of a predominately political nature: it is difficult not to notice that Guernica Editions' decision to retranslate a novel by a writer who had been associated with the separatist journal *Parti pris* came in the wake of the nationalists' defeat in the 1980 referendum and English-speaking Canada's perceived victory over Quebec's fight for sovereignty. One could, therefore, interpret this choice as an attempt to send a thinly veiled reminder to over-confident federalists of the cultural, linguistic, and socio-economic factors responsible for the irruption of Quebec nationalism in the 1960s. Such an interpretation was borne out by ex-Partipriste poet and prominent Péquiste politician Gérald Godin in his preface to *Broke City*: "If you want to understand how violent Quebec was back then, what a steaming volcano it was, read *Broke City*. And the volcano's still churning, don't you worry. Or maybe you should worry, ladies and gentlemen" (*Broke City*, "Twenty Years Later" 6).

Godin rightly sensed a literary and ideological blind spot regarding the Quiet Revolution, which was to a large extent a translation effect. Indeed, the absence of English translations of Partipriste writing is intriguing. As a result, many otherwise informed anglophone readers had no access to the literary movement that spawned the Quiet Revolution, in spite of increasing awareness of Quebec culture and politics throughout the 1960s. Again, the reasons were most probably of a political nature, given that, by 1984, many of the equally difficult, but less politically threatening post–Quiet Revolution authors (including Michel Tremblay, Roch Carrier, and Jacques Godbout) had been rendered into English. As we shall see, Homel's retranslation strategies suggest that perhaps he felt the time had come to provide (provoke?) English-language Canadian readers with a more accurate picture of Quebec literature and society both during the 1960s and – as Godin slyly intimates – in 1984. That he chose *Le cassé* rather than another Partipriste novel is not surprising, insofar as in Quebec it was considered to possess the greatest literary value and Renaud had become one of the Quiet Revolution's most representative writers.

The second reason for the retranslation of *Le cassé* is undoubtedly of a more aesthetic and ethical nature. Despite the disclaimer provided by Guernica Editions to the effect that the "publication of the present translation should not be construed as a critical refutation of *Le cassé*'s first translation," published the same year as the original (1964) by Gérald Robitaille under the title *Flat Broke and Beat, Broke City* as a retranslation is not only a product of the post-referendum political climate some readers may feel it indirectly responds to, but also it conveys a rather strong statement about the implications of Robitaille's translation choices. Again, all retranslations carry significant aesthetic weight insofar as they suggest, for instance, that the previous translation is no longer in keeping with contemporary reader perceptions or expectations and that, as a consequence, the new translation is both a necessity and an improvement; however, in the context of the Canadian literary institution of the early 1980s, when government-funded retranslations could only be deemed a luxury, Guernica's decision to produce a new rendering of *Le cassé* implies that the aesthetic and ethical dimensions were of particular concern. In his introduction to *Broke City*, Ray Ellenwood picks up on this aspect of Homel's retranslation when he notes, on the one hand, that *Le cassé* "had to wait twenty years for a decent translation" and, on the other, that Robitaille's translation had "disappeared without a trace like its Montreal publishers, Editions du Bélier" due, one may hypothesize, to its poor quality ("Welcome to *Broke City*" 7).

This, however, is only the tip of the iceberg. Underlying these two rather obvious responses are a number of issues that go far beyond mere surface-level political and aesthetic considerations. Three reviews of *Broke City* provide a good starting point, for not only do they offer a glimpse of some of the immediate effects of Homel's translation, but also they enable us to ask new questions. The title of Michael Mirolla's review, which appeared in the Montreal *Gazette*, is self-explanatory: "Even the Art of Translation Can't Revive Dated Work." According to Mirolla, "the quality of a literary translation depends [...] on [the original's] intrinsic value as a work of art, and the translator's ability to recreate that value" (D8), something he feels Homel did not achieve. Stripped of the original's politically connoted language, *joual*, the translation reads as a "misfired attempt at anti-art [... that] doesn't stand up as anything other than a curiosity of its time" (D8). Kathy Mezei poses the question differently in a review published in the

University of Toronto Quarterly. While she agrees that Homel's choice of street slang – "a generalized, big-city, working-class, northern, white dialect" (Homel, "The Way They Talk in *Broke City*," 24) – to render Renaud's *joual* "unquestionably recreates the violence and alienation of the source text," Mezei points to other essential aspects that have been lost, notably, the notion of Quebec's colonial status, and adds: "Whether or not the reader agrees with this or that rendition of slang is irrelevant; the question is whether the reader agrees with Homel's decision to produce an equivalent text" ("Translations" 389). Estelle Dansereau's review in *Quarry* offers a response to Mezei and a rejoinder to Mirolla: Homel has found a "suitable" equivalent for *Le cassé*'s proletarian speech that manages to capture all but the original's sense of place. She furthermore asserts that "*Broke City* will remain in the [Canadian] literary canon for its daringly unilateral story and discourse," thanks in part to the paratextual contributions from Godin, Ellenwood, and Renaud himself, which confirm that "this work is relevant […] when placed in its historical, cultural, and ideological context" (105–6). In this view, *Broke City* aimed at producing very specific historical, cultural, and literary – that is, translation – effects.

So, we now have another series of questions that can be formulated as follows: To what extent was the retranslation relevant to readers in 1984? What aesthetic, ideological, and ethical issues did it entail? How was the intrinsic value of the original perceived in 1964? How was it perceived in 1984? What is literary *joual*? How had it evolved since the 1960s? How could it be rendered in English in 1984? How had it been rendered prior to 1984? What was at stake when the translator opted for an equivalent speech register? What new images of Quebec society, culture, and identity did the retranslation foster with respect to the original text, Robitaille's version, and previous English translations of *joual*? In brief – what were the far-reaching causes and effects of Homel's retranslation?

I shall begin by recalling several historical and literary facts, some of which are by now well known, notably, those related to the politically charged decision of the Parti pris writers to reject the linguistic norms of standard French, seen as a source of cultural domination and alienation. By resorting to the use of *joual*, a lexically impoverished, grammatically incorrect, phonologically deviant, heavily anglicized, hence, "polluted" variety of French spoken in the working-class neighbourhoods of East End Montreal, these writers hoped to achieve a high degree of social realism and authenticity. More importantly, they sought to violently expose the tragedy of the French Canadians whose substandard speech was seen as symptomatic of their economic and social colonization by English Canada. As Renaud stated in a 1967 interview:

> *Le cassé* est une œuvre maudite [...], nihiliste. Et quant au *joual* [...], ce n'est surtout pas un style mais un mode de penser, un mode d'être. Le *joual*, c'est plus que le seul langage du Cassé, c'est sa condition de paria. Le *joual* est le langage à la fois de la révolte et de la soumission, de la colère et de l'impuissance. C'est un non-langage et une dénonciation. (*"Le cassé*, c'était l'enfer" 41)[2]

Of all the literary works in *joual* published by Les Éditions du Parti pris prior to its demise in 1968, Renaud's *Le cassé* is arguably the one that had the greatest impact due to the scandal it unleashed and the central position it has subsequently occupied in the history of modern Quebec literature. To a certain degree, this can be attributed to the novel's out-of-control hero, its unprecedented thematic violence, together with its innumerable blasphemies and obscenities. It was, however, the equally unprecedented presence of *joual* in the narrative passages, traditionally the preserve of civilizing grammatical norms and reassuring authorial distancing effects, that caused the greatest uproar. Henceforth, an integral part of the narrative voice rather than an inoffensive element of characterization, this under-privileged speech could no longer be defined as the expression of an alienated social class; rather, it had been exposed as the expression "de notre infériorité culturelle et sociale" (Langevin 119) and, above all, "[du] refus de se suicider" (Renaud, "Comme tout le monde," 21).[3]

What was initially perceived as the overriding presence of *joual* in the narrative passages led to two quite different contemporary assessments of *Le cassé*'s intrinsic value. Most critics of the period chose to read it not as a literary work per se but as a personal testimony, a psychological or a social document, thereby highlighting the novel's ontological and existential authenticity, as well as its semi-autobiographical status. This reading led them to draw attention to the political efficiency of the novel's primary unresolved contradiction: on the one hand, *joual* is, for the dispossessed, downtrodden characters, "une condition d'existence" for which there is no remedy; it is a non-language that could hardly be deemed revolutionary.

On the other hand, the narrator, who manifestly speaks *joual*, is nonetheless able, unlike his characters, to revert at will to standard French; in this respect, *joual* becomes "une arme, un étendard qu'il peut brandir à volonté" (Major, "Le joual comme langue littéraire," 50), so as to shake bourgeois readers out of their linguistic and political indifference. It is only by reading *Le cassé* as a social document wherein *joual* is depicted as a non-language invested with a latent violence that one can capture its revolutionary political thrust.

Conversely, a few contemporary critics highlighted the novel's aesthetic avant-gardism, its rejection – however politically charged – of traditional narrative constraints, thereby underscoring the stylistic specificity of written *joual*, defined less as a non-language than as a subsystem of standard French rife with innovative possibilities for creative freedom. *Le cassé* was described not as an authentic social document but as the product of an aesthetic practice (artifice) that should be analysed as such, insofar as it raised problems related both to the written transcription of oral speech and to the interplay between multiple, conflicting registers of language within the narrative voice.

Significantly, none of the Parti pris writers believed *joual* to be a literary language with a future, let alone a national language. Indeed, literary *joual* was, above all, a language of combat and a call for action rendered necessary by social and historical circumstances that, once revealed, acknowledged, and transcended, would no longer require its services. To choose to write in *joual* was to exorcize a collective humiliation and thus dialectically pave the way for the much-awaited birth of a national language, literature, and identity that could be defined in positive terms (see Major, "Le joual politique"; Filteau). By 1968, writers and critics had already begun to refer to the *joual* movement as a phenomenon of the past and the Parti pris group had disbanded. The same year, Michel Tremblay's highly successful *Les belles-sœurs*, the first Quebec play to be written entirely in *joual*, nevertheless, gave a new impulse to the movement which, over the course of the next decade, would become a symbol of national and literary self-affirmation in the works of a second generation of *joual* writers. By the mid-1970s, however, as the Parti Québécois was gearing up for its first electoral victory, literary *joual* had lost most of its powers to provoke and reveal in exchange for cultural legitimacy and positive identitarian connotations: overdone, overvalued, repetitious, reified, *joual* had become a fashionable stylistic device closer to folklore or cultural snobism than to authentic social realism or revolution and, as such, ideologically suspect, as the 1974 publication of Marie-Claire Blais' parody of novelistic *joual*, *Un joualonais, sa joualonie*, made abundantly obvious. Her book signed the death warrant of "le *joual* de combat" as it had been defined throughout the 1960s.

Insofar as *Le cassé* was concerned, the stylistically oriented readings outlined above had by now become standard fare, fostering a less socio-political, more literary appreciation of the book. Critics were at pains to emphasize the at best conservative, at worst unoriginal characteristics of Renaud's so-called stylistic innovations together with the greater presence of standard French in the narrative passages than initially thought. Despite the odd deformation, Renaud's syntax was described as based not on bona fide a-grammaticality, but on a variety of perfectly acceptable structures such as parataxis, repetition, parallelism, and bare-bone sentences that suggest, via a tense, syncopated, unconstrained rhythm, a sense of sociolinguistic impoverishment, economic desperation, and seething inner violence. As for *joual*'s main distinguishing feature, anglicisms, they were found, on closer reading, to be few and far between. In short, *Le cassé* was much less avant-garde, context-specific, and linguistically homogeneous than the quarrel it ignited had led readers to believe.

When Homel agreed to retranslate Renaud's novel, not only had issues of national identity receded into the background, but Quebec French was well on its way towards standardization and its distinguishing characteristics were no longer stigmatized (see Bouchard). Homel was fully aware of this mutation; he also recognized the ethical and ideological problems of "using the language of a group of people for whom their very language is a sign of humiliation and poverty and isolation" ("The Way They Talk in *Broke City*" 24), even though Renaud, who was from that same group, as Homel knew, could hardly have been accused of being condescending. Put differently, in the context of post-referendum Quebec, it was no longer possible to construe *joual* as a non-language or *Le cassé* as a social document overlaid with a revolutionary call for political action. Nor was it possible to consider *joual* a reliable marker of place. *Le cassé* could only be (re)read – and (re)translated – against the dual backdrop of its evolving status as literary monument and *joual* as a stylized, banalized, partially delocalized, politically defused literary device open to universal concerns.

Renaud's use of anglicisms, however sparse, deserves more attention, for they are the distinguishing feature of *joual* and at the crux of the translation issues I now wish to briefly address. As David Homel points out, "not only does *joual* accept English words into its lexicon, it also distorts them once they are inside, in a kind of sabotage action against a linguistic occupying force [...] these English words better betray the domination, both economic and linguistic, under which these people live" ("The Way They Talk in *Broke City*" 23–4). In *Le cassé* this sabotage action is exerted by phonetic transformation ("bum" becomes "bomme"), calques ("broke" becomes "cassé"), and morphological integration ("to pitch" becomes "pitcher/pitché") that "assimilate" the English words into French linguistic patterns; however, rather than politically empowering the characters, such sabotage only accentuates their sense of abjection and despair. How, then, in the Canadian context, was political *joual* to be translated? More precisely, if, as Homel also remarks, "joual was the manifestation of a key historical moment for Quebec writing, but at present, one would turn no heads by writing in it" (24), then the question becomes: How was *joual* to be translated in 1984? Which image – or images – of Quebec could/should be conveyed – or not? Which ones were relevant to the expectations of a contemporary Canadian readership? And what might be the influence of translators who had already tackled the problem of *joual*?

While Homel's decision to retranslate *Le cassé* twenty years later was, to a large extent, motivated by the challenge presented by *joual* and the desire to give Anglo-Canadians a view of 1980s Montreal, it was also motivated by the fact that he felt *joual* had been poorly rendered not only by Robitaille, but also by those few translators (Sheila Fischman, Ray Chamberlain, Ralph Manheim, John Glassco, John van Burek) who had been courageous enough to translate a few select second-generation novels.[4] Although he was more than aware that these problems were unsolvable and that his own particular translation strategies would, per force, be unable to properly reproduce the colonized state of the characters' speech or re-enact the political and identitarian "dévoilement et dépassement" so crucial to Parti pris' call for action, his choice of equivalency, in contrast to his predecessors' more literal approaches based on Gallicisms, foreignizing sentence structures, and/or word-for-word renderings, did not reflect a desire to appropriate by conforming to target expectations, long grounded in the notion of Quebec's untranslatable otherness. On the contrary, Homel's choice of equivalency reflected a desire to offer, over and above a more accurate view of the Quiet Revolution, as Godin pointed out, new, unfamiliar images of post-colonial, urban Quebec that eschewed questions of untranslatability, otherness, and local colour by challenging target values and perceptions.[5]

This, perhaps, is the first most significant effect of Homel's retranslation. His against-the-grain choice of a radical *Parti pris* novel openly contested the canon of francophone literature in translation by calling into question the aesthetic, ethical, and ideological assumptions of canon formation in English-language Canada, whereas his choice of equivalency just as openly contested the condescending literal translation practices that had helped to foster these assumptions. In this respect, equivalency was a paradoxical strategy designed to simultaneously conform to (due to its target-culture orientation and accessibility) and criticize Anglo-Canadian reader (mis)perceptions, stereotypes, and blind spots in effect since the 1960s by preserving the original's political and identitarian dimensions.[6] Furthermore, his choice of North American street slang as opposed to other plausible equivalents such as Black, rural, or Atlantic dialects represented, on a stylistic level, a deliberately violent alternative to English renderings of literary *joual* published between 1964 and 1984. According to Homel, who grew up in Chicago, this choice was designed to allow readers to have "a literary experience in a language they were not used to," insofar as previous translators of *joual* had "had no thought for alternative English, as if no one knew how the lower classes spoke in Canada. [They] couldn't look outside Toronto for equivalent English" (Conversation with the author). From a translational viewpoint, resorting to street slang enabled Homel to select hegemonic target values, attitudes, and normalizing processes with the intention of overturning them, especially the supposedly neutral activity of bridge building so prevalent in the English-Canadian conception of cultural exchange throughout the 1960s and 1970s. This was unmasked as an ideologically oriented illusion for the bridge was essentially a one-way street (from Quebec to English-speaking Canada) in the same way linguistic contamination in Quebec and North America has always been a unilateral process: "English invades French, not the other way around" ("The Way They Talk in *Broke City*" 24). Put differently, the expected domesticating thrust of target-oriented approaches is short-circuited. On the one hand,

Le cassé resists complete assimilation into (standard) English and the Canadian literary canon by remaining outside the normative. On the other hand, *Broke City* flouts the ethnographic discourses of cultural curiosity, rapprochement, and cordial co-habitation informing previous translations of *joual* by virtue of a translation project that calls attention to the foreign (the excluded, the stigmatized, the voiceless) within – rather than without – the linguistic and sociocultural parameters of the domestic.

Broke City can, therefore, be seen as occupying a key position in the history of literary translation in Canada. Herein lies, I believe, the second, more far-reaching effect of Homel's retranslation. By using the evolving identity preoccupations of the source society as a springboard to challenge target-reader habits and condescending perceptions, the translated text put forth images of sociolinguistic forces at play in both societies. It deftly scrambled the ideologically suspect "bridging" approach underlying the foreignizing strategies that had been mobilized by previous translators to deflate the threatening aspect of Quebec's otherness and thereby avoid confronting head-on issues of linguistic marginalization, colonization, and (counter)violence located not only within Quebec, but also within English-speaking Canada. Quaint amusement was definitely not the reaction Homel wished to convey or elicit as a translator, as the following comparison with extracts from Robitaille's literal translation make clear:

> C'est cassé pis ça donne des ordres
> GR: Flat broke and it gives you orders.
> DH: He's broke and he's spoutin orders like a faucet

> Ti'Jean avale sa salive.
> GR: Ti'Jean swallows his own spit.
> DH: Johnny swallowed hard.

> Chiennerie de vie.
> GR: What a bitchy life.
> DH: Bitch of a life.

Urban street slang was as unprecedented in Canadian translations of Quebec prose writing as Montreal proletarian speech had been in the Quebec novel twenty years prior. While it is true that it could capture neither the original's intense sense of place nor "the domination and linguistic and economic poverty lurking in the simple sentence Il s'est assis sur le tchesteurfilde" (Homel, "The Way They Talk in *Broke City*" 23), it could nonetheless produce surprisingly similar effects, most notably, the potential to awaken in the anglophone reader a "surconscience linguistique" (Gauvin, *Langagement*) able to apprehend the negative power of grammatical norms and recognize in Homel's rejection of dominant literary and translation conventions a gesture of defiance and denunciation. The notion of diglossia (colonization of one language by another) can, by analogy, be extended to include situations of internal diglossia (colonization of a non-standard register by a standard register). If invested with anti-social, emotionally explosive connotations, a non-standard register such as slang can produce equivalent effects of "intranquillity" that are perceived as unfamiliar and foreignizing (as opposed to domesticating) from a target-reader perspective. Stigmatized by tyrannical, "colonizing" grammatical norms, *joual* and slang can both be seen as a liberating form of counterviolence and revolt.

Urban street slang was, moreover, strangely in keeping with what Girouard had described in 1964 as the logical evolution of *joual* as a non-language, "[qui] ne peut que devenir argot, ce serait sa place normale, ou bien marquer la dernière étape vers l'anglicisation" ("En lisant *Le cassé*" 64); in this sense, *joual* represented an equivalent speech register that quite literally exemplified its imminent deterioration and the characters' corresponding hopelessness. Homel's slang also avoided the artificiality of foreignizing literalisms and semantically opaque Gallicisms, far too removed from the unilingual Canadian anglophone public's own linguistic reality to serve as markers of social realism or sites of (forced) reader identification, infusing *Broke City* with a sociolinguistic authenticity and an author-reader relationship akin to the original's. Indeed, with very few exceptions (e.g., Yves; Berthe), Homel steadfastly refused to retain even the most conventional markers of québécitude. All nicknames, topographical references, and most proper nouns are anglicized ("Ti-Jean" – "Johnny"; "Bouboule" – "Bubbles"; "la rue Crescent" – "Crescent Street"), contrary to Robitaille's version. In this way, he was able to avoid the polarizations of ethnographic translations and to capture one of Parti pris' central preoccupations, namely, problems of cultural poverty and dispossession are a part of "our" society, not just a part of "their" reality. As for slang's delocalized, timeless dimension, on one level, it resonated with the tendency of previous translators to compensate for the loss of place by adhering to the original's universal themes; on another level, however, it enabled Homel to propose, again within the confines of a paradoxical domesticating translation strategy, an image of the new attitudes towards language and identity emerging in contemporary Quebec, where the liberation of *joual*'s long-suppressed universalizing properties had opened up new possibilities for the literary translator.

Broke City was thus very much a product of its time, a translation event aimed at creating concrete translation effects. In subsequent interviews, Homel remarked that not only should a translated text improve on the original (see McGillis), but also, insofar as retranslations are concerned, "pour les livres très importants, chaque génération a sa lecture. On peut faire une relecture-retraduction pour l'époque présente" (Interview with Charette). One may hypothesize that the reviews of *Broke City* were symptomatic of the more complex, albeit conflicting responses available to English Canadians by 1984: ongoing tendencies to assimilate (Dansereau); disavowal of post-referendum Quebec's nationalist aspirations (Mirolla); recognition of the legitimacy of Quebec's political claims and cultural specificity (Mezei). Not only does this third response "suggest that in the 1980s, critics and audiences were more able to 'cross the cultural intersection'" (Koustas, "From 'Homespun' to 'Awesome'" 94), but Homel's disquieting choice of equivalency further suggests that translators no longer needed to highlight the origin of the translated text and the otherness of Quebec society. Indeed, both target and source texts could henceforth be read according to wider linguistic, cultural, and aesthetic horizons.

Over and above its capacity to consolidate *Broke City*'s resolutely contemporaneous status, Homel's choice of equivalency served to promote an emerging shift in literary translation practices in Canada and the corresponding rise of a new, target-oriented translation paradigm suddenly able to "see" what until then had remained invisible: the existence of potential equivalents for rendering *joual* in English. For translation paradigms, too, have their blind spots, and the source-oriented, literal options favoured throughout the 1970s, along with the political, aesthetic, and ethical assumptions they carried, were products of a historical moment when Anglo-Canadian images of Quebec's otherness were grounded in (exotic) assumptions of untranslatability. That the new translation paradigm had its own blind spots, notably, the erasing of difference in the name of fluidity (sameness), would become evident in the ensuing debates of the 1980s and 1990s; however, it is now apparent, thirty years later, that Homel's non-conformist, paradoxical approach to equivalency not only points us to where these translational blind spots would be found, but, more importantly, to how they could be challenged. If, as translation scholars such as Sherry Simon would later conceptualize, assimilative forces are always at work because translation is always a reflection of attitudes prevalent in a society at a given time, then the effects of Homel's translation in the Canadian context today are to be found in the continuing relevance of a domesticating model of translational *intranquillité*, or disquiet, which operates from a conflictual, yet lucid position that is neither completely outside nor completely within the confines of binary thinking and practices. *Broke City*, like the original, has aged well, bearing with it the salutary message that the homogenizing processes inherent to globalization and the ever-expanding hegemony of Anglo-American culture may be resisted through the very act of translating into English.

Notes

1 Examples of both views can be found in Gervais (*Emblématiques de l' "époque du joual"*).

2 By qualifying *joual* as a non-language, Renaud reinforced *Le cassé*'s sociopolitical message, together with the link between non-language, non-identity, and non-existence in which this message was rooted. *Joual* as non-language was central to the Partipristes' theory *and* personal experience of alienation; it was also what the second generation of *joual* writers would reject, retaining only the colonized status of *joual* from which it derived.

3 By making *joual* synonymous with Quebec French in general, Parti pris relativized the initial sense of place it evoked and underscored its potential to become the universal symbol of all dominated languages.

4 There were other, more personal, motivating factors, notably, Homel's relationship to a variety of "shameful ungrammatical" English he had been told by a schoolteacher not to speak ("If you can't speak well, you shouldn't speak at all," in "The Way They Talk in *Broke City*" 24) – slang, like *joual*, was condemned by the same state and cultural institutions – his ensuing sense of voicelessness and alienation (as a Jew growing up in a Christian neighbourhood),

similar economic hardship (due to unemployment), as well as shared political convictions. To some degree, *Broke City* is as much a personal testimony and cathartic experience as *Le cassé*, insofar as Homel's choice of an anti-normative equivalent for *joual* allowed him to "liberate" his earlier spoken language. This was what had initially attracted him to translating this book (Homel, conversation with the author).

5 Anglophone readers of works in *joual* had been conditioned by translators to "understand" Quebec via the effects of local colour generated by literal translation strategies couched in otherwise standard English. Gallicisms were particularly high in local colour and had the added advantage of portraying Quebec as an untranslatable reality that no target idiom could capture. In this way, "we" can pride ourselves on our desire for rapprochement while at the same time "constructing a politically neutral Canadian canon, in which the problems of Quebec society are examined only at a discreet and dispassionate distance" (Malone 47). Homel's translation project rejected these criteria, with the notable exception of realism, which he buttressed by resorting to paratextual confirmation of *Broke City*'s value as a contemporary social document.

6 In Translation Studies, "equivalency" has been associated with domestication, that is, with conservative translation practices designed to suppress otherness by aligning the source text with target-language expectations, whereas "neo-literalism" (i.e., not word-for-word renderings such as Robitaille's but renderings that respect the original's "poeticity") has usually been associated with foreignizing practices designed to retain the "otherness" of the original. In the first instance, the translation must read as if it were an original; in the second instance, the translation must read as a translation by allowing the original to "show through." Homel's translation reveals that these binaries are not necessarily pertinent to the Canadian context when one is dealing with the problems raised by literary *joual*.

Works Cited

Bouchard, Chantal. *La langue et son nombril: Histoire d'une obsession québécoise.* Montréal: Fides, 1998.

Dansereau, Estelle. "Jacques Renaud, *Broke City*." *Quarry* 35: 3 (1986): 103–7.

Ellenwood, Ray. "Welcome to *Broke City*." *Broke City*. Jacques Renaud. Trans. David Homel. Montreal: Guernica, 1984, 7–11.

Filteau, Claude. "*Le cassé* de Jacques Renaud: Un certain parti pris sur le vernaculaire français québécois." *Voix et images* 5 (1980): 271–89.

Gauvin, Lise. *Langagement*. Montréal: Boréal, 2000.

Gervais, André, ed. *Emblématiques de l' "époque du joual": Jacques Renaud, Gérald Godin, Michel Tremblay, Yvon Deschamps*. Montréal: Lanctôt, 2000.

Girouard, Laurent. "En lisant *Le cassé*." *Parti pris* 2: 4 (1964): 62–4.

Godin, Gérald. "*Broke City*, Twenty Years Later." *Broke City*. Jacques Renaud. Trans. David Homel. Montreal: Guernica, 1984, 5–6.

Homel, David. "The Way They Talk in *Broke City*." *Translation Review* 18 (1985): 23–4.

– Conversation with the author. 22 Apr. 2008.

– Interview with Christiane Charette. Radio Canada. Spring 2008.

Koustas, Jane. "From 'Homespun' to 'Awesome': Translated Quebec Theatre in Toronto." *Essays on Modern Quebec Theatre*. Ed. Joseph J. Donohue and Jonathan M. Weiss. East Lansing: Michigan State University Press, 1995, 81–107.

Langevin, André. "Une langue humiliée." *Liberté* 6: 32 (1964): 119–23.

Major, Robert. "Le joual comme langue littéraire." *Canadian Literature* 75 (1977): 41–51.

– "Le joual politique: Sur *Le cassé* de Jacques Renaud." *Emblématiques de "l'époque du joual": Jacques Renaud, Gérard Godin, Michel Tremblay, Yvon Deschamps*. Ed. André Gervais. Montréal: Lanctôt, 2000, 69–84.

Malone, Paul. "'Good Sister' and 'Darling Sisters': Translating and Transplanting the Joual in Michel Tremblay's *Les belles-sœurs*." *Theatre Research in Canada* 24: 1–2 (2003): 39–57.

McGillis, Ian. "Award Gives Translators Their Day: In City Where Language Pre-occupies, They're Unsung but Flourishing Breed." *Gazette*, 14 Nov. 1998, J8.

Mezei, Kathy. "Translations." *University of Toronto Quarterly* 54: 4 (1985): 383–99.

Mirolla, Michael. "Even the Art of Translation Can't Revive Dated Work." *Gazette*, 2 Mar. 1985, D8.

Renaud, Jacques. *Le cassé*. Montréal: Parti pris, 1964.

– *Dead Broke and Beat*. Trans. Gerald Robitaille. Montréal: Les Éditions du Bélier, 1964.

– "Comme tout le monde ou le post-scriptum." *Parti pris* 2: 5 (1965): 20–4.

– "*Le cassé*, c'était l'enfer." Interview with Jean Bouthillette. *Perspectives* 11 (Nov. 1967): 38–41.

– *Broke City*. Trans. David Homel. Montreal: Guernica, 1984.

– "Afterword." *Broke City*. Trans. David Homel. Montreal: Guernica, 1984, 93–5.

Tremblay, Michel. "Mort le *joual*? Pantoute!" *L'Actualité* 16: 13 (1991): 21–2.

16

1989: The Heyday of Feminist Translational Poetics in Canada: *Tessera*'s Spring Issue on *La traduction au féminin comme réécriture*

Alessandra Capperdoni

> I am a translation because I am a woman.
> – Susanne de Lotbinière-Harwood

What is the relationship between translation and women's language and writing? Is there a feminist practice of translation? Is a feminist poetics a translational one? Is a feminist translation theory being produced in Canada, and if so, what role can it play in Translation Studies internationally? In the spring of 1989, the Canadian feminist bilingual journal *Tessera* dedicated issue no. 6, "La traduction au féminin / Translating Women," entirely to these questions. That in the same year four works exemplifying the intersection of feminist writing and translation were published can hardly be a coincidence. Québécois avant-garde poet Nicole Brossard reassembled the cycle of exploration on translational poetics and feminist writings in her collection of poetic sequences, *À tout regard*. At the same time, the publication of Fiona Strachan's translation of Brossard's *Le sens apparent* (1980) as *Surfaces of Sense* and Susanne de Lotbinière-Harwood's translation of Lise Gauvin's *Lettres d'une autre* (1984) as *Letters from an Other* brought the theoretical preoccupations of fiction theory to bear on the practice of feminist translation. With Susanne de Lotbinière-Harwood's translation into French of the influential experimental novel *Heroine* (1987), by anglophone Québécoise Gail Scott, the interrelationship of a feminist theory of writing and the practice of feminist translation became fully apparent. The 1989 *Tessera* issue captured the energy of this unique moment through the publication of essays, translations, and theoretically engaged conversations that marked a turning point in the development of Canadian

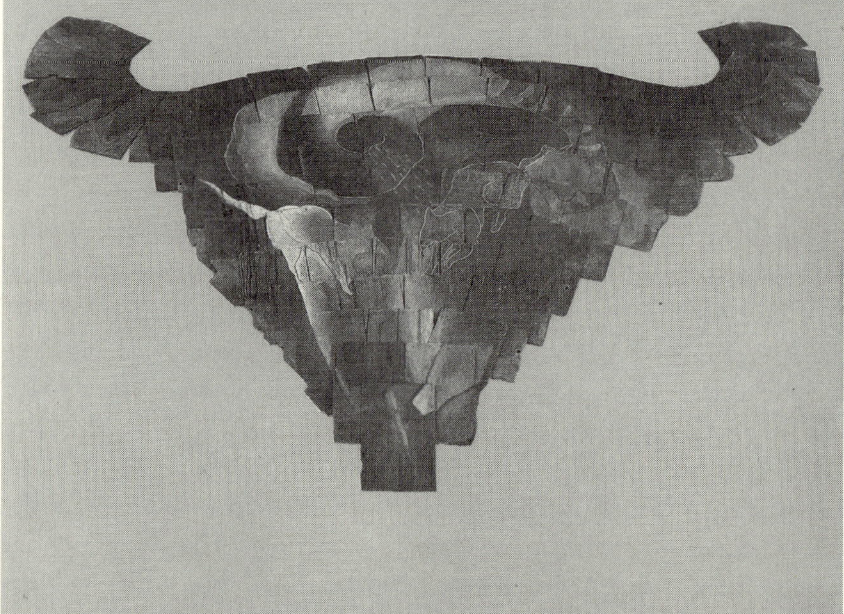

Figure 16.1
Cover of *Tessera*, Spring 1989.

writing.[1] Indeed, the theorization of writing and translation, along with the translation of avant-garde Quebec and English-speaking Canadian women writers into the other language, to which *Tessera* dedicated much of its work in the 1980s and 1990s, had the effect of contributing to the shaping of a Canadian and Québécois theory of feminist poetics and translation that was to be disseminated at an international level. But it is the issue's highlighting of the interrelationship of feminist writing, translation, and theoretical investigations into the discursive construction of gendered subjectivity that marks it as the catalyzer of a key moment in the development of a Canadian and Québécois feminist *poiesis* and, thus, as a "translation event."

Since its inception, in 1984, the work of *Tessera* focused on the critical exploration of the nexus of writing, language, and gender/sexuality, which informed the practice of feminist translators throughout the 1980s. A bilingual periodical, *Tessera* dedicated its pages to intercultural and feminist work. In the vision of the first editorial collective, formed by Barbara Godard, Daphne Marlatt, Kathy Mezei, and Gail Scott, *Tessera* was "a journal where we could continue the dialogue between Francophone and Anglophone writers and critics" (Marlatt, *Readings from the Labyrinth* 9), a dialogue that is translation as relation of differences.[2] Its first numbers appeared as guest issues of well-established journals, featuring themes that pertained directly to the question of writing, women's language, and translation.[3] It is this interrelationship of creative and theoretical writings energizing the feminist exchanges between Quebec and English-language Canada that is at the heart of *Tessera*'s project as a translational dialogue. As feminist critics responded to the gendered politics of translation of women's texts, questions of language and gender came increasingly to the forefront of feminist politics in ways that resonated with theoretical investigations into language by Québécois theorists and writers. Indeed, questions featured in the first two issues of *Tessera*, "Doubleness in Language" and "Reading as Writing / L'écriture comme lecture," highlighted the notion of translation as *réécriture au féminin* and the "movement across" languages, theories, genres, and writing practices of emerging feminist writing. This scrutiny of language was recognized as an urgent question, or, as Brossard explained, "*question d'écriture* [...] *comme question féministe*" (*La lettre aérienne* 9), where re-writing was articulated as a way to displace and reappropriate language through difference to challenge the structures of patriarchal discourse. This complex and ambiguous movement refers, at the same time, to the process of translation, for aren't these tactical interventions into language implicit in the process of feminist translation itself? Translation, therefore, is both transformance and performance (Godard, *Encyclopedia of Literary Translation into English*), for a feminist writing practice actively manipulates the text in order to produce meaning. It is no surprise, then, that the first issues dedicated to the question of writing and language are followed by an issue on translation.

The conceptualization of writing as a translational practice has been central to the articulation of a feminist theory of writing in Canada and Quebec since the late 1960s and 1970s when feminist writers, artists, and theoreticians critically examined the constitution of the subject in language and the specificity of female subjectivity in relation to patriarchal discourse. The centrality of language and writing for feminist theory and practice is foregrounded by the exclusion of women from the production of thought, images, and symbols operating through the a priori exclusion of the feminine from the symbolic order (exemplified for Nicole Brossard, in her essay "L'e muet mutant," by the mute sign of the terminal "e" of the feminine form) and the re-signing of women's difference within the patriarchal logic of the (masculine) Same. Excluded from the orders of the symbolic and unable to speak her/self in language, woman lives in a condition of linguistic displacement and fragmented subjectivity. In *La venue à l'écriture* (1977), Québécoise critic Madeleine Gagnon aptly articulated this condition as one of alienation which, for the female Québécoise subject, is further complicated by the unequal power relations between francophone and anglophone cultures and between minority and dominant language. Feminist writing, then, can only be a theft of language, a reclaiming of what has been excluded from the structures of representation, a process unleashing the *jouissance* of desirous language. Echoing Hélène Cixous' playful conceptualization of women's writing as *vol/voler* (theft/flying) that constitutes *écriture féminine* ("Le rire de la méduse"), Gagnon describes feminist writing as a *travail* of translation, a critical transformation of the subject in language which is also, and always, a movement of alterity:

> Yet I snatch this language that is foreign to me and turn it about in
> my fashion. I thread together truths that will be reproduced. But on
> the slate I wrote with a sovereign chalk. It told which part of me

was to prevail. I am a foreigner to myself in my own language and I translate myself by quoting all the others. (179–80)

In translation the boundary between theory and creative act is dissolved. For in writing her condition of alienation within language – a process of self-translation in Gagnon's words – woman challenges the violence of rhetoric and representation. Against the silences and erasures that have signified for centuries the condition of female subjectivity and sexuality, her translational writing enters the chains of signification of patriarchal discourse through its holes and gaps, vertigoes of language that mark the undecidability of her signature and the production of new meaning. This translational *poiesis* became a central aspect of the feminist poetics of Canadian avant-garde writers such as Nicole Brossard, Daphne Marlatt, Madeleine Gagnon, Lola Lemire Tostevin, and Erin Mouré, who produced some of the most interesting textualities in recent decades in North America. It also shaped the *travail* of feminist translators engaged in significant experimentations throughout the 1980s and 1990s.

As Godard points out in her essay, "Theorizing Feminist Discourse/ Translation," questions of language and gender were central preoccupations both of feminist theory and feminist translation. Feminist translators had already attended to the problematic of language and gender in translation studies – for example, in articles by Barbara Godard ("Translating and Sexual Difference") and Kathy Mezei ("The Question of Gender in Translation") from 1984 and 1986, respectively. Mezei discussed this question in relation to F.R. Scott's translation of Anne Hébert's *Le tombeau des rois* (1953), following which Hébert had remarked in *Dialogue sur la traduction* (1970) that the translator had failed to realize the gender and theme of the poem – a young girl and a ritual rape. Barbara Godard's work on gender and language was already evident in her translation of Antonine Maillet's *The Tale of Don l'Orignal* (1978), and Patricia Claxton's translation of Brossard's *French Kiss* in 1986 also showed a keen awareness of the problematic of gender in writing and translation. But it was the encounter with Québécois theories of *écriture au féminin* that productively energized the work of feminist translators. This is perhaps most evident in Godard's trajectory as theorist and translator and her role in *Tessera* in showing the ways in which translation, too, represented a *"question d'écriture [...] comme question féministe."* Her work comprises a long list of translations, prefaces, critical and theoretical articles, and conference presentations,[4] but it is her essay, "Theorizing Feminist Discourse/Translation," published in this issue of *Tessera* that marks the passage from the experimentation on translation of feminist writings to the theorization of translation as feminist intervention into dominant discourse – an intervention articulated as emancipatory practice. The border between theory and practice is problematized and undone. More specifically, Godard emphasized the political import of feminist translation, which is, to all effects, feminist poetics: "Ce discours avance une théorie du texte comme transformation critique: le discours féministe travaille le discours dominant dans un mouvement complex et ambigu entre discours" ("Theorizing" 42). This complex movement "in-between," which brings to light the doubleness of language as well as the potential subversiveness of feminist translation and its challenge to the dominant notion of the transparency of language, is more clearly expressed by the author: "Ici, au contraire, l'auteure avance une théorie de la traduction comme trans(dance)form, comme transformation et performance [...] La traduction féministe est un mode privilegé de réécriture" (42). The significance of Godard's essay, and the whole of the *Tessera* issue, is reflected in the intense activity of feminist translators throughout the 1980s, which the essay frames in theoretical terms, culminating with Susanne de Lotbinière-Harwood's translation of Nicole Brossard's *Le désert mauve* in 1990, a novel that thematizes the notion of feminist writing as translation and whose translation into English exemplifies Godard's notion that "la traduction féministe est un mode privilegié de réécriture" ("Theorizing" 42).[5]

Tessera's 1989 "translation event" was not an isolated occurrence, for *Tessera*'s work should be read in the context of the cultural activism of small presses, feminist magazines, conferences, and the cross-cultural encounter between anglophone and Québécois writers and critics. *Tessera*, indeed, served as a key site for creative exchanges among writers, translators, critics, and academics; far from being a self-originating instance, this translation event is a catalyzing moment of the work of Québécois *écriture au féminin*, the activism of feminist translators, avant-garde writing, and the incessant work of critics and theorists associated with *Tessera*. Godard, for example, explored the theory and practice of feminist translation in academic essays and papers presented at several conferences, thus building a corpus of criticism, including prefaces, highly influential in the articulation of a feminist theory of translation. Sherry Simon's *Gender in Translation: Cultural Identity and the Politics of Transmission* (1996) originated with the conference she had organized at Concordia in 1984. Interestingly, it was during this conference that the joint reading of Nicole Brossard and Barbara Godard of *Journal Intime* took place, with the translated texts being read before the "original." Brossard commented on the affective relation to reading herself in translation. The movement between translation and writing in relation to the constitution of gendered subjectivity in language was brought to the fore through the materiality of sound – the matter of language – and what Godard would call "*transformance*" and "*performance*" ("Theorizing" 42). It was thus by being translated that Brossard's interest in writing as translation and its relation to gender emerged (Godard, e-mail message to author). And, on this occasion, Susanne de Lotbinière-Harwood's interest in feminism and translation turned into a feminist translational practice (ibid.). Then, in 1986, Simon organized with David Homel the Montreal international conference on the art and politics of translation with a panel on feminist poetics featuring Susanne de Lotbinière-Harwood, Sherry Simon, Barbara Godard, and Kathy Mezei and whose proceedings were published as *Mapping Literature: The Art and Politics of Translation* (1988). She also edited an issue on gender and translation in *TTR: Traduction, traductologie, rédaction* 4 (1991).

Two conferences, in particular, played a key role by creating spaces for the elaboration of feminist discourse and the context for *Tessera*'s translational work. The Dialogue Conference that Barbara Godard organized at York University in 1981 set in motion the idea of a feminist journal which would address women's ex-centric relation to knowledge and foster women's art, thinking, and writing. It was especially the "theoretical energy of the feminist writers from Quebec" (*Readings from the Labyrinth* 9) during this conference, Marlatt claims, that sparked the idea of a feminist journal and the formation of the first *Tessera* editorial collective. *Tessera* started in the winter of 1982, and the first issue was completed when the collective met again during the Women and Words / Les femmes et les mots conference that Betsy Warland, Victoria Freeman, and Daphne Marlatt together with a women's support group organized in Vancouver in 1983. On this occasion, they decided to have their conversations recorded as an introduction to the first issue. The emergence of the periodical and its dissemination, therefore, were intimately tied to conferences that were central to the articulation of a feminist theory and to feminist writing in Canada. But the network of feminist relations that *Tessera* embodied, a translational/ dialogical space best exemplified in issue no. 6 on translation, was also imbricated with the collaborative projects and translational encounters of a network of periodicals, from *La Nouvelle Barre du jour* and *Room of One's Own* to *Ellipse*.[6]

At this key moment in the history of feminist writing and translation in Canada, the articles and translations featured in *Tessera* 6 picked up the threads of the many engagements of feminists with the *topoi* of translation. Kathy Mezei highlighted the interrelationship of language, writing, and translation in her introduction to the issue, appropriately entitled "Traverse/*Traversée*." The process of translation foregrounds the condition of language in producing subjectivity and the subject positions that our identities inhabit. Whenever we speak, we translate ourselves but, at the same time, the articulation of our subjectivities is bound by the language we enter at birth. Our relationship to language marks, therefore, the position we occupy in the larger (and dominant) symbolic systems, the articulation of the speaking subject thus involving what Roman Jakobson calls an intersemiotic process. Feminist writing/translation always requires courageous choices, for women who venture into unexplored grounds and imagine alternative realities to the logic of the Same need to use the possibilities of language while subverting its constraining effects; but translation is also "traversal" and entails rearticulation, for the language that constitutes us is also language of the other. Feminist writing/translation is, therefore, reenunciation, re-creation, and *poiesis*. This process was made visible in the sequence of translations for this issue that were also re-writings into English of Lola Lemire Tostevin's poem in the French language, *"extrait d'espaces vers."* A bilingual poet living within the interstices of both languages, Lemire Tostevin resorted to a strategy of contamination to undo the structures of patriarchal nationalistic discourse, grounded in the discrete boundaries of the "two founding nations," and produced, instead, a relation of differences – a strategy she explained in "Contamination: A Relation of Differences" with which the sequence of translations by Susan Knutson, Kathy Mezei, Daphne Marlatt, Barbara Godard, and Gail Scott were in conversation. Translation as rendering and exchange ("Vers-ions con-verse: A Sequence of Translations"), these re-creations re-write the *auteure's* words and images by delving into the pleasures and the intensity of language, and visibly inscribe the reading act in the labour of the translator. The dialogue established between *auteure* and translator is caught by the reader, and is carried on in the musings that follow each of the texts: a translational *lieu* as dialogue/conversation that further points to the importance of interrelationships and productive contaminations. Indeed, this translational space and acts of translation were the matrix for a feminist exchange between Quebec and English-language Canada which generated key works in feminist poetics and theory: feminist collaborations that blurred the boundaries between theory and creative act and produced a unique Canadian feminist *poiesis* in the articulation of *fiction-theory / la théorie-fiction*.

It comes as no surprise, then, that a central text in the articulation of feminist theory and translation, Barbara Godard's "Theorizing Feminist Discourse/Translation," was featured in this issue of *Tessera*. Here Godard brings together theories of language and translation as re-enunciation and production, rather than re-production, of meaning and the role of the writer/translator in reading and re-writing writing. If the metaphor of translation suggests a poetics of equivalence (the "carrying over" of meaning from one language to another) grounded in the illusory notion of the transparency of language, feminist writing emphasizes the notion of inter-semiotic translation which, by doubling and refracting phallogocentric language, produces difference, rather than equivalence, and opens up to the multiplicity of women's experiences. In her essay, "Translating *Mauve*: Reading Writing," also included in *Tessera 6*, Daphne Marlatt reflected with Nicole Brossard on this process in relation to the writing and translation/recreation of the poetic sequences *Mauve* and *Character / Jeu de Lettres* and described it as "erotic transgression of borders, both cultural and linguistic, where meaning seeps through the poem from one brain to another" (30) – a process of "*transformation*" and "*performance*" that Godard had articulated as "*trans(dance)form*" ("Theorizing Feminist Discourse" 42).[7] Marlatt's essay shows a keen awareness of the way in which translation is embodied in the tension between women's subjectivities and the constraints of patriarchal language, while Ginette Legaré's visual textual pieces with Lacanian echoes explore the relation of translation to the construction of the (female) self. Within the specificity of Canadian history, language also participates in the construction of colonial relations and the construction of the racial other, and, as Susanne de Lotbinière-Harwood best put in her piece, "Deux mots pour chaque chose," the female subject living through the effects of colonial relations can best express her subjectivity as "Je suis une traduction" (24). Well before the rise of identity politics in the 1990s, then, the issue also dedicated several pieces to the question of ethnicity and subjectivity in regards to the language of the other (Marguerite Andersen's "Se traduire," Ilma Rakusa and Rada Ivekovi 's "The Translator Being Translated: An IRRI Project," and Clea H. Notar's "My Gentleman of the White Knights"), which was unravelled further in relation to the language of the mother in Dôre Michelut's splendid essay, "Coming to Terms with the Mother Tongue."

But *Tessera*'s issue, and *Tessera*'s work on feminist writing, theory, and translation, also had a resonance in literary criticism and cultural studies. For example, "Theorizing Feminist Discourse/Translation" was presented first at the Literary Translators' Association Conference in Montreal in 1986 and then at the Beyond Translation Conference in Warwick in 1988. It was subsequently included in *Translation, History and Culture*, the conference proceedings of the Warwick conference edited by Susan Bassnett and André Lefevere, who noted the central contribution of Godard's essay to the "cultural turn" in translation studies.[8] Godard's essays were also translated into several languages. Marlatt's translational writing further explored the dimensions of self-translation into the holes and gaps of the language of the other and the possibilities of articulation through lesbian desire, and many young writers in English were influenced by this prolific moment of the feminist avant-garde. Writing in the feminine intervened substantially in the writing practices of English Canada leading, in Gail Scott's words, to "new directions" and "exciting discoveries" (Godard, "Theorizing Fiction Theory" 9).

The intricate relations of writing, theory, academic conferences, reading events, and publications continued throughout the 1990s. Significant contributions came from Susanne de Lotbinière-Harwood's translation of Brossard's bilingual auto-fiction essay *Elle serait la première phrase dans mon prochain roman / She Would Be the First Sentence of My Next Novel* (1998);[9] and Luise von Flotow, whose doctoral research at the University of Michigan resulted in two articles, "Feminist Translation: Contexts, Practices, and Theories" (1991) and "Translating Women of the Eighties: Eroticism, Anger, Ethnicity" (1995), and a monograph, *Translation and Gender: Translating in the "Era of Feminism"* (1997). Clearly, the productive intersection of translation and feminism, Québécois and English Canada, creative writing and theory, which is at the heart of feminist translational practice (feminist writing as translational writing), was effectively captured by *Tessera*'s issue on translation and had a direct impact on the formation of a *poiesis* of feminist translation in Canada.

The feminist groups, writers, artists, cultural activists, reading groups, dialogues, theorists, academics, and conferences were a matrix of relations that made possible the carving of a new space of translational writing and the elaboration of a feminist theory of translation. A matrix of relations and "creative interchange" (Simon 22), feminist translation during the 1980s was key to the development of a feminist theory and practice in Canada that critically examined, and troubled, the margins of language and nation through a *poiesis* of "performance" and "transformance" (Godard, *Encyclopedia of Literary Translation into English*). It is this translational writing as *traduction / réécriture au féminin* that *Tessera* 6 performed and celebrated, and which anticipated a *jouissance* of feminist avant-garde poetics, theorizing about translation, and dialogue among feminists to come.

Notes

1 Brossard introduced the term "fiction-theory" in *L'Amèr*. The term has been used differently by different generations of writers, as the correspondence among Barbara Godard, Daphne Marlatt, Kathy Mezei, and Gail Scott in "Theorizing Fiction Theory" (*Tessera* 1986) points out. Gail Scott further notes that in Québécois writing, where the term is older, "the theory has been assimilated into the form" because "the theoretical discussion has done its work to a certain extent" (7). Writers also emphasize differently "fiction" and "theory," but it is useful to cite Kathy Mezei's summary of Brossard's understanding of *la fiction théorique*: "But her '*fiction théorique*' is something else – the text as both fiction and theory – a theory working its way through syntax, language and even narrative of a female subject, a fiction in which theory is woven into the texture of the creation, eliminating or trying to, distinctions between genres, between prose, essay, poetry, between fiction and theory" (8).

2 A selection of articles and creative pieces from *Tessera* was republished in *Collaboration in the Feminine: Writings on Women and Culture from Tessera*, edited by Godard in 1994.

3 Issue 1, "Doubleness in Language," hosted in *Room of One's Own* 8: 4 (1984);

Issue 2, "L'écriture comme lecture: Reading as Writing / Writing as Reading," hosted in *La Nouvelle Barre du jour* 157 (1985); Issue 3, "Fiction Theory," hosted in *Canadian Fiction Magazine* 57 (1986); Issue 4, "The State of Feminist Criticism," hosted in *Contemporary Verse* 2, 11: 2/3 (1988). Issue 5, "Dialogue / conversation / une écriture à deux" (1988), was the first to be published by *Tessera* on its own.

4 In 1981, Godard translated a section of Nicole Brossard's *Amantes* for the poet's reading at a "Writers in Dialogue" event held in Toronto in 1981. This "experiment" was followed by the translation of Brossard's fiction-theories on lesbian desire, *L'Amèr, ou, Le chapitre effrité* (1977) and *Amantes* (1980), which was published as *These Our Mothers, or, The Disintegrating Chapter* (1983) and *Lovhers* (1986) with important prefaces on the translation process. Godard's close involvement with Brossard's writing continued in the years to come. In 1986, she translated a few excerpts from *Journal intime, ou, Voilà donc un manuscrit* (1984) for Adele Wiseman's *Canadian Women Writers Engagement Calendar* (the complete text appeared as *Intimate Journal, or, Here's a Manuscript* in 2004 with her introduction "The Moving Intimacy of Language"), and in 1991, she produced the translation of Nicole Brossard's *Picture Theory* (1982) with a lengthy critical preface. In the same year, she published a collection of several texts by Québécois writer and theorist France Théoret (*Bloody Mary*, 1977; *Une voix pour Odile*, 1978; *Vertiges*, 1979; and *Nécessairement putain*, 1980) under the title *The Tangible Word*, prefaced by her introduction "Translating Translating Translation."

5 In the same period, Yvonne Klein translated Jovette Marchessault's experimental plays, *Triptique lesbien* (1980), published as *Lesbian Triptych* (1985) and introduced by Barbara Godard's preface, "Flying Away with Language," and Patricia Claxton published Brossard's *French kiss: Étreinte-exploration* (1974) as *French Kiss, or, A Pang's Progress* (1986). Susanne de Lotbinière-Harwood translated both Brossard's *Sous la langue* as *Sous la langue / Under Tongue* (1987) and Gail Scott's English-language novel *Heroine* (1987) about radical Quebec politics and lesbian subjectivity into French as *Heroïne* (1989). In 1988, Marlene Wildeman published the translation of Brossard's auto-fiction essay, *La Lettre aérienne* (1985), as *The Ariel Letter*. The following year, Fiona Strachan translated Brossard's *Le sens apparent* (1980), as *Surfaces of Sense*.

6 In Quebec, the avant-garde journals *La Nouvelle Barre du jour* and *Les Têtes de pioches* played a central role in the production of a radical culture; *La Nou-*

velle Barre du jour published groundbreaking theoretical and creative feminist work in the 1970s, e.g., "Femme et language," in *NBJ* 50 (1975), and "le corps, les mots, l'imaginaire," in *NBJ* 56/57 (1977) – essays that Godard and Josée Michaud proposed translating for *Room of One's Own* – and in 1985 it hosted the second issue of *Tessera*. But important translational work, marking the encounter between francophone and anglophone avant-gardes, was also carried out by the bilingual journal *Ellipse*, *Writing*, as well as *Room of One's Own* (which would also host *NBJ* 56/57 (1977) in 1978), *Fireweed*, and the American periodical, *Trivia*.

7 Brossard's poetic sequences and Marlatt's translations were first published by the journals *Writing* and *La Nouvelle Barre du jour* in 1985 and 1986, and then republished in Brossard's *À tout regard* (1989) and Marlatt's *Salvage* (1991).

8 Godard's theory of feminist poetics and translation is also grounded in her work as an editor of the Coach House translation series in the 1970s, as well as a project on gendered differences in French-Canadian women's writings translated into English for *Women Writers in Translation: An Annotated Bibliography*, which came out under the editorship of Marjorie Resnick and Isabelle de Courtivron in 1984.

9 See Agnès Conacher's article, "Susanne de Lotbinière-Harwood: Totally Between" (*Writing between the Lines*) on Susanne de Lotbinière-Harwood's translation of short prose writings, poems, and theory by writers Anne-Marie Alonzo, Michèle Causse, Louise Cotnoir, Louise Desjardins, Jauvette Marchessault, Daphne Marlatt, and Sharon Thesen throughout the 1980s.

Works Cited

Andersen, Marguerite. "Se traduire." *Tessera* 6 (1989): 70–5.

Bassnett, Susan, and André Lefevere, eds. *Translation, History, and Culture*. London: Pinter, 1990.

Brossard, Nicole. *À tout regard*. Montréal: Éditions NBJ, 1989.

– *Amantes*. Montréal: Quinze [1980]. *Lovhers*. Trans. Barbara Godard. Montréal: Guernica, 1986.

– *French kiss: Étreinte-exploration*. Montréal: Éditions du jour [1974]. *French Kiss, or, A Pang's Progress*. Trans. Patricia Claxton. Toronto: Coach House Quebec Translations, 1986.

– *Journal intime, ou, Voilà donc un manuscrit*. Montréal: Les Herbes rouges

[1984]. *Intimate Journal, or, Here's a Manuscript*. Trans. Barbara Godard. Toronto: Mercury, 2004.

– *L'Amèr, ou, Le chapitre effrité*. Montréal: Quinze [1977]. *These Our Mothers, or, The Disintegrating Chapter*. Trans. Barbara Godard. Toronto: Coach House, 1983.

– *La lettre aérienne*. Montréal: les éditions du remue-ménage [1988]. *The Aerial Letter*. Trans. Marlene Wildeman. Toronto: Women's Press, 1988.

– "L'e muet mutant." *La Nouvelle Barre du jour* 50 [1975]: 10–27. Trans. *Ellipse* 23/24 (1979): 44–63.

– *Le désert mauve*. Montréal: Éditions de l'Hexagone [1987]. *Mauve Desert*. Trans. Susanne de Lotbinière-Harwood. Toronto: Coach House, 1990.

– *Le sens apparent*. Paris: Flammarion [1980]. *Surfaces of Sense*. Trans. Fiona Strachan. Toronto: Coach House, 1989.

– *Picture Theory*. Montréal: Nouvelle Optique [1982]. *Picture Theory*. Trans. Barbara Godard. New York: Roof Books, 1990.

– *She Would Be the First Sentence of My Next Novel / Elle serait la première phrase dans mon prochain roman*. Trans. Susanne de Lotbinière-Harwood. Toronto: Mercury, 1998.

– *Sous la langue / Under Tongue*. Trans. Susanne de Lotbinière-Harwood. Montreal: L'essentielle/Gynergy Books, 1987.

Brossard, Nicole, and Daphne Marlatt. *Mauve* and *Character / Jeu de lettres*. Montréal: NJB, 1986 and 1986. Rpt. in *À tout regard*. Montréal: BQ, 1989, 83–93, 95–108.

Cixous, Hélène. "Le rire de la méduse." *L'arc* [1975]. Trans. "The Laugh of the Medusa." *Signs* 1: 4 (1976): 875–93.

Conacher, Agnès. "Susanne de Lotbiniere-Harwood: Totally Between." *Writing between the Lines: Portraits of Canadian Anglophone Translators*. Ed. Agnes Whitfield. Waterloo: Wilfrid Laurier University Press 2006, 245–66.

De Lotbinière-Harwood, Susanne. "Deux mots pour chaque chose." *Tessera* 6 (1989): 24–6.

– *Re-belle et infidèle: La traduction comme pratique de réécriture au féminin / The Body Bilingual: Translation as a Rewriting in the Feminine*. Montréal/Toronto: Les éditions du remue-ménage / Women's Press, 1991.

Gagnon, Madeleine. "Corps I." Hélène Cixous, Madeleine Gagnon, and Annie Leclerc, *La venue à l'écriture*. Paris: UGE [1977]. "Body I." *New French Femi-*

nisms. Ed. Elaine Marks and Isabelle de Courtivron. Trans. Isabelle de Courtivron. Amherst, MA: Schocken Books, 1981, 179–80.

Gauvin, Lise. *Lettres d'une autre*. Montréal: L'Hexagone [1984]. Trans. Susanne de Lotbinière-Harwood. *Letters from an Other*. Toronto: Women's Press, 1989.

Godard, Barbara. "Translating and Sexual Difference." *Resources for Feminist Research / Documentation sur la recherche féministe* 13: 3 (1984): 13–16.

– "Theorizing Feminist Discourse / Translation." *Tessera* 6 (1989): 42–53.

– "Gender and Gender Politics in Literary Translation." *Encyclopedia of Literary Translation into English*. Ed. Olive Classe. Vol. 1. London: Fitzroy Dearborn, 2000, 501–12.

– Personal e-mail message, 31 March 2009.

– ed. *Collaboration in the Feminine: Writings on Women and Culture from* Tessera. Toronto: Second Story, 1994.

– Daphne Marlatt, Kathy Mezei, and Gail Scott. "Theorizing Fiction Theory." *Tessera* 3, *Canadian Fiction Magazine* 57 (1986): 6–12.

Homel, David, and Sherry Simon, eds. *Mapping Literature: The Art and Politics of Translation*. Montreal: Véhicule, 1988.

Knutson, Susan, Kathy Mezei, Daphne Marlatt, Barbara Godard, and Gail Scott. "Vers-ions Con-verse: À Sequence of Translations." *Tessera* 6 (1989): 153–61.

Maillet, Antonine. *Don l'Orignal*. Montréal: Lémeac [1977]. *The Tale of Don l'Orignal*. Trans. Barbara Godard. Toronto: Clarke Irwin, 1978.

Marchessault, Jovette. *Tryptique lesbienne*. Montréal: Éditions de la pleine lune [1980]. *Lesbian Triptych*. Trans. Yvonne M. Klein. Toronto: Women's Press, 1985.

Marlatt, Daphne. "Translating *Mauve*: Reading Writing." *Tessera* 6 (1989): 27–30.

– *Salvage*. Red Deer: Red Deer College, 1991.

– *Readings from the Labyrinth*. Edmonton: NeWest, 1998.

Mezei, Kathy. "The Question of Gender in Translation: Examples from Denise Boucher and Anne Hébert." *Tessera* 3 (1986): 136–41.

Michelut, Dôre. "Coming to Terms with the Mother Tongue." *Tessera* 6 (1989): 63–71.

Notar, Clea H. "My Gentleman of the White Knights." *Tessera* 6 (1989): 76–80.

Rakusa, Ilma, and Rada Ivekovi . "The Translator Being Translated: An IRRI Project." *Tessera* 6 (1989): 59–62.

Resnick, Margery, and Isabelle de Courtivron. *Women Writers in Translation: An Annotated Bibliography, 1945–1982*. New York: Garland, 1984.

Scott, Gail. *Heroine*. Toronto: Coach House [1987]. Trans. Susanne de Lotbinière-Harwood. *Héroïne*. Montréal: Les éditions du remue-ménage, 1989.

Simon, Sherry. *Gender in Translation: Cultural Identity and the Politics of Transmission*. New York: Routledge, 1996.

Théoret, France. *The Tangible Word*. Trans. Barbara Godard. Montreal: Guernica, 1991.

Tostevin, Lola Lemire. "Contamination: A Relation of Differences." *Tessera* 6 (1989): 13–14.

Von Flotow, Luise. "Feminist Translation: Contexts, Practices, Theories." *TTR: Traduction, traductologie, rédaction* 4 (1991): 69–84.

– "Translating Women of the Eighties: Eroticism, Anger, Ethnicity." *Culture in Transit*. Ed. Sherry Simon. Montreal: Véhicule, 1995, 31–46.

– *Translation and Gender: Translating in the "Era of Feminism."* Ottawa: University of Ottawa Press, 1997.

17

1992: Translating Montreal's Yiddish Poet Jacob Isaac Segal into French

Pierre Anctil Translated by Deborah Shadd

Yiddish is a language spoken in Montreal since the beginning of the twentieth century, and although it has given birth to an important body of writing in the city, this Yiddish literature was not connected with the francophone literary corpus until relatively late. Not until 1992 was Montreal's Yiddish poetry translated into French for the first time and presented to a readership that, for the most part, had never before been able to grasp its meaning or understand its contribution to their literary culture. The appearance in 1992 of *Poèmes Yiddish*, by Jacob Isaac Segal, a collection bringing echoes of the Eastern European Jewish world, was all the more startling since the book was organized in the Hebrew manner – from a Western point of view – with the order of pages reversed. Published by Éditions du Noroît, the volume included the original texts in Hebrew script, presented side by side with their French translations, a format curiously chosen despite the fact that those most interested in the translation could not read the original, nor even decipher its basic elements. The surprise that resulted from this publication, moreover, was not limited to the francophone population discovering this unpronounceable author, but even extended into the contemporary Jewish community to which Jacob Isaac Segal belonged. For while a fair number of Montreal's Jews could no doubt read a Yiddish poem with a little effort, many of them did not know French well enough to understand the version relayed by the translator. On both sides, then, the simultaneous presentation of Yiddish and French initially produced an overwhelming sense of inadequacy, as though the interaction of these two languages, which had practically never come together before in the Canadian context, could only result in mutual incomprehension.

This sense of uncertainty about the unreadable Jew, however, had already long been present in the collective imagination of francophone Montrealers, not least because the language and its script had during a certain period been boldly displayed in the city's streets, most notably along St Laurent Boulevard and on adjacent streets during the interwar years. Yiddish had also been abundantly heard in the markets and businesses of Montreal's largest immigrant quarter, reverberating with its unique guttural sonority and leaving indelible traces in certain works by, for example, Gabrielle Roy and Yves Thériault. Still remotely present in memory like a vague shadow falling on a western-facing wall, Yiddish somehow continues to captivate by its absence and by its silence, now so unchanging in the city:

> Yiddish is for me the perfect example of a language that I do not know at all, not even the alphabet, and yet that I can never class among those languages that are foreign to me. [...]

> What, then, is this familiarity, so mysterious and opaque, that binds me to Yiddish? [...]

> Yiddish lives in me even though I am not Jewish. It is an integral part of my cultural universe, a part of that great adventure of languages – an adventure that is at once universal and particular to Montreal – that every writer senses is near, that every writer and intellectual in Montreal experiences in the deepest part of themselves where languages seek life, creating against all odds, warding off those forces of nature that, sooner or later, bend them, deform them, and often utterly destroy them. (Nepveu 72–6)

The publication of *Poèmes Yiddish* thus prompted an awakening, as if the veil had been lifted, at least in part, from the identity and the appearance of someone who had vanished, that few really remembered ever having near, but that remained like a haunting memory from the distant past. Suddenly, the language was familiar again, readable, and almost audible, and it brought with it a series of evocative images familiar to every Montrealer: the port, the mountain, Jeanne-Mance Park, the narrow streets of Plateau Mont-Royal.

The movement from one alphabet to another also shed light on the vulnerability of the author, his long journey to North America from the Ukraine, the suffering he experienced, and above all, his desire to remain Jewish even while grasping at literary modernity with all his being. Nothing similar had ever appeared in French in Montreal up to that point. And although, according to Pierre Nepveu, "in the context of Montreal, Yiddish is a language that never stops rising to the surface, whether through allusion or reference," this time Segal's work brought it forth in all its splendour – rich, perplexing, and somehow so near to the heart of Montreal's francophones. A door was opened that would never again be closed, and through this ever tenuous opening, a radical redefinition of Montreal's literary corpus would eventually emerge, challenging perceptions of a reality that, up to that point, was thought to be shared by only two.

Yiddish belongs to a vast constellation of eastern and southern European languages, dialects, and regional vernaculars that first took root in Canada at the beginning of the twentieth century, among also German, Polish, Russian, Ukrainian, and Italian, most often in non-conventional varieties and non-standard forms. It is difficult to be more precise than this, however, in the absence of research yet to be done on the many publications, periodicals, and newspapers that appeared in Canada over the past hundred or so years. Most often, the abundance and vitality of such writing was found only within communities that were clearly delimited both geographically and socially; and for the most part, the leading figures within these communities did not pass on their mother tongues as an enduring inheritance for their Canadian descendants. Community association reports, parish bulletins, the personal memoirs of immigrants, record books from the *landsmanshaftn*, political campaign posters, literary monthlies, newspapers, and regional newsletters, not to mention the countless manuscripts never published, represent as many reflections of this production in non-official languages, covering a vast and diverse array of topics, depending on the time period and organization considered. The emotions of immigrants at the moment of their arrival in Canada were recorded on the pages of simple notebooks, of bound volumes, and of printed newspapers, the obstacles that they met along the way were described, and the aspirations they held as new citizens were revealed.

In the midst of this multilingual abundance on Canadian soil, however, one language in particular stood out, distinguished by the quality of its literary production, the scope of its inspiration, and the force of its creativity: Yiddish (Baumgarten). Although spoken by little more than 2 per cent of the immigrants who arrived as part of the influx between 1905 and 1914, Yiddish benefited from several advantages in Canada, one of which was that nearly all of those who spoke or wrote it were grouped together in three large, booming cities: Montreal, Toronto, and Winnipeg. Within these leading urban centres, Eastern European Jewish institutions quickly became so common that Yiddish newspapers began to appear even before the First World War, the first of them in Montreal in 1907. Yiddish-language libraries and cultural centres, intellectual and literary circles, schools, and political parties soon combined to create a fertile cultural environment, complete with debates and activities of all sorts (Anctil, "Les communautés juives de Montréal"). By grouping in this way on Canadian soil, Eastern European Jews reproduced the conditions they had traditionally known in the Old World, where they had most often lived in mid-sized cities. They were by far the most educated of the immigrants who arrived during this period (Rosenberg), and they were also the most likely to be engaged in literary writing in the modern sense of the term.

Given this context, Yiddish soon developed the most significant body of literature in a non-official language in twentieth-century Canada (Anctil, "À la découverte de la littérature yiddish montréalaise" and "Writing as Immigrants: Yiddish Belles-Lettres in Canada"). In 1980, a biographical dictionary of Canadian authors who wrote in Yiddish or Hebrew appeared in Montreal, penned by Haim-Leib Fuks and entitled *Hundert yor Yidishe oun Hebreyshe literatur in Kanade*. It presented a record of 429 authors of Eastern European descent who had published in this country at one point or another in their careers (Fuks). In the Yiddish-Canadian sphere, writing initially produced for strictly pragmatic, collective, or journalistic purposes was soon transformed into a veritable literary outburst. And as immigration slowly resumed in the years following the First World War, young Yiddish-speaking immigrants found in their hearts the inspiration to begin writing poetry, and in the world around them, the material resources needed to print their first collections. In 1917, in Winnipeg, for example, Ezekiel Bronstein (Brownstone) published a short manuscript of 64 pages entitled *Blitsen* (Flashes). Most notable of all, though, was Jacob Isaac Segal, a young factory worker turned teacher at Montreal's Peretz School, who in 1918 published a sixty-seven-page collection under the title *Foun mayn velt* (Of My Universe). It was a remarkable work, not only for its literary maturity, but also for its decidedly Canadian inspiration. This was followed, over the course of the 1920s and 1930s in the three aforementioned Canadian cities, by the publication of a whole series of serious literary monthlies, including *Nyuansn* (Nuances), *Royerd* (Virgin Ground), *Epokhe* (Epoch), *Baginen* (Dawn), *In gevirbl* (In the Whirlwind), *Kanade* (Canada), *Heftn* (Notebooks), and *Montreal*.

The pages of these periodicals introduced not less than twenty or so literary talents worthy of note, most of whom later published at least one collection of Yiddish poetry. Among the most talented of these authors were Jacob Isaac Segal, Ida Maze, Sholem Shtern, Abraham Shlomo Shkolnikov, Noah Isaac Gotlib, Esther Segal, and Yudika. After the Second World War, one last group of Yiddish-speaking survivors arrived in Montreal, among them several poets and literary figures who earned recognition stretching well beyond the city limits. Here the exceptional contributions of Rokhl Korn, Chava Rosenfarb, Melekh Ravitch, and Mordechai Husid deserve to be underlined. Nevertheless, despite the brilliance of these Yiddish-Canadian literary accomplishments and the subsequent diffusion of these writings through a number of European, North American, and Latin American cities during the first half of the twentieth century, no significant mark was made on the country's cultural sphere. Yiddish as a literary language was, in the end, a matter of only one generation in Canada, a generation that had been born in Eastern Europe. Only those who had grown up with the language from their earliest childhood and who had arrived in the New World in an era when Jewish Canadians still spoke it on a daily basis chose to write in Yiddish. Of the 429 authors listed by Haim-Leib Fuks in 1980, only six were born in Canada, into families that held onto their linguistic and cultural heritage in a more lasting way. After 1942, for reasons due in large part to their education in the city's Protestant school system, young Jews drawn towards a literary career judged without exception that, in the long run, it would be easer and more profitable for them to pen their works in English.

This abrupt linguistic turn, led by authors such as Irving Layton, A.M. Klein, Mordecai Richler, and Leonard Cohen, did not prevent Montreal's Yiddish literary scene from continuing to develop and assert itself right through the 1960s and 1970s, until the domain of these Canadian immigrants inexorably began to shrink. Yiddish literature, however, did not completely disappear from the landscape of Jewish Montreal even after that date; still today, one can find venues celebrating its accomplishments and triumphs, but little by little, it has withdrawn into smaller and more private circles. Although common to all Jews prior to the Second World War, today Yiddish has come to belong primarily to those whose parents and grandparents survived the Holocaust and for whom this language is the best way of commemorating the enormous struggle of the inhabitants of the ghettos and their supporters who fought against Nazi oppression. Yiddish literature is unknown today to most of the Jews born in Canada, many of whom seem to have forgotten that they are descended from immigrants assimilated into English only one generation ago. And, until very recently, Yiddish literature had never crossed the linguistic and cultural divide that separates the Ashkenazi community of Montreal from the francophone majority.

In the beginning, Yiddish-Canadian literature was translated by immigrants and the descendants of immigrants, all of whom followed their natural inclination towards English, the receptive society's language of cultural assimilation. The first to attempt bridging this gap was Miriam Waddington who, in 1969, translated eight of Jacob Isaac Segal's poems for inclusion in an American anthology edited by Irving Howe and Eliezar Greenberg (*A Treasury of Yiddish Poetry*). In 1976, Abraham Boyarsky and Lazar Sarna undertook an anthology that presented English translations of Yiddish literature drawn solely from Montreal, aided by the work of A.M. Klein, Seymour Levitan, Seymour Mayne, and Judith Rotstein, among others (Boyarsky and Sarna). Sholem Shtern, himself a Polish writer who immigrated to Canada in 1927, sought to further this trend by obtaining a grant from Multiculturalism Canada to translate his own poetry into the country's two official languages. Judith Rotstein was entrusted with the task of translating the poems into English and Guy Maheux that of translating them into French, although the latter worked from the English text rather than the original, without any direct reference to Yiddish culture and tradition (see Shtern, *Au Canada*; *In Canada*; *La famille au Canada*; *The Household of Professor Sydney Goldstein / La maisonnée du professeur Sydney Goldstein*; *Nostalgie et tristesse: mémoires littéraires du Montréal yiddish*; *Velvl*; and *The White House*). Unfortunately, the result was far from convincing, in part, because the translators were not up to the task, particularly where the French was concerned, but also because the volumes in question were not published by recognized firms and their circulation was, in the end, almost negligible. Moreover, the author, despite all his good intentions about intercultural dialogue, did not speak French and, to the day he died, never developed the social skills that would have allowed him to move freely within the more influential francophone cultural circles (Margolis).

In the years that followed, three Anglo-Canadian translators, Seymour Levitan, Rivka Augenfeld, and Seymour Mayne, compiled their work to produce several small volumes, each containing about thirty poems, some of which appeared in a Yiddish-English bilingual edition, all of which had very limited circulation (Korn, *Generations: Selected Poems* and *Paper Roses*; Ratvitch). Some of these poems were later republished in *The Penguin Book of Modern Yiddish Verse* (Howe at al.), another American anthology, which appeared in 1987 and particularly seemed to highlight three Canadian poets: Rokhl Korn, Melekh Ratvitch, and Jacob Isaac Segal (even if in the first two cases the pieces chosen belonged mainly to the pre-Holocaust, European phase of their writing). Other significant translations from Yiddish into English included those done by Goldie Morgentaler of works written by her mother, Chava Rosenfarb – an author who arrived in Montreal immediately after the Second World War – including a trilogy called *Der boym foun lebn* (*The Tree of Life: A Trilogy of Life in the Lodz Ghetto*). More recently, Morgentaler brought together in a single English volume entitled *Survivors: Seven Short Stories* Rosenfarb's short stories about life in Canada for survivors of the Nazi concentration camps. Mervin Butovsky and Ode Garfinkle's translation of the diary of Yaacov Zipper, a Montreal teacher and Yiddish author originally from Poland (Zipper, *The Journals of Yaacov Zipper*), should also be noted here, along with Rhea Tregebov's anthology of Yiddish writers, *Arguing with the Storm*.

These efforts, although quite successful in terms of fidelity to the text and literary in form, did not, for the most part, reach Quebec's francophone readers, many of whom were not even aware of the existence of such quality Yiddish literature in Montreal. As is so often the case in these situations, the seeds that were planted could not germinate and grow, lacking a soil truly prepared for intercultural exchange on a broad scale. The most decisive turn came with the adoption of the Charter of the French Language in 1978 and with the subsequent enrolment of Montreal's young allophone immigrants in the Francophone school system. Over the course of the decade that followed, it became increasingly evident that welcoming linguistic and religious diversity had become an important responsibility of the Francophone majority and that the nationalist sentiments of one portion of the population, in fact, called for an openness towards difference. Only then did it become possible to truly advance the discovery of other literary traditions in Montreal (Anctil, "Sortie de crise linguistique au Québec"). Confident that their own language would survive, francophones suddenly realized that there were other communities, including Yiddish-speaking Jews, who were even more minoritized and also struggling to maintain their existence in Montreal. Two events that occurred in the same year served as catalysts for this unanticipated discovery, one of which was the presentation of Goldie Morgentaler's Yiddish translation of *Les belles-sœurs*, by Michel Tremblay, at the Centre Saidye-Bronfman in the spring of 1992 (see the chapter by Rebecca Margolis in this volume); the other was Éditions du Noroît's autumn publication of an anthology of poems by Montreal's great Yiddish poet, Jacob Isaac Segal, prepared by the author of this essay.

That Tremblay could find a place so near to the heart of the Jewish community, thanks in no small part to Dora Wasserman, that great lady of Yiddish theatre, carried extraordinary resonance and captured the attention of the francophone media. And Segal, in turn, found his place side by side with the francophone poets of the day, published in a Yiddish-French bilingual edition by a publisher well known for the seriousness and quality of its production. This time, Yiddish entered the francophone cultural sphere by the front door, against a background now favourably set to recognize the cultural and linguistic pluralism that had existed in the city since the beginning of the twentieth century. Other translations followed through the late 1990s and early 2000s, including translations of memoirs of immigrants who arrived in Canada prior to 1914 (see Belkin; Elberg; Medresh; Wolofsky). Montreal soon emerged as the only city of the Eastern European Jewish diaspora where Yiddish works were translated simultaneously into two languages for the benefit of two separate readerships. Several chapters of Sholem Shtern's *Shrayber vos ikh hob gekent, esayn un memuarn* later reappeared in 2006, this time under the title *Nostalgie et tristesse: mémoires littéraires du Montréal yiddish*. Ironically, the poet who thirty years earlier had been unable to break into the francophone book market for want of appropriate resources now posthumously found a place in the collection *Chemins de traverse*, published by Éditions du Noroît, in the company of leading authors like Saint-Denys Garneau, Jacques Brault, and Fernand Ouellette.

In the gradual process of rendering Yiddish literature readable and familiar, even for the Québécois Jews themselves, translation has played and continues to play a key role. It is thanks to translation that we can now look back from where we stand and retrace the movement of the impetuous torrent of Montreal's Yiddish creativity, finding its source in the previous century's flood of immigration from Eastern Europe. It is thanks to translation that we can trace it even further back, finding its roots in the writing of the Hebrew alphabet begun much longer ago. In this way, nearly a hundred years of Yiddish literary activity in Canada seems to be taking shape for the first time before our very eyes, and translators are the only ones who can patiently unearth this tradition from the nearly impenetrable clay into which the forgetfulness of some and the ignorance of others have caused it to sink. And what is thus revealed is not merely the scattered vestiges of a misunderstood corpus but rather a fully developed structure with its foundations still intact. Slowly, but surely, Yiddish literature is assuming its place beside the two other Montreal literatures that have long been explored and that are still active today. What a surprise to discover that over the course of the twentieth century the city gave birth not to two, but to at least three literary corpuses, each inspired by a distinct European intellectual and artistic tradition. Who would have thought that the culture of Montreal, so long perceived as a well-synchronized duet, would now have to make room for new performers in its concert? Although still very few in number, translators of Yiddish literature face a task already laid out in a literary field that has only just begun to flourish. It is the task of making available to readers the texts that reflect the surprised expressions of young allophone immigrants arriving in Canada in an era when the country was for the first time displaying all the allure of its cosmopolitan cities and the power of its industrial machine.

Works Cited

Anctil, Pierre. "Les communautés juives de Montréal." *Le patrimoine des minorités religieuses du Québec, richesse et vulnérabilité*. Ed. Marie-Claude Rocher and Marc Pelchat. Quebec City: Presses de l'Université Laval, 2006, 37–60.

– "À la découverte de la littérature yiddish montréalaise." *New Readings of Yiddish Montreal / Traduire le Montréal Yiddish*. Ed. Pierre Anctil, Norman Ravvin, and Sherry Simon. Ottawa: University of Ottawa Press, 2007, 19–30.

– "Writing as Immigrants: Yiddish Belles-Lettres in Canada." *What Is Your Place? Indigeneity and Immigration in Canada*. Ed. Hartmut Lutz. Augsburg: Wißner-Verlag, 2007, 118–42.

– Norman Ravvin, and Sherry Simon, eds. *New Readings of Yiddish Montreal / Traduire le Montréal yiddish / Taytshn oun ibertaytshn yidish in Montreal*. Ottawa: University of Ottawa Press, 2007.

– "Sortie de crise linguistique au Québec: L'apprentissage du français par les immigrants selon les données du recensement fédéral de 2001." *Revue d'études canadiennes / Journal of Canadian Studies* 41: 2 (2007): 185–212.

Baumgarten, Jean. *Le yiddish, histoire d'une langue errante*. Paris: Albin Michel, 2002.

Belkin, Simon. *Le mouvement ouvrier juif au Canada, 1904–1920 / Di Poale-Zion Bavegung in Kanade, 1904–1920*. [1956]. Trans. and preface Pierre Anctil. Sillery: Septentrion, 1999.

Boyarsky, Abraham, and Lazar Sarna. *Canadian Yiddish Writing*. Montreal: Harvest House, 1976.

Bronstein (Brownstone), Ezekiel. *Blitsen* [Éclairs]. Winnipeg: Dos Id. Vort, 1917.

Elberg, Yehuda. *L'Empire de Kalman l'infirme / Kalman Kalikes Imperye*. [1983]. Trans. Pierre Anctil. Montréal: Leméac/Actes Sud, 2001.

Fuks, Haim-Leib. *Cent ans de littérature yiddish et hébraïque au Canada / Hundert yor Yidishe oun Hebreyshe literatur in Kanade*. [1980]. Trans. and pref. Pierre Anctil. Sillery: Septentrion, 2005.

Howe, Irving, and Eliezer Greenberg. *A Treasury of Yiddish Poetry*. New York: Holt, Rinehart and Winston, 1969.

– et al. *The Penguin Book of Modern Yiddish Verse*. New York: Penguin, 1987.

Korn, Rokhl. *Generations: Selected Poems*. Trans. Rivka Augenfeld et al. Oakville: Mosaic, 1982.

– *Paper Roses*. Yiddish-English Edition. Trans. Seymour Levitan. Toronto: Aya Press, 1985.

Margolis, Rebecca. "Sholem Shtern, Bridging the Gaps." Ed. Pierre Anctil, Norman Ravvin, and Sherry Simon. Ottawa: University of Ottawa Press, 2007, 93–102.

Medresh, Israël. *Le Montréal juif d'autrefois / Montreal foun nekhtn.* [1947] Trans. and preface Pierre Anctil. Sillery: Septentrion, 1997.

– *Le Montréal juif entre les deux guerres / Tsvishn tsvey velt milkhomes.* [1964] Trans. and preface Pierre Anctil. Sillery: Septentrion, 2001.

Nepveu, Pierre. "Traduit du yiddish: Échos d'une langue inconnue." *New Readings of Yiddish Montreal / Traduire le Montréal Yiddish.* Ed. Pierre Anctil, Norman Ravvin, and Sherry Simon. Ottawa: University of Ottawa Press, 2007, 72–6.

Ravitch, Melekh. *Night Prayer and Other Poems.* Trans. Seymour Mayne with Rivka Augenfeld. Oakville: Mosaic, 1993.

Rosenberg, Louis. *Canada's Jews: A Social and Economic Study of Jews in Canada in the 1930s.* [1939]. Montreal and Kingston: McGill-Queen's University Press, 1993.

Rosenfarb, Chava. *Survivors: Seven Short Stories.* Trans. Goldie Morgentaler. Toronto: Cormorant Books, 2004.

– *The Tree of Life: A Trilogy of Life in the Lodz Ghetto / Der boym foun lebn.* [1972]. Trans. by the author with Goldie Morgentaler. 3 vols. Madison: University of Wisconsin Press, 2004.

Segal, Jacob-Isaac. *Foun mayn velt* [De mon univers]. Montreal: City Printing, 1918.

– *Yidishe lider / Poèmes yiddish.* Bilingual ed. Yiddish-French. Trans. Pierre Anctil. Montréal: Éditions du Noroît, 1992.

Shtern, Sholem. *In Canada: A Novel in Verse / In Kanade.* [1963]. Trans. Judith Rotstein. Montreal: Jewish School Publishing House, 1984.

– *The White House: A Novel in Verse / Dos vayse hoyz.* [1967]. Trans. Max Rosenfeld. Montreal: New York: Warbrooke, 1974.

– *The Family in Canada: A Novel in Verse / Di mishpokhe in Kanade.* [1975]. Trans. Judith Rotstein. Montreal: Published privately, 1984.

– *The Household of Professor Sydney Goldstein: A Novel in Verse / La maisonnée du professeur Sydney Goldstein: Un roman en vers / Dos hoyzgezint foun profesor Sidni Goldshteyn.* [1975]. Trans. Judith Rotstein (Yiddish to English), and Guy Maheux (English to French). Montreal: Published privately, 1984.

– *Velvl: Roman.* Trans. Guy Maheux. Montreal: Société de belles-lettres Guy Maheux, 1977.

– *Au Canada: Un roman en vers.* Trans. Guy Maheux. Montreal: Published privately, 1984.

– *La famille au Canada: Un roman en vers*. Trans. Guy Maheux. Montreal: Published privately, 1984.

– *Nostalgie et tristesse: Mémoires littéraires du Montréal yiddish / Shrayber vos ikh hob gekent, esayn oun memuarn*. [1982]. Trans. (in part) preface and comments Pierre Anctil. Montréal: Éditions du Noroît, 2006.

Tregebov, Rhea, ed. *Arguing with the Storm: Stories by Yiddish Women Writers*. Toronto: Sumach, 2007.

Wolofsky, Hirsch. *Mayn Lebns Rayze: Un demi-siècle de vie yiddish à Montréal et ailleurs dans le monde / Mayn lebns rayze: Zikhroynes foun iber a halbn yorhundert yidish lebn in der alter oun nayer velt*. [1946]. Trans. and preface Pierre Anctil. Sillery: Septentrion, 2000.

Zipper, Yaacov. *The Journals of Yaacov Zipper, 1950–1982: The Struggle for Yiddishkeit*. Trans. Mervin Butovsky and Ode Garfinkle. Montreal and Kingston: McGill-Queen's University Press, 2004.

18

1992: Through Translation, Mordecai Richler's *Oh Canada! Oh Quebec!* Generates Controversy in English and French

Julie McDonough Dolmaya

In mid-September 1991, days before Mordechai Richler's essay "Inside/ Outside" appeared in the 23 September 1991 *New Yorker*, excerpts from it were already coming out in French translation, starting with an article in *La Presse* (Leblanc A1). And well before the book that developed from this essay (*Oh Canada! Oh Quebec! Requiem for a Divided Country*, 1992) was translated into French by Daniel Poliquin (1992) and published by Les Éditions Balzac, various excerpts from it had appeared in numerous newspapers and magazines and been discussed on the air, in political cartoons, letters to the editor, and even in Canada's House of Commons, causing controversy that had such an impact it was still being cited years later in Richler's obituaries in 2001. The controversies circulated around a number of topics, including antisemitism in Quebec, Lionel Groulx's influence on Quebec's birth rate, unemployment in Newfoundland and Prince Edward Island, and the ostensibly lowly roots of some Quebecers and other Canadians.

This study of the effects of the French translations on the reception of Richler's work focuses on translations produced by and published in the media, comparing them to the influence of the "official" translation by Daniel Poliquin.

French Translations of "Inside/Outside" and *Oh Canada! Oh Quebec!*

In September 1992, only five months after the release of the English book, Les Éditions Balzac published a French translation of *Oh Canada! Oh Quebec!* by Daniel Poliquin. Although Poliquin originally had some misgivings about the book, he realized after reading it that, "[it] was innocent, [it was] nothing [...] I said, 'No, there's something wrong there.' We are being told by Lise Bissonnette in *Le Devoir* and other people not to read that book. There was even a Member of Parliament who said that the book should be banned. And then I said, 'No, this is the Inquisition, this is the auto-da-fé, the act of faith'" (Interview with the author). Accordingly, Poliquin's goal for the translation was to give Richler a chance; if francophones listened to Richler, Poliquin believed they would realize what he said was "really no big deal." Moreover, Poliquin wanted to give francophones the opportunity to read the full text, since the only French versions of *Oh Canada! Oh Quebec!* available prior to Poliquin's translation were short excerpts in the press (Interview with the author). These articles, which appeared in such French-Canadian periodicals such as *L'Actualité* and *La Presse*, sparked what came to be called "the Richler affair."[1]

On 17 September 1991, *La Presse* published an article by Gérald Leblanc about "Inside/Outside" with two translated passages, each in quotation marks. One is Richler's prediction that Montreal will continue to decline because anglophone Quebecers feel unwelcome in Quebec and will continue to leave. The other is a passage that was widely lambasted in the French-Canadian press: "Ce pénible niveau de reproduction, basé, me semble-t-il, sur la notion que les femmes étaient des truies, a été encouragé par le chanoine Groulx, le champion de la revanche des berceaux" (A1).[2]

Then, in March 1992, *La Presse* published another article about Richler with two more translated citations, this time from the book, *Oh Canada! Oh Quebec!* They are as follows:

> Examinez la question sous cet angle. Plusieurs des Québécois pure laine ou de vieille souche sont, en fait, les rejetons des filles du roi, ces prostituées amenées en Nouvelle-France par l'intendant Jean-Baptiste Talon pour satisfaire aux besoins primaires de ses soldats illettrés.

> Les troupes loyalistes n'ont guère une descendance plus noble, poursuit [Richler], eux qui sont sortis de la cuisse de "réactionnaires obsédés ou de repris de justice [...] de voleurs, de prostituées et d'arnaqueurs de deuxième ordre." Quant au premier ministre René Lévesque, "il n'a jamais été à la hauteur de sa réputation d'honnêteté." (Girard B1)[3]

Finally, on 1 April 1992, *L'Actualité* published a book review/article about *Oh Canada! Oh Quebec!* with numerous citations from the book, all of which had presumably been translated into French by Jean-François Lisée, the author of the article. These translations are different from the version eventually published in September 1992 by Daniel Poliquin. While more than ten passages are quoted in Lisée's article, several examples here will suffice:

> [Richler] met en parallèle "le cri racial plaintif 'Le Québec aux Québécois!' entendu dans les rues de Montréal et la révolte des nerds de l'Ouest, c'est-à-dire la montée du Reform Party."

> [Richler] informe aussi ses lecteurs que "la majorité des habitants de Terre-Neuve et de l'Ile-du-Prince-Édouard passent traditionnel-lement l'hiver en chômage." (B1)

> L'amère vérité est que la Sûreté du Québec n'assommaient pas les autochtones plus souvent que la police de l'État de Californie ne fait éclater la tête des Noirs ou des Hispaniques ou – et je déteste avoir à l'admettre – que les soldats israéliens ne brisent les os des enfants palestiniens. (11)[4]

Other articles in the French-Canadian press also cite passages from "Inside/Outside" or *Oh Canada! Oh Quebec!* before the book was available in translation, but *La Presse* and *L'Actualité* are the only sources to use quotation marks, thus giving the translations greater effect, as they are not intended to be received as paraphrases, but rather as Richler's exact wording. Whether these are accurate renderings of Richler's English is a question best answered by examining these translations, comparing them with the work done by Poliquin, and studying their effect in Canada.

The Effect of the "Official" Translation in the Richler Affair

One way to assess the effect of a translation is to determine whether it was read and prompted responses. An influential work could be expected to be reviewed and discussed in the press, thus helping circulate the author's ideas. This is obviously what happened with the English version of *Oh*

Canada! Oh Quebec! as the numerous editorials, book reviews, letters to the editor, and television and radio interviews attest.[5] But what about Poliquin's French version, *Oh Canada! Oh Québec! Requiem pour un pays divisé*? A search through the archives of the French-Canadian Press reveals that Poliquin's translation seems to have passed almost unnoticed.[6]

While Richler's book was quoted in the French-Canadian press on several occasions after 1992, Daniel Poliquin's translation, for the most part, was not. The first post-1992 reference to *Oh Canada! Oh Quebec!* is in *L'Actualité*, which notes that "À propos du taux de fécondité dans les années 30, [Richler] expliquait que, encouragés par l'abbé Lionel Groulx, les Québécois 'prenaient leurs femmes pour des truies'!" (Vastel 62). This is not Poliquin's translation,[7] nor is it identical to other versions circulating in the French-Canadian Press in the early 1990s. It appears to be yet another journalistic creation. Another reference to *Oh Canada! Oh Quebec!* appeared in a 2001 obituary for Richler published in *Le Devoir*:[8] "[Richler] ridiculise par exemple les 'miliciens autoproclamés de la cause linguistique,' gardiens féroces des exigences souvent loufoques de la loi sur l'affichage commercial traquant les mots anglais, honnis, bannis, comme des injures" (Baillargeon, "Mordecai Richler, 1931–2001," A1); once again, this translation is not Poliquin's.[9] Whose is it?

One year later, another reference to *Oh Canada! Oh Quebec!* can be found in a letter to the editor of *Le Devoir*, where an entire paragraph from page 98 of Richler's book was reprinted, but in English (Legault A6). Two other quotes were printed in *Le Soleil* in Richler's 2001 obituary: "En 1992 [...] l'auteur écrivait que 'depuis le début, le nationalisme canadien-français a été fortement teinté de racisme'" and "Dans son livre *Oh Canada! Oh Quebec!* Richler s'était attaqué à René Lévesque qui, selon lui, 'ne méritait pas sa réputation d'honnêteté'" (Tremblay A6). These two quotations are taken directly from the translated excerpts in Lisée's April 1992 article in *L'Actualité* that appeared well before Poliquin's official translation in September 1992. They demonstrate the lasting effect of this journalistic representation of Richler's work on French-speaking Canadians.

A second obituary, this time in *La Presse*, also included quotes from *Oh Canada! Oh Quebec!* and here, for the first time, the French translation is identical to Poliquin's version published by Les Éditions Balzac; however, the author of the article does not cite Poliquin's translation as her source: "J'ai retrouvé la citation exacte dans le bouquin de Nadia Khouri, *Qui a peur de Mordecai Richler?"* (Petrowski C3). In this instance, then, Poliquin's translation is quoted only indirectly. A final reference to *Oh Canada! Oh Quebec!* occurs in 2007, when a letter to the editor was published in *Le Devoir.* This time, the French quotation is from *Oh Canada! Oh Québec! Requiem pour un pays divisé,* virtually the only citation from Poliquin's official work (Thilges-Lanners A10).

While these six articles are certainly not the only ones in the French-Canadian press to refer to *Oh Canada! Oh Québec!* after its official 1992 publication, they are the only examples with direct quotations from Richler. They seem to indicate that Poliquin's French translation had little effect in French Canada, as it was seldom consulted when journalists or the general public quoted Richler. Indeed, Poliquin notes that Les Éditions Balzac had been hoping *Oh Canada! Oh Québec!* would sell well (Interview with the author), since it was such a controversial book, but this was not the case: of the 3,000 copies initially printed, fewer than a thousand had sold three years later (Slopen H13), and of the French-language periodicals to review the book (e.g., *Spirale, L'Actualité, Le Devoir*), only *Le Devoir* reviewed the "official" French version (Saletti D1), although without mentioning the translator's name or commenting on the translation itself, further demonstrating the minimal effect Poliquin's translation had on the Richler Affair.

However, it would be a mistake to conclude that translation was not a vital element in the Richler Affair. Let us return to the media translations in *La Presse* and *L'Actualité,* and to the Member of Parliament referred to earlier.

The Media Translations of Richler and Their Effects

In the House of Commons on 16 March 1992, Bloc Québécois MP Pierrette Venne demanded that *Oh Canada! Oh Quebec!* be banned under section 319 of the Criminal Code, which addresses public incitement and wilful promotion of hatred. She explained that "when you describe the Quebec people as a nasty, racist tribe, that is hate propaganda" (cited in Fraser A1). And, key to assessing the importance of translation, Venne acknowledged that her request came not because she had read the book itself, but rather because she had read the excerpts printed in the *Gazette* and *L'Actualité.* She asserted, "What I have seen here, in *L'Actualité* and the *Gazette* is really, in its entirety, hate propaganda" (A1).[10] While Venne did consult an

English newspaper (the *Gazette*), as well, the fact that she drew conclusions from the *L'Actualité* article is important. It exemplifies the broader trend: many journalists and letter writers had read translations of *Oh Canada! Oh Quebec!* only in the French-Canadian press and based their reactions to the book on these French excerpts rather than on the original English text. In fact, these translations had such a lasting effect on Canadians that they continued to be quoted long after the more "official" translation was published by Les Éditions Balzac.

But how accurately do these translations portray Richler's ideas? They served as the basis for labelling his work "hate propaganda" and were quoted for years after their initial publication, perpetuating a decidedly negative image of Richler's book.

Lisée, in *L'Actualité*, clearly made an effort to select excerpts that depicted Quebec and Quebecers unfavourably: of the ten paragraphs that he quotes directly or indirectly from *Oh Canada! Oh Quebec!* virtually all say something negative. One criticizes René Lévesque, another Lionel Groulx, French-Canadian nationalism and Pierre Bourgault, a third the 1991 Fête nationale parade, and another Richler's omission of surveys contradicting his data that Quebecers were more antisemitic than other Canadians. When Lisée did quote a passage about another Canadian group (say, the inhabitants of Newfoundland and PEI, as cited above), his translation contains shifts that make these comments seem less offensive: in the English text, Newfoundlanders and Prince Edward Islanders "traditionally wintered on welfare" (*Oh Canada!* 149), while, in Lisée's translation, they "passent traditionnellement l'hiver en chômage" ("Mordecai Richler Rides Again" 11). A slight shift, but in Lisée's version, citizens of Newfoundland and PEI are merely unemployed, while in Richler's version they are living on taxpayers' money. In another passage about a non-Quebec group, Lisée omits a key term from his translation. When he mentions "la révolte des nerds de l'Ouest, c'est-à-dire la montée du Reform Party," Lisée omits the qualifier "equally xenophobic," which Richler used to describe the Reform Party,[11] thus removing Richler's strong criticism of this anglophone movement. In both cases described above, the effect is to make Richler less critical of English constituents, and more aggressive towards the French.

Lisée was not the only journalist to introduce translational shifts that made Richler seem more critical of Quebec and less critical of other groups. The 1992 *La Presse* translation also omits important qualifiers in its translation of the "filles du roi" passage. In *Oh Canada! Oh Quebec!*, Richler described "some of the Québécois pure laine," "mostly functionally illiterate soldiers" and "many of those United Empire Loyalists," but in Girard's translation, *some* of the Québécois pure laine become *plusieurs*, creating ambiguity in the French text, since "plusieurs" can mean "several" or even "many," in its Canadian sense. In other words, "some Québécois pure laine" become "many Québécois pure laine." In other instances, Richler's qualifier is simply omitted; the *mostly* functionally illiterate soldiers become completely illiterate, and the critical comments about many United Empire Loyalists in the English version are applied to *all* of them in the French. In the English text, these qualifiers temper Richler's words; when omitted in the translation, they reposition Richler as being far more provocative than he actually was. Finally, in Girard's version, the "illiterate" loyalist troops, the "troupes loyalistes" are not identified as ancestors of both French- and English-speaking Canadians, as in Richler's text, but exclusively of Quebecers, again suppressing Richler's criticism of both linguistic groups.

Likewise, the 1991 *La Presse* translation omits various details, without indicating to readers that cuts were made to the quoted text: in the French version, l'Abbé Groulx is the "champion de la revanche des berceaux," while in the English version, it was Groulx's newspaper *"L'Action française*, founded in 1917 [that] preached la revanche des berceaux, the revenge of the cradles, which would enable French-Canadians to become the majority in Canada" (Richler, "Inside/Outside," 49).

And so, although the official translation *Oh Canada! Oh Québec! Requiem pour un pays divisé* did not play a large role in the Richler Affair, the inaccurate press translations did, generating controversy that continued to circulate for months and even years afterward. While Richler certainly did criticize Quebec figures, institutions, and legislation, the journalists' French translations of his work depicted him as being far more critical of Quebec and far more one-sided than he actually was.

Notes

1 This term was used by many writers to label the controversy surrounding the publication of *Oh Canada! Oh Quebec!* and the *New Yorker* article that preceded it (see, e.g., Gagnon B3; Simon 52–4; Latouche A8; and Zerbisias A12).

2 This is a translation of a passage from p. 49 of "Inside/Outside" (and which

became, with a few minor alterations, pp. 13–14 of *Oh Canada! Oh Quebec!*):
"This punishing level of reproduction, which seemed to me to be based on
the assumption that women were sows, was encouraged with impunity from
the sidelines by l'Abbé Lionel Groulx, whose newspaper *L'Action française*,
founded in 1917, preached *la revanche des berceaux*, the revenge of the cradles,
which would enable French-Canadians to become the majority in Canada"
(Richler, "Inside/Outside," 46).

3 This is a translation of two passages from *Oh Canada! Oh Quebec!* The first
is from p. 102: "Look at it this way. Some of the *Québécois pure laine* or *de
vieille souche* are in fact the progeny of *les filles du roi*, or hookers, imported
to New France by Jean-Baptiste Talon to satisfy the appetites of his mostly
functionally illiterate soldiers. And many of those United Empire Loyalists –
from whom, Walter Stewart has written, one out of six English-speaking Canadians is descended – were either obdurate reactionaries or – *pace* Mrs C.M.
Day – refugees from justice, men without fixed principles, or designing and
unscrupulous adventurers." The second is from p. 132: "[René Lévesque]
nevertheless did not merit his reputation for honesty."

4 These are translations of three passages from *Oh Canada! Oh Quebec!*:
"Hence the plaintive racial cry in the streets of Montreal of '*Le Québec aux
Québécois!*' and out west the revolt of the nerds, that is to say, the sudden rise
of the equally xenophobic Reform Party" (101); "This meant that Mulroney's
constitutional fix could be undone by tiny Prince Edward Island or Newfoundland, most of whose citizens traditionally wintered on welfare" (149); and
"The sour truth is that the Sûreté didn't beat natives to pulp more often than
the California State Police cracked open the heads of blacks or Hispanics or –
much as I hate to admit it – Israeli soldiers broke the bones of Palestinian
children" (176).

5 For interviews, see Frum (*The Journal*) and Gzowski (*Morningside*). For book
reviews, essays, and letters to the editor, see, e.g., Bissonnette (A8); Graham
(C20); Granatstein (56); King (B2); Latouche (A8); McGoogan (B7); Saletti
(D1); Simon (52–4); and Zerbisias (A12).

6 This includes such periodicals as *Le Devoir, La Presse, Le Soleil, L'Actualité,*
and *Voir.*

7 Poliquin's translation: "Cette fécondité exténuante, qui *revenait à prendre les
femmes pour des truies*, était impunément encouragée en coulisses par l'abbé

Lionel Groulx, dont la revue *L'Action française*, fondée en 1917, prêchait *la revanche des berceaux**, qui permettrait aux Canadiens français de constituer la majorité au Canada" (Richler, *Oh Canada!* 24; emphasis added). Note: Poliquin used asterisks throughout his translation to indicate instances where words or phrases were originally in French in the English source text.

8 This quotation is identical to the one that appeared in an article by the same author published in *Le Monde* in 1999 (Baillargeon, "Mordecai Richler, le trublion").

9 This is a reference to p. 1 of *Oh Canada! Oh Quebec!*: "the photographer was one of a number of self-appointed vigilantes who, on lazy summer days off from work, do not head for the countryside to cool off in the woods or to fish; instead, they dutifully search the downtown streets for English-language or bilingual commercial signs that are an affront to Montreal's *visage linguistique*." Poliquin translates Richler's "self-appointed vigilantes" (*Oh Canada!* 1) with "justiciers improvisés" (*Oh Canada! Oh Quebec!* 11) instead of "miliciens autoproclamés."

10 This is likely a quotation from a comment originally made in French, but I was unable to find the French source.

11 "Hence the plaintive racial cry in the streets of Montreal of '*Le Québec aux Québécois!*' and out west the revolt of the nerds, that is to say, *the sudden rise of the equally xenophobic Reform Party*" (Richler, *Oh Canada!* 101; emphasis added). In Lisée's translation, "[Richler] met en parallèle 'le cri racial plaintif *Le Québec aux Québécois!*', entendu dans les rues de Montréal et la révolte des nerds de l'Ouest, c'est-à-dire *la montée du Reform Party*" ("Mordecai Richler Rides Again" 11).

Works Cited

Baillargeon, Stéphane. "Mordecai Richler, le trublion." *Le Monde*, 19 mars 1999, 3.

– "Mordecai Richler, 1931–2001: Écrivain surdoué, polémiste mordant." *Le Devoir*, 4 juillet 2001, A1.

Bissonnette, Lise. "Comme à Salisbury." *Le Devoir*, 18 mars 1992, A8.

Fraser, Graham. "BQ Urges Ottawa to Ban Richler's Book." *Globe and Mail*, 17 March 1992, A1, A2.

Frum, Barbara, host. *The Journal*. CBC. Television broadcast. 10 March 1992. http://archives.cbc.ca/arts_entertainment/media/topics/368-2023/

Gagnon, Lysiane. "L'affaire Richler." *La Presse*, 21 sept. 1991, B3.

Girard, Maurice. "Loin de condamner les écrits de Mordecai Richler, Joe Clark défend sa liberté d'expression." *La Presse*, 17 mars 1992, B1.

Graham, Ron. "Less Requiem than Rant." Rev. of *Oh Canada! Oh Quebec! Requiem for a Divided Country, by Mordecai Richler. Globe and Mail*, 28 March 1992, C20.

Granatstein, J.L. "Richler's Canadian Tragicomedy." Rev. of *Oh Canada! Oh Quebec! Requiem for a Divided Country*, by Mordecai Richler. *Quill & Quire* 58 (1992): 56.

Gzowski, Peter, host. *Morningside*. CBC. Radio Broadcast. 27 March 1992. http://archives.cbc.ca/IDCC-1-68-753-4613/arts_entertainment/mordecai_richler/

Khouri, Nadia. *Qui a peur de Mordecai Richler?* Candiac, QC: Balzac, 1995.

King, Norman. "Richler 'Should Apologize to Quebecois.'" *Gazette*, 24 Oct. 1991, B2.

Latouche, Daniel. "Le grand silence." *Le Devoir*, 28 mars 1992, A8.

Leblanc, Gérald. "Mordecai Richler se déchaine contre le Québec français." *La Presse*, 17 sept. 1991, A1.

Legault, Josée. "L'anglais, langue de travail." *Le Devoir*, 28 juin 2000, A6.

Lisée, Jean-François. "Mordecai Richler Rides Again." Rev. of *Oh Canada! Oh Quebec! Requiem for a Divided Country*, by Mordecai Richler. *L'Actualité*, 1 avril 1992, 11.

McDonough, Julie. "Framed! Translations, Paratexts and Narratives of Nationalism, Independence Movements and the 1980/1995 Referenda in Canada, 1968–2000, with Special Focus on Mordecai Richler's *Oh Canada! Oh Quebec!* and Pierre Vallières' *Nègres blancs d'Amérique*." Doctoral dissertation, Canadian Studies, University of Ottawa, 2009.

McGoogan, Kenneth. "Richler Reacts with Anger." Rev. of *Oh Canada! Oh Quebec! Requiem for a Divided Country*, by Mordecai Richler. *Calgary Herald*, 21 March 1992, B7.

Petrowski, Nathalie. "Goodbye Mordecai." *La Presse*, 5 juillet 2001, C3.

Poliquin. Daniel. "Interview with the author, 25 June 2008." Framed! Translations, Paratexts and Narratives of Nationalism, Independence Movements and the 1980/1995 Referenda in Canada, 1968–2000, with Special Focus on Mordecai Richler's *Oh Canada! Oh Quebec!* and Pierre Vallières' *Nègres blancs d'Amérique*. Julie McDonough, doctoral disseration, Canadian Studies, University of Ottawa, 2009.

"Richler's Distorted Mirror: Antisemitism Charges Are Excessive." *Gazette*,
   21 March 1992, B2.
Richler, Mordecai. "Inside/Outside." *New Yorker*, 23 Sept. 1991, 40–92.
– *Oh Canada! Oh Quebec! Requiem for a Divided Country*. Toronto: Penguin,
   1992.
– *Oh Canada! Oh Quebec! Requiem pour un pays divisé*. Trans. Daniel Poliquin.
   Candiac, QC: Balzac, 1992.
Saletti, Robert. "Mordecai Richler donne son âme au diable." Rev. of *Oh Canada!
   Oh Quebec! Requiem pour un pays divisé*, by Mordecai Richler. *Le Devoir*,
   3 oct. 1992, D1.
Simon, Sherry. "The Richler Affair." *Matrix* 38 (1992): 52–4.
Slopen, Beverley. "Richler Gains Allies on View of Quebec." *Toronto Star*, 22 April
   1995, H13.
Thilges-Lanners, Djo and Norbert. "Un mal-aimé?" *Le Devoir*, 13 nov. 2007, A10.
Tremblay, Régis. "Mordecai Richler, 1931–2001: La controverse s'éteint avec
   l'homme." *Le Soleil*, 4 juillet 2001, A6.
Vastel, Michel. "Le cas Richler." *L'Actualité*, 1 nov. 1996, 62.
Zerbisias, Antonia. "'Silence' over Richler Disturbs Quebecers." *Toronto Star*,
   21 March 1992, A12.

19

1998: The Artefactual Voice Within:
Terry Glavin's "Rain Language" Is Published

George Lang

> *Konoway tiillciums klatawa kunamokst klaska mamook okoke huloima chee illahie.*
> Everyone was thrown together to make this strange new country.
> – Iona Campagnolo, former Lieutenant-Governor of British Columbia
> (citing a line from "Rain Language")

"Rain Language" is a seventeen-page poem composed in alternating lines of English and Chinook jargon – henceforth, *Wawa*, its endonym, the name of the language in the language itself. "Rain Language" is the centrepiece of *A Voice Great within Us*, a defence and illustration of Wawa by the west coast poet and regional historian Charles Lillard. The poem itself is by Terry Glavin, who collaborated with Lillard and then, after Lillard's death in 1997, edited the manuscript for publication.

A Voice Great within Us is, beyond the pieces by Lillard and Glavin, a compendium of artefacts, visual and textual, which speak to the history of Wawa, the "hidden language of the Pacific Northwest" (Holton). There are extracts in and on Wawa, as well as a bilingual lexicon. "Artefacts" is meant here in the sense of objects that give information about the culture of their creators and users, but the question remains whether artefacts consisting of language should be considered natural objects or not, a distinction founded on the Aristotolean differentiation between things that "exist by nature" and things that are "products of art" or "artificial products." Within this framework, Risko Hilpinen argues that languages and words "can be [either] natural entities (without identifiable creators) or artefacts which have been intentionally designed for a certain purpose. In fact, many 'natural' languages, especially their written forms, can be regarded as artefacts" ("Artifact"). For instance, the choice and imposition of an orthography for any language already betrays the heavy hand of intention and is, therefore, artificial. Contact languages like pidgins and creoles and, in particular, the "special case of creolization," which is Wawa (Zenk), are natural linguistic phenomena, normal. But they are usually implicated in social projects aimed at promoting and defending them, or alternatively, at stomping them out, which amounts to the same type of project.

As an assemblage of artefacts, *A Voice Great within Us* is thus caught up not only in the ambiguities attached to any cultural artefact – an object said to represent a cultural practice – but also, and more compromisingly, in the contradictions inherent in the polemic construction of any language's history. Any narrative or theory of linguistic genesis contains a pre-emptive vision of who has spoken that language, how it should be spoken, and to whom that language belongs. If the language in question is "hidden" or "within us" and revealed only through exposition of its artefacts, then neutrality is even more problematic.

The roots of Wawa go back to the first contact of marine fur traders with the Nootka (now Nuuchahnulth) on the west coast of Vancouver Island, notably, at the time of Captain Cook. Although the default lingua franca on the northwest coast during most of the nineteenth century, Wawa was spoken fluently almost exclusively by Aboriginal peoples or those in close and frequent contact with them. The two most vital communities of speakers surviving into the twentieth century were residents of the Grand Ronde reservation southwest of Portland, Oregon, which continues to lay claim to Wawa as a heritage language, and the cluster of Central Salish speakers around Kamloops, for whom it was a vehicle of Christian proselytization and communion. It continued to flourish along the British Columbia coast during the first half of the twentieth century wherever interethnic communication was a necessity and English had not yet imposed itself. Glavin put it nicely: "The greatest assaults on Chinook [jargon] were all those forces that combined to undermine the *interdependence* of settler and aboriginal communities" ("Damned Rascal" 37). There is thus something of a contradiction between Glavin's personal judgment that Wawa hinged on the interdependence of settler and Aboriginal societies and the sanguine and typically multicultural "new Canadian" vision evoked by Lieutenant-Governor Iona Campagnolo in the epigraph above, itself from "Rain Language": "Everyone was thrown together to make this strange new country" (27). But some of us were thrown together more than others, with the general intention that these others were to be thrown out. To imagine that Wawa offers an inner voice for the post-settler society that has long since taken virtually full possession of the land is (poetic) fantasy.

But why not? "Rain Language" is a poem, and *A Voice Great within Us* as a whole is poetic in its intentions, a projected vision of British Columbia and the Pacific northwest rooted in the poetic traditions of west coast writers on both sides of the 49th parallel. Although I have qualified Wawa as "the notional 'national' language of a unified and ecologically correct Cascadia" (Lang 141), that poetic field, as it were, stretches beyond Cascadia as usually defined. And it is with reference to those poetics that Terry Glavin composed "Rain Language," a strangely inverted self-translation, since the Wawa phrases come first, although it is safe to conclude that English was the guiding hand as he wrote. This is not to impugn Glavin's control of Wawa, but only to recognize the precarious and dependent state of Wawa in the contemporary world.

The seven sections of "Rain Language" recount the history of Wawa, making it in Pound's terms an epic, a poem about history, although this is epic in minor key. The metaphoric frame is the familiar North American practice of drag-racing, a duel between a Ford and a Chevrolet, the driver of the Ford winning because "pe Ford man mamook klahwa / the Ford guy slowed down / kopet colley, yaka halo mamook fly / soon enough to avoid going airborne / oakut opoots / at the end of the road" (17). The victor was *skookum chikchik*, the skookum car. *Skookum* is, accordingly, the reigning epic virtue in the poem, and in *A Voice Great within Us* there is indeed a short essay by Lillard on the "natural history" of *skookum*. Like other prime words of Wawa cited in the first section, *skookum* is a familiar expression borrowed from Wawa into regional English, alongside *cultus* (bad), *saltchuck* (salt water or ocean), and *klootchman* (woman). Its meaning (strong or powerful) is displayed in various artefactual contexts by Lillard. It typically occurs in compounds like *skookum chuck* (river rapids), *skookum haws* (power house or prison), or *skookum wawa* (strong argument). The word was attested in white-Aboriginal exchange as early as 1813 by the fur trader Alexander Ross, and derived from Lower Chinook *i-skukm* "powerful creature" – Ross had *is-co-com* and glossed it "Good spirit." Lower Chinook, colloquially Old Chinook, was spoken at the mouth of the Columbia River and provided a significant percentage of the base vocabulary of Wawa, as did incidentally, Nuuchahnulth, for example, *chuck*, water, and the aforementioned *wawa* (Lang 74).

The motif of the *skookum chikchik* returns in the final section of "Rain Language," where the narrator wonders if Wawa, in another sense *skookum wawa*, a strong language, did not in fact take leave of the road and become airborne, leaving only fragments, artefacts of its voice here and there in the collective memory; "Klonas yaka halo mamook klahwa, halo kopet cooley / Maybe he did not slow down soon enough / pe yaka momook fly / and he became airborne" (33). This memorial departure and departure itself is a ubiquitous theme throughout the poem, and for good reason. The artefacts of Wawa that Glavin has gathered tend to evoke disappearance and separation, as if the language were prone to express absence. Elsewhere (Lang 140), Wawa has been characterized as a diaspora language, which "lost its homeland as the region became radically transformed. It became by and large an obsolete language in which disparate and scattered communities now seek traces of their past." This is another way of saying that all that remains are artefacts. These artefacts themselves seem to have already borne within the inscription of their departure, their condition as "airborne."

Like *A Voice Great within Us* as a whole, "Rain Language" is a pastiche, an accumulation of other texts, but most strikingly of the old songs (*ole chantie*) in Wawa, which were recorded and transcribed by Franz Boas in 1888 at a cannery in New Westminster, the first of which occurs at the end of the first section of "Rain Language": "Hyas tlakowa nika / I am so happy / Spose steamboat klatawa yukwa / When the steamboat arrives, / Tlonas nika cly / I think I will weep / Spose steamboat klatawa / When the steamboat leaves" (18). In fact, sections IV and V largely consist of these transcriptions by Boas, which are duly referenced in the authors' bibliography. Not by accident are these songs the most moving passages in "Rain Language." Unlike much of the rest of the poem, expository and explanatory in nature, they are, or rather were, living Wawa, although they were artefacts from the moment Boas transcribed them in his self-conceived role as "salvage ethnographer" whose goal was to collect and preserve evidence of the disappearing Aboriginal cultures of the Northwest Coast. Glavin deftly exploits the nostalgia expressed by multiethnic Wawa-speaking workers in the canneries, who had been geographically displaced with the new regional economy, by transposing this yearning into a consonant memory of "our" historical loss of Wawa: "Konoway sun nika cly. / Always, I weep. / Siah illahie nika mitlite alta. / Far away is my county now" (22).

Readers conversant with Pacific northwest history will recognize other quotes from the extant corpus of Wawa. The introduction to section IV of "Rain Language" begins: "Elip wawa / The first word / yaka mitlite cloosh / was good" (23). The next phrase makes clear, to those in the know, that the first word of the first full sentence documented in Wawa was in fact "good" (*cloosh*), this in the phrase transcribed in 1805 by William Clark: *clouch musket, wake com ma-tax musket* (that is a good musket, I do not understand this musket). Another well-known phrase, often cited as an example of the inventive powers of Wawa, is alluded to in the same section: "Opitsha, / Knife / Opitsha yahka siks / Knife, his friend" (23). This first appears to be a riddle, the answer to which is "fork," the utensil that customarily, at least in common American etiquette, sits alongside the knife. The metaphor can be extended in Wawa, since a well-matched man and wife can be referred to as *opitsha pe opitsha siks* (knife and fork friend), but the turn of phrase allows Glavin to link the history of Wawa, a language in constant and rapid evolution, to the names of the things that were imported into the country, as opposed to those that were native: "Alki, lapooset, chako la fourchette / Soon, lapooset from la fourchette"(23). During the 1820s, a large number of artefacts arrived via the fur trade. The majority took French names in Wawa, since French was the language of the imported Laurentian fur trade technology and its accompanying ideology. On the other hand: "Tillicums elip yukwa potlatch / The people here first gave / lukutchee, ollallie / clams, berries / mowitch, mawamuks / deer, otters / kalakwhatie, pe youtl / cedar bark and pride" (23). Put more abstrusely, as Wawa developed, things already naturally present in the landscape and denoted in Aboriginal languages (e.g., *snass*, "rain") were supplemented by imported artefacts bearing first French and then English names. There was, accordingly, a tendency within Wawa for natural things to have Aboriginal overtones, and artefactual things to have French and then English associations, another way that the dichotomy nature/object played out within Wawa and its view of the world.

On several occasions the words of Wawa that remain (*tenas wawa*) are likened to abandoned implements, relics of material culture:

Alta yukwa mitlite ketling / Now, there is a kettle here,
keekweeklie powitsh stick / under the crabapple trees,
pil ikta kopa chickamin chako halo ikta / rusting to nothing.
Yahwas / There,
eneti kullaghan / on the other side of the fence,
koksut leshaloo / a broken plough
mitlite kow kopa ollallie / tangled in the blackberries [...]
Kopa snass, / in the rain (22).

This emblematic image is developed further in the final lines of the poem, where the residual word-artefacts of Wawa are again enmeshed in the enduring natural scheme of things on the northwest coast, caught in brambles, shards of language in the rain.

In a final step, the landscape itself, the quintessential naturally existing thing, is attributed a kind of artefactuality, at least those points of it that received Wawa names: "[...] nems / [...] in names / tzum kopa illahie / written on the country." Here and elsewhere in the poem Glavin recites a litany of place names: *Tzum Point, Boston Bar, Chikaman Bay, Snass Creek.* *Tzum* means "mark," hence "writing"; *chikamin* first "copper" and then any metal and eventually "money"; and *snass,* "rain." But isn't "Boston" an English word? Yes, but it is also the Wawa word for American, *Basten,* alongside *Kinchotsh* ("King George") for the British or what became Canadians, and *Pasaiooks* ("blanket people") for the French (Canadians). Boston Bar was, in fact, at first a well-known gathering place for prospectors from the United States. Among the artefacts collected in *A Voice Great within Us* is a 1930 *Geographical Gazetteer* and map of Wawa-derived place-names in British Columbia updated by Lillard before his death. Among these monuments to the presence of the language are Eena (beaver) Lake, Illahee (earth) Meadows, Memaloose (death) Creek, and Waugh (pour out or vomit) Creek. As this range of names show, the landscape itself is now a translational artefact, their residual primary meaning echoing through the minds of the informed readers, the landscape a signifier of what has been lost.

Appropriation and distantiation are bipolar terms, both in the sense that they are dichotomies, but also in something akin to a psychological sense, since like mania and depression they can quickly convert from one to the other, given their relativity to each other. As a translational strategy, for example, distantiation (aka foreignizing) has the goal of conveying a more accurate impression of the source language and text than a transparent translation might have. To be sure, transparency and accuracy are defined by the translator and, eventually, the reader. But in the final analysis, distantiation aims at an eventual naturalization of the new norms. Such naturalization is inherently artefactual, as is appropriation, since translations cannot by definition simply exist – to reprise the Aristotelean distinction – but must be knowingly and deliberately created. In the case of a self-translation or "co-translation" like "Rain Language," both languages are present, juxtaposed in the alternating interlineal way found in pedagogical texts or in linguistic analysis. The play or balance between appropriation and distantiation thus proceeds in a special way.

The polemic aim of "Rain Language" is to demonstrate that English is the foreign, intrusive language in the Pacific northwest, Wawa the original stratum that has been supplanted by the invading settlers' tongue. The aforementioned strategy of placing Wawa first followed by the English gloss also tends, per the conventions of translation, to lend it priority as the source, English being the target language. Throughout, the English attains a stripped-down eloquence reminiscent of American modernism – because of the broken plough, perhaps, one thinks easily of William Carlos Williams' "The Red Wheelbarrow." It is composed with restraint, aiming not to call attention to itself, rather to turn attention to the parallel text without trying to replicate idiomatic or stylistic features of the source, only, on occasion, highlighting vocabulary that has already been borrowed into English. This would normally be appropriative or assimilative translation.

But there is an additional layer of paradox. "Rain Language" is one of the exceedingly rare poetic texts composed in Wawa in recent times. It has been over a century since Boas' *Chinook Songs* were transcribed, and most contemporary texts in Wawa are functionally prosaic. This is some measure of Glavin's ambition, which is admirable despite quibbles with the way he writes Wawa. For example, his recurrent use of *mitlite* as copulative instead of intransitive can be considered odd with its restricted meaning of "sit, reside, or be associated with" thus reflecting English usage – the denotation in the Old Chinook etymon *mi-thlayt* was "sit down" (these glosses from Holton 103). Indeed, absence of copulatives is the rule in varieties of Wawa spoken in Native communities, Grand Ronde but also in Kamloops at the beginning of the twentieth century among them. Notably, *mitlite* is used only in the restricted context of sitting or staying in the quoted songs from 1888.

To put it another way, Glavin's Wawa is a concocted register, an artefact. Fluent readers of English can readily determine the nature and qualities of Glavin's English, its stylistic features, but very few readers of the poem will realize that its Wawa is a dialect, "dialect" here in the sense of a variety characteristic of a given speech community, in this case the practices of the English-speaking settler community and the vocabulary and conventions defined by the English lexicological tradition begun, roughly with Horatio Hale's 1841 word list, amplified in Shaw (1909) and Thomas (1935) – all are in the bibliography at the end of *A Voice Great within Us*.

This brings us finally to a consideration of the translation effects produced in and by "Rain Language." A co-translation that aims at restoring knowledge of a dead language not as scholarship but as poetry and no doubt intended to be performed is, perforce, a quixotic endeavour. It is, nonetheless, a speech act, one reflecting west coast cultural history and beliefs, and which can be defined in terms of Austin's typology. "Rain Language" is locutionary, saying the things it says about the history of Wawa. It is perlocutionary insofar as it demonstrates its own possibility, an illustration more than a defence. But it is fundamentally illocutionary, engaging the reader with its promise of new poetry in Wawa, attempting to gain from the reader a counterpart promise to appropriate and assimilate the Wawa co-present in the text, transferring to the reader an artefactual voice within.

Works Cited

Austin, J.L. *How to Do Things with Words: The William James Lectures Delivered at Harvard University in 1955.* Ed. J.O. Urmson. Oxford: Clarendon, 1962.

Glavin, Terry. "Rain Language." In Charles Lillard and Terry Glavin, *A Voice Great within Us: The Story of Chinook.* Vancouver: Transmontanus/New Star Books, 1998, 17–34.

– "Damned Rascal, Son of a Bitch. A Discussion." In Charles Lillard and Terry Glavin, *A Voice Great within Us: The Story of Chinook.* Vancouver: Transmontanus/New Star Books, 1998, 35–54.

Hilpinen, Risto. "Artifact." *Stanford Encyclopedia of Philosophy.* 2004. Accessed 23 Dec. 2009. http://plato.stanford.edu/entries/artefact/#2

Holton, Jim. *Chinook Jargon: The Hidden Language of the Pacific Northwest.* San Leandro, CA: Wawa Press, 2004.

Lang, George. *Making Wawa: The Genesis of Chinook Jargon.* Vancouver: UBC Press, 2008.

Lillard, Charles, and Terry Glavin. *A Voice Great within Us: The Story of Chinook.* Vancouver: Transmontanus/New Star Books, 1998.

Zenk, Henry B. "Chinook Jargon and Native Cultural Persistence in the Grand Ronde Indian Community, 1856–1907: A Special Case of Creolization." Doctoral dissertation, University of Oregon, 1984.

20

1999: Cross-Purposes: Translating and Publishing Traditional First Nations Narratives in Canada at the Turn of the Millennium

Philippe Cardinal

In 1999, Canadian poet Robert Bringhurst published his retranslation of the Skidegate Haida nation's traditional founding narrative. He was later accused of having produced a work that is "emphatically designed to appropriate Haida stories into a Western art canon and the value-laden sense given by modern artistic specialization" (Willmott 125).

In 1999, Canadian ethnographer Dominique Legros published his textualization of a Northern Tutchone Elder's self-translation of his nation's traditional founding narrative. The Elder's family,[1] and the Northern Tutchone Selkirk First Nation government, now accuse him of doing it without their permission and of failing to share the royalties with them.

What is the reading public to make of this? Canadians know very little about traditional Aboriginal narratives, and what they do know has reached them through the filter of translation. It is, however, unlikely that many have ever given this any thought, let alone asked who the translators are, what their goals and working methods might be, or wondered what Aboriginal Canadians might think of such translations as published by mainstream publishing houses. In North America, there are two rival traditions of translating Aboriginal narratives: the ethnographic tradition and the literary tradition. A typical contemporary example of the literary tradition is poet Robert Bringhurst's retranslation of the traditional narratives of the Haida First Nation. A contemporary example of the ethnographic tradition is the recording, translation, and textualization in English of the founding narrative of the Northern Tutchone First Nation, "The Story of Crow," by Canadian ethnographer Dominique Legros, who then translated his own English-language publication into French and had it published by prestigious French international publisher, Gallimard. This French version is of particular interest because Gallimard insisted that Legros heed the advice of a well-known French poet named Jean Grosjean to produce the French-language translation.

In Canada, the literary tradition can be traced back to the seventeenth century with Marc Lescarbot, who recorded some fragments of the Souriquois (Mi'kmaq) First Nation's narratives in 1606, and Jesuit missionary Paul Le Jeune's translations of Innu (Montagnais) traditional narratives published in the Jesuits' *Relation de ce qui s'est passé en la Nouvelle France*, beginning in 1633. In Canada and the United States, the ethnographic tradition began late in the nineteenth century when Franz Boas, who is generally considered "the father of American anthropology" (Tambiah 65), and his students began recording and translating traditional Aboriginal narratives for the ethnographic and linguistic data this could yield.[2] Boas wanted to establish the then brand new academic discipline of anthropology as a science. He did all he could to sharply separate his own work from anything that had been done before. When he translated North American traditional Aboriginal stories, Boas deliberately translated "against" the older literary tradition, whose work he charged with being "amateurish, vague and impressionistic" (Krupat 7).

The Literary Tradition

One of the earliest English translations of an Aboriginal verbal production is that of a "Cherokee war song" by Henry Timberlake, published in London in 1765 (*The Memoirs of Lieut. Henry Timberlake* 56–7). Timberlake textualized his translation in the form of heroic couplets, the most popular poetic form of his day (Swann, *On the Translation* xvi), thereby establishing an enduring pattern for the North American English-language literary tradition of translating Aboriginal traditional narratives. Half a century later, Henry Rowe Schoolcraft was recording and translating the Ojibwa First Nation's traditional narratives: "Schoolcraft believed that one of the most important discoveries he had made among the Ojibwa involved their literary propensities" (Clements, *Native American Verbal Art* 115). He and his contemporaries perceived North American Aboriginal narratives as "inchoate literature, rich in raw material that needed only the disciplinary guidance of the civilized literary artist to take its rightful place among the world's literatures" (101). Schoolcraft's translations were later reworked by Henry Wadsworth Longfellow into such widely known literary offerings as *The Song of Hiawatha*.

Today, when we look at the work of well-known contemporary translators such as Dell Hymes, Dennis Tedlock, and Jerome Rothenberg in the United States, and Robert Bringhurst in Canada, we can see that the practice of textualizing translations of Aboriginal narratives in forms that closely mirror those of the day's fashionable verse poetry remains the norm of the literary tradition. In 1970, Jerome Rothenberg and Dennis Tedlock founded *Alcheringa*, proclaiming it "the first magazine of the world's tribal poetry."[3] The venture lasted a decade, and its influence on the textualization of translated Aboriginal narratives has been considerable. The three main proponents of what can be termed the "poetizing approach" to textualizing translations of Aboriginal narratives into English, Jerome Rothenberg, Dennis Tedlock, and Dell Hymes, were major contributors to both issues. Rothenberg's 1972 anthology, *Shaking the Pumpkin*, featured "workings" of Aboriginal songs and narratives that often appear on the page in the form of concrete poetry, and what Rothenberg calls "total translation," by which he means the inclusion of all the vocal sounds of Aboriginal "poets," even those that are mere sounds and have no meaning as words ("Total Translations"). Such an approach is useful when the translator is working with sound recordings, but Rothenberg also insists that total translation seeks "to develop special means for re-creating oral works within a literate culture" ("We Explain Nothing" 70), even for narratives that were recorded in writing only. William Clements allows that Rothenberg's approach has been a popular success, but he cautions that "some students of Native American verbal art have been uncomfortable with *Shaking the Pumpkin*, especially with the 'workings' or versions reconstructed from previous translations" (*Native American Verbal Art* 43). Some critics charge that Rothenberg's workings are more concerned with producing a good English poem than a truly Aboriginal one. Native American writer Leslie Marmon Silko has charged Rothenberg with "appropriation" (quoted in Clements, ibid. 44–5). Clements argues that Rothenberg's notion of total translation "may reflect more of his own primitivistic aesthetic than the real artistry of the [...] original" (50).

Brian Swann has argued that "if translation itself is problematic, the translation of Native American literatures is twice so. To questions of paraphrasis and metaphrasis, parataxis and syntactics, to epistemological, aesthetic, and theoretical considerations, are added problems of transcription and recording, as well as moral and political dimensions" (*On the Translation* xvi). Swann's own "translations" have, however, also been criticized for much the same reasons as Rothenberg's, but Swann readily allows that his offerings do not constitute true translations, but "poetic versions" of Native American verbal art that he has himself called "white man's poetry" (Krupat 14).

Beginning in 1972, Dennis Tedlock retranslated a series of traditional Zuni narratives first recorded and translated by Frank Hamilton Cushing in the nineteenth century and retranslated by Ruth Bunzel in the 1930s. About Tedlock's offerings, William Clements writes, "While Difference in medium emerges from what amounts to typographic manipulation, Tedlock actually does little more than Bunzel to signal linguistic/cultural Difference" (*Native American Verbal Art* 27). Dell Hymes, one of the main contributors to *Alcheringa*, has argued that while most Aboriginal oral narratives were originally textualized as prose, a close study reveals that they are actually poetry and, as such, ought to be textualized as verse poetry: "Hymes investigates structures in transcribed texts, especially those of the Northwest cultures, employing rhetorical patterns that reveal themselves as repetitions or recurrent adverbial particles, to produce 'measured verse'" (Swann, *Coming to Light* xxviii). Hymes', Tedlock's, Rothenberg's, and their numerous followers' obsessive insistence on textualizing Aboriginal narratives in verse poetry format is, however, puzzling. Their understanding of what constitutes "poetry" appears oddly limited to texts with formal line breaks and in which there is rather more white space than there are printed characters on the page. One can't help but wonder if they are aware of the existence of prose poetry. An opposing view holds that most Aboriginal verbal productions and especially textualizations of narrative storytelling are most accurately represented in written form as prose devoid of formal line breaks. That view, moreover, holds that the prose form is eminently well suited to represent the poetic aspects of such narratives without being chained by the constraints attending "the serious idea of Poetry with a capital P," as Frances Mayes puts it.[4] As to which Aboriginal verbal productions are best represented as verse and which as prose, Paul G. Zolbrod contends that formal verse should be reserved for "lyric poetry which is sung or chanted" and that prose be used for what he calls "colloquial poetry."[5] Before settling on a verse or prose format to represent Aboriginal verbal productions in written form, translators and editors might, moreover, be well advised to read and compare the two versions of Baudelaire's poem, "La chevelure," first composed in 1857 as a verse poem for *Les fleurs du mal* (1975), and recomposed in 1869 as a prose poem for *Le spleen de Paris* (1972) under the slightly modified title of "Un hémisphère dans une chevelure." They would see for themselves that verse and prose are equally capable of serving as a vehicle to fully convey the full extent of any poetry. As to which form should be chosen for a given Aboriginal verbal production, Zolbrod's reasoning – that verse be reserved for lyric poetry which is sung or chanted and prose for everything else – makes the most sense.

Sophie McCall condemns the re-production of Aboriginal and Inuit culture in out-of-context bits and pieces, and the appropriation by Euro-Canadians (or even by southern Aboriginal Canadians such as David Daniel Moses) of Inuit Orature, which they re-present in modified form that closely approximates forms of Western literary art, or which they use as inspiration to create a Canadian literature that romanticizes the original Inuit Orature into something largely foreign to its original creators' intent (24–5).[6]

The only real change that seems to have occurred since the early days of the literary tradition is that while Timberlake and Schoolcraft and the early Jesuit missionaries personally interacted with the Aboriginal peoples whose narratives they translated and published, their current intellectual offspring have virtually ceased to collect raw material directly from the First Nations, relying instead on narratives first recorded, translated, and published by ethnographers, or even those that were previously recorded, translated, and published by earlier practitioners of the literary tradition. Although such efforts generally purport to "correct" their predecessors' "errors," the net result is often little more than an updating of the text to bring it more in line with current literary aesthetics.

True to this practice, Robert Bringhurst's recent translations of Haida narratives were of stories that were all recorded, translated, textualized, and published at the turn of the twentieth century by ethnographer John Swanton, a student of Franz Boas. Bringhurst retranslated and re-textualized these Haida narratives as verse poetry. Bringhurst believes that the Haida narrators around 1900 were oral poets (*A Story as Sharp as a Knife* 16) whose work he equates with that of the ancient Greek poet Homer (67). And although he allows that Haida storytellers' narration is not verse, he argues that being essentially oral, it is not necessarily prose either (111), and so, to make it all the more obvious that it is indeed poetic, he has chosen to textualize it as verse poetry. And to ensure that his readers would not fail to recognize the poetic quality of his text, he sometimes added poetic phrases of his own creation, one example of which is the phrase "down through the clouds" (55), repeated three times in a single stanza, even though there was no equivalent phrase in the Haida source text.[7]

Bringhurst's Haida translations have had their share of detractors. Nicholas Bradley argues that Bringhurst's translation strategy renders "the English-language poetry forever open to questions of authenticity and accuracy" ("'We Who Have Traded Our Voices for Words'" 145). Glenn Willmott contends that Bringhurst's Haida translations "constitute a commodification for commercial purposes of appropriated Aboriginal traditional narrative" (125). His case against Bringhurst rests largely upon the fact that "Bringhurst's work, published by a mainstream national press, is emphatically designed to appropriate Haida stories into a Western art canon and the value-laden sense given by modern artistic specialization" (ibid.). Willmott compares Bringhurst's retranslation of "Raven Traveling," the founding narrative of the Skidegate of the Haida First Nation, with a retranslation of the same Haida narrative by linguist John Enrico. He writes that in Enrico's publication "the stories are presented fully in Haida and English on facing pages and clearly may be used by an English-speaking reader learning to understand written (and, with the orthography appendix, also spoken) Haida" (125–6). He is correct. Bringhurst's translation "is emphatically designed to appropriate Haida stories into a Western art canon."[8] But Willmott fails to mention that Bringhurst also presents a substantial portion of his translations next to their Haida source texts, and his argument that an English-speaking reader could learn to read, and even speak Classical Haida on the sole basis of Enrico's side-by-side (although by no means word-for-word) translation would be merely absurd if it weren't so tragically (and ethnocentrically) ignorant of the complexities of learning as sophisticated a language as Classical Skidegate Haida.

The Ethnographic Tradition

The translations of the ethnographic tradition have also attracted their share of criticism over the years,[9] among other things, for neglecting to account for or to convey any real sense of the "artfulness" of Aboriginal "oral performance" (Berman; Clements, *Native American Verbal Art* and "Tokens of Literary Faculty") – in other words, of translating mechanically, generally "word for word," and failing to translate the rhythm and the poetry of the original narrative. Ethnographer Dominique Legros' English- and French-language publications of Central Yukon's Northern Tutchone First Nation's founding narrative, the "Story of Crow,"[10] published in Canada in English in 1999 and in 2003 in French, are contemporary examples of the work of the ethnographic tradition. As such, Legros' translations present a unique opportunity: first, they allow us to measure what changes, if any, have occurred within that tradition since the days of Franz Boas; second, they allow us to map each step of the transformation of a traditional Aboriginal oral narration into a published book; third, they make it possible to determine just what the Aboriginals whose traditional narrative it is think of such a book.

Dominique Legros first tape-recorded Northern Tutchone Elder Tommy McGinty's telling of the "Story of Crow" in the Tutchone language in 1984. A few days later, Mr McGinty translated his own earlier telling into elementary English. According to Legros, McGinty wanted to "provide public schools in Tutchone villages with a written version of his narratives" (*Tommy McGinty's Northern Tutchone Story of Crow* 23). This may, however, have only been the most obvious of his reasons for collaborating with the anthropologist,[11] for as McGinty prepared to narrate the "Story of Crow" for the anthropologist and his tape recorder, land claims and self-government negotiations were going on between his and other Yukon Aboriginal nations and the governments of Yukon and Canada – negotiations that had been dragging on for decades. It is, therefore, likely that the stagnating state of those ongoing negotiations had an effect upon Tommy McGinty's storytelling.[12]

In due course, Legros' student research assistants transcribed McGinty's 1984 oral self-translation. Then, in 1990 and 1991, Legros recorded Tommy McGinty retelling the crow story twice more in English. These were also transcribed by Legros' research assistants. Producing these transcriptions is no easy task, and it is not at all unusual for a transcriber to precede a significant number of words and even entire sentences throughout the transcription with the words "sounds like" followed by the transcriber's best guess as to what it was that the speaker might actually have said. It is from those three separate transcriptions, plus a significant number of interviews conducted with McGinty over several years for the express purpose of eliciting as much ethnographic data as the Elder could recall, that Dominique Legros distilled the English-language text that was published in 1999.[13]

Tommy McGinty's "Story of Crow" actually takes up only 132 of the book's 268 pages. The rest of the book consists of a lengthy foreword and an even lengthier afterword in which Legros describes the ethnography of the Northern Tutchone and explains how he arrived at his final textualization. This is typical of recent ethnographic publications. As ethnographer Phyllis Morrow explains, current academic anthropology insists on ethnographic explanations of Aboriginal narrative while according little, if any, credit to books made up exclusively of Aboriginal Elders' narration (43). Considering that, in 1905, ethnographer John Swanton published a 448-page book made up entirely of the Haida First Nation's traditional narratives except for his own two-page introduction, some might suggest that some regression has occurred since his day.

The attribution of authorship in ethnographic publications of Aboriginal traditional narratives is a troublesome consideration. Although the name of the Aboriginal narrator is mentioned on the front cover of each book, actual authorship of both the English and the French publication of elder Tommy McGinty's "Story of Crow" is attributed to the ethnographer only. When I asked Dominique Legros why Tommy McGinty was not credited as the author or even as co-author on the front cover of the Gallimard edition – the precise wording as it appears on the front cover of the Gallimard edition is: "*L'histoire du corbeau et Monsieur McGinty*, par Dominique Legros. Traduit et adapté de l'anglais (Canada) par l'auteur" ['The Story of Crow' and Mister McGinty, by Dominique Legros. Translated and adapted from English (Canada) by the author] – Legros answered that he (Legros) is the sole author of the entire book, and that Tommy McGinty is not even a co-author. During the interview, he explained:

> I am the author of a photographic snapshot; a moment that I re-worked much like a photographer retouches his photographs before exhibiting or selling them. Mister McGinty retells a story created, not by him, but by an endless number of ancestors. He is not the author of that story; he is like a pianist, the interpreter of that story in the same way that a concert pianist is the interpreter of a musical partition. The ideal title would have been something like, 'The Story of Crow according to Dominique Legros.' That would have been ideal. The author of a dictionary claims authorship of it even though he did not invent any of the words. Mister McGinty and I had also planned to publish a book on the animals of the Yukon. That would have been a co-authored book. (Personal interview, translation by the author)

Legros' argument notwithstanding, by any current literary standard, is this not a co-authored book? Should McGinty not at the very least have received full co-billing together with Legros as one of the two authors of the entire book? That he did not is, however, not surprising, for that is the norm in ethnographic publishing.

For example, when we look at the 1992 book, *Life Lived Like a Story: Life Histories of Three Yukon Native Elders* (written by Julie Cruikshank, in collaboration with Angela Sidney, Kitty Smith, and Annie Ned), at first glance, the title appears ethical enough since all of Cruikshank's collaborators are duly named on the book's cover. But isn't this ambiguous title, in fact, meant to obscure a disquieting reality? Is this book a co-authored effort or not? As a closer look shows, only Cruikshank is named as author (by Julie Cruikshank), while the other three women are merely her "collaborators," a term that anthropology uses as synonymous with "informant," and not authors in their own right. And yet, as anyone who reads the book discovers, the greatest part of it consists of narratives that Sidney, Smith, and Ned told Cruikshank. That Cruikshank reworked their narratives before publishing them hardly makes them any less co-authors of the book.

What could possibly motivate a respected academic to resort to such an ambiguous title page? Her own profession's expectations, answers Phyllis Morrow, who, in her own collaborative publications with Yup'ik Elsie

Mather, was confronted with precisely the kind of dilemma that Cruikshank faced. As the academic member of the team, Morrow had to struggle with her discipline's expectation that her contributions to "the literature" would only be acceptable inasmuch as they were her own, original insights. This, of course, created considerable pressure for her to "go out on an intellectual limb" to say something new or at least express herself in a unique way. She argues that "the academy is suspicious of collaboration at the same time that it applauds the presence of Native voices [...] if Elsie Mather is assumed to be the 'real' author, then her byline must be mere tokenism. There is no room for coequal collaboration within the author function" (43).

In order to receive full credit from his peers for his work with the Northern Tutchone Elder, Dominique Legros had little choice but to claim sole authorship of the "Story of Crow," even though Tommy McGinty should have received full credit as the co-author. That neither he nor Julie Cruikshank's "collaborators" get that credit – and that this remains standard practice in ethnographic publication – is but one more indication that, as ethnographer Paul Rabinow suggested more than twenty years ago, an ethnography of ethnography which examines such practices is long overdue (252–3).

At first glance, the French version of the "Story of Crow," published in 2003 by Gallimard, is a fairly straight translation of the English text, but there are some innovative solutions to thorny problems. In his original French textualization, French-born Dominique Legros transposed McGinty's elementary "Yukon steamboat sailor's" English and sometimes coarse language into Parisian street French.[14] This proved unacceptable to his Gallimard editor, the well-known French poet Jean Grosjean, who objected that "your Amerindian appears to be a Parisian, and you have embellished ['fleuri'] his language compared with the original English" (Legros, Personal interview). Legros then retextualized his French translation into Québécois *joual*. This met with Grosjean's approval well enough because it created distance between the narrator and French readers. It was Legros' Québécois colleagues who now objected, arguing that Legros' Yukon Indian now sounded like an uneducated Québécois. Faced with a seemingly impossible dilemma, Legros enlisted the help of classical cellist Nicolas Cousineau to help him make the text more "vibrant and rhythmic" (*L'histoire du corbeau et Monsieur McGinty* 10). Together, they hit upon the clever idea of using *joual* and argot side by side throughout the French translation. It was a clever and undoubtedly elegant way of solving a thorny problem. While some French readers might temporarily have difficulty accepting a Yukon Aboriginal Elder speaking typical French street argot, before they have half a chance to decide whether or not this is appropriate, they find themselves reading a sentence featuring vaguely familiar, although difficult to understand typical low register Québécois speech that feels as if it might have been lifted out of a Rabelais novel. Grosjean, who wanted a translation that created distance between the narrator and the French reader, is well served. Similarly, the abundance of Franco-Français low-register words and expressions, most of which are difficult to understand for Québécois readers, can't but create a real distance between Québécois readers and the old Tutchone storyteller. This juxtaposition of *joual* and argot is all the more elegant a solution to a knotty translation problem that it is difficult to imagine a more effective way of rendering Tommy McGinty's Tutchone-inflected "Yukon River Sternwheeler English" into French.

Northern Tutchone Reception of the Published Story of Crow

In 2006, I travelled to the Yukon with two specific objectives in mind. First, I had Mr McGinty's original 1984 Northern Tutchone telling retranslated by Mrs Lizzie Hall, a contemporary Elder of that nation and Tommy McGinty's matrilineal niece. In Northern Tutchone traditional kinship reckoning, a man's matrilineal niece or nephew – in other words, his own sister's child – is considered far more closely related to him than even his own children. In the Tutchone tradition, a person automatically always belongs to her or his mother's moiety;[15] consequently, a man's niece or nephew is perforce a member of his own moiety, while his children – whose mother is always a member of the opposite moiety – necessarily always belong to their mother's – or opposite to his own – moiety. Mrs Hall agreed to collaborate with me on two conditions; one, that I give her and the McGinty family my word that I would never publish her retranslation but restrict my use of it to short excerpts for research purposes and, two, that I produce a transcript of her oral retranslation and that I make it available to the McGinty family so it can use it as the basis for a new publication of its patriarch's version of the "Story of Crow" for the education of Tutchone schoolchildren.

My second objective was to determine how the Northern Tutchone have received Legros' publications. I soon found out that they are not at all pleased with these publications of their founding narrative for a variety of reasons, perhaps the most significant being that they say that Legros did it without their permission and that he made a lot of money from the sale of the book and yet never shared any of it with the people whose traditional narrative it is. As far as the French publication goes, they say that they had not even been aware of its existence before I asked them what they thought about it. On 25 March 2008, I conducted a lengthy interview with Dominique Legros, who insisted that it was at Tommy McGinty's own request that he published his narratives. He also told me that he has received no money at all for the English publication since the Canadian Museum of Civilization only agreed to publish it provided he (Legros) cede it the book's copyright, and that this is standard Museum policy with all of its authors in the Mercury Series.

I was able to verify the accuracy of these last two facts with the Museum's official spokesperson and Curator of Plateau ethnology, Ms. Nicholette Prince, who told me that the book's copyright has always been and is still owned by the Canadian Museum of Civilization Corporation. No royalties of any sort have ever been paid for this book to anyone. Legros says he received an undisclosed small sum of money from Gallimard for translating the English version into French, but he insists that this actually works out to approximately 7 cents per word. Finally, he said that he told Tommy McGinty's eldest daughter by telephone early in 2006 that a French version of her father's stories had recently been published. "But she must have forgotten," he suggested.

Regarding the permission to publish, in all fairness, it must be pointed out that although it is true that Dominique Legros did not have the Selkirk First Nation's formal permission, the very notion that such permissions might in any way be needed is very recent, so recent, in fact, that the Selkirk First Nation's government has yet to finalize its permission-granting protocol. In 1984 and in 1991, when the book's manuscript was beginning to take shape, it never occurred to anyone that SFN government permission should be sought or granted. An inquiry among Mr McGinty's relatives has, moreover, made it almost certain that the Tutchone storyteller had indeed agreed to, and possibly even requested that, Dr Legros publish his version of the "Story of Crow."

Conclusion

It is evident that the McGinty family and the Northern Tutchone have but a vague understanding of the world of academic publication. Since this lack of understanding is generally widespread among Canadian First Nations, any past, present, and immediate future publications of translations of Aboriginal narratives by non-Aboriginals are not likely to be well received by the nations whose traditional narratives they are. But it isn't simply a question of money. The literary tradition makes the elders sound like mainstream English-speaking lyric poets whose very mode of expression is utterly foreign to Aboriginal ears. The ethnographic tradition's practice of publishing Elders' narratives embedded within ethnographic monographs designed primarily to explain those stories for their predominantly non-Aboriginal and largely academic readers is precisely the opposite of the traditional Aboriginal practice of telling stories without ever presuming to tell anyone (not even small children) what the stories should mean to them (Mather, quoted in Morrow 27–8). Traditional Aboriginal stories should not be equated with Western traditional stories. In the Western tradition, folk stories come with a moral. The Aboriginal tradition differs markedly. Its stories almost never have an obvious moral. Individual listeners may decide what the story means for themselves, if they choose, or not.[16]

In light of the foregoing, it is clear that neither the productions of the literary tradition, nor those of the ethnographic tradition fulfil the needs of the First Nations. The Elders may not understand the world of academic publication, but they understand very well that if they do nothing, their youngsters will soon take the Whites' reinvention of their culture for the genuine article. Eurocanadians should, therefore, not be surprised that Aboriginal peoples are now doing everything in their power to regain full control over their own cultural productions.

Notes

1 Mr Tommy McGinty passed away in 1993.

2 It could be argued that the ethnographic tradition also goes back to the work of Jesuit Paul Le Jeune, given the care he took to record what amounts to ethnographic data about the Aboriginal peoples whose narratives and oratory he translated.

3 They cautioned that *Alcheringa* would "not be a scholarly 'journal of ethnopoetics' so much as a place where tribal poetry can appear in English translation and can act (in the oldest and newest of poetic traditions) to change men's minds and lives" (Rothenberg and Tedlock, *Alcheringa* 1: 1).

4 Frances Mayes writes: "Some critics maintain that the writer of prose poems didn't take the trouble to find a form; it's some aberration, like the fish in Florida that crawls out of water and walks. But the short block of prose *is* the form. Line breaks aside, the prose poem keeps the craft tools of free verse working as hard as in other forms. Density can give an implosive quality to a subject; the lack of white space intensifies the impression that everything is happening at once. Some prose poems have a relaxed appearance, skipping lines or including conversation. Because of the prose appearance, the writer, at times, seems freed from the serious idea of Poetry with a capital *P* and admits more humour, conversation, description, or irony into the poem" (373).

5 Paul Zolbrod writes: "I expand the term *poetry* to include both what is written and what is recited, and I define it more broadly to include the art whose primary medium is language whether written, spoken, or sung. For my purposes, then, I do not apply *poetry* just to *verse* as that word is conventionally understood, or to language deliberately spaced line by line on a page. Loosely speaking, what is seen on the page as *verse* represents what I call *lyric poetry*, whose language takes on properties of song, such as rhyme, fixed measures of rhythm, or other such carefully assembled patterns of sound. What appears as *prose*, on the other hand, I take as a term associated with the way print appears on a line from margin to margin. It designates properties of the conventional voice, which I call *colloquial poetry*, in contrast with *lyric poetry*, which is sung or chanted" (306).

6 Sophie McCall further charges that Canadian anthologies that include Aboriginal and Inuit songs – such as Daniel David Moses and Terry Goldie's *An Anthology of Canadian Native Literature (1992–1998)* – "have constructed the songs as imagist poems and isolated them from their original contexts. The presentation of the songs as isolated fragments ignores the storytelling interactions and the social contexts of the telling" (21).

7 As Arnold Krupat writes, literary translators of First Nations traditional stories believe in the "necessity of the textual conventions of Western poetry for conveying the artfulness of [Aboriginal] narrative" (12).

8 Robert Bringhurst's avowed goal is to ensure that the works of classical Haida

poets take what he perceives as their rightful place among the world's classical art productions (15, 51, and passim).

9 Tejaswini Niranjana maintains, for example, that "implicitly or explicitly, ethnography always conceived of its project as one of translation [...] the transformation of ethnology into a scientific discipline also endowed the fieldworker with the professional 'tools' that would enable her/him to construct entire cosmologies on the basis of a one- or two-year acquaintance with a tribe and its language. It was often emphasized that the anthropologist need not be absolutely fluent in the language. One could always depend on native interpreters. The idea of translation in such a context is a metonymy for the desire to achieve transparent knowledge and provide for a Western audience immediacy of access to 'primitive thought'" (68–70).

10 The Northern Tutchone First Nation's "Story of Crow" is but one example of numerous instances of raven creation stories found among many Aboriginal nations of northern and western North America (including the far north's Inuit), northeastern Siberia, and according to Jesuit Paul Le Jeune, among the Eastern Woodland Montagnais/Innu as well. The Northern Tutchone's "crow" is, in fact, no crow at all but a raven. There are no crows in Yukon. Early fur traders, missionaries, and gold seekers coming into the territory, evidently unaware of the basic difference between those two distinct bird species, mistakenly dubbed the much larger black birds they met there "crows." In the absence of real crows, the name has stuck.

11 Anthropologist Julie Cruikshank argues that First Nations Elders who tell stories at Whitehorse's International Storytelling Festival have very different motivations from those of their non-Aboriginal fellow storytellers at the same festival, who are primarily public entertainers, while Aboriginal tellers, contends Cruikshank, seek most of all to reinforce their nation's position in ongoing land claims and self-government negotiations, even if the larger part of their mostly white audiences may not always be aware of this (*The Social Life of Stories* 149). Cruikshank further argues that "oral traditions are not natural products. They have social histories, and they acquire meaning in the situations in which they are used, in interactions between narrators and listeners" (40).

12 In *A Story as Sharp as a Knife*, Robert Bringhurst argues that turn of the twentieth-century Haida narrators chose to tell their people's founding narrative at an exceptionally politically charged moment in their history – decimated and demoralized as a result of a catastrophic (some estimates range as high as a 90

per cent rate of mortality) loss of population due to so-called virgin soil epidemics – they had already as good as capitulated before the combined onslaught of Christian missionaries and Eurocanadian officialdom bent on transforming them into Christianized English-speaking (albeit second-class) citizens. For Tommy McGinty, however, even though the moment was just as politically charged for the Northern Tutchone as it had been for the Haida eighty years earlier, the situation was nearly the exact opposite as, for the first time in nearly a century, his and other Yukon First Nations felt that they were negotiating from a position of relative strength as sovereign nations facing another sovereign nation (Canada) across the negotiating table.

13 Dominique Legros states that none of the numerous Northern Tutchone narrators that he knew ever told all of the known episodes of the crow story in a single session, and this includes Tommy McGinty, who always omitted a number of major episodes from each one of his tellings – this is why Legros, in an attempt to be exhaustive, resorted to combining McGinty's 1984 narrative together with his 1991 narratives (*Tommy McGinty's Northern Tutchone Story of Crow* 242–3). And yet Legros would be first to allow that this is still not a truly "complete" version of the crow story. And as long as Northern Tutchone narrators continue to tell their people about crow's deeds at the beginning of time, it's a safe bet that they will be moved from time to time by evolving sociopolitical developments to create ever new episodes to account for such changes.

14 Mr McGinty learned his somewhat eccentric version of English while working as a deckhand on the steam-powered sternwheelers that plied the Yukon River between Whitehorse and Dawson City well into the 1950s.

15 Social scientists use the word "moiety" (after the French "moitié") to designate each of the two descent groups into which the populations of certain human groups fall.

16 Elsie Mather, a Yup'ik native and educator, believes explications are best avoided: "The Yupiit know and feel that the world is experienced in different levels. There is much to wonder about. To learn to live comfortably in this is being Yup'ik. The world speaks to us, of one, in and by our feelings. It does not articulate clearly, but we make inferences and leave it at that. I feel strongly that interpretations should be very limited, leaving the information in the stories open. We are on shaky ground when we presume to know what the message is for the Native hearers" (Mather, quoted in Morrow 27–8). Mather is also concerned about the often hidden neo-imperialist agenda behind some

of the educational material currently being produced for Aboriginal schoolchildren: "Most often, someone else writes something in English, and then it
is the so-called language specialist's job to translate it. Too often, the result is
books that have very little appeal as far as language expression is concerned –
to say nothing of the content. We, as translators, are, in effect, cogs in a
machine – a machine used in the business of transmitting English concepts to
the Natives" ("With a Vision Beyond Our Immediate Needs" 22). She is well
aware, however, that Aboriginals can't turn back the clock. They, just like the
rest of us, are compelled to live in a world where the young no longer learn
their culture directly from their elders: "We now have village libraries, and we
expect our students to use these facilities. So we have to come to terms with
this monster that's upon us – this dependency on books. I call it a monster
because of the distance it puts between us and our sources. Nevertheless, it is
a necessary monster, and we have to deal with it" (ibid. 20).

Works Cited

Baudelaire, Charles. *Le spleen de Paris*. [1869]. Paris: Livre de Poche, 1972.

– *Les fleurs du mal*. [1857]. Paris: Gallimard-La Pléiade, 1975.

Berman, Judith. "Oolachan-Woman's Robe: Fish, Blankets, Masks, and Meaning
in Boas's Kwakw'ala Texts." *On the Translation of Native American Literature*.
Ed. Brian Swann. Washington, DC: Smithsonian Institution Scholarly Press,
1992, 125–62.

Bradley, Nicholas. "'We Who Have Traded Our Voices for Words': Performance,
Poetry, and the Printed Word in Robert Bringhurst's Translations from Haida."
Textualizing Orature and Orality. Special issue of *Essays on Canadian Writing* 83
(2004): 140–66.

Bringhurst, Robert. *A Story as Sharp as a Knife: The Classical Haida Mythtellers
and Their World*. Vancouver: Douglas and McIntyre, 1999.

Clements, William M. "'Tokens of Literary Faculty': Native American Literature
and Euroamerican Translation in the Early Nineteenth Century." *On the Translation of Native American Literature*. Ed. Brian Swann. Washington, DC: Smithsonian Institution Scholarly Press, 1992, 33–50.

– *Native American Verbal Art: Text and Context*. Tucson: University of Arizona
Press, 1996.

Cruikshank, Julie. *The Social Life of Stories: Narrative and Knowledge in the
Yukon Territory*. Vancouver: UBC Press, 1998.

– in collaboration with Angela Sydney, Kitty Smith, and Annie Ned. *Life Lived*

Like a Story: Life Histories of Three Yukon Native Elders. Lincoln: University of Nebraska Press, 1992.

Enrico, John. *Skidegate Haida Myths and Histories*. Skidegate, BC: Queen Charlotte Islands Museum Press, 1995.

Krupat, Arnold. "On the Translation of Native American Song and Story: A Theorized History." *On the Translation of Native American Literature*. Ed. Brian Swann. Washington, DC: Smithsonian Institution Scholarly Press, 1992, 3–32.

Legros, Dominique. *Tommy McGinty's Northern Tutchone Story of Crow: A First Nation Elder Recounts the Creation of the World*. Hull, QC: Canadian Museum of Civilization, 1999.

– *L'histoire du corbeau et Monsieur McGinty*. Paris: Gallimard, 2003.

– Personal interview. 25 March 2008.

Le Jeune, Paul. *Relation de ce qui s'est passé en la Nouvelle France, en l'année 1633, Envoyée au R.P. Barth. Iacquinot, Provincial de la Compagnie de Jésus en la Province de France par le p. Paul le Jeune de la mesme compagnie, supérieur de la résidence de Kébec*. Paris: Sébastien Cramoisy, 1634.

McCall, Sophie. "'I Can Only Sing This Song to Someone Who Understands It': Community Filmmaking and the Politics of Partial Translation in Atanarjuat, the Fast Runner." Textualizing Orature and Orality. Special Issue of *Essays on Canadian Writing* 83 (2004): 19–46.

Mather, Elsie. "With a Vision Beyond Our Immediate Needs: Oral Traditions in an Age of Literacy." *When Our Words Return: Writing, Hearing, and Remembering Oral Traditions of Alaska and the Yukon*. Ed. Phyllis Morrow and William Schneider. Logan: Utah State University Press, 1995, 13–26.

Mayes, Frances. *The Discovery of Poetry*. 2nd ed. Fort Worth: Harcourt Brace, 1987.

Morrow, Phyllis. "On Shaky Ground: Folklore, Collaboration, and Problematic Outcomes." *When Our Words Return; Writing, Hearing, and Remembering Oral Traditions of Alaska and the Yukon*. Ed. Phyllis Morrow and William Schneider. Logan: Utah State University Press, 1995, 27–51.

Niranjana, Tejaswini. *Sitting Translation: History, Post-Structuralism and the Colonial Context*. Berkeley: University of California Press, 1992.

Rabinow, Paul. "Representations Are Social Facts: Modernity and Post-Modernity in Anthropology." *Writing Culture: The Poetics and Politics of Ethnography*. Ed. James Clifford and George E. Marcus. Berkeley: University of California Press, 1986, 234–61.

Rothenberg, Jerome. "'We Explain Nothing, We Believe Nothing': American Indian Poetry and the Problematics of Translation." *On the Translation of Native American Literatures*. Ed. Brian Swann. Washington, DC: Smithsonian Institution Scholarly Press, 1992, 64–79.

– "Total Translation: An Experiment in the Translation of American Indian Poetry." 2007. Accessed 23 Dec. 2009. http://www.ubu.com/ethno/discourses/rothenberg_total.html

– ed. *Shaking the Pumpkin: Traditional Poetry of the Indian North Americas*. New York: Doubleday, 1972.

– Rothenberg, Jerome, and Dennis Tedlock, eds. *Alcheringa* 1 (1970) and 2 (1971).

Swann, Brian. *Coming to Light: Contemporary Translations of the Native Literatures of North America*. New York: Vintage, 1994.

– ed. *On the Translation of Native American Literatures*. Washington, DC: Smithsonian Institution Scholarly Press, 1992.

Swanton, John R. *Haida Texts and Myths: Skidegate Dialect*. Washington, DC: Bureau of American Ethnology Bulletin 29 (1905).

Tambiah, Stanley Jeyaraja. *Magic, Science, Religion, and the Scope of Rationality*. Cambridge: Cambridge University Press, 1990.

Timberlake, Henry. *The Memoirs of Henry Timberlake: Who Accompanied Three Cherokee Indians to England in the Year 1762*. London: Ridley, Nicoll and Henderson, 1765.

Willmott, Glenn. "Modernism and Aboriginal Modernity: The Appropriation of Products of West Coast Native Heritage as National Goods." Textualizing Orature and Orality. Special issue of *Essays on Canadian Writing* 83 (2004): 75–139.

Zolbrod, Paul G. "The Flight of Dzilyi Neeyáni." *Voices from the Four Directions: Contemporary Translations of the Native Literatures of North America*. Ed. Brian Swann. Lincoln: University of Nebraska Press, 2004, 303–8.

21

22 February 2001: Les Allusifs Enter the Publishing Scene

Hélène Buzelin

Publishing houses offer a strategic perspective for understanding the making of culture. In a position to decide what is worth reading and what is not, who is in and who is out, they act as gatekeepers. They can enhance some voices and repress others. As such, they also have the power to set new trends. This power is exercised in interaction with political actors, specifically in Canada, with civil servants who implement cultural policies, and with the media. Analysing the relationships of these groups permits the highlighting of tensions that underlie the construction of a collective identity. Sherry Simon aptly notes, "Canada has a rich and varied history of translation, but much of it yet remains to be discovered beneath the cover of official bilingualism" (15). Les Allusifs, an independent press located in the Plateau Mont-Royal district of Montreal, was founded in 2001 with a mission to publish international fiction. It exemplifies that claim.

Ten years after its creation, Les Allusifs has released more than a hundred titles, 75 per cent of them translations into French from some twelve different languages. Les Allusifs is not the first literary press in Canada to develop an editorial line consisting of translations,[1] although very few have relied on translation to such an extent.[2] Its originality with respect to the Canadian context lies, rather, in its desire and ability to bring new literary voices to an international French-speaking audience, both North American and European, regardless of the authors' countries or languages of origin, and thus regardless of the Canadian national translation/publishing policies. This publisher thus deserves attention for its input to the Canadian cultural field and identity, but also – and maybe more importantly – for its role in promoting an alternative agenda for literary translation in Canada. In many ways, the recent development of this publishing company reveals both the influence and the limits of institutional translation policies (in Canada and abroad) as well as the specific cultural agendas underlying them.

Building a Network of Translators

To build a catalogue made up of translations from so many different source languages, Brigitte Bouchard, Les Allusifs' creator and former director, set up a network of polyglot collaborators. In the initial stages, this network boiled down to family and friends. The first four titles, therefore, partly reflect the milieu to which this publisher belongs – a milieu composed primarily of artists from the performing, visual, and literary arts, based in Montreal for many years but often with European backgrounds. Most of them are polyglots for whom writing involves a choice of language, for example, between Polish or English for Tecia Werbowski, between English and French for Pan Bouyoucas.

Apart from the titles by writers who have settled in Canada, the first books published in translation came primarily from Latin America. Although there is a community of Latino-Canadian artists dating back at least to the 1970s (see Hugh Hazelton in this volume), in the case of Les Allusifs, the connection developed along more formal lines. In April 2001, Quebec was the host city of the third Summit of the Americas. On that occasion, Brigitte Bouchard met Chilean writer and diplomat Jorge Edwards, who agreed to submit one of his unpublished texts and introduced her to fellow Latin American novelists, such as Roberto Bolaño from Chile and Horacio Castellanos Moya from El Salvador. Moya's translator, Robert Amutio, became a key resource in providing foreign manuscripts from that region.

Amutio was not the only translator who served as a literary scout for Les Allusifs. The titles translated from Brazilian and Mozambican Portuguese, for example, were discovered thanks to Paula Salnot, another translator. Likewise, Lise Chapuis, Gojko Luki , and Gabriel Iaculli proved to be valuable collaborators not only for their translation skills (from Italian and Serbo-Croatian), but also for the literary networks they brought with them. Bouchard readily acknowledges the key role translators have played in the development of her publishing house. She admits having discovered many authors through them, although as the company expanded, this role was passed gradually to literary agents and foreign colleagues (occupying a similar niche abroad). However, the publisher stresses that translators who have acted as literary scouts have rarely been Canadian. In her opinion, "the tradition whereby a translator goes to a publisher with a new title or author in mind does not exist in Quebec, except maybe for English-Canadian literature, but even then" (personal interview).

This statement deserves attention. It is generally agreed that translation in the Quebec literary press started to spread in the early 1970s, and the tradition that has since developed, influenced by Canadian public policy, has concentrated primarily on English-Canadian authors. However, a comparative look at interviews that Patricia Claxton and Charlotte Melançon, two former presidents of the Literary Translators' Association of Canada (LTAC), gave to the press in 1977 and 1998, respectively, suggests an interesting change of perspective over the years. In 1977, two years after the LTAC's founding and five years after the official launch of Canada's national translation grant program, Claxton stated that "all literary translation projects [in Canada] are realized under the aegis of the Council for the Arts that offers grants to publishers" (quoted in Marchand 79, my translation) and that Canadian literary translators confined themselves to the translation of Canadian texts published in the country, paying little attention to titles produced abroad (81). Twenty years later, Melançon stressed that LTAC members often worked for foreign publishers. As such, she felt that the national translation policy – once justified – had become too restrictive, reflecting neither the Association's reality nor its members' needs. In terms of Quebec literary presses that publish more and more foreign texts in translation, these translations are more often than not done abroad by a foreign co-publisher. So, although Brigitte Bouchard's statement constitutes a perception stemming from her own experience, it may also contain a grain of a more general truth.

In the same vein, Bouchard has mentioned her difficulty in finding professionals on the local scene to translate from so-called third languages, that is, languages other than Canada's two official ones. The recognition of translation skills beyond the official languages has always been an issue among LTAC members, and it was raised as early as the second general meeting, as Patricia Claxton recalled. Although "it was felt that [...] the listing of languages and direction of translation should be limited to those in which a member had done major work" (9), actions were taken to promote translation projects from third languages and to call upon the Canada Council for the Arts (CCA) to make translation grants available to third languages or foreign writers from the Americas (Melançon). However, resources for translation from third languages among LTAC member remains limited, with the exception of Spanish.[3] Bouchard emphasizes that finding professional literary translators from Italian, Dutch, Serb, Danish, or Polish to French always requires extensive research and that the result has not always been successful. While it has worked in some cases (for Russian or Spanish, in particular), in others, she finally decided to look for translators abroad – a decision that had both direct consequences, in terms of funding, and indirect but far-reaching ones, as her translation network gradually moved and expanded away from Canada.[4]

In Search of Funding

If I publish Tecia Werbowski, for example, who lives in Montréal but writes in Polish, I can't find anybody to translate from Polish to French in Québec, so I go and look in Europe. But then the book is no longer eligible for a grant, even for a publishing grant or the tax credit, because at this stage what matters is the translator's nationality.
– Brigitte Bouchard

Most rich countries invest public funds into the promotion of their national literature (i.e., for its translation and exportation abroad). Some, such as France, also support the translation of foreign literature into their national language. The CCA, whose mission is to promote Canadian artists and culture, has two translation grant programs. The first, mentioned above, encourages national translation by subsidizing translation fees for Canadian publishers releasing a first translation of a Canadian text in one of the country's two official languages. The second program, created in 1985, is designed for non-Canadian publishers who undertake to translate Canadian literature in third languages for distribution abroad. The national translation grant is one of the several book publishing support programs administrated by the CCA. To apply for this translation grant, a publisher must have been previously considered eligible for either the "emerging publisher grant" or the "block grant," which, in turn, involves other criteria, the main requirement being a catalogue of four to sixteen eligible titles (in the first case) or more than sixteen eligible titles (in the second instance). "Eligible titles" are titles that "contain at least 50 percent Canadian-authored creative content (text graphic)" (CCA). Les Allusifs quickly qualified for the emerging publisher grant and received a translation grant for almost all the Canadian authors it has published in translation, whatever the source language. This amounts to about thirteen titles over seven years.

Meanwhile, the company has also regularly received translation grants from the Centre national du livre (CNL) in Paris for almost thirty titles that were ineligible for CCA translation grants. Whereas the objective of the CCA national translation program is to support the circulation of Canadian literature in both official languages, the CNL in-translation program is primarily concerned with promoting the translation of "high quality" foreign literature into French. The selection process is based on the close examination, by an academic expert, of the literary quality of the original title and that of its translation. The application and the expert's report are then analysed and discussed within a committee. While the literary experts look at translation accuracy and literary as well as stylistic mastery, the committee will also consider other factors such as linguistic diversity (encouraging projects in source languages other than English) and potential readership (encouraging non-commercial projects). In this framework, "high quality" is often tantamount to "non-commercial." This opposition between symbolic and economic profit is a structuring feature of the literary field as described by Pierre Bourdieu ("Le champ littéraire"). As such, CNL could be regarded as a key actor in the reproduction and development of this field, at both national and international levels.

Critical as they are, translation grants represent only the tip of the iceberg. The main and most regular source of public funding for a small literary press comes from publishing support grants. As mentioned, to be eligible for the CCA "block grant," a company must have published at least sixteen "titles with at least 50 percent Canadian creative content." So the publication of any foreign text increases the time it takes to reach that threshold. For Les Allusifs, this sixteenth title was published in 2005 and was the thirty-third in the catalogue. Within the framework of the Book Publishing Industry Development Program (BPIDP, since 2009 called the Canada Book Fund) the main book-publishing grant in Canada administered directly by Canadian Heritage, the company's performance is determined by a formula based on eligible sales.[5] The publishing grant system prevailing in Quebec and administrated by SODEC follows the same logic. In any case, Les Allusifs, which primarily produces foreign titles and posts limited sales, seems rather in tune with CNL's agenda, but is partly at odds with that of federal Canadian agencies.

Moving Away from Conventional Frames

In the media and among literary commentators, Brigitte Bouchard's editorial project has raised much enthusiasm. Since its beginnings, Les Allusifs received warm support, and its products rave reviews. Portraits of the company that appear in the press are similarly laudatory (see, in particular, Beaumier; Desmeules; Lepage; Welcomme). "Originality," "rigour," and "audacity" are traits often ascribed to the firm. Such unanimous approval may seem surprising considering the very specific aesthetic line followed by this publisher. Could it be that Les Allusifs is appreciated not only because of the books it produces but also because of the cultural ideal and image it promotes?

Let us recall that this company entered the scene at the turn of the millennium. At the time, the wave of mergers that had led the industry to unexpected and unprecedented levels of concentration was subsiding and a new generation of independent publishers was emerging (in Québec, the main shock wave was actually felt in October 2005 when Quebecor bought the publishing group Sogides). These structural changes led, in public as well as in specialized discourses, to a polarization between "small" independent publishing and "big" corporations, a dichotomy heavily loaded with moral values – independent publishing being regarded as a guardian of cultural diversity and editorial freedom. In this landscape, Les Allusifs appeared as a positive symbol of both resistance (in following a strict, demanding editorial line free from political and economic pressures) and success (in its ability to think and work internationally within its own niche). Along the way, the company has also come to be depicted, both in Quebec and in the French press, as representative of a new generation of publishers "who wish to perform better by moving away from conventional frames" (Bolduc 7, my translation; for articles on this new generation of publishers, see Bolduc; Brunelle; Lalonde; Thibault; Welcomme).

In a detailed study of the evolution of independent publishing, Gilles Colleu portrays this new generation. In his view, "the new publishers have become more professionalized: their creative skills are obvious and sometimes validated by many years of working in larger groups or their subsidiaries. They are also certainly less 'naïve' about the commercial side of publishing than most of the publishers of the former 'golden generation' who could be more of a dilettante nature and who tended to minimize market considerations" (73–4, my translation). This description aptly fits Brigitte Bouchard, who spent years working for a large publishing company before launching her own house and who definitely has both a literary flair and a sense of marketing. Bouchard, states Alexandra Bolduc, believes in "concept books" as much as in aesthetics. "Some may consider it a mere marketing strategy, but Brigitte Bouchard specifies that the creation of her company stemmed from a personal wish and a desire to mark her entry into the industry in red letters" (7, my translation).

These "new publishers" also believe strongly in the power of the Internet, as well as in the use of close-knit or alternative social networks, with respect to marketing their products. They value flexibility – the flexibility both to adapt to various constraints and to surprise their audience by playing on and mixing ready-made categories. Here again, with its delocalized and customized mode of production, its ability to create a strong image while renewing it regularly, its use of social networks such as Facebook, Les Allusifs provides a good example (for more details on the production process, see Buzelin 2007). This readiness to adapt suggests that, within this framework, translation – both in the strict and the metaphorical sense, as a genuine intersemiotic and interlingual transfer or as a way of recycling older forms and ideas – becomes a key actor.

Translation Effects

As the book industry has internationalized, publishers in Canada and elsewhere have become increasingly conscious of the importance and the limits of their local market and, hence, of the value of translation. Along the way, the old (and somewhat misleading) argument that "only those who translate are translated" has been resurfacing. Publishers and policy makers do at least agree on one point: translation is important. This being acknowledged, the question is: what will be translated and for whom? Depending on their position, publishing-industry actors provide different answers.

Some, like the publishers who supported the "New National Translation Grant Program" that originated among ANEL's general publishers, are happy with the nationalist agenda, but argue for an opening of translation grants to non-literary works. Others, like LTAC, Les Allusifs, and a growing number of small literary presses, call for this program to be opened to third languages or foreign literatures. The institution's position, on the other hand, is univocal. Since the early 1970s, the translation policy has been set to serve the development of a national literature and its circulation between "the two solitudes." Canadian Heritage's March 2009 announcement of a $5 million investment over four years in literary translation as part of the Roadmap for Linguistic duality suggests that this agenda is not about to change (Canadian Heritage). And, as reported by Brunelle (5–6), the policy supporting the Canadian book publishing industry, through BPIDP, is not likely to change, either.

Despite the institutional status quo, Les Allusifs has succeeded in consolidating its position in the publishing and literary milieus worldwide, continuing to win prizes and maintaining its output,[6] while developing new genres such as biography and graphic albums. In doing so, it has contributed to making available new literary talents, some of whom are also part of the Canadian literary landscape, including French-speaking Sylvain Trudel and André Marois, Neil Smith and Timothy Taylor (in translation from English), and Tecia Werbowski and Vladimir Tasic (in translation from Polish and Serbo-Croatian, respectively), to name but a few. In a way, this press could be regarded as a high-brow talent scout for a selective readership and for bigger companies. Indeed, reflecting, in part, the sensitivity and tastes of its owner, the titles composing Les Allusifs' catalogue, most of which come from so-called migrant writers, could also very well be the vectors of an "emerging internationalized aesthetics," to take up Emily Apter's words (1). Those narratives often tell us about otherness, death, identity, and human violence using a swift, sharp, incisive style that goes straight to the essentials.

The emergence of this publishing house in twenty-first-century Canada is also significant for the contrast it has created with the established publishing field, and for the debates on translation it has stimulated. Very much at odds with the official national agenda, Les Allusifs reminds us of this agenda: translation should serve Canada's official policy of bilingualism and strengthen the national book industry. The company's emergence also highlights the compelling character of this agenda: if you wish to move away from it, you have to be ready to pay the price. Finally, the story of Les Allusifs may illustrate the side effects of this agenda: translation competence from or into third languages has little visibility and is not encouraged; literary publishers have little incentive to look beyond Canada and develop relationships with foreign colleagues. And yet a growing number of small presses do look outwards – or at least wish to do so – participating in an alternative form of literary globalization, driven not so much by the search for economic profit through mass-market products, but by the search for symbolic capital and social distinction.

Epilogue

A lot has happened to Les Allusifs since the above was initially written, in the summer of 2009. In the course of the following year, 55 per cent of the shares of this small independent press were taken over by Leméac, another independent literary press from Montreal, founded in 1957. In May 2011, the company celebrated its tenth anniversary at the Quebec Delegate-General's residence in Paris. The event was also acknowledged in the Canadian press. On that occasion, journalist Lise Bissonnette dedicated her weekly review on the national French-speaking radio broadcast to literary translation, and more particularly to Les Allusifs: "Literary translation seems to be undergoing major changes worldwide," claimed Bissonnette, before presenting Les Allusifs as a successful small Quebec press that is representative of these changes, and that seems to be "showing the way" to other small presses. Stressing the international literary recognition this company has acquired, she concluded on the following note:

> The surprising thing is that those small presses are not eligible for publishing grants, apart from general publishing grants, as the CCA only subsidizes translation of Canadian works. This idea that only translation of Canadian authors ought to be subsidized is generally accepted, particularly between English and French, but as the world is changing, I think it may be time to question this. I know this debate started some time ago, but it has never gone very far. (Bissonnette, my translation)

On 2 October 2012, *Le Devoir* reported that Les Allusifs was going bankrupt (Nadeau, "Les Éditions Les Allusifs déclarent faillite"). While putting most of the blame on Bouchard's "jet setting" lifestyle, Leméac director Lise Bergevin reasserted that Les Allusifs was a cultural and business project that she still believed in, and that new books would be released under this brand. In a letter written to *Le Devoir*, a significantly toned-down version of which was published a week later, Bouchard ("Édition – Rétablir la vérité des éditions Les Allusifs") responded to Bergevin's statement and gave her vision of the facts. She reminded readers that Les Allusifs had stemmed out of a passion for literature regardless of linguistic and cultural origins. It had grown out of constant hard work, risk taking, struggles for independence, and commitment to the people who shared this passion.

A couple of months later, on 29 November, *La Presse* announced that the founder of Les Allusifs was "embarking on a new adventure," this time on the other side of the Atlantic. She would become head of Notabilia, a new collection for the Switzerland-based publishing house Noir sur Blanc. It was also stated that the editorial line of this new collection would remain close to that of Les Allusifs, and that most of the authors who had been previously published by Bouchard would follow their former publisher in her new adventure. The first title of this collection, *Dernier voyage à Buenos Aires* by Louis-Bernard Robitaille, was released in March 2013 (Nadeau, "Après un parcours du combattant"). At the time of writing, April 2013, the rules and objectives of the CCA translation grant program have remained unchanged.

Notes

1 "Literary press/publisher" refers here to a company dedicated to the publication of genres defined as "literary" by the Canada Council for the Arts (CCA), i.e., fiction, poetry, drama, graphic novels, children's books, and literary non-fiction. Accessed 23 May 2009. http://www.canadacouncil.ca/grants/writing/ap127723094273982142.htm

2 For example, before specializing in children's literature, Éditions Pierre Tisseyre contributed to the translation of many English-Canadian authors in Quebec. Les Écrits des Forges, one of the two principal publishers of poetry in Quebec, has translated many titles from English Canada and abroad while exporting those of Quebec artists. Since the early 1990s, these translations have been

part of a strong internationalizing process taking place thanks to a policy of reciprocal co-edition (for more details, see Buzelin 2008). At Boréal and Fides, the publishing of translated works has never been the main activity (representing traditionally about 5 per cent to 15 per cent of the catalogue), but it has been on the increase since the 1990s as these companies have not only strengthened their relations with their English-Canadian counterparts but have also embarked on several large-scale translation projects with foreign publishers (e.g., the Biography series for Fides and the Myths project for Boréal). At Leméac, the increase in the number of titles published in translation is closely related to co-publishing agreements with French publisher Actes Sud.

3 Indeed, in the 2008 LTAC directory, one may find a dozen translators who can work from Spanish to English or French, but resources are scarcer when it comes to other languages, especially for translation into French. The association recognizes one translator who works from German to French (compared with six who translate from German to English), one from Italian to French (and four from Italian to English), and one from Russian to French, but nobody who translates from Portuguese to French.

4 Although significant in the firm's early years, the percentage of translations by Canadian translators released by Les Allusifs has declined over time.

5 The program encourages "the ongoing production, marketing, and distribution of Canadian-authored books," with sales of each title weighted by a coefficient that varies according to the title's "passport." The highest coefficient (3.75) is given to Aboriginal or official translations of Canadian-authored titles; the second highest (3) is for all other Canadian-authored books. Foreign-authored books translated in Canada have a coefficient of 0.5. Foreign books translated by foreign translators are not mentioned. The budget is shared proportionately among applicants according to each applicant's relative performance.

6 Les Allusifs has won the Governor General's Literary Award for best translation in French twice in 2007 (*Dernières notes*, translated by Lori St-Martin and Paul Gagné [*Last Notes and Other Stories* by Tamas Dobozy]) and in 2008 (*Tracey en mille morceaux*, translated by Claire Chabalier and Louise Chabalier [*The Tracey Fragments* by Maureen Medved]).

Works Cited

Apter, Emily. "On Translation in a Global Market." *Public Culture* 13: 1 (2001): 1–12.

Beaumier, Jean-Paul. "Les Allusifs: Une nouvelle maison qui voit grand." *Nuit Blanche* 84 (2001): 4–5.

Bissonnette, Lise. *Ouvert le samedi*. Radio Canada Première chaîne. 14 mai 2011. AccessedOnline. 13 July 2011. http://www.radio-canada.ca/audio-video/pop. shtml#urlMedia=http://www.radio-canada.ca/Medianet/2011/CBF/Ouvert LeSamedi20110514215_1.asx

Bolduc, Alexandra. "La relève chez les éditeurs travaille à allumer des feux." *Livre d'ici* (mai 2001): 7–8.

Bouchard, Brigitte. Personal interview. Montreal. 5 Dec. 2005.

– "Montréal, capitale mondiale?" *Liberté* N°271 (2006): 20–2.

– "Édition – Rétablir la vérité des éditions Les Allusifs" *Le Devoir*, 9 oct. 2012.

Bourdieu, Pierre. "Le champ littéraire." *Actes de la recherche en sciences sociales* 89: 1 (1991): 3–46.

Brunelle, Anne-Marie. "L'édition a atteint un moment charnière: Le soutien aux petits éditeurs est effectivement une nécessité." *Livre d'ici* (oct. 2005): 5–6.

Buzelin, Hélène. "Translations in the Making." *Constructing a Sociology of Translation*. Ed. Michaela Wolf and Alexandra Fukari. Philadelphia/Amsterdam: John Benjamins, 2007, 135–69.

– "Les contradictions de la coédition internationale: Des pratiques aux représentations." *Les contradictions de la globalisation éditoriale*. Ed. Gisèle Sapiro. Paris: Nouveau Monde Éditions, 2008, 45–79.

Canada Council for the Arts (CCA). Accessed 23 May 2009. http://www.canada council.ca/grants/writing/0f127227340679531250.htm

Canadian Heritage. Accessed 5 March 2009. http://www.pch.gc.ca/pc-ch/info Cntr/cdm-mc/index-eng.cfm?action=doc&DocIDCd=CJM082442

Claxton, Patricia. "Introduction: Looking back." *Meta* 45: 1 (2000): 7–12.

Colleu, Gilles. *Éditeurs indépendants: De l'âge de raison vers l'offensive*. Paris: Alliance des éditeurs indépendants, 2006.

Desmeules, Christian. "Brigitte Bouchard, tête chercheuse: Contre vents et marées, la petite maison québécoise *Les Allusifs* célèbre ses cinq ans." *Le Devoir*, 18 mars 2006, F1.

Lalonde, Catherine. "Les stratégies de marketing des petits éditeurs." *Livre d'ici* (fév. 2006): 6.

Lepage, Jocelyne. "Brigitte Bouchard: Le dur défi de durer." *La Presse*, 26 fév. 2006, cahier arts et spectacles, 13.

Marchand, Pierre. "Conversation avec Patricia Claxton (présidente de l'Association des traducteurs littéraires)." *Meta* 22: 1 (1977): 79–87.

Melançon, Charlotte. "Pour connaître nos deux littératures nationales: 25 ans après." *Circuit* (automne 1998): 4–5.

Nadeau, Jean-François. "Les Éditions Les Allusifs déclarent faillite." *Le Devoir*,
    2 oct. 2012.
– "Après un parcours du combattant – Retour au front de l'édition." *Le Devoir*,
    30 mars 2013.
Simon, Sherry. "Translation and the Making of Canadian Culture." *Traduire
    depuis les marges / Translating from the Margins*. Ed. Denise Merkle, Jane Kous-
    tas, Glen Nichols, Sherry Simon. Montreal: Éditions Nota bene, 2008, 11–24.
Thibault, Geneviève. "Les visages de l'autre édition." *Le libraire* (2007). Accessed
    May 2009. http://www.lelibraire.org/article.asp?cat=14?id=2405
Welcomme, Geneviève. "Les petits éditeurs dans la mêlée." *La Croix*, 17 avril
    2008, 14.

PART FOUR

Translating Drama

31 March 1973: Michel Tremblay's *Les belles-sœurs* in Toronto: Theatre Translation and Bilingualism

Louise Ladouceur Translated by Deborah Shadd

The English-language production of Michel Tremblay's *Les belles-sœurs*, which ran from 31 March to 28 April 1973, at the St Lawrence Centre in Toronto, was a resounding success. Herbert Whittaker of the *Globe and Mail* described it as a "milestone play [...] a historic document of some significance" ("*Les belles sœurs* Milestone Play" 13), while the *Toronto Citizen*'s David McCaughna praised the success of the translation in retaining "the flavour and earthiness" (quoted in Koustas, "From Gélinas to Carrier" 118) of the original's common, everyday Québécois speech.[1] The rave reviews given the play by Toronto critics established Tremblay as a leading Canadian playwright and set the stage for the immense popularity he would later enjoy throughout English-speaking Canada. The success of Tremblay's play in Toronto, particularly at a time when many were focused on the formation and development of a distinctly Canadian drama repertoire, was the result of a series of circumstances that serve to highlight the issues and concerns at stake in translation. Moreover, the portrayal put forward by Bill Glassco and John Van Burek in their translation of what turned out to be the founding play of a repertoire that would thereafter be known as "Québécois" had a profound impact on the way it was perceived and received on English-Canadian stages. Nevertheless, despite their novelty, the translation strategies Van Burek and Glassco applied to the play created a traditional image of Quebec in contrast to the source text – which deliberately broke with tradition.

Even before the 1973–74 season, numerous French-Canadian plays from Quebec had been presented in English translation in Toronto. Traditionally, the majority of these plays had neatly conformed to the rules of "proper" speech in both their English and French versions.[2] Increasingly, however, this had ceased to be the case. Written and translated in a highly accentuated vernacular idiom, plays such as Jean-Claude Germain's *Notes from Quebec*, presented at Theatre Passe Muraille in 1970, or Jean Barbeau's *The Way of Lacross* and *Manon Lastcall*, both staged at the Poor Alex Theatre in 1972, revealed a Quebec emerging transformed from the Quiet Revolution, a revelation not at all reassuring to anglophone audiences in Toronto. Not only did Toronto critics judge the subject matter of the plays to be irrelevant to Torontonians, but the vernacular level of language and the numerous profanities on display contrasted sharply with a tradition of refinement "established through the playing of English imports" (Whittaker, "Bright Light" 14).

An earlier play by Tremblay had been performed in Toronto in 1972. Directed by Bill Glassco, in a translation he had produced with John Van Burek, *Forever Yours, Marie-Lou* was staged at the Glassco-directed Tarragon Theatre. Despite a lukewarm critical reception, the production met with popular success, even winning the Chalmers Award, a prize given to the best Canadian play of the season in Toronto. Whittaker, however, deplored the sense of "déjà-vu" he experienced in watching it: "As we appreciated the skill with which Tremblay led us over old rocky ground, we had to suppress an urge to pop up and say 'I knew that! Teacher, I knew that. Everybody knows that!'" ("*Forever Yours*" 12). He added that for "an Ontario audience in the mainstream of North American psychological drama for the past quarter-century, the surprise is that Quebec's novelty today was ours earlier" (ibid.). It is possible that it was precisely this sense of familiarity with the portrait of Quebec society presented by Tremblay that contributed to its success with Toronto audiences. Curious as to what had caused such disruption in Quebec and brought about the violent events of the early part of the decade, the anglophone audience was met by impoverished characters, belonging to an underprivileged social class, powerless and still subject to traditional religious dogma and morality. It thus proposed a representation of Quebec that was non-threatening and reassuring, an image to which anglophones were actually rather attached. As Jacques Saint-Pierre noted, "Michel Tremblay perpetuates a fantasy for anglophones, a vision of Québécois society from the years before the Quiet Revolution" (65, my translation), a task more readily accomplished as the translation had smoothed out so many of the rough spots that could have hindered the reception of the work.

From the start, the English text was purged of the distinct markers of vernacular speech that were such a revolutionary element of Tremblay's writing in French. Just like *Forever Yours*, the translation of *Les belles-sœurs* used what Vivien Bosley described as "standardized [...] generic North American" (141), a form of neutral written English commonly used in North America. However, the addition of numerous swear words to the translation lowered the level of language spoken by the characters. Thus, in a section of the 1968 original version of *Les belles-sœurs* containing three swear words or mild curses, such as "Ma grand-foi du bon Dieu" (10) and twice "Mon Dieu" (14), the 1974 English version has acquired fourteen: "Sweet Jesus" (7), "Jesus," "Christ," "goddamn show" (9), "Mother of God" (10), "Jesus" (11), "Jesus," "goddamn thing" (14), "goddamn thing" (15), "my God" (18), "the God's truth" (20), "Goddamn sex" (21), "Dear God," and "Goddamn it" (23). Not only are they clearly more numerous in English, they are also much more intense, and this intensity is heightened by the fact that it is in sharp contrast with the rather conservative tone of the rest of the dialogue. This further underscores the hypocrisy of the sisters-in-law, who claim to be very religious and for whom certain of these curses would be forbidden (see Ladouceur, "Canada's Michel Tremblay").

The decision not to employ a highly accentuated form of vernacular speech in the translation can be explained by the fact that the vernacular is unable to fulfil the same function in English-speaking Canada as in Quebec. *Joual* is the result of historical conditions that caused the language to evolve in isolation for centuries, juxtaposing archaisms, pronunciations, and turns of phrase from early colonial times with expressions borrowed from Indigenous languages and anglicisms derived from the dominant English culture (see also Gillian Lane-Mercier's contribution in this volume). It is an oral language characterized by striking regionalisms specific to Quebec that serve to clearly distinguish *joual* from standard French, thus allowing Quebecers to claim a distinct linguistic identity. This is not the case with most Anglo-Canadian vernaculars within the context of North America (see Ladouceur, "La langue populaire québécoise").

Unlike *joual*, vernacular variations of spoken English in Canada are insufficiently distinct to signal a specifically Canadian linguistic identity, with the possible exception of that spoken in Newfoundland. In fact, this is precisely what Bill Glassco underscored when he compared his translation of *Les belles-sœurs* with the Scottish version produced by Bill Findlay and Martin Bowman (*The Guid Sisters*): "What we were doing in English was so far away from being faithful to the spirit of the French. [In the Scottish version] the spirit of the play was there because the colour and the energy of the language were there in a way that John Van Burek and I simply couldn't get in English" (quoted in Steward and Knowles). Elsewhere, he elaborated, "I suspect that many Quebec plays could profit in English by being transposed to Newfoundland. The two provinces are not only Canada's most distinct societies, but they also have the most distinctive ways of speaking" (quoted in Rudakof and Thomson 146). Still bearing signs of the strong influence of Irish immigrants, the Newfoundland dialect, when compared with standard English, is indeed distinct enough to fulfil a symbolic function equivalent to that of *joual*. However, given that the dialect is almost incomprehensible to those living elsewhere in Canada, it would hardly be appropriate for an uninitiated anglophone audience. Consequently, outside of Newfoundland, the question of dialect remains unresolved.

Translating the play into a vernacular lacking any distinctive social function or symbolic weight comparable to that of *joual* would have been a risk, for it could have shocked and puzzled an audience for whom identity is not anchored in linguistic affirmation. It could also have hindered the reception of the work at a key moment when it was destined to contribute so significantly to the formation of a nascent Canadian drama repertoire. Adjustments were thus required for the translation to portray the Canadianness of Tremblay's text. To do this, the translators resorted to a technique that had rarely been used in the English translations of French-Canadian plays. Aside from *Tit-Coq*, a play by Gratien Gélinas staged in Toronto in 1951 and whose title is also the name of the principal character, only Anne Hébert's *Le Temps sauvage*, produced in Toronto in 1972, had retained the French title in its English version. Beginning in 1973, however, French titles were retained for the translations of a number of Tremblay's plays, a technique that would become their trademark. Used first for *Les belles-sœurs* (1973), this strategy was taken up again for *Hosanna* (1974), *Bonjour, Là, Bonjour* (1975), *Surprise! Surprise!* (1975), *En Pièces Détachées* (1975), *La Duchesse de Langeais* (1976), *Trois Petits Tours* (1977), and *Damnée Manon, Sacrée Sandra* (1981). While a bilingual variation was adopted for *Sainte-Carmen of the Main* (1981), the practice of keeping the French title was once again employed for *La Maison Suspendue* (1991). With these titles, the translations immediately displayed their colours, attesting to an untranslatable reality that had no cultural equivalent in the receptive context.

This translation technique found its extension in the many Gallicisms sprinkled throughout the English dialogue, reproducing words and expressions in French borrowed directly from the source text. Thus, the English version, entitled *Les Belles Sœurs*, retained all the characters' French names and forms of address, despite the difficulty performers had in pronouncing them correctly. As a result, they address one another this way: "Thanks Mlle. [*sic*] Verrette. You're so kind" (*Belles Sœurs*, 1974, 25), "Mme. [*sic*] Brouillette, your language!" (17). The audience also hears of "Monsieur Turgeon" (44), who was known as Dubé in the original, and of the "Abbé Castelneau" (107). In addition to these French names and forms of address, other Gallicisms can be found in expressions such as "a whore on la rue St-Laurent" in *Forever Yours, Marie-Lou* (50); "I got what I wanted, I got my Anglais," in *Bonjour, Là, Bonjour* (29); countless "stupide," "oui, allô," "ah oui," "ben oui," "hein," "aie," "ouais," "ayoye," "dégoûtant," "câlice," and "sacrement," as well as an allusion to the "poses voluptueuses et provocantes" in *Hosanna* (29). The use of such Gallicisms was even more accentuated in the revised version of the translation, entitled *Les Belles-Soeurs* (with the addition of a hyphen), published in 1992, where "mama" was replaced by "maman" (29) and "college" becomes "cours classique" (27). This technique reached its height in the translation of *La Maison Suspendue*, where a dozen examples can be found in a monologue of only two hundred words (see Ladouceur, "Canada's Michel Tremblay").

Blending the languages in a way that did not correspond to any actual usage in a Canadian context where anglophones are rarely exposed to the influence of French, these translations replaced the realistic aesthetic of the source-text dialogue with an artificial bilingualism that served to underscore the play's alterity in the target language. Vivien Bosley described the effect produced on the audience this way: "It is my contention that, instead of identifying with what is happening on stage, we become observers of an ethnological situation which strikes us as interesting and amusing and quaint" (139). This ethnographic point of view prevented anglophone audiences from identifying with what was happening on stage, inviting them instead to distance themselves from the less-than-flattering social portraits that Tremblay's early works presented. This facilitated the reception of the plays for, rather than being directly implicated in the play's subject matter, audiences could instead observe a reality that seemed somehow foreign to them. This insistence on the alterity of the Québécois text contributed greatly to the success of Tremblay's plays in English. According to Stephen Mezei, "In Toronto it scored mainly because Tremblay's characters belong to a class that does not exist in Toronto and the women on the stage represented something alien with an exotic flavour" (26).

Despite its artificiality, the blended language attributed to Tremblay's characters in their English incarnation nonetheless presented a form of linguistic specificity that was most pertinent at the time. These plays were among the first to receive translation grants through a program launched by the Canada Council for the Arts in 1972, just two years after the October Crisis, with the intention of encouraging dialogue and exchange between Canada's francophone and anglophone communities. At a time when relations between the two linguistic communities were at their most tense, this blended language served to promote bilingualism through a model of linguistic cohabitation by way of translation. Furthermore, the English version's integration of the country's two official languages exhibited a Canadian linguistic specificity within the North American context as it affirmed the multiculturalism of the Canadian "mosaic" as opposed to the "melting pot" of its American neighbour.

If English translations could use such an artificial language to represent Tremblay's *joual*, it was because the relationship to the oral language of theatre was decidedly different in each context. Not threatened in terms of their linguistic identity, English-speaking Canadians had no need to see the existence of their language affirmed on stage. Theirs was a language sure of itself, and it would be pointless to insist on it. Indeed, the question of language was so unimportant that they failed to take into consideration the translation process involved in producing Tremblay's texts in English. This was what prompted Robert Wallace to complain, in 1990, of "a general insensitivity to the issues surrounding translation that permeates Canadian culture" (222–3), citing as an example the English publication of Tremblay's *The Real World* that fails to mention on the cover that the work is a translation. "This oversight," wrote Wallace, "along with a long statement by Tremblay printed on the back cover, could lead the reader to conclude that Tremblay wrote the play in English" (223). The first thirteen works by Tremblay published in English by Talonbooks all neglected to indicate on the cover that they were translations, providing only the title of the play and the name of the author (see Kathy Mezei's contribution in this volume). It is only with the publication of *The First Quarter of the Moon*, in 1994, that the cover would henceforth indicate that the English texts were translations.

While such an omission certainly signalled a lack of sensitivity towards translational issues, it did have the advantage of allowing Tremblay to be more directly integrated into the world of English-Canadian theatre. This integration was further facilitated by the absence of any preface or metatext that could enlighten the reader about the process of translation that the work had undergone. In the case of *Les belles-sœurs*, this silence is particularly surprising given that it was not only the first of Tremblay's plays to be published in English, but also the one that had just revolutionized Québécois theatre by establishing *joual* as a language of the stage. Failing to mention the mediating effects of translation gave the impression of an identical reproduction presumably made possible by a total compatibility of languages and cultures. Tremblay's work could thus be readily integrated into an emerging Canadian drama repertoire to which it would significantly contribute, not only through the number of plays produced but also by the prominence of the author on both the national and international scenes.

Well aware of the difficulties inherent in the transposition of *joual* into English, theatre critic Urjo Kareda did initially question the very translatability of texts written in *joual*. However, he did not press the point and hastened to celebrate the arrival of the young Canadian playwright on Toronto's stages. At the height of all the enthusiasm following the 1975 return of *Forever Yours, Marie-Lou*, he acknowledged that "Tremblay himself would say that he's a Quebec playwright, not Canadian at all, but never mind" (quoted in Hulan 49). Indeed, it was the success of a Canadian author that the anglophone critics in Toronto and in Montreal celebrated in Tremblay (see Sabbath). Given the way it was translated, the play offered an essentially Canadian version of Tremblay's work to the anglophone public, and it was in light of Canadian standards that it would be measured.

Since "the assumption, all too prevalent in Canadian criticism, [is] that the best theatre reveals universal truths" (Wallace 10), the merit of the plays was thought to reside in their universal qualities. This interpretation was certainly helped along by a translation that had removed the subversive potential inherent to *joual*, the form of speech that had been so crucial to the shock waves produced by Tremblay on Quebec stages, replacing it with a neutral language generously seasoned with curses to underline its earthiness and with Gallicisms to accentuate its non-threatening alterity. While these strategies may have, indeed, constituted a linguistic innovation in English-Canadian theatre, as had *joual* on Quebec stages, this was an innovation that had the effect of offering a traditional image of Quebec, whereas the original had marked a break with tradition.

The validation of a work based on its universal qualities is certainly not exclusive to the Canadian context; rather, it is one of the most favoured means of consecration on the international literary scene. According to Pascale Casanova, "The dominant literatures reduce literary works from elsewhere to their own categories of perception, established as universal norms, suppressing the context [...] that would allow them to be understood without reduction" (214, my translation). This, of course, presupposes a network of absolute norms and representations shared everywhere by everyone. But if we accept that every representation of the world is historically determined and informed by its context, this notion of the universal poses a problem. Rather than resulting from a referential consensus, it arises from an ideological construct formulated by those whose interests they serve. At a time when Canadian theatre was just coming into its own, the universal quality assigned to Tremblay's plays served to distance them from their immediate political context, a deterritorialization that eased the process of appropriation.

The translation techniques used by Glassco and Van Burek, most particularly the use of Gallicisms in their English versions of Tremblay's work, truly shaped the representation of the Quebec drama repertoire in English. Not only did they firmly fix this notion in the collective imagination of the English-Canadian public, who from then on would recognize this as the definitive marker of a Québécois play, they also profoundly influenced the practice of theatre translation in Canada. For some, these techniques have become the required English equivalent to *joual*.

Such was the conviction of Canadian playwright Judith Thompson, who was recently asked by the Centre des auteurs dramatiques (CEAD), a Quebec-based organization of French-Canadian authors, to translate Serge Boucher's *Motel Hélène* into English, starting from a literal translation done by Morwyn Brebner. Written in a highly accentuated *joual*, the play features working-class characters with few resources and little education who are crippled by personal tragedy. They are descendants of the destitute cast-offs who people Tremblay's universe. Exhibiting a highly accentuated English vernacular, the translation proposed a level of language comparable to that of the source text, but repeated the process inaugurated by Glassco and Van Burek of incorporating Gallicisms into the target text. Thus, the English translation kept many expressions and most of the abundant curses in their original French. Despite a warning from the CEAD, which supervised the project and advised against this technique, Thompson refused to revise her translation. The model set out by Glassco and Van Burek thirty years earlier had become unavoidable for her when translating *joual* into English. Although this version of the play was staged at the Tarragon Theatre in 2000 and published that same year by the Playwrights Union of Canada, it was ultimately rejected by the CEAD, which entrusted its revision to Crystal Béliveau and Serge Boucher, who promptly eliminated all the Gallicisms. This revised version, dated 2001, is the only one now available at the CEAD.

Resorting to Gallicisms for forms of address remains an active strategy in the English translations of Québécois texts, notably, in the corpus of works translated by Linda Gaboriau. A high-profile translator responsible for the English versions of some eighty plays by a number of Quebec's most famous playwrights, Gaboriau has also held key positions in organizations responsible for educating and training new translators for the theatre, in the process becoming an unavoidable model herself in the world of Canadian theatre translation. Following in the footsteps of Glassco and Van Burek, Gaboriau completed the English translations of Tremblay's five latest plays – *Assorted Candies* (2006), *The Driving Force* (2004), *Past Perfect* (2004), *Impromptu on Nuns' Island* (2002), and *For the Pleasure of Seeing Her Again* (1998). Gallicisms analogous to those in previous versions occasionally appear in these translations, such as "Madame Forget's kitchen table" (11) and "Madame Oligny" (51) in *For the Pleasure of Seeing Her Again*, produced in Montreal in 1998. However, they are much less frequent in Gaboriau's work than in that of her predecessors.

Certain forms of address have also been retained in French in Gaboriau's English translations of many plays by other contemporary authors. In Michel Marc Bouchard's *Lilies*, for example, produced in Toronto in 1991, Timothée addresses the countess and her son as "Madame [and]

Monsieur" (27). Audiences later meet "Madame Tessier" (19), "Madame Giroux" (46), and "Madame Tanguay" (46) in *The Orphan Muses*, a play by the same author that was staged in Vancouver in 1996. More recently, in the 2007 Toronto production of Wajdi Mouawad's *Scorched*, the only reference in the entire text to the setting of the play is to "Saint-François Hospital in Ville Emard" (5), and one of the story's central characters is addressed as "Madame Newal" (73). While this French form of address may not be too surprising in the English translation of a play obviously set in Quebec and in which other geographical references have also been kept in French, this is decidedly not the case here. This is the only Gallicism found in the second part of the play, where the action has moved to a far-away Arab country. Such a reference to the Québécois language of the source text seems highly incongruous since it occurs in a conversation with an Arab protagonist who is unfamiliar with Newal's personal history. Moreover, the French pronunciation of the two principal characters' names, Simon and Janine, was retained throughout the English production,[3] further emphasizing the francophone alterity of a play in which the action unfolds within a vague frame of reference that precludes situating it in any precise American or Middle Eastern location.

Although the English translation of Quebec's drama repertoire no longer responds to the same needs and is no longer called upon to perform the same functions within an English-Canadian dramatic tradition now well established, certain techniques adopted in the wake of the first English translations of Tremblay's works are still being employed today. The use of Gallicisms to indicate the origin of the play and the language in which it was first written have particularly influenced the way Quebec theatre is commonly represented in English. That this strategy continues to be used in the English versions of more recent Quebec plays, which have set aside the discourse of identity prevalent in the 1970s to explore other discursive territories through other linguistic means, attests to the enduring importance of this mode of translation. Found only in Canadian plays translated from the Québécois repertoire, this use of Gallicisms is a translation device specific to the English versions destined to represent Quebec theatre on Canadian stages.

Notes

1 Newspapers at the time made mention of a first version, by René Dionne, which was rejected three weeks before the play's premiere.

2 For further information, see Koustas' article "From 'Homespun' to 'Awesome,'" as well as Ladouceur's book-length study, *Making the Scene*. Up until the end of the 1960s, Québécois cultural productions were still part of the French-Canadian repertoire and were designated as such.

3 First performed in February 2007 at the Tarragon Theatre, in a co-production with the National Arts Centre, and then re-presented on a Canadian tour.

Works Cited

Béliveau, Crystal, and Serge Boucher, eds. *Motel Hélène*. By Serge Boucher. Trans. Morwyn Brebner. English adapt. Judith Thompson. Ms. at Le Centre des auteurs dramatiques, Montréal, 2001.

Bosley, Vivien. "Diluting the Mixture: Translating Michel Tremblay's *Les belles-sœurs*." *TTR: Traduction, traductologie, rédaction* 1: 1 (1988): 139–45.

Bouchard, Michel Marc. *Lilies or The Revival of a Romantic Drama*. Trans. Linda Gaboriau. Toronto: Coach House, 1990.

– *The Orphan Muses*. Trans. Linda Gaboriau. Victoria: Scirocco Drama, 1995.

Casanova, Pascale. *La république mondiale des lettres*. Paris: Seuil, 1999.

Gélinas, Gratien. *Tit-Coq*. Trans. Kenneth Johnstone and Gratien Gélinas. Toronto: Clarke and Irwin, 1967.

Hébert, Anne. *Le Temps Sauvage*. Trans. Elizabeth Mascall. Toronto: Firehall Theatre, 23 Nov. 1972.

Hulan, Renée. "Surviving Translation: *Forever Yours Marie-Lou* at Tarragon Theatre." *Theatre Research in Canada* 15: 1 (1994): 48–57.

Koustas, Jane. "From Gélinas to Carrier: Critical Response to Translated Quebec Theatre in Toronto." *Studies in Canadian Literature* 17: 2 (1992): 109–28.

– "From 'Homespun' to 'Awesome': Translated Quebec Theatre in Toronto." Ed. Joseph I. Donohue Jr and Jonathan M. Weiss. *Essays on Modern Quebec Theatre*. East Lansing: Michigan State University Press, 1995, 81–107.

Ladouceur, Louise. "Canada's Michel Tremblay: Des *Belles-Sœurs* à *For the Pleasure of Seeing Her Again*." *TTR: Traduction, traductologie, rédaction* 15: 1 (2002): 137–63. http://www.erudit.org/revue/ttr/2002/v15/n1/006804ar.html

– *Making the Scene: La traduction du théâtre d'une langue officielle à l'autre au Canada*. Québec: Nota bene, 2005.

– "La langue populaire québécoise au Canada anglais: Fonction distinctive et équivalence." *Études françaises* 43 (2007): 29–42. http://www.erudit.org/revue/ etudfr/2007/v43/n1/index.html

Mezei, Stephen. "Tremblay's Toronto Success." *Performing Arts in Canada* 10 (1973): 26.

Mouawad, Wajdi. *Scorched*. Trans. Linda Gaboriau. Toronto: Playwrights Canada Press, 2005.

Rudakof, Judith, and L.M. Thomson. *The Process of Dramaturgy*. Toronto: Playwrights Canada Press, 2002.

Sabbath, Lawrence. "*Belles Sœurs*: Canadian Masterpiece." *Montreal Star*, 11 Oct. 1973, C10.

Saint-Pierre, Jacques. "Michel Tremblay, dramaturge québécois et canadien: Bilan de la réception d'une pièce et sa traduction." *Littérature québécoise: La recherche en émergence*. Actes du deuxième colloque interuniversitaire des jeunes chercheur(e)s en littérature québécoise. Centre de recherche en littérature québécoise. Québec: Nuit blanche, 1991, 57–69.

Steward, Jesse, and Ric Knowles. "Turning an Elephant into a Microphone: A Conversation on Translation and Adaptation." *Canadian Theatre Review* 114 (2003). http://www.utpjournals.com/product/ctr/114/114_Thompson.html

Thompson, Judith, English adapt. *Motel Hélène*. By Serge Boucher. Trans. Morwyn Brebner. Toronto: Playwrights Union of Canada, 2000.

Tremblay, Michel. *Bonjour, Là, Bonjour*. Trans. John Van Burek and Bill Glassco. Vancouver: Talonbooks, 1975.

– *For the Pleasure of Seeing Her Again*. Trans. Linda Gaboriau. Vancouver: Talonbooks, 1998.

– *Forever Yours, Marie-Lou*. Trans. John Van Burek and Bill Glassco. Vancouver: Talonbooks, 1975.

– *The Guid Sisters and Other Plays*. Trans. Martin Bowman and Bill Findlay. London: Nick Hern Books, 1991.

– *Hosanna*. Trans. John Van Burek and Bill Glassco. Vancouver: Talonbooks, 1974.

– *La Maison Suspendue*. Trans. John Van Burek and Bill Glassco. Vancouver: Talonbooks, 1991.

– *Les belles-sœurs*. Montreal: Holt, Rinehart and Winston, 1968.

– *Les belles sœurs*. Trans. John Van Burek and Bill Glassco. Vancouver: Talonbooks, 1974.

– *Les belles sœurs*. Trans. John Van Burek and Bill Glassco. Rev. ed. Vancouver: Talonbooks, 1992.

Wallace, Robert. *Producing Marginality: Theatre and Criticism in Canada*. Saskatoon: Fifth House, 1990.

Whittaker, Herbert. "*Les belles sœurs* Milestone Play." *Globe and Mail*, 4 April 1973, 13.

– "*Belles sœurs* Bright Light for St Lawrence." *Globe and Mail*, 7 May 1973, 14.

– "*Forever Yours* Offers Some Familiar Novelty." *Globe and Mail*, 5 June 1972, 12.

1974: Small West Coast Press Talonbooks Makes a Bold Move and Publishes Four Quebec Plays in Translation

Kathy Mezei

Why did Talonbooks in Vancouver, along with other small publishing houses across Canada in the 1970s, turn to the translation of Quebec writers? What effects did Talonbooks' translations – the choice of translations, the process of obtaining them, and the conditions of production – have on the making of modern Canadian culture?[1] Although Talonbooks can claim neither the first English translation of a modern Quebec play,[2] nor the first translation of a writer from Quebec's Quiet Revolution,[3] its unprecedented publication of four contemporary Quebec plays in 1974 signalled a pivotal moment in the history of literary translation in Canada. Within a space of a few months, this small Vancouver press at the periphery of the country's cultural production brought out Robert Gurik's *API 2967* (translated by Marc Gélinas), and his *The Trial of Jean-Baptiste M.* (translated by Allan Van Meer), followed swiftly by Michel Tremblay's controversial and popular *Hosanna* and *Les belles-sœurs* (translated by theatre producers John van Burek and Bill Glassco). These publications signalled that it was time to ensure the wider availability of Quebec francophone drama in the wake of successful and prize-winning productions of *API 2967* at the 1969 Venice Biennale, *The Trial* in Paris and Athens in 1974, and Tremblay's *Les belles-sœurs* (St Lawrence Centre 1972),[4] *Forever Yours, Marie-Lou* (Tarragon Theatre 1972), and *Hosanna* (Tarragon Theatre 1974) in Toronto. And, as Talonbooks became "forever" the English-language publisher of Tremblay's plays, novels, and memoirs through persistent negotiation and strategies of acquisition,[5] the field of literary production and the dominant producers were seemingly challenged from the margins – the margin of size as well as the margin of location (see Hayward). Then, as Talonbooks achieved renown for its translations of Tremblay in attractively designed paperbacks, several translators from Montreal began to approach them with suggestions, including David Lobdell, Patricia Claxton, Linda Gaboriau, and David Homel. Talonbooks subsequently went on to develop an impressive list of translations of experimental Québec and francophone playwrights and novelists (e.g., Jovette Marchessault, Larry Tremblay, Michel Marc Bouchard, Marie-Claire Blais, Madeleine Gagnon, and Lise Tremblay). Observing the trajectory of this press, Kathleen Scherf remarked that "the life of Talonbooks closely documents and reflects the life of Canadian literary culture since 1967, with a West Coast twist" (132). The following traces the history, conditions, and effects of Talonbooks' trajectory of translation (see Figure 23.1).

This audacious step in 1974 propelled Talonbooks to the edge in two significant ways.[6] First, perched on the west coast, far from the publishing centres of Toronto and Montreal, this young, struggling press took a chance on publishing a playwright whose counterdiscourse disrupted forever not only normative French speech in Quebec literature, but also theatrical forms and conventions by writing in the vernacular about working-class women in Montreal's Plateau Mont-Royal. After much negotiation, Talonbooks finally convinced John Goodwin, Tremblay's literary agent, to award them the contract. In the words of Toronto theatre critic, Urjo Kareda:

> For some time last year, there was a dispute about which Canadian publishing house would acquire the English-language rights to the plays of Quebec dramatist Michel Tremblay [...] Well, the battle was won by Talonbooks, a small but energetic publishing company in Vancouver. (F6)[7]

As Talonbooks boasted in its introduction to the winter 1986/spring 1987 catalogue, the press was "well known for its translations of works from Quebec – notably, for bringing Michel Tremblay's plays and first novel into print in English." It has been no mean feat to maintain this relationship from Vancouver with Quebec's most prolific writer, while juggling Quebec publishing houses, barriers of language and customs, agents, translators, authors, and the Canada Council bureaucracy, in what Karl Siegler has compellingly described as a "a cascade of challenges" (Personal interview).[8] Embedded in this history of acquisition is the story of how canons are

Figure 23.1

Cover of Michel Tremblay's *Les Belles-Soeurs* (Talonbooks, 1974).

created – in this case of a certain aspect of Quebec writing – humorous, carnivalesque, Montreal-centred, sometimes offering the perspective of homosexuals, sometimes that of children, or working-class women.

Second, Talonbooks, which began publishing poetry books in 1967 under the editorship of Jim Brown, David Robinson, and Gordon Fidler, shifted its attention to contemporary Canadian drama with the arrival of Peter Hay in 1969 as drama editor: a risky but, in the end, profitable gamble.[9] The publication of drama, like that of translations, is a layered and complex process of production, involving scripts, notations, stage directions, agents, the variables of spectators and audience, playwrights, and directors. In his study of the press, Michael Hayward offers one reason for this venture: "Unable to locate Canadian play texts to teach [at Simon Fraser University], he [Peter Hay] eventually approached Talonbooks with the rights to two plays [James Reaney's *Colours in the Dark* and George Ryga's *The Ecstasy of Rita Joe*]" (4). Karl Siegler suggests another: "Canadian publishers such as Talonbooks, by continuing to publish poetry and drama titles into a marketplace too small to make such titles financially viable, are performing an important role in defining and maintaining Canadian culture" (quoted in Hayward 12). In a number of communications, Siegler is adamant that Talonbooks become the "major play publisher in English Canada" (Letter to Naïm Kattan).

But why and how "forever Tremblay"? Chance, timeliness, and synchronicity played their role for, according to Siegler, Leméac Editions, which was the prime publisher of Quebec theatre just as Talonbooks had become the publisher of anglophone contemporary theatre, was searching for an English analogue, while at the same time, Talonbooks, at the urging of Hay, was looking for a Quebec analogue (Personal interview). Yves Dubé, Leméac's director, had noted the quick succession and success of plays published by Talonbooks and the resulting national and international productions and laudatory reviews. Early in 1974, Dubé made a special trip to Vancouver expressly to check out Talonbooks and meet with David Robinson, Peter Hay, and Siegler. Although it was Robert Gurik who was on the agenda, Dubé sang Tremblay's praises; intrigued, Talonbooks decided to pursue this connection (Personal interview).[10] And, indeed, by October 1974, *Hosanna* was out in print.

In order to understand the felicitous conjunction of the emergence of small presses like Talonbooks with the turn to translation in the 1960s and

1970s and its effects on the making of modern Canadian culture, we need
to examine how this emergence was fostered by specific cultural and institutional conditions. As David Robinson explained in response to George
Woodcock's query about the rise of so many new publishing houses in the
previous five years:

> [It was] the discovery, among ourselves, that *we* have the writers –
> poets, playwrights, novelists, short story writers, even artists and
> film makers, *and* that they need books – as a service to *their* com-
> munity and to the community at large. (Quoted in Woodcock 52)

Cultural Conditions and the Rise of Small Presses in the 1960s and 1970s

Often started by writers and staffed by the writers and their (girl)friends,[11]
small presses are ideological rather than profit-driven, associated with modernism and the avant-garde – and justified by their lack of readership and
mass audiences! In the 1960s and 1970s, several circumstances converged
to create an explosion of small presses across Canada. Between 1965 and
1975, there were several dramatic changes in Canadian publishing. More
and more, the major Toronto houses concentrated on mass-circulation titles
and rejected books that lacked nationwide sales appeal. Because many of
these firms were evolving into public companies and/or subsidiaries of international corporations, publishing decisions often had more to do with
the bottom line than the vision of any one person. By contrast, small press
owners maintained hands-on control over all aspects of publishing from
the manuscript to the finished book. The development of offset presses and
computerized printing made possible the production of low-cost, attractively designed books, most of them in soft cover editions (Parker).

Reacting against the tradition of realism in Canadian fiction and in the
publishing sphere, writers like Dennis Lee and Dave Godfrey (Anansi), and
Victor Coleman (Coach House Press) set up venues for experimental writers in adventurously designed and well-crafted books, independent of the
editorial and marketing constraints of the big publishing houses. To that
mix, Talonbooks added the desire to counter "the pan-Canadian, New

Canadian Library, patriotic agenda in favour of articulating the local" (Scherf 137). As David Robinson remarked, "Talonbooks' impetus to begin publishing was local" (quoted in Woodcock 57), and several emerging presses such as Talonbooks in Vancouver, Coteau Books in Regina, and Fiddlehead Books in the Maritimes defied the centrifugal pull and power of the centre, concentrating instead, on the local and deliberately flaunting their peripheral status: "[I] try to bring new blood in, but also, to move things out" (60). However, as its extensive drama list from 1969 on indicates, and its significant translation list further corroborates, Talonbooks, having accumulated substantial cultural capital, perceives itself now as a federalist press, a Canadian literary publisher (Robinson, Personal interview).[12]

Other small presses that pursued and published translations included Harvest House in Montreal, from 1965 to 1995, with their French Writers in Canada series; House of Anansi, beginning in 1967, which was persuaded by Sheila Fischman to produce the Roch Carrier trilogy; Michael Macklem's Oberon Press, from 1966; and Coach House Press, from 1965, which under the direction of Barbara Godard and Frank Davey created the Quebec Translation series, 1975–1989. Coach House, whose first translation was Victor-Lévy Beaulieu's *Jack Kerouac: A Chicken-Essay*, was instrumental in bringing Nicole Brossard's poetry, fiction, and feminist theory to the attention of English Canada.[13] Later in the 1980s, the Women's Press, among the second wave of small presses, focused on feminist texts from Quebec.[14] By the mid-1970s, Talonbooks' translation list had expanded to include fiction, and by the late 1970s, non-fiction.[15]

The flexibility and adventurousness of small presses, the hands-on (although sometimes testy) relationship between editors, designers, translators, and authors along with attractive and accessible book designs and the continuing marketability of translations as course adoptions appealed to authors and their translators. At the same time, translations of writing from Quebec that experimented with form and language enhanced the small anglophone presses' reputation as avant-garde and exploratory.

Additional sociopolitical conditions influencing the appeal of translating the other included the following: the patriotism generated by centennial celebrations and Expo 67 in Montreal, the rise of Canadian nationalism and the desire to discover and forge a "Canadian" identity accompanied by anti-Americanism sentiments, the anti–Vietnam War protests, the peace and civil rights movements, campus activism and radicalism, and Paris 1968. Events in Quebec also conspired to spark the interest of anglophone writers and publishers: the Quiet Revolution of the 1960s; the Quebec independence movement; the 1970 October Crisis with its alarming and anti-democratic crackdown on writers, artists, musicians, and performers; the close ties between leftist politics and culture; and the explosion of experimental writing in Quebec grounded in a radical sense of place and language.

This mounting interest in translations from French to English in the 1970s was thus linked not only to the oft-expressed but seldom reciprocated desire to bridge the cultural gap between the two solitudes, but also to the wish to understand the turbulent situation in Quebec. As Peter Hay chided in his introduction to Gurik's *The Trial of Jean-Baptiste M.*:

> One of the commonest commonplaces of Canadian culture is to remark about the absence of cross-fertilization between its two official languages [...] Yet, there is only one thing rarer than a French Canadian play produced by an English Canadian theatre, and that's vice versa. (5)

Describing Anansi's program of publishing French-Canadian books in translation, John Metcalf admitted that while "such translations or bilingual editions are usually pious exercises fuelled by government gold," and that "hardly anyone on either side of the divide actually reads them," the "[Roch] Carrier trilogy was a genuine and popular success" (9). John Van Burek's advice to David Robinson was simply to choose good plays and plays of historical or social interest.[16] In retrospect, however, these gestures of mediation and bridge building were, nevertheless, marked by an uncritical acceptance of anglophone dominance and hegemony. For example, the correspondence between Talonbooks and Lémeac and Gurik was entirely in English.

Another powerful incentive for translating and publishing Quebec writers stemmed from envy of the vibrant and avant-garde cultural scene in Quebec and led to a propensity to embroider a narrative construction of Quebec as an eroticized and exoticized imagined community. As Frank Davey recalled:

A frequently important element in the anglophone desire for connection with Quebec was a romantic view of its francophone culture as more passionate, violent, and creative than much of anglophone culture – not only an FLQ Quebec where nationalists paraded with flags, planted bombs, kidnapped officials, and exploded themselves in parliamentary washrooms, but also a Gilles Vigneault-Pauline Julien Quebec where people were believed to care deeply about poetry, culture, and collective creativity [...] and a site of libidinal excess. ("A History of the Coach House Press Translations")

And, finally, there were timely and specific institutional factors, emerging out of the volatile political climate and social context that enabled small presses like Talonbooks to publish Quebec writers in translation.

Institutional Factors

In response to its Royal Commission on Bilingualism and Biculturalism, which had warned that Quebec's simmering discontent indicated that Canada was passing through the greatest crisis in its history (1965), the federal government enacted the Official Languages Act, 1969, which was intended to enhance the status of French federally and implement bilingualism in Parliament and federal institutions, and began to promote official bilingualism and biculturalism. On a smaller scale, literary translations received support through the Canada Council translation grant program, starting in 1972,[17] which was also the year in which block publishing grants were inaugurated.[18] Publishers like Talonbooks also took advantage of federal programs like Opportunities for Youth and Local Initiatives to hire assistants; these grants also enabled theatrical troupes to produce and tour contemporary Quebec plays, as Allan Van Meer did throughout British Columbia in 1972 with his translated versions of Tremblay, Gurik, and Dominque de Pasquale (Talonbooks Fonds, MsC 8.4.13.14), versions that then found their way to Talonbooks and other small presses.

A crucial boost to small presses and the publication of Quebec literature in translation was the educational capital created by the demand for course books due to the rapid rise of new universities, the expansion of established ones, and the gradual development of courses in Canadian literature and Canadian Studies. In other words, course adoptions and the educational system conferred a "legitimate mode of consumption" (Bourdieu 37). An enduring effect, therefore, of the 1974 venture into translating Gurik and Tremblay is that about a quarter of Talonbooks' list now consists of translations, and that a corpus of Quebec playwrights are accessible and available for study in schools and universities and for mounting productions nationally and internationally. Another effect is its contribution to the creation of a canon of Quebec writers for anglophone students and readers that privileges Tremblay's plays and novels. However, like other presses, Talonbooks has recently expanded its list to include francophone literature outside Quebec (Jean Marc Dalpé) and translations from other languages. New emerging small presses – Broken Jaw Press in Fredericton, Butschek Books in Ottawa, Cormorant Books in Toronto, Ekstastis in Victoria – join older presses like Oberon, Vehicule (est. 1973), Guernica (est. 1970), and Exile Editions (est. 1976) in publishing not only translations from French, but also from Spanish, Gallician, First Nations, German, Russian, Polish, Yiddish, Italian, and Arabic languages. In 2011/2012, the Canada Council awarded ninety-seven translation grants to forty-eight Canadian publishers.

Talonbooks is thus a prime example of the margin surprising and inflecting the centre. Its leading edge and edginess as a publisher of drama, in pursuing the federal and the BC government for funding, and in its choice of texts to be translated implies a realignment of the field of cultural production. However, despite the valiant and persistent efforts of Talonbooks and other small presses, the rest of Canada's experience of writing in Quebec is worryingly contingent, for it remains limited by what gets translated, how and by whom it is translated, how adequately it is funded, and the necessity to attract readers and spectators.[19] The canon of translated texts is eclectic and, even in the case of small, independent, ideologically driven presses, dependent less on any considered program of selection than on recommendations by translators, who can be seen as gatekeepers of the other culture, the vagaries of the translation grant Program, publishers' preferences, contracts and rights negotiations, the allure of prize winners, and marketability. "Name-stuff," as translator David Lobdell once admonished David Robinson, tends to be published over lesser-known figures, thus ironically, vitiating the radical function of the small press and potentially blunting its edginess (Letter to David Robinson, 25 Jan. 1977).[20]

Notes

1 The extensive Talonbooks Fonds (Special Collections and Rare Books, W.A.C. Bennett Library, Simon Fraser University, Burnaby, BC, accession number MsC 8) has been an invaluable resource for this article. I am most grateful to Eric Swanick, Tony Power, Keith Gilbert, and Judith Polson for their attentiveness and assistance with these materials. Conversations and correspondence with Karl Siegler are very much appreciated, and I warmly thank Ian Chunn and Michael Hayward for their information and advice.

2 Gratien Gélinas's *Bousille and the Just* appeared in 1961 and must be considered the first modern Quebec play translated into English.

3 Roch Carrier's *La Guerre, Yes Sir!* was published in 1970; Marie-Claire Blais' *Mad Shadows* had been published by 1960, and David Lobdell had hoped to retranslate it for Talonbooks (Letter to David Robinson 25 Jan. 1977); in 1955, Contact Press published *Nine Poems* by Saint-Denys-Garneau, *Seven Poems* by Gilles Hénault, and *Six Poems* by Paul-Marie Lapointe, all translated by Jean Beaupré and Gael Turnbull. New Press, started by former Anansi publisher David Godfrey, along with James Bacque and Roy MacSkimming, created the short-lived New Drama series (New Press was taken over by General Publishing in 1974), which offered several Quebec plays in translation in 1972, including Marcel Dubé's *The White Geese* and Robert Gurik's *The Hanged Man*. These plays lie within a more traditional realist tradition than Tremblay's oeuvre, and for this reason they, along with the two Gurik plays published by Talonbooks, have not been in demand as course adoptions and, therefore, are no longer in print.

4 *Les belle-sœurs* "set off a storm of controversy, firstly because of the language (a particularly raucous – some say vulgar – joual), and then because it dared to portray working class women doing working class things. Also, it went after men. None of this sounds particularly special today, but in 1968, theatre in Quebec was just releasing itself from religious and morality plays and joining (late) in the Quiet Revolution; although Marcel Dubé and Gratien Gélinas had been writing about 'normal' folk for years, they had not been doing it quite like this." (http://www.canadiantheatre.com/dict.pl?term=Les%20belles-soeurs). For the translation history of *Les belles-sœurs* and for an analysis of issues such as the translation of *joual*, see Louise Ladouceur and Gillian Lane-Mercier in this volume. Ladouceur notes the omission of the translators' names on the cover of the Talonbooks editions – thus, as she points out, giving the impression that they were not translations but written in English in the first place.

For additional elaborations, see Ladouceur's *Making the Scene: la traduction du théâtre d'une langue officielle à l'autre au Canada* and "Recently Canadian: versions franco-québécoises du théâtre canadien-anglais,"as well as Vivien Bosley's "Diluting the Mixture: Translating Michel Tremblay's *Les belles-sœurs.*"

5 Van Burek and Glassco translated seven plays; from *For the Pleasure of Seeing Her Again*, which appeared in 1998, the plays have been translated by Linda Gaboriau; Sheila Fischman has the option on the novels, and Linda Gaboriau and Fischman have, respectively, translated his memoirs and autobiographies.

6 The 1963 poetry magazine *Talon* had transformed into the Talonbooks publishing house by 1967 and began publishing poetry collections.

I use the word "edge" deliberately here because of its playful evocation of the counterculture of Vancouver and Talonbooks in the 1970s. The poetry published by Talonbooks (bill bissett, George Bowering, Frank Davey, b.p. nichol) was avant-garde and alternative, on the edge, edgy, tuned more to experimental American language poets like Robert Creeley, Denise Levertov, Charles Olson, and Robert Duncan than to poets in central Canada; Vancouver as a city felt itself culturally removed from the centre, and sits on the western edge of the country and continent. There is also a tone of edginess in the self-conscious bravado about the cultural positioning of west coast writing and publishing that we can trace in the correspondence of Karl Siegler and David Robinson. While I am aware that terms like "margins," "periphery," "edge" can reify hierarchical positions, I think the term "edge" captures the spirit of the 1970s.

7 Kareda comments on the popularity of Tremblay's plays at the Tarragon Theatre and St Lawrence Centre in Toronto; he also notes that there was a demand for making translations available for the "expanding Canadian drama courses at high schools and universities" (F6).

8 Karl Siegler joined Talonbooks in January 1974 as business manager and, by 1984, with his wife Christy, had taken over as owner and publisher. In 2008, Kevin and Vicki Williams became majority shareholders in the press, while Karl continued as editor and publisher and Christy, as production manager, until September 2011, when, after four dedicated decades, they turned over their shares to Kevin and Vicki, and left the press.

9 Siegler claims that Talonbooks sells between 500 and 1000 copies of *Les Belles-Sœurs* annually (personal interview).

10 In a postscript to a 21 June 1974 letter to Robinson about a contract for David Freeman's *Battering Ram*, Goodwin was cryptic: "I am meeting with Dubé and

will clear the other matter at that time" (Letter to David Robinson). Gurik
seems to have played a role as advocate and intermediary, writing to Peter Hay,
"I talk to Dubé of Leméac and he is waiting tomorrow for an answer from the
biggest edition house of Toronto on Michel Tremblay's play. After talking to
him he said he will be willing to have you publish one of Tremblay's play. He
did [not?] elaborate which one" (Letter to Peter Hay). Gurik was referring to
McClelland and Stewart; New Press was also angling for Tremblay. On 29 July
1974, Gurik wrote to David Robinson, "I talk to Dubé this morning and I am
happy that you finally got all the Tremblay's" (Letter to David Robinson).

11 For a concise history of small presses in Canada, see George Parker's "Small
Presses"; David McKnight's "Small Press Publishing"; and Roy MacSkimming's
The Perilous Trade. Jim Brown reminisced, "I remember my girlfriends got
stuck with the job of typing it – I always had girlfriends who were good
typists" (*Line* 105).

12 Robinson's emphasis on the local may refer to the preponderance of BC and
Vancouver poets published by Talonbooks in the 1960s and early 1970s (e.g.,
bill bissett, Lionel Kearns, George Bowering, Frank Davey, Phyllis Webb,
Jamie Reid, and Peter Trower).

13 Ironically, Talonbooks declined to translate Brossard because she didn't have
enough of a reputation outside of Quebec (Letter from David Lobdell to
David Robinson, 28 Nov. 1977).

14 Susanne de Lotbinière-Harwood, *Re-belle et infidèle: La traduction comme
pratique de réécriture au feminin / The Body Bilingual: Translation as a Rewriting in the Feminine*; Lise Gauvin, *Letters from an Other*; and Nicole Brossard,
The Aerial Letter.

15 In 2011, Talonbooks published Hugh Hazelton's translations of Yannick
Renaud's two volumes of poems (*Taxidermie, La disparition des idées*); thus,
their translation program finally encompasses all four genres, fulfilling one
of the long-term goals of the press (Siegler, 28 March 2011).

16 Roy MacSkimming's more tempered rationale was that "Anansi also advanced
English-speaking Canadians' knowledge of the other solitude" (*Making Literary History* 17).

17 In 1977, aid to translations included grants for the translation of plays for
production. Translation grants were awarded as subsidies to publishers, not
to translators; the publisher then paid the translator.

18 Correspondence in the Talonbooks archive reveals a prickly, cantankerous relationship in the late 1960s and 1970s with Canada Council officials, like Naïm

Kattan (who claims to have initiated the Translation Grant program), Robert
Fink, and Robin Farr as Talonbooks continually renegotiates its position in
relation to "institutionalized cultural authority" (Bourdieu 39). Jim Brown
recalled concerns about the Council's role in determining what should be published and "the question of autonomy," noting that the Vancouver scene tended
to be paranoid about central Canadian and federal interference: "The Canada
Council is going to become the editor for small presses – and it did happen"
(118).

19 For example, until recently, publishers could not have more than six Canada
Council–supported translations underway at any one time.

20 For example, prize winners, especially the Governor-General's Fiction or
Drama prize winners often tend to have priority.

Works Cited

Beaulieu, Victor-Lévy. *Jack Kerouac: A Chicken-Essay*. Trans. Sheila Fischman.
Toronto: Coach House, 1975.

Blais, Marie-Claire. *Mad Shadows* [*La Belle Bête*]. Trans. Merloyd Lawrence.
Toronto: McClelland and Stewart, 1960.

Bosley, Vivien. "Diluting the Mixture: Translating Michel Tremblay's *Les belles-
sœurs*." *TTR: Traduction, traductologie, rédaction* 1: 1 (1988): 139–45.

Bourdieu, Pierre. *The Field of Cultural Production: Essays on Art and Literature*.
Ed. Randal Johnson. Trans. Claud DuVerlie. Cambridge: Polity Press, 1993.

Brossard, Nicole. *The Aerial Letter*. Trans. Marlene Wildeman. Toronto: Women's
Press, 1988.

Brown, Jim, and Barry McKinnon. "Vancouver Writing Seen in the 60s." *Line* 7/8
(Spring/Fall 1986): 94–123.

Carrier, Roch. *La Guerre, Yes Sir!* Trans. Sheila Fischman. Toronto: House of
Anansi, 1970.

Davey, Frank. "A History of the Coach House Press Translations."
http://publish.uwo.ca/~fdavey/c/daveymain.htm

– "The Beginnings of an End to Coach House Press." *Open Letter: A Canadian
Journal of Writing and Theory* Ninth Series no. 8 (Spring 1997): 40–77.

De Lotbinière-Harwood, Susanne. *Re-belle et infidèle: La traduction comme pratique de réécriture au féminin / The Body Bilingual: Translation as a Rewriting in
the Feminine*. Montréal/Toronto: Les éditions du remue-ménage / Women's Press,
1991.

Dubé, Marcel. *The White Geese*. Trans. Jean Remple. Toronto: New Press, 1972.

Gauvin, Lise. *Letters from an Other*. Trans. Susanne de Lotbinière-Harwood. Toronto: Women's Press, 1989.

Gélinas, Gratien. *Bousille and the Just*. Trans. Kenneth Johnson and Joffre Miville-Dechêne. Toronto: Clarke Irwin, 1961.

Goodwin, John. Letter to David Robinson, 21 June 1974. MsC 8.2.14.4. Talonbooks Fonds. Special Collections and Rare Books. W.A.C. Bennett Library, Simon Fraser University, Burnaby, BC (hereafter, Talonbooks Fonds).

Gurik, Robert. *The Hanged Man*. Trans. Philip London and Laurence Bérard. Toronto: New Press, 1972.

– Letter to David Robinson, 29 July 1974. MsC 8.3.2.4. Talonbooks Fonds.

– Letter to Peter Hay, n.d. [?1974.] MsC 8.3.2.5. Talonbooks Fonds.

Hay, Peter. Introduction. *The Trial of Jean-Baptiste M*. Vancouver: Talonbooks, 1974.

Hayward, Michael. "Talonbooks: Publishing from the Margins." Unpublished essay. April 1991. Talonbooks Fonds.

Kareda, Urjo. "Small Publisher Wins Play Rights." *Toronto Star*, 19 Sept. 1974: F6.

Ladouceur, Louise. "Recently Canadian: Versions franco-québécoises du théâtre canadien-anglais." *Tendances actuelles en histoire littéraire canadienne*. Québec: Nota bene, 2003, 131–48.

– *Making the Scene: La traduction du théâtre d'une langue officielle à l'autre au Canada*. Montréal: Nota bene, 2005.

Lobdell, David. Letter to David Robinson, 25 Jan. 1977. MsC 8.a, Box 21. Talonbooks Fonds.

– Letter to David Robinson, 28 Nov. 1977. MsC 8.a, Box 21, 82. Talonbooks Fonds.

MacSkimming, Roy. *Making Literary History: House of Anansi Press, 1967–1997*. Concord, ON: House of Anansi, 1997.

– *The Perilous Trade: Book Publishing in Canada, 1946–2006*. Toronto: McClelland and Stewart, 2007.

McKnight, David. "Small Press Publishing." *History of the Book in Canada, 1918–1980*. Vol. 3. Ed. Carole Gerson and Jacques Michon. Toronto: University of Toronto Press, 2007, 302–18.

Metcalf, John. "A Collector's Notes on the House of Anansi." *Canadian Notes and Queries* (Spring/Summer 2002): 3–11.

Parker, George. "Small Presses." *The Canadian Encyclopedia*. 21 Nov. 2009. http://www.thecanadianencyclopedia.com/index.cfm?PgNm=TCE&Params=A1ARTA0007459

Scherf, Kathleen. "A Legacy of Canadian Cultural Tradition and the Small Press:
   The Case of Talonbooks." *Studies in Canadian Literature* 25: 1 (2000): 131–49.
Siegler, Karl. Letter. Letter to Naïm Kattan, 18 Sept 1972. MsC 8.4.5.18. Talon-
   books Fonds.
– Personal interview. 14 Apr. 2008.
– Talonbooks Spring 2011 Catalogue. 28 Mar. 2011.
Talonbooks Fonds. Accession number MsC 8. Special Collections and Rare Books.
   W.A.C. Bennett Library, Simon Fraser University, Burnaby, BC.
Van Burek, John. Letter to David Robinson, 12 July 1975. MsC 8.4.13.12.
   Talonbooks Fonds.
Woodcock, George. "New Wave in Publishing." *Canadian Literature* 57 (1973):
   50–64.

24

1977: Michel Tremblay's *Bonjour, là, bonjour* in English at the Saidye Bronfman Centre Theatre: Jouissance, Translation, and a Choice of Taboos

Gregory J. Reid

Prior to the first election of the independentist Parti Québécois in 1976, Michel Tremblay had refused to allow his plays to be produced in English in Quebec. The Quebec premiere of John Van Burek's and Bill Glassco's English translation of Tremblay's *Bonjour, là, bonjour* at the Saidye Bronfman Centre (now the Segal Centre for Performing Arts) in Montreal in 1977 was, therefore, the first time that a Tremblay play had been presented in Quebec in English. The event was a crossroads of many histories, and even now, more than three decades later, we are still challenged to grasp its full significance.

The production came almost ten years after the landmark premiere of Tremblay's *Les belles-sœurs* at Théâtre du Rideau Vert. By 1977 the 35-year-old Tremblay was well established as Quebec's playwright laureate while challenging convention at every turn. His plays had already taken on one taboo after another: using *joual* in poetic, empathetic portrayals of working-class housewives, homosexuals, and transvestites. With every Tremblay play, director André Brassard would seem to invent yet another new dramaturgical style. Nonetheless, *Bonjour, là, bonjour* marked a new level of radicalism in both style and content. For the Saidye Bronfman production, Brassard opted for largely static blocking, with the cast of eight sitting around a huge table that dominated the stage. Tremblay's text not only dealt with the taboo of sibling incest, as the play's hero, Serge, returns from a sojourn in Paris and tries to come to terms with the affair he had begun with his sister Nicole, but also the play concludes in the "happy ending" of their decision to live together and take in their aging, hearing-impaired father.

The play premiered in Ottawa at the National Arts Centre in 1974, produced by the Compagnie des Deux Chaises, before touring Quebec. In his essay in Gilbert David and Pierre Lavoie's *Le monde de Michel Tremblay*, Stéphane Lépine qualifies *Bonjour, là, bonjour* as "la pièce central du Cycle de Belles-sœurs" (125). According to Lépine, the incest theme is "décoratif […] une métaphore de la rupture (souhaitée) avec la Loi," whereas "l'enjeu essentiel de la pièce demeure très certainement ce renouement avec le père" (127). The play is dedicated to Tremblay's father, and Armand, the father-character of the play, is clearly based on Tremblay's own father who, as Tremblay has revealed elsewhere, suffered from hearing loss. There is, then, ample evidence that the play's dominant theme is the traditional patriarchal reconciliation of father and son. Lucie Robert pursues this patriarchal theme, arguing:

> le personnage de Serge dans *Bonjour, là, bonjour* […] tombe amoureux de sa sœur, avec qui il a une relation incestueuse mais malgré tout présentée comme égalitaire et profondément narcissique: Nicole peut être vue comme le double de Serge, comme cette féminité détachée de lui-même, mais encore assez proche pour qu'il en tombe amoureux. Cette division du féminin et du masculin permet également au personnage d'entreprendre la réconciliation avec le Père. (371)

Robert concludes that, in effect, *Bonjour, là, bonjour* is the first play in the Belles-sœurs cycle in which the "father" assumes a real presence rather than simply being put on stage to signify his own insignificance. However, in contrast to this view of the play as a return to patriarchy, Dominique Lafon argues that even if *Bonjour, là, bonjour* can be read as "la première pièce du Cycle où le père assume une réelle présence, n'ayant été jusque-là mis en scène que pour désigner son insignifiance" (95), the denouement of the drama signals the weakness of the father-figure who is welcomed into an unlikely family unit based on sibling incest. That the Father acquiesces to this union, which he admits to having known about all along, not only puts into question the verisimilitude of the play, but in exercising and accepting the incest taboo, the play challenges patriarchal, familial tradition and the "law of the father" (Lafon 95).

The sibling incest taboo, because it is so forthrightly presented and ultimately embraced within the play, overshadows the various other taboos displayed in *Bonjour, là, bonjour*. Within structuralist anthropology from

Lévi-Strauss onwards, taboos are generally understood as contravening the binary structures that are taken to be the organizing principle of all cultures. Most cultures maintain fairly obvious binary categories separating the "marriageable" and the "unmarriageable." The incest taboo signals that we must marry someone outside the family on the family/not-family binary axis. Traditionally, most societies have maintained other marriage taboos in line with a general us/them, same/different binary compelling individuals, in varying degrees, to remain within their own race, class, generation, tribe, religion, and so on. The matriarchal figure, Lucienne, Serge's oldest sister, is the transgressor of many of these other taboos at issue in *Bonjour, là, bonjour*.

Not only is Lucienne a social-climbing, materialistic, egocentric bourgeois and an avowed adulteress, her sexual appetites run towards younger men. Lucienne consistently occupies an interstitial taboo space between poor and rich, working class and ruling class, young and old, propriety and impropriety. However, within the play, her most unmitigated taboo is to have crossed the linguistic line between English and French and married "un Anglais." Consequently, throughout the play she is referred to, bitterly, by her relatives as "l'Anglaise." In the present context, this particular taboo is of interest for a number of reasons, not the least of which is the paradox that the play itself being presented in English translation in Quebec seems to repeat the same taboo.

As Muriel Gold outlines in her history of the Saidye Bronfman Centre Theatre, *A Gift for Their Mother*, the eventual production of *Bonjour, là, bonjour* was anticipated and inspired by the creation of Théâtre Rencontre in 1973, a collaboration among Allied Jewish Community Services, the Saidye Bronfman Centre, Playwrights' Workshop Montreal, and Le Centre d'Essai des Auteurs Dramatiques to produce plays in both English and French at the Saidye "to develop ways of rapprochement between Anglophones and Francophones and to sensitize the entire Jewish community to the need to recognize the importance and significance of the French language and culture" (Sabbath, quoted in Gold 234). However, after two seasons, the project fell through because, as Gold recounts, audiences were becoming increasingly English, and "some members of Le Centre d'Essai felt that the word 'bilingue' connoted English and they preferred to present their own plays in French in a totally French environment" (236). "With the demise of, and inspired by, Théâtre Rencontre," beginning in 1976,

Gold, as artistic director of the Saidye Bronfman Centre Theatre, implemented a policy of including in each five-play season "one Québécois play in translation in order to expose English-speaking audiences to Québécois plays and artists" (237; see also Rachel Margolis in this volume).

Tremblay's debut in English in Quebec, consequently, was one of a number of productions at the Saidye that were significant "translations": one of which was not a translation and another not Québécois. That is, in addition to presenting plays in English translation such as Michel Garneau's *Quatre à Quatre*, Tremblay's *Bonjour, là, bonjour* and *L'impromtu d'Outremont*, as well as Gratien Gélinas' *La passion de Narcisse Mondoux*, the Saidye also produced English premieres of John T. McDonough's *Charbonneau et le Chef* which had become a classic in French in Quebec, although it was originally published in English, and Antoinine Maillet's Acadian classic, *La Sagouine*.

Gold also describes the "post-performance discussions," the "teach-ins at the Saidye," which "Brassard and Tremblay often participated in" (245). The one I attended took place in a classroom on the downtown campus of Concordia University during the run of *Bonjour, là, bonjour* at the Saidye. Tremblay began the meeting by telling the audience that he did not intend to give a speech, but if we had any questions he would be happy to answer them. After a brief, stunned silence, Tremblay gestured as if to leave, sending a collective gasp through the audience. As three or four spectators precipitously raised their hands to ask questions, Tremblay smiled at us impishly.

The first question I remember was the obvious "question of the evening": why had Tremblay changed his policy and allowed his play to be presented in English? Tremblay responded that now that there was a government in place to take care of such things, it was not his "job" to be responsible for Quebec's language policy. At least one audience member wanted to know why Tremblay insisted on writing in a form of French that people who had learned French in school found very difficult to understand. Tremblay's answer was that he did not consider himself a French teacher, but ultimately, he did not consider the gentleman's problem a very important one.

What followed and, in my recollection occupied the better part of our meeting, were a series of what I would now describe as very English, bloke-ish, square-head euphemistic questions about the "sources," "family background," and "autobiographical elements" of *Bonjour, là, bonjour*. For the better part of an hour, Tremblay feigned innocence and struggled to answer these questions literally by pointing out how he has been inspired by Greek tragedy and by music, that Quebec is a family, and family is always important in Quebec, and yes, everything he writes is autobiographical. Finally, he interrupted himself in an "oh-by-the-way" manner to say: "I think I perhaps should tell you that I am an only child, but if I was going to have a sexual affair with a sibling, it would be with my brother."

Perhaps sensing that the joke had been too good and at the audience's expense, Tremblay took a deep breath to signal a change of register. I remember quite clearly what Tremblay said next because, although simple and straightforward, it would remain the core of my understanding of Tremblay's work for the next thirty years. He began, "What I tried to say in this play, it's what I say in all my work, if you have the chance [...] it doesn't matter what it is." He paused to gesture, pointing, "even if it's a chicken walking down the road." Tremblay winced slightly, already a bit unhappy with his own analogy, then continued, "If you have a chance for happiness, for love, you take it, no matter what!"

The word for what Tremblay is describing here, I have since concluded, is *jouissance*. The word, which covers both sexual orgasm and religious ecstasy, the thrill of transgressing a taboo and the right and satisfaction of possession, has no equivalent in English. The concept of jouissance, to a degree, resolves the either/or debate of the critics as to whether the play overturns or embraces patriarchy. Both sibling incest and paternal reconciliation are potential sources of jouissance; the romantic fantasy of being able to enjoy them both is the play's ultimate example of jouissance. In his overview and analysis of Tremblay's career, Craig Walker extensively develops "an idea that lies close to the heart of Tremblay's poetic theatre: that religion and sexuality often spring from a common source" (202). A word that could cover this "idea" is, once again, jouissance.

That translation is a form of transgression and betrayal has become a bromide, but less discussed is the idea that this transgression is a *cause* of jouissance. As Louise Ladouceur outlines in *Making the Scene: La traduction du théâtre d'une langue officielle à l'autre au Canada* (see Louise Ladouceur's contribution to this volume), Michel Tremblay is English Canada's most translated francophone playwright. This fact, in itself, seems tinged with taboo as we might note in Craig Walker's justification of the inclusion of Tremblay in his study of six of Canada's best known play-wrights in English-language theatre against the perception that "it has become customary to treat the French and English literatures of Canada separately" (viii). Van Burek, alone and with Glassco, has been responsible for the English translations of a dozen Tremblay plays, with *Les belles-sœurs* (1974) and *Hosanna* (1974) preceding *Bonjour, là, bonjour* (Ladouceur, *Making the Scene* 89, 94, and 95). The English translation of *Bonjour, là, bonjour* premiered in Toronto at the Tarragon Theatre in 1975 – that is, two years before the Saidye production.

Inevitably something gets broken in the process of translation. Either the French original, for example, must be fractured to fit the Procrustean bed of English cultural expectations and linguistic requirements, or the original must be allowed to do some damage to the language and expectations of the target audience. In the former case, we have what Lawrence Venuti would call the "invisibility" of the translator and a "domesticating" mode of translation; in the latter, a "foreignizing" (81) process. Invariably, attempts to mitigate, compromise, or mask what gets broken by these alternatives are, or are perceived as, a kind of cover-up.

For example, Ladouceur characterizes Van Burek and Glassco's use of French names for persons and places, and a number of Gallicisms and calques within the English translations of Tremblay as reducing the threat of difference. Ladouceur argues that *joual*, in addition to being the sociolect of a disavantaged class, "s'est aussi imposé comme langue dénonciatrice d'une alienation linguistic et culturelle ainsi que symbole d'affirmation identitaire" (*Making the Scene* 108; see also Ladouceur's contribution to this volume). Since it is seemingly impossible to translate *joual* into Canadian English, ultimately, in Ladouceur's view, the "québécitude" of Tremblay's text is reduced to curses and Gallicisms: "une québécitude non menaçante à laquelle le public Anglophone est très attaché" (*Making the Scene* 108). Do Ladouceur's observations apply to *Bonjour, là, bonjour* as performed at the Saidye in 1977? Since Ladouceur's basic argument is that anglophone audiences are given insufficient context within which to appreciate the subversive import of Tremblay's plays, it would be significantly less applicable to an anglophone audience in Montreal shortly after the first election of the sovereignist Parti Québécois in 1976. However, Ladouceur's argument that the inclusion of various markers of linguistic alterity creates a false sense of authenticity (*Making the Scene* 109) would seem to apply. As Alan

Filewod points out in *Performing Canada*, throughout its history Canadian theatre, including what was known as the alternative theatre movement throughout the 1970s, has been driven by the "imagined cultural authenticity" (1) of the nation, of regions and communities. The translations of Tremblay's plays, as Ladouceur underlines, were an important contribution to English-Canadian "alternative theatre." In concluding her discussion of the Saidye's rich history of presenting Québécois plays in translation, Gold offers the opinion that:

> Québécois plays should not only be presented in English but they should be cast with Québécois actors to retain the flavour of the characters. With Tremblay plays in particular, especially in Quebec, where English theatregoers are either bilingual themselves, or at the very least, exposed daily to the French language, I am still of the opinion that the use of English actors weakens the plays' authenticity. (248)[1]

In his review of *Performing Canada*, Denis Salter offers a final, perfunctory word on the "authenticity" question as he declares, "The quest for the real is a mug's game. There is no single originating moment for anything or anyone, least of all for something as large, multifarious, and contestatory as a nation" (152).

If cultural authenticity is always imagined, always a myth, then Tremblay's original French texts are as much in question as representations of "reality" as are the English translations. However, the question remains: was *Bonjour, là, bonjour* at the Saidye "non menaçante" for English audiences relative to the French original? One significant adaptation in the English translation is that Lucienne is referred to as "L'Anglaise" in the French version, but "Lady Westmount" in the English. This change would significantly reduce the number of reiterations signalling Lucienne's linguistic betrayal. However, there are other instances in the script where the point is made. For example, Serge mocks the idea that Lucienne is serious about her affair with his friend Robert, the painter, and adds:

> Look, you're married to a doctor, an Anglais on top of that, you've got a seventy thousand dollar house in Cartierville, a charming son who's started to knock up the neighbourhood girls, and two lovely

teenage twins who flatly refuse to learn French because their father speaks nothing but English. Now how could you leave all that, Lucienne? You love it too much. (*Bonjour, là, bonjour* 25)

Nonetheless, the impossibility of translating the linguistic situation becomes obvious, for example, when we consider Van Burek and Glassco's translation and inclusion of the stage direction: "The actress should bear in mind that in the original, Lucienne speaks French with a slight English accent as though she has lost the habit of speaking her mother tongue" (*Bonjour, là, bonjour* 15). How to convey the idea, while speaking English, that you have lost some of your ability to speak French is a conundrum, which even the most talented of actresses would be challenged to resolve.

Despite the inevitable loss of some of the play's linguistic subversion, *Bonjour, là, bonjour* does manage to repeat the larger musical structure of Tremblay's play. Serge's relationship with his father and his sister are sublimated themes throughout much of the play. The tangible elements of the incest theme are displaced and presented through Serge's interactions with his sister Denise, who repeatedly and overtly claims to be sexually aroused by her brother. Serge's attempts to communicate with his father are repeatedly blocked by the countervailing speeches of his aunts. Nicole and Armand are minor verbal presences through much of the play, but in the symphonic structure of the play they and the themes associated with them (incestuous love and filial devotion) rise to dominance in the episodes labelled "No. 27 Solo" and "No. 31 Final Duet," the climax and denouement of the drama, respectively. As this structure is preserved in the translation, so too, is the comparative significance of the incest and the language taboos of the play.

Lucienne fills the stereotype of the *comprador*, living the empty, decadent life of a wealthy Anglo. It is Bob, Lucienne's husband, who has corrupted her with his wealth and trapped her in a boring, loveless marriage. Bob, the doctor, is also responsible for supplying Serge's sister Monique with the prescription drugs that she has become addicted to. Bob, the father of son Bob the profligate, and cuckold of young Bob the painter, is the play's ultimate scapegoat, without a voice or a physical presence in the play, or even a distinguishing name. The linguistic taboo remains unredeemed and devoid of *jouissance* – or does it?

Although *Bonjour, là, bonjour* had already been presented in Toronto, the Quebec premiere, because of Tremblay's anterior policy, stands out as the ultimate transgression, paradoxically, a greater transgression of the linguistic taboo than Lucienne's marrying a unilingual anglophone doctor. Before judging this apparent contradiction too quickly, it is judicious to remember the degree to which Quebec nationalism and the independence movement were taboo subjects in English-speaking Canada in the early 1970s. The censoring of George Ryga's play, *Captives of a Faceless Drummer*, by the board of the Vancouver Playhouse in 1971 is an obvious example. Not only was the play cancelled using "financial and administrative excuses" (Hay 7), but even supporters of the play attempted to dissociate it from the October Crisis by insisting that such a connection was "a simplistic distortion of the meaning of Ryga's play and its dramatic intent" (Hay 9). In the early 1970s, the only kind of comment on Quebec nationalism that English Canada seemed prepared to hear was condemnation. It is hardly surprising that the only kind of comment that Franco-Quebec was ready to hear from its playwright laureate about Quebec's English economic elite in 1974 would have to be critical and sardonic.

By 1977, much had changed, and the Saidye production of *Bonjour, là, bonjour* was a significant marker of the change. These days, there is a risk of reaching overly simplistic conclusions by drawing a straight line from the Saidye production to the headlines in *La Presse* and *Le Devoir* in April 2006 that "Michel Tremblay dit ne plus croire à la souveraineté" ("Michel Tremblay"). The headlines provoked virulent reactions against Tremblay, in particular, from film director Pierre Falardeau, writer Victor-Lévy Beaulieu, and former premier Bernard Landry, who vowed to never again attend a Tremblay play. As Tremblay pointed out in a subsequent interview with Matt Radz in the *Gazette*, "I was not misunderstood, but this [brouhaha] was one proof of the damage the headline of an article can do" (quoted in Radz E12). Tremblay's objection to the sovereignist project was to "the way they are trying to sell it to us now, which is about money, about the economy" (ibid.).

This perspective might cause us to reconsider Lucienne's transgressions as being along a materialist/idealist axis as much as a linguistic taboo. Our interpretation of Tremblay's vilification of Doctor Bob, in 1974, should perhaps also be tempered by his comments in 2006 to the effect: "I don't want to have a country against Ottawa. I want to have a country for my-self. Now they are demonizing Ottawa, and it is only against Ottawa" (ibid.). Tremblay reports that he gave up his membership in the Parti Québé-cois in 1971 "because I wanted to keep my, uh, independence" (ibid.).

Van Burek and Glassco's *Bonjour, là, bonjour* goes a long way in in-forming anglophone audiences and encouraging empathy with the frustra-tion and alienation that Quebec francophones have felt in attempting to pursue their culture and fulfil their lives in the place they call home. Despite what could not be translated, the play, even in English, effectively makes the point by comparing incest to surrendering language, culture, and iden-tity for money, and concluding, even if the conclusion challenges credulity, that the former is a better choice of taboo. The production at the Saidye and the discussions that followed broke the linguistic ice and were a source of *jouissance* for anglophone audiences and, I suspect, for Michel Tremblay.

In fact, the 1977 production of *Bonjour, là, bonjour* was the beginning of a fairly extensive history of collaborations between Michel Tremblay and the Saidye. In addition to the other Tremblay plays the Saidye would produce, this first collaboration would also lead, as Gold describes in her history, to Tremblay's sharing the stage with the "grande dame" of Yiddish theatre in Montreal, Dora Goldfarb Wasserman, in June of 1991 for read-ings in French and Yiddish, and ultimately to the translation and interna-tional tour of *Les belles-sœurs* in Yiddish (251–8).

Bonjour, là, bonjour at the Saidye was an early demonstration (con-firmed in 2006) that Tremblay's nationalism is not narrow, dogmatic, xeno-phobic ethnocentrism. The point is reconfirmed by the extensive work Tremblay himself has done as a translator and adapter, translating a dozen Tennessee Williams' plays (see Ladouceur's article, "Les voix de la marge: Tennessee Williams et Michel Tremblay") and other American dramas, and adapting Chekov and Aristophanes. Tremblay's perspective is most obvi-ously presented in his play *Encore une fois, si vous permettez* (1998) in which he, as narrator, begins by sketching the variegated universe of his literary influences and ends by revealing that his mother, the play's only character, was from Saskatchewan.

Tremblay's gestures and comments, like those of Robert Lepage, who has been under similar attack from certain Quebec nationalists, are itera-tions of what Premier Lucien Bouchard told anglophones of Quebec in a speech at the Centaur Theatre in March 1996. After pointing out that "here in this very room, French and English Montrealers sat side by side, laughed and were moved, by one of the most popular plays this city has ever seen: *Balconville* by David Fennario. You know it well: it's about a group of Montrealers in Point St Charles, French- and English-speaking, who disagree about politics but are bound together by their shared experiences of life," Premier Bouchard assured his audience that "Quebec nationalism [...] no longer seeks to be homogeneous, but instead embraces diversity and pluralism" ("Address to Anglophones").[2] The premier's claim has been contested and tested, in particular, by what came to be known as the "Michaud Affair," when Bouchard invoked a motion of censure against long-time Parti Québécois member Yves Michaud for his having publicly chastised Montreal's Jewish community for voting against sovereignty in the 1995 referendum. *Bonjour, là, bonjour* at the Saidye Bronfman Centre was an early warning that the stakes were high, that the debate would be heated, heartfelt, and difficult, but that dialogue was possible – and a better choice of taboo than the incestuousness of linguistic solitudes.

Notes

1 In this conclusion Gold is clearly responding to the negative reaction, in particular, from Robert Lévesque, theatre critic for *Le Devoir*, to the Theatre 1774 production of *Echo* at the Saidye directed by Robert Lepage. Lepage was criticized for using Franco-Québécois actors in a play that turned out to be entirely in English (Gold 164, 247–8; see also the NFB film *Breaking a Leg*).

2 The speech was also accessed in French translation on the Government of Quebec's official "Site du Premier Ministre" under the title "Allocation du premier ministre du Québec, M. Lucien Bouchard, devant la communauté Anglophone du Québec." Accessed 17 May 2009. http://premier.gouv.qc.ca/salle-de-presse/discours/1996/mars/1996-03-11.shtm. Acessed 28 June 2011. http://english.republiquelibre.org/Speech_of_the_Premier_of_Quebec,_Mr._Lucien_Bouchard,_before_the_Anglophone_community_of_Quebec

Works Cited

Bouchard, Lucien. "Parts of Premier Lucien Bouchard's Address to Anglophones: 12 March 1996." Acessed 26 June 2006. http://www.geocities.com/SouthBeach/Breakers/2368/politics_address.html

Breaking a Leg: Robert Lepage and the Echo Project. Dir. Donald Winkler. Montreal: National Film Board of Canada (NFB), 1992.

David, Gilbert, and Pierre Lavoie, eds. *Le monde de Michel Tremblay: Des*

Belles-sœurs *à* Marcel poursuivi par les chiens. Montréal: Cahiers de théâtre Jeu /
  Éditions Lansman, 1993.

Filewod, Alan. *Performing Canada: The Nation Enacted in the Imagined Theatre.*
  Kamloops, BC: Textual Studies in Canada, 2002.

Gold, Muriel. *A Gift for Their Mother: The Saidye Bronfman Centre Theatre,
  A History.* Montreal: MIRI, 2007.

Hay, Peter. Preface. *Captives of the Faceless Drummer.* George Ryga. Vancouver:
  Talonbooks, 1971.

Ladouceur, Louise. *Making the Scene: La traduction du théâtre d'une langue
  officielle à l'autre au Canada.* Montréal: Nota bene, 2005.

– "Les voix de la marge: Tennessee Williams et Michel Tremblay." *TTR: Traduction, traductologie, rédaction* 19: 1 (2006): 15–30.

Lafon, Dominique. "Un air de famille." *Le théâtre québécois 1975–1995.* Ed.
  Dominique Lafon. Ottawa: Fides, 2001, 93–110.

Lépine, Stéphane. "*Bonjour, là, bonjour.*" *Le monde de Michel Tremblay: Des
  Belles-sœurs à Marcel poursuivi par les chiens.* Ed. Gilbert David and Pierre
  Lavoie. Montréal: Cahiers de théâtre Jeu / Éditions Lansman, 1993, 125–32.

Lévi-Strauss, Claude. *The Raw and the Cooked.* Trans. John and Doreen Weight-
  man. New York: Harper and Row, 1969.

"Michel Tremblay dit ne plus croire à la souveraineté." *Le Devoir,* 10 avril 2006.
  Accessed 29 May 2008. http://www.ledevoir.com/2006/04/10/106469.html

Radz, Matt. "Tremblay Still Feels the Sting of Landry's Attack." *Gazette,* 4 Nov.
  2006, E12.

Robert, Lucie. "L'impossible parole des femmes." *Le monde de Michel Tremblay:
  Des Belles-sœurs à Marcel poursuivi par les chiens.* Ed. Gilbert David and Pierre
  Lavoie. Montréal: Cahiers de théâtre Jeu / Éditions Lansman, 1993, 359–76.

Tremblay, Michel. *Bonjour, là, bonjour.* Montréal: Leméac, 1974.

– *Bonjour, Là, Bonjour.* Trans. John Van Burek and Bill Glassco. Vancouver:
  Talonbooks, 1975.

– *Encore une fois, si vous permettez.* Montréal: Leméac, 1998.

Salter, Denis. "Staging Canada." Review of *Performing Canada: The Nation
  Enacted in the Imagined Theatre. Theatre* 34: 3 (2004): 146–52.

Venuti, Lawrence. *The Translator's Invisibility: A History of Translation.* New
  York: Routledge, 1995.

Walker, Craig Stewart. *The Buried Astrolabe: Canadian Dramatic Imagination and
  Western Tradition.* Montreal and Kingston: McGill-Queen's University Press,
  2001.

25

1984–2009: Robert Lepage Meets the Rest of Canada

Jane Koustas

When asked about his dual loyalty to Canada and Quebec, Robert Lepage once stated, "Quebec is a small, incestuous society that I am proud to be a part of" (Grescoe 132). And, commenting on his creative inspiration, he confessed to being still very much a kid "always more interested in playing with the box than with the gift that came in it" (Winsor).

Lepage here introduces ideas central to understanding the notion of identity and its role in his work. First, he is a proud Quebecer and, while recognizing the limits of this perhaps sometimes closed society, he also understands the importance of the ties that bind, however tightly. With respect to the box, Lepage suggests an entirely different take on the overused expression "thinking outside of the box." Instead, he plays with the box itself, reshaping and transforming it to make it do and mean new things.[1] If Canadians are hemmed in or contained by the box of our language, binary translation practice, culture, and geopolitical space, we can rethink the box itself rather than trying to manipulate or change the contents. And this is not thinking outside the box, this is making the box work for us. If we are boxed in by a small incestuous society, for example, we can try to redefine the limits and the shape of the box while still recognizing the importance of boundaries for our sense of identity and belonging. This is one way to look at the work of this extraordinary dramaturge who has redefined the shape of theatre and who has reconfigured the "boxes," the standard linguistic, cultural, geographical, geopolitical boxes into which Canadians place themselves and others.

Among the many boxes that come to mind when discussing the Canadian identity question is that of the two solitudes. This decidedly overused, and arguably outdated expression – there are multiple solitudes – still serves as shorthand to describe the relationship between Quebec and English-speaking Canada. Coined by the eminent translator and translation scholar Philip Stratford, the ROC, the Rest of Canada, is used to describe the "other" solitude, the non-Quebec, non–French-speaking factor in the "two solitudes" equation. While Stratford himself suggested the more accurate and more contemporary image of the double helix rather than that of the two solitudes (131), cultural exchange between French and English Canada, nonetheless, remains at the forefront in the discussion of Canadian literary systems and translation practice. Titles such as *Two Solicitudes, Échanges entre les deux solitudes*, or even the trailer for the 2006 Quebec film, *Bon Cop, Bad Cop*, which announces "cet été les deux solitudes se rencontrent," clearly rely on this common currency. Even Lepage himself, commenting on a 1990 joint anglophone-francophone project noted, "The theatre company was fired up by the idea of getting Montreal's anglophone and francophone actors to work together, something that never happens. It's like the Berlin Wall, and that wall hasn't cracked" (quoted in Crew).

It may seem narrow to discuss Robert Lepage from this perspective given that the Quebec actor, cineaste, dramaturge, and director has earned an international reputation for himself and his Quebec-based theatre company Ex Machina. He is recognized as a world leader in the production of innovative theatre for a global community. Recipient of the Governor General's Award for Lifelong Achievement in 2009, the Europe Theatre Prize in 2007, and numerous other prestigious awards, Lepage's success on the national and international scene is well established and documented.[2] Furthermore, scholarship on Lepage insists on the global trajectory and global impact of his work. These studies, however, also highlight a key element in Lepage's theatre, namely, that his theatre centres on the question of identity frequently defined through the concept of recognition by an- or the Other or as dialogism like that described by Bakhtin.[3] This essay considers Lepage's encounter with a more immediate, significant Other, namely, English-speaking Canada, or the ROC, through the study of Lepage's importance as a player on both the Canadian and international theatre scenes and on the landscapes of political, cultural, and linguistic identity and concomitant translation practice. While the success and popularity of Lepage's theatre is very much global, the artist's relationship with the ROC remains a central component of the identity question consistently addressed in his work.

In his influential essay on the Canadian geopolitical, cultural space, Canadian political philosopher Charles Taylor reflects on the importance of the Other in determining one's own identity:

> This crucial feature of human life is its fundamentally dialogical character. We become full agents, capable of understanding ourselves, and hence of defining our identity through our acquisition of rich human languages of expression [...] People do not acquire the languages needed for self-definition on their own. Rather, we are introduced to them through interaction with others who matter to us – what George Herbert Mead called "significant others." We don't learn the languages in dialogue and then go to use them for our own purposes [...] We define our identity always in dialogue with, sometimes in struggle against the things our significant others want to see in us. (32)

Lepage's work in both theatre and film was influenced by his own upbringing in which confrontation with the Other was a daily occurrence. Born in predominately francophone Quebec City in 1957 into a working-class family, Lepage grew up with three siblings, two of whom were adopted and were English-speaking. His parents, largely because of displacement during the Second World War, were also fluent in English. Lepage explains that his family was unusual because "it was a mix of all kinds of things: children who had been adopted and children who were biological and the two adopted children were adopted in English Canada, so they were brought up in English and we [he and his sister Lynda] were brought up in French" (Dundjerovic 5). This bilingual upbringing was exceptional in 1950s–60s working-class Quebec City, and collision or confusion between French and English, over the choice of television programs, for instance, frequently occurred. Relating this daily confrontation with otherness to the larger Canadian-Quebec political scene, Lepage stated, "My family is a metaphor for Canada. I have this strong impression that we are of the same flesh even if it is not the case" (quoted in Johnson 56). This notion of originating from the "same" flesh, of being in negotiation rather than in conflict with the Other, of sharing, but not belonging to a cultural linguistic community underlies his performances. And while the success and popularity of Lepage's theatre is certainly global, his complex relationship with English-speaking Canada – and, in particular, his ongoing "love affair" with Toronto – remains a central component of the identity question consistently addressed in his work (Wagner, "All the World's a Stage"). Labelled, somewhat arbitrarily, as a French-Canadian Quebecer or even Montrealer by critics, Lepage was quickly recognized as a major voice from Quebec, his openly declared separatist stance posing little problem for his rapid entry onto the Toronto scene in the mid-1980s.

Lepage's arrival in Canada's largest theatre scene, and thus in the "rest of Canada," was not the city's first taste of Quebec theatre (Koustas, "From 'Homespun' to 'Awesome'"). Gélinas triumphed in the 1950s, and Michel Tremblay drew crowds consistently for over two decades between 1972 and 1997. However, Tremblay was produced in English translation, which highlighted the language divide. Indeed, Tremblay's status as a francophone Quebecer and ardent nationalist became somewhat blurred. Reviewing Tremblay's openly political *Hosanna*, to which the notion of identity is central, theatre critic David McCaughna commented, "It does not hit home that this play has a great deal to do with Quebec" ("Tremblay Scores Again"). Still, in spite of Tremblay's popularity and Toronto's appropriation of his theatre, the need to translate drew attention to the French-language origins of the plays and stamped them with the "made in Quebec" label. In short, up until the arrival of Lepage, Quebec theatre in Toronto was French-language theatre in English translation, in which, therefore, the concepts of source and target language and culture remained central: Quebec and Toronto (and the rest of Canada) were not seeing the same Tremblay.

In 1984, with *Circulations*, however, Lepage introduced Toronto to multilingual theatre that bypassed and transformed conventional notions of translation that normally set source and target languages, audiences and cultures in binary opposition: the Quebec and Toronto versions of *Circulations* were identical. The positive response to, and emphasis on, Lepage's ability to plunge the rest of Canada into another sort of otherness, deracinated from the traditional bi and bi (bilingualism and biculturalism) model,[4] has continued throughout Lepage's presence in Toronto where he remains in the critical limelight. In 2002, Lepage was listed in *Maclean's* as number five in a list of the fifty most influential Canadians on the contemporary cultural scene (Macleans.ca). Significantly, the article congratulates Lepage, "Quebec's biggest theatrical export," for having "spanned the cultural divide that is English and French." As Lepage's history on the Toronto scene demonstrates, his work, internationally marketed global theatre for the computer-wired age, defies both traditional linguistic and geographical boundaries by revolutionizing ways of viewing and doing theatre; hence, Lepage proposed to Toronto, and to the world, productions beyond translation and national origin rather than Quebec theatre in English translation staged for only Canadian audiences. If Tremblay and other Quebec playwrights initiated the Toronto audience to positive and negative translation effects through plays that struggled, for example, with the translation of *joual* (see Gillian Lane-Mercier's and Louise Ladouceur's contributions to this volume) while nonetheless introducing the dynamism of Quebec theatre, Lepage deliberately chose to either exploit and expose translation in productions like *Circulations* and *Lipsynch* or to circumvent translation difficulties in a play such as the globally oriented solo production, *The Far Side of the Moon*, in which he simply "switches" into English. Translation, then, was no longer an obstacle to be overcome. It was a source of creative inspiration, energy, and engagement.

Like all Ex Machina productions, *Circulations*, staged in 1984, was inspired by a "concrete visual source" (Ex Machina Archives, Publicity File), in this case, a road map. When Louise, the Québécoise heroine leaves a miserable home life to "voir le monde," she does so in both senses of the expression: she sets out to see the world but also to learn about life. However, the audience is expected not only to follow Louise's geographical and existentialist journey, but also to explore with her the question of language. Although billed as trilingual, "one third French, one third English, one third movement," "in French and English" does not imply here the simultaneous translation usually associated with Canadian bilingualism – "bi and tri" here mean the combination of languages as all are used without translation (Ex Machina Archives, *Circulations*). There is, therefore, neither an original nor a target language; it is a "play" on the very idea of translation. Phrase-book English, especially when spoken by Louise with her Quebec accent, appears foreign to both French and English audiences. It is, in fact, more like a third language that spans the two. Just like Louise, the audience must "circulate" between cultures and languages, finding itself curiously uprooted and at a cultural intersection.

The meeting, collision, and confusion of languages and cultures remain a central trope in Lepage's Toronto and global repertoire. *Vinci*, a solo performance by Lepage staged in 1986, is a play on Caesar's victorious boast uttered as the cultural conqueror acquired new territories. The title also refers to the creator of the Mona Lisa, the international culture icon. Languages (Quebec and continental French, Italian, and English) and identities blend and clash creating both comic and poignant scenes: a girl, played by Lepage, in a Paris Burger King discourses on the meaning of "Burgerkingness," turns her face, and becomes the Mona Lisa. *The Dragons' Trilogy*, the longest-running and most frequently studied Lepage production, first played in Toronto in 1985; it toured for seven years in over thirty cities and a remake opened the Festival transamériques in Montreal in 2003. Here, the audience is taken on a cultural and linguistic voyage that spans seventy-five years and three cities: Quebec, Toronto, and Vancouver. As in *Circulations*, the confrontation of cultures and the volatile nature of the "Other" form the framework of the play. It was originally a trilingual (English, French, and Chinese) production and recent versions include Japanese. This now quadrilingual production was billed as a "lyrical epic about the meeting of cultures" (Ex Machina Archives, *The Dragons' Trilogy*). Language difference, although central to the play, poses few difficulties. Indeed, the play centres on the intertwining and layering of languages and cultures. The stories of the English, Québécois, and Chinese individuals and communities that inhabited Chinatown in Quebec City prior to the Second World War and before the space was transformed into a parking lot, have combined to create a storied landscape in which they, and their languages, are united.

Similar explorations of the clash of languages and cultures underpinned other Toronto productions such as *Tectonic Plates* (1998), *Polygraph* (1990), *Needles and Opium* (1995), *The Seven Streams of the River Ota* (1995), and *The Geometry of Miracles* (1998), which covered subjects from the aftermath of Hiroshima and the Berlin Wall to organic architecture, as well as failed and frustrated human relationships. Featuring a wide and wild set of characters from Miles Davis, Jean Cocteau, and Jean-Paul Sartre to Frank Lloyd Wright, the plays took audiences from the isolation of a Paris hotel room to journeys across time zones, continents, and languages, thus destabilizing customary notions of "us" versus "the Other" and of target and source languages and cultures. Like numerous Lepage characters caught in a liminal geopolitical, temporal, and linguistic zone, Philippe in *The Far Side of the Moon* (2000) is "lost in space." A failed, or at least failing, academic, he attempts to explain, in philosophical terms, the need for the moon landing, while, at the same time, preparing a video destined for space aliens in which he explains life on earth. He is clearly searching for a new audience that exists outside the box of his own experience, including that of binary, official bilingualism.

Lepage returned to Toronto in 2009 with *Lipsynch* after a nine-year absence. In the meantime, critics maintained a sustained, if occasionally long distance, relationship with the superstar. While not staged in Toronto, *Zulu Time* (Taylor), *Kâ* (Ouzounian), a joint production with Le cirque du soleil, the remake of *La triologie des dragons* (Whiting) and *Busker`s Opera* (Cotner), were nonetheless reviewed in Toronto. Furthermore, Lepage was honoured as one of the world's creative geniuses along with fellow Quebecer Guy Laliberté in the 2001 Harbourfront extravaganza, "World Leaders: A Festival of Creative Genius." Lepage's return with *Lipsynch* was announced eight months in advance. He triumphed again in the fall of 2009 with his joint production with the Canadian Opera Company of Stravinsky's *The Nightingale and Other Short Fables*. Toronto anxiously anticipated his return in 2010 with *Eonnogata* and *The Andersen Project* and the press enthusiastically covered his success at the Met. In June 2010, Toronto awarded him the prestigious Dora Mavor Moore Award.

Like all Lepage productions, *Lipsynch,* relies on the interference, interaction, and interconnection among languages and cultures as suggested by the Northern Stage billing which describes this joint production as "a theatrical extravaganza of nine stories, magically interweaving continents and lifetimes in a search for origins, voice and identity" (Whetstone). The original six-hour production was expanded to nine when the play was included in the 2009 Luminato program in Toronto. While the challenges and rewards of the multicultural form the trope of *Lipsynch* , Lepage overtly challenges, overturns, and exploits conventional notions of dubbing, voiceover, sur- and subtitling, and translation and their role in overcoming language difference and the barriers associated with the multicultural experience. Through his creative and provocative use of the traditional "technical" means of supplying voice, Lepage demonstrates, by isolating, mismatching, reconfiguring, and even subverting standard screen translation techniques, their interdependence as well as their relationship to voice, language, culture, and identity. He also reveals the potential for miscommunication associated with these processes. Lepage challenges preconceived notions of the seemingly smooth obstacle-free passage from one language to another as well as the idea of the entirely harmonious coexistence of languages and cultures, as globalization might have us believe, and as portrayed in numerous film and theatre productions in which dubbing and subtitling appear both problem-free and reliable. In *Lipsynch*, the rough, underside of the supposedly seamless transition from one language, community, culture, or voice, and hence, identity, to another is exposed.

In the *Andersen Project*, a one-man show (Yves Jacques replaced Lepage in Toronto), Frédéric Lapointe, jet-lagged, disoriented, and lonely, attempts to understand why he, a Québécois writer, was commissioned by the Palais Garnier to prepare the libretto for an opera to celebrate Andersen's anniversary. He quickly learns that he is merely the token non-European in an equally token European Union gesture of inclusion, a sort of "Europudding," as the director of the Palais Garnier tells him. His Quebec French standing in sharp contrast to the Parisian opera director's deliberately stilted and condescending commentary (in the French-language versions), his English failing him during a meeting with the Danes, Frédéric, like other Lepage characters, wrestles with issues of language, identity, and belonging in confrontation with the Other.

In Toronto, Frédéric spoke English while Arnaud spoke in French, with subtitles, thus confounding traditional notions of otherness and placing the ROC-Quebec balance in a new light. It is worth noting that not all critics welcomed this approach – not because of the linguistic politics it may have suggested, but rather because it complicated the staging. However, there is a new twist in the production as the struggling artist of previous productions has now become a cog, and a somewhat disposable one, in the wheel of the much larger intercultural mill. Lepage thus leads his ROC audience into a theatre world in which concepts of national, international, and intercultural lose their determinacy, if not their relevance, on the stage and elsewhere.

In *Eonnagata*, the ROC was taken on an international journey on which it was neither a thematic stop nor a reference point. There is almost no spoken text in *Eonnagata*. Lepage and his fellow dancer/actors recount, through dance and martial arts, the story of Charles de Beaumont, the Chevalier d'Éon, who was a cross-dressing spy and swordsman for Louis

XV. Having dressed as a woman while "on duty" in the Russian court, de Beaumont was sent to England as a diplomat, where he was stranded after the French Revolution. Among his diplomatic duties, he participated in the Treaty of Paris, which gave New France to the British.

Drawing, in part, on the Japanese Kabuki dance Onnagata, hence the title, which features male actors impersonating women, the production borrows and bends Western and Asian concepts of dance, gender, and theatre and their concomitant relationship to identity. The positive reviews of this "Japanese ballerina transsexual samurai kung fu dance show" (Knelman) suggest that the Toronto audience embraced the theme of duality, of gender bending, and of the fragility of our constructs of belonging which are staged through dazzling transformations such as that of the kabuki dancer to the swordsman or of the samurai warrior to the fan dancer. Swords, fans, plumes, and poles transform from scene to scene as symbols of male and female power. The boxes of belonging are continually reformatted.

In sum, all of Lepage's productions staged in Toronto have centred on issues of identity and language and have thus engaged translation, often as a theme, as in *Lipsynch*. While Lepage was initially identified as an ardent separatist, Toronto reviewers, and presumably audiences, did not focus on Lepage's personal or professional nationalist stance; instead, Toronto was enamoured with the global, universal, multicultural, international, and multilingual Lepage rather than preoccupied with his political sentiments. Indeed, Lepage's own interpretation of his Quebecness seems increasingly vague. He recently stated that he identifies as "Québécois" when in Canada but views himself more as a Canadian when working in Europe or Asia (Audet). However, it is not merely that outside of Quebec he felt, and was seen, as being Canadian more than "Québécois," but also that his work, viewed from the ROC's perspective, encouraged audiences to see beyond the traditional "two solitudes," to appreciate theatre that was international both in scope and method, and to position itself at the interface between languages, signs, cultures, and theatrical practice.

Indeed, attempts at more conventional "side-by-side" "bi and bi" were unsuccessful. In a 1989 Quebec-Saskatoon co-production, which "dr[ives] home the reality of the two solitudes" (Lacey), Lepage and Gordon McCall staged *Romeo and Juliette* [*sic*] in Verona, Saskatchewan. In this bilingual, updated version, the francophone Capulets are feuding with the anglophone Montagues suggesting the representation of somewhat stereotypical power vectors with Quebec as the weaker, more feminine partner. The final scene found the doomed protagonists stretched across the TransCanada highway, a symbol of supposed unity. While it was a box office success, albeit in a very small venue, there were no further joint efforts between the theatre companies. Lepage tried again with *Echo*, a bilingual adaptation of the prose poem *A Nun's Diary*, by Montreal anglophone writer Ann Diamond, which was staged at the Theatre Passe Muraille in 1990. This was a joint project with the then newly formed Theatre 1774 founded by Marianne Ackerman and Clare Schapiro and dedicated to bilingual theatre.[5] The script was prepared in both French and English and thus represented a return to more traditional, binary, notions of French- and English-language theatre and the need for translation. The play was a critical and box office failure.

As Sarah Hood notes, Lepage demanded that the audience approach theatre differently and with greater awareness of the power of language, including its aesthetic value, thus transforming standard translation practice:

> Lepage explains that he likes to let the audience participate actively in making connections and piecing together the story. One way of doing this is to use languages that are not familiar to the listeners; it forces them to pay attention to the different parts of the narrative [...] A [third] reason for his repeated use of many tongues is simply aesthetic: Lepage is as much aware of the sound of his work as of the visual elements. (11)

Lepage's theatre thus responds to the cultural duality bind of Canada, but also to the need to escape from this translation position of language and cultural politics by reconfiguring and reimagining the identity boxes.

Lepage's success in Toronto was conditioned both by his need, as a Quebecer, to escape the linguistic enclosure and seek recognition from the Other as defined by Taylor, and by Toronto's need to recognize, or demonstrate recognition, of a major voice from Quebec. Furthermore, his being "home away from home" and "chez lui" (Dansereau) in Toronto hint at the duality or doubling, a key element in Lepage's work.

If Lepage's own dual belonging drew him to the ROC and inspired much of his work, the Toronto theatre community was, in a similar play of contrasts, eager to claim him as a fellow Canadian while playing the card of his Quebec origins and international star status. Just as Lepage's theatre evolved between the first Toronto production in 1985 and those in 2010, the Toronto theatre scene also changed. The success of gay theatre such as Buddies in Bad Times, of feminist companies such as Nightwood Theatre, of women's drama or of projects by the Ontario Multicultural Theatre Association or by Cahoots Theatre Projects, which focused on visible minority playwrights, also challenged traditional social, cultural, and linguistic boundaries bringing new voices, new writers, and theatre that corresponded to the pluralistic demographics of Canadian society. Similarly, Carol Frechette, Daniel Danis, Serge Boucher, Yvan Bienvenue, immigrant writers such as Wajdi Mouawad, and other Quebec dramatists arrived on the Toronto scene and, while staged in English translation, their plays, unlike Tremblay's in the 1980s, did not focus on Quebec nationalism and, therefore, did not directly invite reflection on the "bind of binarism." Furthermore, as suggested by the du Maurier World Stage, begun in the 1980s, Toronto increasingly sought artistic internationalism that would complement the city's economic and multicultural transnationalism. Thus, the evolution of Lepage's theatre, from his early *Circulations*, which drew on the place of Quebec in North America, to the 2010 productions of *Eonnagata* and *The Andersen Project* with a much wider international focus, cast, and itinerary, corresponds as well to the Toronto theatre scene's desire to "go global," to seek out other horizons.

Although not the only significant other in Lepage's personal and dramatic universe, Toronto, English Canada, or the ROC participated in the dialogue as Lepage and his characters constructed identity, searched for recognition, and struggled against or with misrecognition by the Other in the Canadian and Quebec cultural, identifactory equation, through theatre that fused and blurred horizons through all of the languages of theatre. Neither Lepage's small incestuous society, nor the box, need to define or confine.

Notes

1 See the Ex Machina website, http://lacaserne.net/index2.php/lacaserne/intro/

2 Theatrical Works by Robert Lepage and Ex Machina (in chronological order): *Circulations* (1984); *The Dragons' Trilogy* (1985–91; 2003–ongoing); *Vinci*

(1986–87); *Polygraph* (1987–91); *Tectonic Plates* (1988–90); *Needles and Opium* (1991–95); *The Seven Streams of the River Ota* (1994–97); *Elsinore* (1995–97); *Geometry of Miracles* (1998–2000); *Zulu Time* (1999–2002); *The Far Side of the Moon* (2000–ongoing); *The Andersen Project* (2005–ongoing); *Lipsynch* (2006–ongoing); Robert Lepage and Gordon McCall, *Romeo and Juliette*, *Shakespeare on the Saskatchewan* (June–Aug. 1989); Robert Lepage and Theatre 1774, *Echo*, Theatre Passe Muraille (Feb. 1990).

3 See Dundjerovic, *The Cinema of Robert Lepage*; Fouquet, *Robert Lepage*; Fricker, *"The Dragons' Trilogy"* / "La trilogie des dragons," "The Globalization of Robert Lepage," and "Robert Lepage: Product of Quebec"; Hébert and Pirelli-Contos, *Théâtre, multidisciplinarité et multiculturalisme.*

4 This is popular shorthand for the Royal Commission on Bilingualism and Biculturalism (the Laurendeau-Dunton Commission), which published its report in 1969 initiating sweeping changes in the then weak legislation on official bilingualism.

5 The name commemorates the restoration of theatre in Quebec with a performance of Moliere by British soldiers after an 80-year ban. The company produced a play, *L'Affaire Tartuffe,* based on the 1774 event.

Works Cited

Atwood, Margaret, and Victor Lévy-Beaulieu. *Two Solicitudes.* Trans. Phyllis Arnoff and Howard Scott. Toronto: McClelland and Stewart, 1998.

Audet, Daniel. "Ich bin ein Lepage." *Le Soleil,* 13 avril 2006, n.p.

Beaudet, Marie-Andrée, ed. *Échanges culturels entre les deux solitudes.* Québec: PUL, 1999.

Canuel, Erik. *Bon Cop, Bad Cop.* Dir. Eric Canuel. Alliance Atlantis Vivafilm, 2006.

Cotner, Alan. "Cheap Slurs Beggar Opera." *Globe and Mail,* 24 Feb. 2004, R4.

Crew, Robert. "Robert Lepage a One-Man Whirlwind." *Toronto Star,* 28 Jan. 28 1990, C1.

Dansereau, Suzanne. "Un triomphe de plus pour Robert Lepage à Toronto avec *Les aiguilles et opium.*" *La Presse,* 11 avril 1994, A12.

Dundjerovic, Aleksandar. *The Cinema of Robert Lepage: The Poetics of Memory.* London: Wallflower, 2003.

Ex Machina Archives. *Circulations.* Publicity File. 103 rue Dalhousie, Quebec City.

Fricker, Karen. *"The Dragons' Trilogy"* / "La trilogie des dragons." [1985] Publicity File. 103 rue Dalhousie, Quebec City.

– "The Globalisation of Robert Lepage: Québécois Cultural Politics and Contemporary Theatre Practice." Doctoral dissertation, Trinity College, University of Dublin, Ireland, 2005.

– "Robert Lepage: Product of Quebec." Paper presented at the Conference on Quebec. Dublin, Feb. 2006.

Grescoe, Taras. *Sacré Blues: An Unsentimental Journey through Quebec.* Toronto: Macfarlane Walter and Ross, 2001.

Hébert, Chantal, and Irène Pirelli-Contos. *Théâtre, multidisciplinarité et multiculturalisme.* Montréal: Nuit blanche, 1997.

Hood, Sarah B. "Bilingual Theatre in Canada / Le théâtre bilingue au Canada." *Theatrum* (Winter 1989/90): 9–13.

Knelman, Martin. "Front St Theatres to Host Lepage Spectators." *Toronto Star*, 11 March 2010, E7.

Koustas, Jane. "From 'Homespun' to 'Awesome': Translated Quebec Theatre in Toronto." *Essays on Modern Quebec Theatre.* Ed. Joseph Donohoe and Jonathan Weiss. Lansing: Michigan State University Press, 1995, 81–109.

Lacey, Liam. "All the World's a Stage for Shakespeare with a Twist." *Globe and Mail*, 7 July 1989, A11.

Macleans.ca. "The Enrichers: 50 Most Influential Canadians." *Maclean's*, 18 Feb. 2002.

McCaughna, David. "Tremblay Scores Again." Metropolitan Toronto Reference Library, File TH 71354 TA. *Motion*, July/Aug. 1974.

Ouzounian, Richard. "*Kâ* Is Talk of Las Vegas." *Toronto Star*, 3 Feb. 2005, A27.

Stratford, Philip. "Canada's Two Literatures: A Search for Emblems." *Canadian Review of Comparative Literature* 16: 2 (1979): 132–40.

Taylor, Charles. *Multiculturalism and the Politics of Recognition.* Princeton: Princeton University Press, 1992.

Wagner, Vit. "All the World's a Stage." *Toronto Star*, 16 April 1998, G11.

Winsor, Christopher. *Eye*, 7 April 1974.

Whetstone, David. "Lepage's Baby about to Be Born." *Journal* [Newcastle, UK], 15 Feb. 2007, 24.

Whiting, Jason. "The Dragons Come Home." *Globe and Mail*, 21 May 2003, R3.

26

1992: *Les belles-sœurs* and *Di shvegerins*: Translating Québécois into Yiddish for the Montreal Stage

Rebecca Margolis

In 1992, the Yiddish Theatre of Montreal's Saidye Bronfman Centre (now the Segal Centre for Performing Arts) produced an original translation of Michel Tremblay's classic Québécois play, *Les belles-sœurs* (The Sisters-in-law) under the title *Di shvegerins*. The plot of *Les belles-sœurs* revolves around a group of French-Catholic working-class women in Montreal's East End who speak in the Québécois dialect of *joual* rather than the standard French that was the convention of the stage when the play was authored in 1965. With its groundbreaking use of *joual* on the stage, and its subtext of social criticism, *Les belles-sœurs* caused a revolution in Quebec theatre, and heralded Tremblay's position in Quebec's nationalist vanguard. Since its stage premier in 1968, *Les belles-sœurs* has become one of the classics of Quebec theatre, internationally performed in the original as well as in translation into various languages. The Yiddish Theatre, under director Dora Wasserman, performed *Di shvegerins* in Montreal from 28 May through 21 June as part of the celebrations marking the city's 350th birthday.

The production marked a watershed moment in Canadian translation. It marked the first time that a French Québécois play was performed in Yiddish. More significantly, it was the first performance of *Les belles-sœurs* in a language other than *joual* in the province of Quebec authorized by Tremblay. The playwright himself, as well as the play's promoters, director, actors, audiences, reporters, critics, and subsequent commentators, characterized the production as a bridge between two Quebec communities that had historically existed in relative isolation from one another: a French population tracing its roots back to colonial times, and a Jewish population largely of twentieth-century immigrant origins. The most enduring effect of the Yiddish *Les belles-sœurs* has been as a nexus for a wider movement of intercultural dialogue between Quebec's French and Jewish communities that spanned the popular press, the political realm, and academia, with the term "bridge" serving as its mantra.

Language and *Di shvegerins*

The dissimilar effects of the original *joual* version of *Les belles-sœurs* and its 1992 Yiddish translation were mitigated by the different historical contexts in which they emerged. *Les belles-sœurs* was originally written during the upsurge of secular nationalism and corresponding language debates of Quebec's Quiet Revolution. The play expressed resistance to both the province's economically dominant English-speaking minority and the existing conventions of local French-language literature and theatre by offering a rare opportunity for French Québécois audiences to hear their own language legitimized on stage. While many critics in the Montreal press objected to its use of *joual* when the play was first performed (Martin 121–5), the play energized the local French-language theatre. Moreover, for many years Tremblay, a fervent supporter of Quebec independence, refused on political grounds to allow the play to be performed in the province in any language other than *joual*. A generation after the first performance of *Les belles-sœurs*, the world it portrayed had largely been replaced by a secular state where the primacy of Québécois French was firmly entrenched.

In contrast, the Yiddish of *Di shvegerins*, the language of a thousand-year-old civilization of the European Jewish diaspora, had lost much of its vitality by the mid-twentieth century. At the end of the nineteenth century, Yiddish served as vernacular for millions of speakers in Jewish centres worldwide: for working-class masses and consumers of the popular press and theatre; for ideologues with strong nationalist or leftist aspirations; and for an emerging intellectual elite promoting the creation of high art in Yiddish. In Quebec, mass immigration from Eastern Europe rendered virtually the entire Jewish community of Quebec Yiddish-speaking in the first decades of the twentieth century, and Montreal formed a local branch of a transnational Yiddish culture that included newspapers, literature, theatre, and schools. However, the overall pattern for Montreal's Yiddish immigrant population was linguistic acculturation into the city's economically dominant English milieu (see Davids). After 1950, in the wake of the decimation of Yiddish life in the Nazi Holocaust and ongoing acculturation,

Yiddish became the purview of a shrinking population of speakers. Although Yiddish in Montreal was bolstered by a strong infrastructure and the arrival of many Yiddish-speaking Holocaust survivors, Yiddish within the mainstream Jewish community crossed into the realm that scholar Jeffrey Shandler terms "postvernacular," where it is tied to heritage rather than active usage with the very act of using the language holding symbolic value (Shandler). In the secular milieu, where there are few fluent speakers, Yiddish has increasingly tended to be used in deliberate and performative ways, in particular, in musical and dramatic productions that do not require audiences to understand what is being sung or said.

Montreal's Yiddish Theatre, founded by Soviet-trained actress Dora Wasserman soon after her arrival in Montreal in 1950, evolved as a bastion of Yiddish. The theatre group, which became the resident company of Montreal's Saidye Bronfman Centre, has produced more than seventy Yiddish classics, musicals, and translations of world theatre. One of the world's few permanent Yiddish theatres, it has endeavoured to continue to present innovative productions in Yiddish. It continues to actively promote literary translation into Yiddish, despite the fact that its Yiddish audience is aging and its younger audiences are unlikely to be conversant in the language (see Abley). All of this raises the question: what were the effects of translating a *joual* play into Yiddish in 1992? The answer has far more to do with intercommunity relations than with language.

Creators

From its inception, *Di shvegerins* was a collaborative effort between members of Montreal's Yiddish and French Québécois communities. *Di shvegerins* was part of Montreal's 350th anniversary celebration, and received funding from its special theatre budget (Donnelly, "Theatre Season Gets Boost"). The play became emblematic of the city's multicultural history, with the Montreal *Gazette* reviewer Pat Donnelly remarking, "Of all Montreal's many 350th anniversary events, the Yiddish premiere of Michel Tremblay's *Les belles-sœurs* (*Di shvegerins*), at the Saidye Bronfman Centre, is one of the most appropriate. As a project, it makes a touching statement of mutual respect between two distinct cultures, underlining the oft-overlooked multi-ethnic nature of our history" (Donnelly, "Tremblay's *Les belles-sœurs* in Yiddish"). Tremblay was an enthusiastic supporter of the project from the outset; according to one report, it was Tremblay who initiated the project of having his play translated and staged, with Wasserman, who was friends with Tremblay, initially resisting the idea but trusting his instincts and finally agreeing to the project (Mietkiewicz). Tremblay remained involved with the production throughout, attending dress rehearsals and instructing the cast's Jewish women about the practices of Roman Catholicism such as the rosary (see Donnelly, "Trials of Tremblay in Translation"). One of the play's early promoters was French Québécois anthropologist and historian Pierre Anctil, author of pioneering studies on the Jews of Quebec as well as translations from Yiddish into French, and founder of "Dialogue St-Urbain," a community group dedicated to rapprochement between French and Jewish Quebecers. (See Anctil in this volume.) Anctil was to translate the play together with Goldie Morgentaler, who was completing a graduate degree in English literature at McGill University; in the end, Morgentaler, a native Yiddish speaker and daughter of renowned Montreal Yiddish writer Chava Rosenfarb, completed the translation from the original *joual* into Yiddish (Morgentaler, "Sole Translator"), with Anctil reviewing the manuscript after completion and involved in the production of the play. Morgentaler translated the play word-for-word in idiomatic, literary Yiddish, including its profanities and obscenities. In some cases, Morgentaler found, the play's puns worked better in Yiddish than in the original French: "When Rose Ouimet suggests that the senile Mme. Dubuc have her mouth plugged with a bottle of Coke, Yiddish offers an irresistible opportunity for word play: Give her a coke, says Rose 'vet di tsekorkevete farkorkevet vern.' 'Tsekorkevet' means someone with a screw loose and 'farkorkevet' means to "plug with a cork'" (Morgentaler, "Tremblay in Yiddish Is Translator's Delight"). For the staging, Wasserman opted to add a sprinkling of terms from the original *joual* into Morgentaler's all-Yiddish script. The staging was filled with lines such as, "*Mon Dieu! s'iz shpet, kh'darf zikh geyn iberton* (My God [*joual*]! It's late, I have to go and get changed [Yiddish]." The effect was praised by critics: "What matters here is that *Les belles-sœurs* is a damned good play. And in Yiddish – with a delightful smattering of French – it works" (Donnelly, "Tremblay's *Les belles-sœurs* in Yiddish"). *Di shvegerins* was geared at a wide audience, with the Yiddish play rendered accessible by a detailed English and French synopsis in the playbill as well as supertitles. Meanwhile, the regular audiences of Wasserman's Yiddish theatre were described by one reporter as "un public endimanché et assez âgé, habitué aux pièces plus traditionnelles du Théâtre yiddish, mais qui fait exception pour un Tremblay" (Boulanger 20). As discussed in more detail below, the play was very well received locally. In contrast, a review of a subsequent Toronto production questioned the suitability of *Di shvegerins* for that city's Yiddish theatre audiences: "But [the Montreal production] was part of the 350th anniversary celebrations of Montreal and a specific example of the possibility of Jewish-French understanding, a rationale absent from its production in Toronto." Situated outside of Montreal, the reviewer would have preferred to see one of the Yiddish classics (Rose 43). The play's production and staging remained very much rooted in its local context.

For the creators of *Di shvegerins*, the play evolved within a contemporaneous movement of dialogue between two linguistic and cultural communities – French Québécois and Jewish – who had historically lived in the same neighbourhoods but with limited contact. For the first half of the twentieth century, Montreal's Jewish immigrant population formed a "third solitude," sandwiched between French and English communities that maintained parallel social, religious, and educational infrastructures. Organized efforts at rapprochement between the French and Jewish communities in the 1950s coincided with the new immigration of French-speaking Jews from the Arab world, with groups such as Le Cercle français bringing together Jews and Franco-Québécois (see Jedwab). However, the rise of Quebec separatism in the 1970s brought about a mass exodus of English-speaking Jewish Montrealers. The 1990s marked a period of renewed dialogue between the communities against a backdrop of constitutional debate about the role of Quebec in Canada, and discussion about whether the province would separate from the rest of Canada.

Even before its staging, *Di shvegerins* was identified in terms of rapprochement. An article in the Montreal *Gazette*, called "Translating *Les belles-sœurs* into Yiddish Bridges Cultural Gulf," explored the connections between the Yiddish and French in Quebec languages despite the historical lack of linguistic and cultural contact between their speakers. The article cited Anctil: "The reason (for the translation) is that in the present context the francophone and Jewish communities need to be brought together through a cultural event understandable to both" (Mennie D14). The ongoing popular and scholarly discourse around Anctil's role in the play (Gagnon; Donnelly; Robitaille; Simon), which in several cases erroneously identified him as the play's translator (Block; Boulanger; Morgentaler "Sole Translator"; Montpetit), would serve to further situate *Di shvegerins* as a politically significant expression of pluralistic nationalism in Quebec.

For director Dora Wasserman, *Di shvegerins* marked continuity in a decades-old relationship between the French and Yiddish theatre in Montreal. For Wasserman, the use of theatre to bridge the French and Yiddish communities was not new: she had worked closely with Gratien Gélinas, one of the founders of French Québécois theatre and an early supporter of Wasserman's Yiddish theatre (see Larrue). The play marked the realization of an older dream of rendering a work of classic Québécois theatre into Yiddish, and the fruition of an idea that was planted when Wasserman first met Michel Tremblay in 1977 to render *Les belles-sœurs* into Yiddish (Mietkiewicz). It also marked a way of promoting the Yiddish language: "We also wanted to prove that Yiddish really is alive and vital. You can write a million books, but the rich roots of the language can't be fully appreciated unless the words are spoken" (ibid.).

At the same time, Wasserman employed the rhetoric of cultural bridge building. In the play's press release, she emphasized the commonalities between Yiddish and French Québécois playwrights (Boulanger 20). The same theme dominated the playbill, where her English greetings pointed to the universal central theme of the play, and her Yiddish-language greetings emphasized the commonalities of the two cultures: "It is laughter through tears, which has been depicted in so many Yiddish creations" (Playbill 3). Michel Tremblay's French-language greeting in the same playbill, which spoke fondly of his long-standing association with Wasserman and the Yiddish theatre, likewise underlined the compatibility of the Yiddish version of the play with the original *joual*: "Que ces belles-sœurs si près des originales, en fin de compte, malgré la difference [*sic*] de religion, vivent longtemps! Vive le Bingo et [...] vive Dora!" (Playbill 5). The play became emblematic of Wasserman's career in Quebec. Of her seventy-odd Yiddish productions, *Les belles-sœurs* was the most discussed in articles on her to appear in print, in particular in conjunction with her subsequent naming to the Order of Canada (1992) and to the Order of Quebec (2003).

The play's translator, Goldie Morgentaler, focused on a different kind of bridge: the challenge of "bridging the linguistic divide" ("Tremblay in Yiddish"). In contrast to her work as a literary translator out of Yiddish, which was prompted by a "sense of mission" to preserve a language with few speakers, *Di shvegerins*, her first translation into Yiddish, was spurred by a sense of "personal adventure": could she convey a play from one highly idiosyncratic language into another? What she found was that the hurdles – religion, obscenities, cultural artefacts, puns – were all surmountable, and that she was able to "speak French in Yiddish" (Morgentaler, "Translating Michel Tremblay's *Les belles-sœurs* from Joual into Yiddish," 107–16). She rejected the discourse around the play that "attempted to stress the similarity of Jews and French Canadians in order to make the idea of a French-Canadian play in Yiddish appear palatable to a Jewish audience, and attractive to a French-Canadian one" as a "mistake." Instead, she argued, literary translators must "never forget that they are dealing with two separate cultures, and two different modes of expression" (ibid. 112). Rather than aim to universalize the play or create links between Montreal's Franco-Québécois and Jewish communities, Morgentaler set out to bridge the linguistic and cultural gap from *joual* to idiomatic Yiddish as a "cultural as well as linguistic emissar[y]" (109).

Media

The English- and French-Canadian media focused on the role of *Di shvegerins* in bringing communities together. The production was depicted in the English press as a barometer for intergroup relations in Quebec. It was cited in the *Globe and Mail* as one of many indications of a growing mood of conciliation in Quebec's language disputes (Gagnon). The *Gazette* theatre critic Pat Donnelly likewise identified the play as part of a sea change in Quebec's political climate, commenting that Tremblay's "distinctly Québécois dramas seem to be hopping over more cultural barricades than usual these days, and it's happening right in his own backyard for a change" (Donnelly, "Theatre Crime of the Season"). Donnelly's subsequent review commented on the apt connection between the city's 350th anniversary and *Di shvegerins* as pointing to the "mutual respect" between cultures and Montreal's multi-ethnic character (Donnelly, "Tremblay's *Les belles-sœurs* in Yiddish"). A review in the French-language weekly *Voir* focused on the positive audience response and underlined the play's universal elements in interviews with audience members. It called the actors "des ambassadrices culturelles plus habiles que bien des politiciens à favoriser le rapprochement entre les peuples" (Boulanger 20).

The play's newsworthiness as a locus of cultural exchange was conveyed in its post-premiere coverage on prime time Canadian radio and television. A story on CBC radio's *The World At Six* repeatedly employed the terms "bridge" in its discussion of the play. It cited Wasserman characterizing the play as "a collaboration between two threatened culture" and further underlined the collaborative aspects of the venture such as Tremblay personally instructing the cast about Roman Catholic practice in Quebec. A clip featured on the Radio-Canada television show *Montréal ce soir* focused on the universality of the play. It cited Tremblay praising the authenticity of the production and identifying art, rather than politics, as a good way to bring people together.

Long-Term Effects

Di shvegerins played an ongoing role in the rhetoric of rapprochement between Jewish and French Quebecers in the province over the subsequent decade, and was often cited as a concrete example of the potential for cultural exchange. If the press is any indication, the effect was particularly marked in French circles, where a number of general interest articles about Yiddish and the Jewish experience in Quebec followed the run of *Di shvegerins*. Montreal's *La Presse* featured a long article in its "News" section titled, "Les racines des juifs; La langue de l'autre majorité" that outlined the origins of Yiddish and its role in the Jewish immigrant community – "C'est dans le même yiddish que vivent toujours les juifs hassidiques d'Outremont et qu'on présente actuellement une traduction des *Belles-sœurs* de Michel Tremblay," the "conversion" of that community to English, and the historic parallels between the two groups. The author posited that the Jewish community, English-speaking but increasingly bilingual, was at a crossroads where intercultural dialogue was bearing fruit (Leblanc). In another article, *Di shvegerins* was cited as an example of a new spirit of cultural exchange in continuity with the "Dialogue St-Urbain" group (Émond). *Di shvegerins* also appears to have sparked a wider interest in the Yiddish theatre in the Québécois press, with Montreal's French-language newspapers reporting on new Yiddish productions as well as milestones in the history of the local Yiddish theatre and the career of director Dora Wasserman (e.g., Cayouette; Chouinard; Legault; Robert Lévesque; Solange Lévesque; Saint-Hilaire, "Dora Wasserman: La bonne fée du théâtre

Yiddish" and "La saison s'allonge à Montréal"; Soulié). These articles emphasized the importance of the local Yiddish theatre and the long-standing mutual influences of Quebec's French and Yiddish theatres.

The Yiddish *Les belles-sœurs* was repeatedly employed within a wider political context. In 1993, Montreal's Federation Combined Jewish Appeal announced the creation of a Comité Rapprochement-Québec to support projects promoting positive relations between local French Quebecers and Jews. An article on the inspiration for the initiative cited "différentes initiatives culturelles dont la présentation en yiddish des Belles-sœurs, de Tremblay, fut l'exemple le plus frappant" (Cauchon). *Di shvegerins* was likewise invoked to refute an article by writer Mordecai Richler entitled "Inside/Outside" which appeared in the *New Yorker* magazine in September 1991 and aroused fury among Quebec nationalists (see Julie McDonough Dolmaya's cntribution in this volume). A rebuttal in *Voir* invoked *Di shvegerins* to respond to Richler's assertion that the exodus of English Montrealers from the city in the 1970s constituted a "subtil [*sic*], non violent ethnic cleansing" by arguing that it did nothing to contribute to the current movement of rapprochement between the province's English- and French-language communities: "À cet égard, il est bon de rappeler par exemple la collaboration entre Michel Tremblay et le centre Saidye-Bronfman, collaboration qui a mené à la présentation en yiddish de la pièce *Les belles-sœurs*" (Travis 8). Most significantly, *Di shvegerins* inspired filmmaker Ina Fichman to produce her 1997 documentary film, *Towards a Promised Land / Vers une Terre Promise*, which explored the relationship between the province's Jewish and Franco-Québécois groups. The film, which was widely screened in theatres as well as on television, was praised for its role in promoting dialogue between the two communities (Fourlanty; Roberge; Venne). Moreover, *Les belles-sœurs* continued to be cited within the context of Franco-Québécois/Jewish relations. For example, in a talk to the Montreal Jewish community in 2001, Quebec Premier Bernard Landry evoked the Yiddish (as well as the 1999 Judeo-Arabic) production of *Les belles-sœurs* in his discussion of the present and future positive relations between Jewish and non-Jewish Quebecers (Landry).[1]

Di shvegerins soon entered academic discourse around the topic of bridge building. In 1993, Morgentaler participated in a round-table session on translating *Les belles-sœurs* at a bilingual conference organized by the Université de Montreal's English Department as part of its mandate for cross-cultural bridge building (Naves).[2] Theatre scholar Jean-Marc Larrue's pioneering 1996 book, *Le théâtre yiddish à Montréal / Yiddish Theatre in Montreal*, discussed the universality of the play: "The Yiddish version of *Les belles-sœurs* did not seem strange to either French-speaking Québécois or Yiddish-speaking Jewish spectators – additional evidence [...] that this drama of daily life has a universal impact" (Larrue 113).

Translation scholar Sherry Simon, who has commented extensively on *Di shvegerins* in her writing on translation in Montreal, offers an alternative understanding of the play as bridge builder. She compared the translations of *Les belles-sœurs* into Yiddish and into Glaswegian Scots (staged in Toronto in 1990 as *The Guid Sisters*) and posited shared affinities between the two minority languages as "more controversial idioms" with implications of "national" recognition for a linguistic community without political status (Simon and St-Pierre 28–9; and Simon, "Hybrid Montreal" 329–30). However, in Simon's understanding, *Di shvegerins* was not "signal" like the Scots translation, which played a central role in the Scots theatre revival. Ultimately, her analysis presents the play as a case of bridges not crossed: "The first sentences of the play, in which *joual* and Yiddish mingle, evoked a strangely dissonant world, defining this common cultural space as largely fictional. Few places could exist where these languages might have mixed in the past [...] and even fewer where they would actually live together today [...] the Yiddish translation points to a history of non-contact, the space of missed opportunities, a realm of impossibility" (Simon and St-Pierre 30).

Conclusions

What have been the effects of the Yiddish *Les belles-sœurs*? The Yiddish translation, unlike that into Scots, has not served to inspire theatre in the vernacular or the nationalist sentiments that lie behind it. A hundred years ago, when Yiddish was being promoted as a national language in Europe, translation into Yiddish proved that the language was on par with all other national languages, and the Jews could be a nation like other nations (see Fishman). However, in 1992, a work of literary translation into Yiddish did not mark a Yiddish national revitalization or cultural revival. Rather, a *joual* play staged in Yiddish translation was invoked as a symbolic act that marked an opportunity to find common ground between Jewish and

French Quebecers as part of a wider movement of dialogue. The production became an emblem for present and future reconciliation between Jews and French Quebecers who had left the world depicted in *Les belles-sœurs* behind and entered a time and place where rapprochement was possible.

Notes

1 Montreal's Saidye Bronfman Centre staged a Judeo-Arabic version of *Les belles-sœurs*, produced by Moroccan writer Solly Levy, in 1999.

2 The bilingual conference was titled "Aux Canadas: Reading, Writing, Translating Canadian Literatures."

Works Cited

Abley, Mark. "Ways of Escape: Yiddish." *Spoken Here: Travels Among Threatened Languages*. Toronto: Vintage Canada, 2004, 201–28.

Block, Irwin. "The Bridge Builder: Pierre Anctil Has Dedicated Himself to Bringing Together French Quebec and the Jewish Community." *Gazette*, 28 Aug. 1993, B3.

Boulanger, Luc. "*Les belles-sœurs* en Yiddish: Il était une fois dans l'ouest." *Voir*, 25 juin 1992, 20.

Cauchon, Paul. "La communauté juive veut se rapprocher des Québécois Francophones." *Le Devoir*, 6 mars 1993, A12.

Cayouette, Pierre. "Place à Lulu." *Le Devoir*, 14 mai 1996, B8.

Chouinard, Marie-Andrée. "Le Saidye a déjà 30 ans." *Le Devoir*, 1 oct. 1997, B8.

Davids, Leo. "Yiddish in Canada: Picture and Prospects." *The Jews in Canada*. Ed. Robert J. Brym, William Shaffir, and Mortin Weinfeld. Don Mills: Oxford University Press, 1993. 153–66.

Donnelly, Pat. "Theatre Season Gets Boost from 350th Anniversary." *Gazette*, 15 Feb. 1992, E3.

– "Trials of Tremblay in Translation: Explaining Rosary to Jewish Cast." *Gazette*, 23 May 1992, E1.

– "Tremblay's *Les belles-sœurs* in Yiddish Underscores City's Rich Ethnic Diversity." *Gazette*, 30 May 1992, E13.

– "Theatre Crime of the Season: Politically Incorrect; But If 'Cultural Appropriation' Were a Crime, We'd All Be Doing Time." *Gazette*, 26 Sept. 1992, E7.

Émond, Ariane. "Voulez-vous faire salon?" Éditorial. *Le Devoir*, 24 fév. 1992, A6.

Fishman, Joshua A., ed. *Never Say Die! A Thousand Years of Yiddish in Jewish Life and Letters*. The Hague: Mouton, 1981.

Fourlanty, Éric. "Vers une terre promise." *Voir*, 12 mars 1998, 37.

Gagnon, Lysiane. "On the Streets, the Hope Is for an Honourable and Decent Peace." *Globe and Mail*, 4 July 1992, D3.

Jedwab, Jack. "The Politics of Dialogue: Rapprochement Efforts Between Jews and French Canadians, 1939–1960." *Renewing Our Days: Montreal Jews in the Twentieth Century*. Ed. Ira Robinson and Mervin Butovsky. Montreal: Véhicule, 1995, 42–74.

Landry, Bernard. "Le Québec, Israël et la communauté juive." Allocution du premier ministre du Québec, M. Bernard Landry, à l'occasion d'un déjeuner-causerie devant la communauté juive au Centre de conférence Gelber. 14 mai 2001. Acessed 28 Dec. 2009. http://archives.vigile.net/01-5/landry-juifs.html

Larrue, Jean-Marc. *Le théâtre yiddish à Montréal / Yiddish Theatre in Montreal*. Montréal: Éditions Jeu, 1996.

Leblanc, Gérald. "Les racines des juifs: La langue de l'autre majorité." *La Presse*, 7 juillet 1992, A5.

Legault, Josée. "Une Vie." Éditorial. *Le Devoir*, 4 fév. 1998, A8.

"*Les belles-sœurs* en yiddish." Radio-Canada. 29 May 1992. Accessed 20 Apr. 2009. http://archives.radio-canada.ca/arts_culture/theatre/clips/4996/

"*Les belles-sœurs* with a Yiddish Twist." CBC Digital Archives. 29 May 1992. Accessed 20 Apr. 2009. http://archives.cbc.ca/arts_entertainment/theatre/clips/5115/

Lévesque, Robert. "Ça bouge au TNM." *Le Devoir*, 4 oct. 1994, B8.

Lévesque, Solange. "Les sorties Houdini réapparait ... grâce au Théâtre Yiddish." *Le Devoir*, 25 mars 2000, 3.

Martin, Michèle. "Modulating Popular Culture: Cultural Critics on Tremblay's *Les belles-sœurs*." *Labour/Le Travail* 52 (2003): 109–35.

Mennie, James. "Translating *Les belles-sœurs* into Yiddish Bridges Cultural Gulf." *Gazette*, 20 June 1991, D14.

Mietkiewicz, Henry. "Michel Tremblay's *Les belles-sœurs* Translated and Performed Yiddish Is Alive, Well and Returning to Page and Stage." *Toronto Star*, 21 Nov. 1992, K18.

Montpetit, Caroline. "La troisième solitude." *Le Devoir*, 27 mai 2000, D1.

Morgentaler, Goldie. "Tremblay in Yiddish Is Translator's Delight." *Gazette*, 30 May 1992, K4.

– "Sole Translator." Letter to the editor. *Gazette*, 17 Sept. 1993, B2.

– "Translating Michel Tremblay's *Les belles-sœurs* from Joual into Yiddish."
Oeuvres en traduction / Writers in Translation. Special issue of *Ellipse* 52 (1994):
107–16.

Naves, Elaine Kalman, "U de M Displays Its English Face: Authors Will Attend
Bilingual Literature Conference." *Gazette*, 10 April 1993, E15.

Playbill. *Les belles-sœurs* = *di shvegerins*, by Michel Tremblay. Dir. Dora Wasserman. Yiddish Theatre of the Saidye Bronfman Centre for the Arts. Montreal:
Yiddish Theatre of the Saidye Bronfman Centre, 1992.

Richler, Mordecai. "O Quebec." *New Yorker*, 30 May 1994, 50.

Roberge, Huguette. "Vers la terre promise: Parce que le dialogue, c'est important!"
La Presse, 15 mars 1998, B7.

Robitaille, Antoine. "Pierre Anctil: Le goy philosémite; Convaincu que les Québécois juifs et Francophones ont depuis trop longtemps des vies parallèles, l'histo-
rien fait des traits d'union entre les deux communautés." *Le Devoir*, 12 mars
1999, B1.

Rose, Ben. "French-Canadian Classic Play Delights in Yiddish Translation." *Canadian Jewish News*, 17 Dec. 1992, 43.

Saint-Hilaire, Jean. "Dora Wasserman: La bonne fée du théâtre Yiddish." *Le Soleil*,
28 déc. 1996, D8.

– "La saison s'allonge à Montréal." *Le Soleil*, 11 juin 1998, C12.

Shandler, Jeffrey. *Adventures in Yiddishland: Postvernacular Language and Culture.*
Berkeley: University of California Press, 2006.

Simon, Sherry. "Hybrid Montreal: The Shadows of Language." *Sites: Journal of the
Twentieth-Century / Contemporary French Studies* 5: 2 (2001): 315–31.

– "Bifurcations: Yiddish Turned to French." *Translating Montreal: Episodes in the
Life of a Divided City.* Montreal and Kingston: McGill-Queen's University Press,
2006. 90–118.

– and Paul St-Pierre, eds. *Changing the Terms: Translating in the Postcolonial Era.*
Ottawa: University of Ottawa Press, 2000.

Soulié, Jean-Paul. "Sur la scène de l'actualité: La personnalité de la semaine: Dora
Wasserman." *La Presse*, 8 fév. 1998, A12.

Travis, Dermond. "Les Grandes Gueules: O Mordecai." *Voir*, 30 juin 1994, 8.

Venne, Michel. "Lucien Bouchard et les leaders de la communauté juive de Montréal ont regardé ensemble le film d'Ina Fichman, *Vers une Terre promise.*" *Le
Devoir*, 28 mars1998, A6.

27

May 2006: East Meets West Coast in Canadian Noh: *The Gull*

Beverley Curran

When Japan bombed Pearl Harbor on 7 December 1941, the consequences were immediately felt by the Japanese diaspora living on the west coast of Canada, who found themselves simultaneously translated into enemy aliens. Citizens and residents of Japanese ancestry were uprooted and interned in camps in the interior of British Columbia and were not allowed to return to the Pacific coast until 1949. Many had worked in the fishing industry, and along with losing their livelihoods, had their boats and other property seized and sold to pay for their incarceration. After the war ended, "repatriation" was encouraged, sending some Japanese Canadians "back" to Japan, a country many had never seen. In Japan, where the population had little knowledge or interest in *Nikkei* and their experiences elsewhere, the Japanese Canadian was visually inconspicuous but culturally different. In Canada, they were considered Japanese; in Japan, they were foreigners. The story of this uprooting, internment, and dispersal, and the effects of its intolerable translation have been the subject of a number of works, most notably Joy Kogawa's *Obasan* (1981), the first fictional account by a Japanese-Canadian writer. Prior to this novel, voices struggling to be heard had been silenced. Roy Miki recalls sifting through records in the National Archives:

Men were shipped to road camps, and women and children ended up in the filthy livestock barns in Hastings Park on the PNE grounds where thousands were cooped up, sometimes for many months. The voices of hardship, confusion and outrage, in the apparent quietude of the indifferent archives, go on and on. It is as if all these voices were trapped in the limbo of inarticulateness, caged in the government's filing systems. ("Redress" 21)

Lifting the words of activist Muriel Kitagawa from their "archival tomb" (26), Kogawa told the story of internment and its aftermath in different voices, using English in various registers and accents, and strategically employing Japanese in the title of her novel and in the narrative to circulate unfamiliar words, such as *obasan* and *nisei*, spoken by and identifying people who turned out to be Canadians.

Hatching *The Gull: The Steveston Noh Project*

The creation of a Noh play by Daphne Marlatt, a west coast anglophone author, and local performers in collaboration with professional Noh artists from Japan not only offers an innovative approach to Noh, but also initiates its recognition as an art form that can be put to use in Canada. However, in order for the traditional Japanese art to take root in Canada, Pangaea Arts director Heidi Specht is convinced that "it has to tell our own stories" (Personal interview). Since its beginning in 1997, Pangaea Arts has recognized Asian elements, including languages, as integral to narratives of the west coast, and for Specht, who grew up there, they are "part of who I am as a person" (Personal interview). The company's productions have employed translators and have often used surtitles to aid audience comprehension, but in the mix of languages that is part of the performance, the actors may be asked to learn a language other then their own.

Noh is based not on a text but on the performer's body, and its performance is focused on movement and music. Richard Emmert worked with Marlatt to adapt the English of her play to the musical sequence of Noh so that the script would interact with the dance choreographed by Matsui Akira, a Noh actor, who also performed the role of *shite*, or main actor, of *The Gull*. Although Matsui speaks English, he was reluctant to have the shite use English in the performance. It became apparent that Japanese, in fact, should be the language used by the shite in performing the role of the Wakayama-born mother of the two fishers. Yoshihara Toyoshi translated the entire script of *The Gull* into Japanese, but the production was bilingual, with the *waki* and *wakitsure*, the older and younger brothers respectively, using English most of the time, and the shite as mother/gull speaking mainly Japanese. Yoshihara is a prolific translator responsible for most of the Canadian drama translated into Japanese for performance in Japan by his own company Maple Leaf Theatre and other

Tokyo units. In spite of his experience as a theatre translator, particularly from English into Japanese, Yoshihara could not complete the final draft of the translation without the assistance of Matsui Akira because he did not have enough knowledge concerning the specifics of the art form to translate the play into the musical form of Noh, the stylized 5–7–5 syllable rhythm of its "chanting."

The production ultimately used a mixed cast, including four Japanese Canadians, and a Tokyo-born stage attendant. Specht felt the lead characters should be played by actors of Asian ancestry, if possible, to "really get at the underlying racism against the [...] Asian population in a white-dominated society" (Personal interview) and to communicate the specific historical themes of the play. The response to the cast call from the Japanese-Canadian community was not particularly strong, partly due to the training required and image of Noh theatre as obscure, but also a certain exhaustion with the theme of internment. For some, though, like David Fujino, who was born in an internment camp, the story was a very personal one, and it was important to be a part of its telling in the role of the *aikyôgen* as an older *Issei* fisherman. Marlatt believes that Noh allows *The Gull* to "sound some of the deeper emotional layers" (quoted in Downey) of the trauma of uprooting, internment, and the delayed return to the coast. Its formal difference helps reveal still hidden aspects of the story that make it more than a narrative that has been officially redressed and laid to rest. Further, it reconfigures the Canadian government's foreignizing translation that left citizens wondering who they were and where their home was.

Littoral Translation

In a 1974 interview with George Bowering, Marlatt described herself as a "local writer, [...] a West Coast writer" (Bowering 32), while poet Phyllis Webb has called Marlatt someone who writes about edges. Whether writing on the Pacific shoreline or "that edge where a feminist consciousness floods the structures of patriarchal thought" (*Salvage*), Marlatt's writing has shown her deep interest in the process of translating text into context in an awareness of "the extensiveness of the cloth of connectedness we are woven into" (*Readings from the Labyrinth* 15). Born in Australia, she lived in Penang until she was about nine; her family immigrated to Canada in 1951. In suburban North Vancouver, where her "foreign" English lexicon was a liability, Marlatt was suddenly aware of herself as many selves and of the place she occupied as multidimensional. She recalls how her "immigrant imagination" began to grasp the mutable nature of the world and language upon arrival in Canada:

> When you are told, for instance, that what you call earth is really dirt, or what you have always called the woods (with English streams) is in fact the bush (with its creeks), you experience the first split between name and thing, signifier and signified, and you take that first step into a linguistic world that lies adjacent to but is not the same as the world of things. (23)

After this early realization of the link between translation and the immigrant experience, and how translation took place within languages as well as between them, Marlatt noticed other things. While writing *Vancouver Poems* (1972), she was struck by the sense of exploitation that ran through the whole of the city's history. Although there was bitterness in those poems, she recalls, "I didn't start getting angry until I started dealing with Steveston" (Bowering 71). In the early 1970s, Marlatt went to the small fishing community on the Fraser River south of Vancouver to collect interviews as part of an oral history project, accompanied by translator Maya Koizumi (who much later would be the Japanese translator of Kerri Sakamoto's *The Electrical Field*), and photographers Robert Minden and Rex Weyler. In the course of the interviews, she found the uprooting of Japanese Canadians from the west coast, their internment, and dispersal entangled in both individual stories and the history of Steveston. Marlatt had felt herself a social outsider as an immigrant but recognized that her skin and speech located her within a Canadian mainstream that had excluded these Japanese Canadians and others of Asian ancestry. Although it was 1974 and lives had resumed on the coast, some very successfully, anger continued to simmer. It still does. It was the emotional aspect of the play, in fact, that fascinated Yoshihara as the translator of *The Gull*: "So many people are so angry but do not know how to express it. Noh is the best way to express quiet anger, which is why I am interested in this particular project. The style and subject perfectly match" (Abell).

To write *The Gull*, Marlatt began by reading English translations of Noh plays, but the story grew out of the nub of a ghost story that Henry

Kokubo, a Steveston fisherman, had told Marlatt back in the 1970s, and which had found its way into Steveston in "Ghost," a poem Marlatt considered "crucial" (Bowering 74):

> "Nobody talks about them
> anymore," the ghosts that used to rise when you, a child, crossing
> the dyke from BC Packers, night, saw, out of the dark this strange
> white light, or covering someone's rooftop, invisible to all but
> stranger, this blue light telling of death.
> [...]
> But then there were places, you say, Chinaman's Hat,
> where you couldn't sleep at night, fresh flower in your cabin, for
> the host of restless souls' unburied hands outstretcht, returning,
> claim their link with the decomposing earth.

The ghost stories that Marlatt collected from the fishermen all referred to China Hat as haunted, but there were two of them up the coast so, as Marlatt explained, "It was very confusing to find out where the original ghost story on which I wanted to base the play actually occurred. Which China Hat was it?" (personal interview). Similarly, although *The Gull* was called a ghost play – *mugen* – in the program, Emmert and Matsui "never agreed on what category [of Noh play] it belonged to – whether it was a woman play or a ghost play – because it has aspects of both" (Personal interview), perhaps due to the ambiguity in the relationship between the *shite* as performer and *waki* as onlooker.

Nevertheless, the play closely follows the structure of Noh, and in a ritualized progression of sequencing, the story unfolds. The *shite* (Matsui Akira) appears in the *maeba* (Act I) as a young Issei woman/gull and in the *nochiba* (Act II) as a middle-aged Issei woman. The *waki* (Simon Hayama) is a Nisei fisherman in his late twenties, and the *wakitsure* (Alvin Catacutan) is his younger brother. It is 1950, postwar and post-internment, and the two brothers have returned to the west coast to resume their lives and livelihoods. The brothers make their journey up the coast of British Columbia to fish. At China Hat (Klemtu), where they tie up at the wharf to ride out a building storm, they encounter the *maejite* (that is, the shite in the first act), who appears to the waki to be a young woman speaking Japanese, "hiding her face in the fold of her sleeve," while the wakitsure sees a gull, "tucking its head under a wing" (Marlatt, *The Gull*, 11). In the *nochiba*, the second act which follows the comic interlude, the *nochijite* (shite) appears again before the groggy brothers dozing on the wharf and they recognize their mother, who speaks of her sense of abandonment in Canada and tells them to go home, back to Wakayama. The waki says that "what was home to you / Mother, was not home to us" (26), revealing within the bilingual dialogue of the play the linguistic and cultural drift that has taken place between the generations. The shite then does a dance of "grief, anger and confusion" (Downey) and then, as the chorus sings of her understanding of the ocean as connection, of "ocean joining here and there" (*The Gull* 27), "quick as a bird" her spirit is released and she disappears.

In *The Gull*, there was "a kind of space" Marlatt was trying to reach through words; she felt the highly metaphorical and symbolic nature of Noh and its "zen feeling" allowed her to approach "a large view of life and death" (Personal interview). Working with levels of association, a Noh play weaves phrases and images from classical Japanese poetry and other plays into its texture; these allusions are "replayed over and over from play to play, and each time they accrue a slightly different meaning" (Personal interview). Marlatt calls the title of her play *The Gull* a "tragic pun," but explains that *The Gull* did not play nearly enough with language:

> There could've been a lot more but I got sidetracked by the story. There is always a psychological pull in a Noh play, but it has to be really present for a Western audience – I was getting that from Heidi [Specht] – so there has to be a strong story line. So textually I used some of the devices of Noh, but I didn't use nearly enough punning. The term "punning" is a kind of diminishment of the potential of such language play – it's the double play, the double-entendre, that comes up over and over again in Noh and gets played out in different ways, sonically and semantically. (Personal interview)

Noh, Nihongo, and Inglish

As translation theatre, the production of *The Gull* localized the Noh stage, costumes, and masks. For example, the traditional pine tree painted on the *kagami ita*, the backdrop of the Noh stage, was replaced with the distinctive coastal landform that had inspired the name China Hat. There were members of the audience who saw *The Gull* whose fathers had been Steveston fishermen; they "loved the details in the play like place-names on the fishing route and names of some of the internment camps," said Marlatt. "There was a feeling that this was their story, very familiar, and they loved the unfamiliarity of Noh that carried it. I think it made their story feel new to them" (quoted in Downey). For others in the audience, the names called up like memories were evocative even when hearing them for the first time. The intertextuality of Noh is also localized in the selection of lines from poems by Roy Kiyooka, Joy Kogawa, and Roy Miki which evoke a particular history that has so much to do with voices gone awry, and bodies read before given a chance to speak.

In its theatre translation, however, *The Gull* has different effects, particularly in the translation of lines from Miki's "Sansei poem." The strategic use of "isolated" Japanese words in Miki's poem operate in Marlatt's play as "text fragments [and] isolated words that penetrate the discourse and replace the so-called normal and original discourse" (Lambert 88) in terms of both English and Japanese. This aligns the play closely with linguistic and cultural translation in terms of performances of processes that involve "appropriation, dominant/subordinate relations, commodification and containment" (Miki, "Can Asian Adian?" 56). Still, the Japanese translation of the lines of Miki's poem does not quite come to grips with the linguistic estrangement that has marked the Nikkei experience in Canada and that includes both the loss of Japanese through assimilation accelerated by internment and a relationship to English that stifled speech. In discussing the writing of Roy Kiyooka, Miki describes that particular dilemma he shared with the artist:

Like [...] other minorities, in like conditions, he had his mother tongue, Japanese, the familial language of childhood and family, overlaid by the English language of the anglo-mainstream [in Calgary]. Learning "English," then, was tied to the need to be accepted and the pressure to conform, i.e., tied to the erasure of the specific and the local. ("Inter-Face" 55)

Kiyooka "had to claim every inch of the language [...] literally syllable by syllable," and to do so, developed a particular "'inglish' inflected by the memory of speaking his mother tongue" and "writing as a means of coming "to an articulateness" in social spaces where he had literally to inscribe himself – as if from scratch" (50). In the lines in "Sansei Poem" Marlatt includes in *The Gull*, Miki uses images of boats and nets to recall another time and place. His poem has as many gaps as details:

once   we said
we say   the world lay

a mixture   the sun
the sea   our children
like marigolds   our boats
our nets we
filled our houses

In translating these lines into Japanese, Yoshihara seeks a syntax that fills in the gaps of Miki's poem in English, linking the children, ocean, and sun – *kodomoto, umito, taiyô* – the nets and boats. The lines in translation no longer contain the absences that allow the poem to operate within the play to impart a sense of the emotional silences and linguistic blockage that are such a profound part of the history of the Nikkei in Canada. The bittersweet delight in the survival of even a few words of *nihongo* more aptly tells the story of the Japanese language in Canada; the play in Japanese translation performs a kind of literary redress.

Location, Location, and Translation

The Gull has so far been performed only in Richmond, British Columbia, but its publication in a bilingual edition by Talonbooks indicates that the play in both English and Japanese would be of interest to Canadian readers. What would be the possible impact of a performance of this Canadian Noh play in Japan? The translation history of Canadian literature into Japanese has been dominated since the 1950s by the works of Lucy Maud Montgomery, and there have been relatively few translations of works by Japanese-Canadian writers; these include Kogawa's *Obasan* and *Naomi's Road*, Kiyooka's *Mothertalk*, and Kerri Sakamoto's *The Electrical Field*, and a translation of Hiromi Goto's *A Chorus of Mushrooms*, which is in the works. A few of Roy Miki's poems have appeared in Japanese ("Winnipeg ni modoru" / "Coming to Winnipeg" and "Furu no shisseki" / "Fool's Scold") translated by Eda Takaomi at Waseda University, but the only book in print is the non-fiction *Justice in Our Time*, an account of the redress movement, written with Cassandra Kobayashi. Like Yoshihara, *The Gull*'s Japanese translator, who is responsible for the bulk of Canadian plays performed on stages in Japan, Maya Koizumi, the translator of *The Electrical Field*, and Masutani Matsuki, who translated *Mothertalk* and *A Chorus of Mushrooms*, are based on the west coast and their translations, destined for the Japanese market, have received Canadian government and Canada Council subsidies. The translations are fascinating because the strategic use of Japanese in the English texts is maintained by the use of *katakana*, the phonetic writing system in Japanese that is used to render foreign words. A production of *The Gull* in Japan might go further to dislodge the stubborn myth of the homogeneity and uniqueness of Japanese culture found only in situ by performing the multiple positions and mutable meanings of "Japanese" found not only in language, and the many possible ways it might be perceived.

In "What's Different about Translation in the Americas," Edwin Gentzler considers the significance of the multicultural, multidirectional nature of translation in the Americas: "It is less something that happens between separate and distinct cultures, and more something that happens between and/or among different but often interconnected hybrid cultures" (9). He points out that most of the critical attention to this multivalent translation has been focused on its relationship to European languages and cultures. In Canada, this interest has largely centred on French and English. Despite the linguistic tensions between these languages, and the theoretical and creative explorations they have provoked, they merge in an officially bilingual state formed by two "heritage" groups that speak for "a state that is already 'foreign' to Natives" (Kamboureli 96) and whose conjunction impedes the production of a discourse of "non-English and non-French ethnic collectivities" (97). *The Gull* draws attention to Japanese and, more broadly, to Asian languages and cultural practices and productions that have shaped and been shaped by the history of the west coast; it shows how complex translation becomes in a community whose bodies have been subjected to racialization and estrangement as both immigrants to and citizens of Canada, and whose "assimilated" tongue is almost the only one left. As a textual theatre translation and a bilingual translation theatre performance,

The Gull: The Steveston Noh Project carries in its collaborative fabric its own history as well as that of the community, and brings attention to the bodies and tongues that perform the story as well as the parts of the story that are missing. Noh's powerful physicality gives "proper weight" to the "silences of all those lives that don't come fully articulated either into history or into fiction" (Malouf 57) at the same time that its somatic and emotional intensity thickens in the elaboration of diasporic stories where linguistic detritus is strategically linked to both memory and absence.

Note

1 A collaboration between Yoshihara and director Kaiyama Takehisa, Maple Leaf Theatre Company, was established in 2000 to introduce Canadian and American plays to Japanese audiences. Its first production was *The Gin Game* by D.L. Coburn, which took place in Tokyo at Sanbyakunin Gekijô in October that same year. It was followed by John Murrell's *Waiting for the Parade* in February 2001.

Works Cited

Abell, Tia. "Noh Plays about *Steveston?*" *Richmond Review*, 12 Sept. 2007. Accessed 24 Dec. 2009. http://www.pangaea-arts.com/press/richmond-review.htm

Bowering, George. "Given This Body: An Interview with Daphne Marlatt." *Open Letter* 4: 3 (1979): 32–88.

Downey, Jean Miyake. "Healing Japanese Canadian History: Multicultural Noh Play *The Gull.*" *Kyoto Journal*, 2 May 2006. Accessed 24 Dec. 2009. http://www.kyotojournal.org/10,000things/043.html

Gentzler, Edwin. "What's Different about Translation in the Americas?" *CTIS Occasional Papers* 2 (2002): 7–20.

Kamboureli, Smaro. *Scandalous Bodies: Diasporic Literature in English Canada.* Don Mills: Oxford University Press, 2000.

Kiyooka, Roy. *Pacific Windows: Collected Poems of Roy Kiyooka.* Ed. Roy Miki. Vancouver: Talonbooks, 1997.

Kogawa, Joy. *Obasan.* New York: Doubleday, 1994 [1981].

Lambert, José. "Literatures, Translation and (De)Colonization." [1995]. *Functional Approaches to Culture and Translation: Selected Papers by José Lambert.* Ed. Dirk Delabastita, Lieven D'hulst, and Reine Meylaerts. Amsterdam: John Benjamins, 2006, 87–103.

Malouf, David. "A Conversation with David Malouf." By Michael Ondaatje. *Brick* 47 (1993): 50–8.

Marlatt, Daphne. *Vancouver Poems*. Toronto: Coach House, 1972.

– *Salvage*. Red Deer: Red Deer College Press, 1991.

– *Readings from the Labyrinth*. Edmonton: NeWest, 1998.

– *The Gull* [Kamome]. Trans. Toyoshi Yoshihara. *Journal of the Noh Research Archives, Musashino University* 18 (2006): 8–29.

– Personal interview. Vancouver, BC. 25 Feb. 2008.

– *The Gull*. With a Japanese translation by Toyoshi Yoshihara. Vancouver: Talonbooks, 2009.

– and Robert Minden. *Steveston*. 3rd ed. Vancouver: Ronsdale Press, 2001 [1974].

Miki, Roy. "Can Asian Adian? Reading the Scenes of 'Asian Canadian.'" *West Coast Line* 33/34 (2001): 56–75.

– "Redress: A Community Imagined," and "Inter-Face: Roy Kiyooka's Writing, a Commentary/Interview." *Broken Entries: Race, Subjectivity, Writing*. Toronto: Mercury Press, 1998, 15–28, 54–76.

– *Saving Face: Poems Selected 1976–1988*. Winnipeg: Turnstone Press, 1991.

– "Winnipeg ni midoru" / "Coming to Winnipeg," "Furu no shisseki" / "Fool's Scold." Trans. Eda Takaomi. *Gendaishi Techo* (2007): 180–5.

Sakamoto, Kerri. *The Electrical Field*. Toronto: Knopf Canada, 1998.

Specht, Heidi. Personal interview. Vancouver, BC. 25 Feb. 2008.

28

February 2008: *The Death of a Chief*: Translating Shakespeare in Native Theatre

Sorouja Moll

On 21 February 2008 "nine human forms, curled around their rocks, nine human forms that wake now, moving from fetal position [...] pulling themselves onto their knees [...] raising their rocks to the sky" (Nolan and Kennedy 387) opened the production of *The Death of a Chief* (hereafter, *Death*) at the National Arts Centre in Ottawa, Ontario. This adaptation of William Shakespeare's historical tragedy *Julius Caesar* was brought to the stage by Toronto's Native Earth Performing Arts Inc,[1] and its co-directors Yvette Nolan and Kennedy Cathy MacKinnon in collaboration with an all-Native company of actors.[2]

As the audience entered the space of the production, instead of the conventional stage tropes denoting Rome, they found a medicine wheel of stones. As the lights went to blackout, the actors made their way onto the stage and crouched over their stones. When the lights went up, the Prologue to the play unfolded; the community lifted the Oracle (Waawaate Fobister), and he pulled long swaths of red silk, not evident at first, from the ceiling. Music started within the circle, with one actor singing, another joining, then the rest. In this production, the company translated *and* adapted Shakespeare's play, exploring and transforming *Julius Caesar*'s theatrical and political structures as well as the relations of power, betrayal, and community that were active in 44 BCE, in 1599, and in the present Aboriginal context. The effects of this complex web of translation, adaption, and production of Shakespeare's *Julius Caesar* serve to emphasize, compare, and voice the social manifestations of power relations within Aboriginal communities and, more specifically, reopen the heterogeneity of cultural, political, and language practices in Aboriginal theatre.

Translation, Adaptation, and the Role of Shakespeare

The play uses several modes of translation, including linguistic transfers between English and Indigenous languages in Canada, the transfusion between and among Western theatre ideologies and Native theatre cosmologies,[3] translations of space (a street in Rome), time (the presence of ancestry), and gender (Caesar as a woman).

Here, the translation event poses a fundamental yet often overlooked question: why is the Native Earth theatre production recognized as "an adaptation" rather than "a translation"? Linda Hutcheon maintains that adaptation is doubly defined as both the "extensive, particular transcoding" of original work into a new form or "product," and "a process" of "creative reinterpretation" (22). *Death* can, indeed, be seen as an adaptation in that the production functions successfully as a "transcoding" of the political structures in Shakespeare's *Julius Caesar*,[4] examining the complexities of community, ambition, power, betrayal, and their relationships to Native peoples in Canada today, "a process that reconfigures the matrix of political hierarchies to make leaders more accountable to the people" (Moll).

Adaptation makes possible a wide range of artistic freedoms for the adapter. In *Death*, the directors transpose the play into a contemporary, social, and political context, thereby helping to classify the work as an adaptation. However, when a play is framed as an adaptation, unlike a translation, language is not necessarily the first point of departure, and because there is no obligation to identify a linguistic locus, the process of translation, and its complexities, is easily elided. Here, *Death* troubles Hutcheon's definition: if the play remains solely an "adaptation," the audience may neglect the process of translation and the leg work needed to identify, engage, and *stay with* the ontology of Native languages. Yet Nolan points out that the first step towards the Shakespearean text is a questioning of how the heterogeneity and complexities of Native languages *translate* Shakespeare. Examining the play through the lens of translation sets the critical focus directly on language, whereas adaptation offers a wider contextual and hermeneutical spectrum in which the importance of language, particularly in Indigenous theatre, can be lost.

In its adapted form, *Death* keeps the larger part of the Shakespearean text intact yet reorders it sequentially. It makes complex structural shifts, moving blocks of passages from their original locations, and omits the theatrical containers of acts and scenes. This speaks to a Native cosmology that sees the borders of European theatre protocol as porous *membranes* through which pan-cultural traditions move with actors who translate and (re)vision specific passages and words.[5] The Prologue, a choreographed piece that mimes the first three Shakespearean acts leading up to Caesar's death, and whose inclusion is an important structural adaptation, weaves in and out of the prophesy and follows Caesar's procession along a road represented by the in-motion red silk leading to the forum, the assassination, and the challenges of political change (see Figure 28.1).

In its structural transpositions, *Death* makes visible the linguistic configurations woven through and through the text that are often rendered invisible when contained inside Western theatre discourses and a patriarchal Eurocentric gaze. Nolan explains, "We had to shift the gaze, from that of a white male writer to an Aboriginal, largely female gaze." Language, in this instance, refuses containment because of the varying nations represented in the theatre company and in Canada, a pan-Indian organization representing the "diaspora" of Cree, Haida, Salish, Mi'kmaq, Métis, and Ojibway, among others (Nolan, quoted in Knowles 55).[6] Native Earth and the production of *Death* are a performative microcosm of linguistic multiplicity that carries with it ancestral borderless land relationships to articulate contemporary urban lives. It operates beyond conventional interlingual translation.

Questions about why Aboriginal theatre practitioners would do Shakespeare at all continue to be asked (Moll and Gruner). Colonial education in the Shakespearean canon produced a cultural bias of *how* Shakespeare should be done. For Aboriginal actors, playwrights, and directors, it remains a continual challenge to enter the British canon – on their terms – whether the work is presented in its traditional form, as a translation, or as an adaptation. *Death*, as a translation, disrupts the traditional understanding of moving "one language" into another and, instead, opens up to an always-present heterogeneity. Language, memory, and ancestry happen as osmosis. Nolan explains: "When genocide happens [...] memory plays out and then we see everything [...] it's not 'I remember when' [...] all the

Figure 28.1
Monique Mojica (Julius Caesar) and Keith Barker (Marcus Brudas) in *Death of a Chief*, National Arts Centre, 21 Feb. 2008.

things are existing at the same time and that's why we can't get over it"
(personal interview).

Federal policies applied in the nineteenth century against Aboriginal
peoples in Canada had genocidal effects that continue to manifest in Native
communities and are shown to play out in the struggles with leadership,
gender, and betrayal in *Death*. Ric Knowles describes *Death* as a process
that "uses Shakespeare's representation of divisions and betrayals at the
roots of Western civilisation to help the Native community in Canada explore real pain over real betrayals within that community, as well as filter-
ing through Shakespeare the real negotiation across many cultures, a
negotiation that constitutes part of the healing of the wounds inflicted by
five hundred years of colonization" (383). *Death* examined as a translation
in the hands of Native practitioners seeks to reverse the hierarchical and
naturalized patterns of Western theatre practices, and place the power
squarely not only in the hands of the production's directors but in those of
each individual member of the cast and technical team. For instance, Jani
Lauzon (who plays Antony) refuses to submit to naturalized theatre etiquette and the aesthetic "purity" of Shakespeare: "[We were told that] you
cannot do Shakespeare unless you think through the colonial mind." Her
reply is firm: "I won't; I refuse" (Moll and Gruner). The refusal to submit
to the *colonial mind* and its linguistic homogeneity reopens the heterogeneity of cultural, political, and language practices always already present in
Aboriginal theatre.

Interlingual Translation

Certain sections in *Death* incorporate conventional forms of translation;
for example, the play's opening lines delivered by the Oracle (Waawaate
Fobister) are spoken in Ojibway only:

Aaniin minik dasing awiya ge-ichigewaad
owe ge-ini-izhiwebag,
bebakaan miziwe gaye, bebakaan ezhi-giigidong? (*Death* 389)

The original Shakespearean lines are uttered by the main conspirator, Cassius, and only appear in Act 3 after Caesar's death: "How many Ages hence
/ Shall this our lofty Scene be acted over, / In States unborn, and Accents

yet unknown?" (*Julius Caesar* 3.1.112). The Native Earth version not only translates but also moves the section to the start of the play to offer both a powerful prediction and to reflect upon current cultural issues in Aboriginal communities.

While the production could be criticized for only using occasional direct translations into Indigenous languages, the sequences that *are* translated stand out dramatically. The opening's translation into Ojibway makes present, for example, the loss of traditional Native languages in Canada as a colonized space. "Accents yet unknown?" as a line reserved for Ojibway speakers, adds an "accent" to the colonial context and points to citizens' accountability and their responsibility to question and determine their sovereignty, a prophesy that is not separated from language, Native cosmology, or *Julius Caesar*.

Nolan points out that "our interlocutors often said they expected a more colloquial text; to wit *Julius Caesar* in rez-speak. 'What's with all the shouting, ennaways? Ever loud, you'" (*Death of a Chief*, Playscript, "Notes to the Production, 1). The call for the "speak" to be familiar to a North American understanding of Native languages replicates the colonial dismantling of Aboriginal communities and the forcible placement into a reserve system that simultaneously controls both land and language (see ss. 18 and 18.1 of the Indian Act). The catalogue of British ideologies, part of the invasion, includes a powerfully constraining patriarchal discourse that was disseminated in literature, like Shakespeare. The expectation of what Native languages "should be" articulates the violence advanced in and by Canadian government policies and education systems that continue to dictate stereotypes and linguistic hierarchies.

It is not surprising, then, that when the Native Theatre company produced *Julius Caesar* for the stage, a translation into Aboriginal languages, from the perspective of what Nolan calls the white gaze, was inappropriate. As Monique Mojica and Ric Knowles emphasize, "These writers [Aboriginal] are quite literarily living in translation, their heads and mouths filled with words and ways of thinking (and therefore perceptions, values and ideologies) that are not their own – but filled, too, with perceptions, values, and patterns that *are* theirs, but that they don't feel the right to claim because the proper words for them don't exist in the only language they have" (vi).

Another effective, if different, mode of translation occurs in the following passage, when Antony mourns Caesar's body. These lines are uttered at the centre of *Death* and stray from the Shakespearean text in only a single word: "Italy" is replaced by "Canada":

> O pardon me, thou bleeding peece of Earth:
> That I am meeke and gentle with these Butchers.
> Thou art the Ruines of the Noblest Chief
>
> That ever lived in the Tide of Times.
> (Which like dumbe mouthes do ope their Ruby lips,
> To begge the voyce and utterance of my Tongue)
> A Curse shall light upon the limbes of men;
> Domesticke Fury, and fierce Civill strife,
> Shall cumber all the parts of Canada. (*Death* 409; *Julius Caesar* 3.1.257–67)

This geographical shift could be seen as a departure into adaptation or, as Linda Hutcheon asserts, a "transcoding" of Rome and its political and social milieu into an Aboriginal community (22). Translating "Rome" with its "Domesticke Fury, and fierce Civill strife" into "Canada" instils metonymic meaning to the land and generates the space to articulate desired responsibilities for its governance and stewardship.

Translation of Space, Time, and Native Cosmology

Nolan wants the audience to think about how time works differently in Native Theatre and, specifically in *Death,* by structuring events through scenes running concurrently. For instance, scenes with Calpurnius and the Conspirators are simultaneous.[7] Consider the following stage direction:

> Upstage of the scrim the Oracle has been preparing Caesar's robe. He now steps into the entrance and offers the robe to Calpurnius who refuses it and exits. Downstage, Brutus enters [...] Now all the conspirators are onstage, circling Caesar. (*Death* 403)

Consider, in contrast, the following direction from *Julius Caesar* 3.1:

Flourish. Enter Caesar, Brutus, Cassius, Casca, Decius, Metellus, Trebonius, Cinna, Antony, Lepidus, Artemidorus, Publius, Popilius, Ligarius and the Soothsayer.

In *Julius Caesar*, the characters "Enter" whereas in *Death*, and Native cosmologies, they are always present. When asked about Native cosmologies, Nolan was quick to respond:

As if there is one! The Native cosmology in *Death* is one we negotiated, agreed to, because every nation has a slightly or hugely different belief system […] For example we agree: our ancestors are with us at all times [and] exist at the same time […] We are connected to the land in a literal, as well as a metaphoric way; there is a balance between male and female […] this balance extends, in our Rome, to a valuing of others – two spirited, youth and elder. (Personal communication)

The continual presence of the characters in the Native Theatre production was not only analogous to solidarity in a heterogeneous belief system but also marked the metaphoric connection to land and, during this event, to the space of theatre. In a significant spatial shift, the stage direction, "A Street," which sets the opening scene in Shakespeare's *Julius Caesar* is translated into a road in Ontario in *Death*. As Nolan explains, it is "outside of any territory, outside of Six Nations.[8] It is actually a community that is invented […] we kept it in Ontario so that we could use those touchstones, because people are so disconnected" (personal interview). Every crack in the "translated" road, in their land, is read differently by each actor and director as Rome, Italy, is transmuted into Rome, Ontario.

The "street" in Shakespeare's Rome becomes a road in *Death* where people actively participate in the political culture; a space where the plebeians, for example, are attempting to regain their voice and their power while dealing with the rhetorical devices and political strategies wielded by their leaders. (See Figure 28.2.)[9]

Translation through the Spine: Caesar and Gender and the Body

Playing the role of Caesar, Monique Mojica considers the translation process on the level of the somatic and gender. That is, translation, for Mojica, comes first "through the spine" (Personal interview); she translates the language of the male dictator, Julius Caesar, into the language of a female warrior:

> My hugest hurdle was how to be powerful without doing a female-to-male impersonation: how to be a powerful Native woman. For example, Kuna culture, which is my ancestry, functions as a modern matriarchy. "Woman" is revered in a way that I don't really have an English vocabulary for, so for me to try to get the translation happening in the production, I had to draw from a language I know. (Personal interview)

The onslaught of colonization in Canada targeted Native women who were active participants in politics, economic activity, and decision making in their communities. The violent racial gendering was enforced in policies such as the Indian Act in which Native women and their children were physically, emotionally, and politically displaced and disenfranchised with their loss of status. An exacting measure devised by the federal government, this ensured a massive reduction and silencing of Canada's Aboriginal populations. The rendering of the Indigenous women's identities into a singular classification excludes them entirely when, under the Act, they lose their status in marrying non-status men. In *Death*, the translation of the male characters of Caesar, Antony, and Cassius into women can be understood not only as a critique of the brutal methods and effects of Canadian nationalism, and its inherent patriarchy, but the ongoing gendered repercussion of these policies within Aboriginal communities. The body of the female Caesar, as a *bleeding peece of Earth*, reflects Indigenous women's forced (dis)connection from the land and language but also paradoxically their ever-present connection to it.

It is significant, however, that in both *Julius Caesar* and *Death* the ghost of Caesar assumes the stance of a warrior; in *Death*, the female successor, Antony, demonstrates not only matriarchal re-empowerment but also a

Figure 28.2

Performance of Prologue, *Death of a Chief*. Workshop at the Festival of Original Theatre, University of Toronto, 18 Feb. 2006. Left to right: Ryan Cunningham, Sara Sinclair, Falen Johnson, Craig Lauzon, Tara Beagan, Cheri Maracle-Cardinal, and Jani Lauzon.

presence and voice that runs through *time and space* and cannot be muted. As Mojica recalls:

> I did not play Caesar as a dictator; I played Caesar as a woman who was bound to her responsibilities to the ancestors and bound to the stars [...] and as a warrior. I think what I used in the northern star speech was that I must be constant. I would hold and define the integrity of belief. (Personal interview)

In *Death*, the line "But I am constant as the northern star" (394; *Julius Caesar* 3.1.60) while exactly repeating the source text becomes transmuted through Mojica's ancestral and linguistic constitution and her Kuna cosmology: "I come from *Nis Bundor* – daughters from the stars" (Personal interview). Thus, Mojica's "northern star" defies Shakespeare's gendered simile signifying a male Caesar and draws a new meaning that reconnects her to her matriarchal roots. The very violence that translation enacts (in that any change is a process of force) provides an intersection from which to understand not only the relationship between colonial ideologies and the counter-force applied in Native theatre but also the linguistic challenges faced within Aboriginal communities.

The erasure of Aboriginal languages advanced in the nineteenth century by the Canadian federal government and its multiple agents, continues to function as a process of cultural genocide. Language, after all, "is one of the most basic markers of colonial authority" (Gilbert and Tompkins 164). In response to the authorized silencing of Aboriginal nations by the state – within the discourse of "Canada as nation" – Native Earth makes present the heterogeneity of Aboriginal linguistic forms while illuminating and critiquing the master narrative of Canada as a "single nation." *Death* stages the exclusions and the states of exception imposed by the sovereign state (Canada), thus showing what continues to be at stake in "founding the nation."

Translation/Adapation: The A/Effects

Translating *Julius Caesar* takes an ironic turn when Native Earth Production Arts asserts their linguistic strength within the very cultural production that was deployed to eliminate their languages. Translation is a transaction of power, an act of authority that is "usually [carried out by] the translator over the translated material – and [shows how] language has the capacity to unsay the world and to speak it otherwise" (176). As observed in both *Julius Caesar* and *Death*: "the abuse of Greatenesse is when it disjoins Remorse from Power" (*Death* 394; *Julius Caesar* 2.1.18).

Death reveals how "there is no one word" to define translation. In Native theatre, "translation [in its conventional and text-based visual sense] rebels against the oral tradition because it's everything we do" (Nolan, personal interview 2008). Through systems of symbols such as the medicine wheel of stones, animal communication, music, specific stage directions, and linguistic transfers, "Shakespeare becomes a Native language [...] a disparate group of people have acquired its arbitrary sounds in conventional ways with conventional meanings in order to be able to communicate amongst themselves" (ibid.).

Death takes over something familiar and conventional (*Julius Caesar*) and makes it unfamiliar, for example, giving stones in the road a language that is firmly attached to the land, to children, dance, struggle, music, and time and space:[x] "and the Elements / So mixt in him" (*Death* 426; *Julius Caesar* 5.5.73). Theatre thus becomes an effective mode of communicating to audiences the experiences that are unique to Aboriginal peoples in contemporary society.[11]

The Death of a Chief comprises a process of coming to language for individuals in a theatre company, individuals whose lives are in continual translation, adaptation, and negotiation. The a/effects remain in the active affirmation of the heterogeneous linguistic structures that are inherent in Native languages and fosters a deeper understanding of the experiences in Aboriginal communities in Canada. Translation is always dynamic; *The Death of a Chief* is an unfinished project and even in its published form will continue to be unfinished, an ongoing process of translation for each reader.[12] The ancestral range of Native languages and their linguistic associations affirm sovereignty, community, and voice; further, this work evokes other traditions: the Indigenous canons of oral storytelling that predate sixteenth-century Shakespearean language plays about leadership, power, and betrayal.

Translation and adaptation, here, provide an unfinished circle where people must work together, using the tools at their disposal to try to figure things out: "We had to build that circle and the other part of the circle remains with our audience and ourselves – so it's not finished yet" (Nolan, personal interview).

Notes

1 The term "Native theatre" is taken from the description by Yvette Nolan, artistic director, Native Earth Performing Arts. The terms "Aboriginal" and "Indigenous" are used interchangeably: although similar, the words do not have the same meaning. However, this is the best method to encapsulate the heterogeneity of nations represented in the theatre production. Whenever possible, specific nations are identified.

2 Information on this performance of *The Death of a Chief* is available on the Native Earth Performing Arts Inc. online.

3 "Aboriginal cultures are many and varied and include Métis, Inuit and First Nations. First Nations are found all over Canada, and some people, mostly Dene and Innu or Ininew, are located further north. Other First Nations include Ojibway, Ininew (Cree), Dakota, Mohawk, Lakota, and so on. All of North America is referred to by many Indigenous cultures as Turtle Island. The Métis were originally people of French and Native ancestry. However, this word has come to describe anyone of mixed Native and European ancestry. Métis is a French word that means "mixed" (Aboriginal Students Association).

4 Shakespeare's history play is based on Julius Caesar (100 BCE – 44 BCE) who was a politician and general of the late Roman Republic. He extended the territories under Roman control before seizing power and making himself dictator of Rome. Caesar was assassinated by the conspirators on the Ides of March (about 15 March) in 44 BCE.

5 Monique Mojica, who is a Kuna and Rappahannock actor and playwright based in Toronto, Ontario, defines "translation," among others ways, as a "membrane."

6 *Indian diaspora* has been called a "dangerous and colonial idea" by Monique Mojica because "we [Indigenous peoples] were always separated by borders and reserves [...] How can we be a diaspora on our own land? In our own homes? In our own bodies?" (personal communication, 26 Oct. 2009).

7 *Death* changes the suffix ending of Shakespeare's feminine "Calpurnia" to the masculine formation, "Calpurnius." The character is played by Lorne Cardinal.

8 The Six Nations (Ontario) includes the Nations of Mohawks, Oneida, Cayuga, Tuscarora, Onondaga, and Seneca. The Caledonia land rights issues must be considered when locating Rome in *The Death of a Chief* on Highway 6. See Bain Lindsay, "Home on Native Land" (the caption states: "According to the Six Nations Confederacy, women are the title holders of the land"); and CBC.ca, "Caledonia Land Claim: Historical Timeline."

9 The February 2006 workshop was performed by eleven actors. See "Kennedy Cathy MacKinnon and Yvette Nolan's "Death of a Chief Multimedia" for biographies. http://www.canadianshakespeares.ca/multimedia/imagegallery/thedeathofachief.cfm

10 *The Death of a Chief*, opening stage direction, 387.

11 Native Earth Performing Arts Inc. Home Page. "About Us."

12 In May 2012, the National Arts Centre of Canada presented Shakespeare's

King Lear in an Aboriginal context. Directed by Peter Hinton, the production was performed by a First Nations cast including Monique Mojica as Goneril and Jani Lauzon playing both Cordelia and the Fool. As explained by Hinton in his Artistic Director's Notes, "Throughout our preparation and rehearsal we were interested in exploring [...] division of lands in the context of 17th century Canada; a world in which English, French and First Nations people endured the struggle of first contact and survived the violent crucible out of which North American society would be constructed" (Hinton 4).

Works Cited

Aboriginal Students Association. ASA Home. 2009. University of Guelph. Accessed 26 Dec. 2009. http://www.uoguelph.ca/~asa/index.shtml

Bain Lindsay, Hillary. "Home on Native Land." *Dominion*, 19 Apr. 2006. Accessed 26 Dec. 2009. http://www.dominionpaper.ca/original_peoples/2006/04/19/home_on_na.html

Canada. Department of Justice Canada. Indian Act. R.S.C. 1985, c. I–5. "Reserves." Section 18. Accessed 26 Dec. 2009. http://laws.justice.gc.ca/eng/I-5/20091226/page-3.html?rp2=HOME&rp3=SI&rp1=indian%20act%20reserves&rp4=all&rp9=cs&rp10=L&rp13=50

cbc.ca. "Caledonia Land Claim: Historical Timeline." cbc *News*, 1 Nov. 2006. Accessed 26 Dec. 2009. http://www.cbc.ca/news/background/caledonia-landclaim/historical-timeline.html

Davin, Nicholas Flood. *Davin Report; Or, Report on Industrial Schools for Indians and Half-Breeds*. Ottawa: Ministry of the Interior, 1879. Accessed 25 Dec. 2009. http://www.canadianshakespeares.ca/multimedia/pdf/davin_report.pdf

Gilbert, Helen, and Joanne Tomkins. *Post-Colonial Drama: Theory, Practice, Politics*. Routledge: New York, 1996.

Hinton, Peter. "Artistic Director's Notes." *Prelude – National Arts Centre*. Ottawa: National Arts Centre, Spring/Summer 2012.

Hutcheon, Linda. *A Theory of Adaptation*. New York: Routledge, 2006.

Knowles, Ric. "*Death of a Chief*: Watching for Adaptation; Or How I Learned to Stop Worrying and Love the Bard." *Shakespeare Bulletin* 25: 3 (2007): 53–65.

– ed. *Shakespeare's Mine: Adapting Shakespeare in Anglophone Canada*. Toronto: Playwrights Canada Press, 2009.

MacKinnon, Kennedy Cathy. *Shakespeare Link Canada*. 2009. Accessed 26 Dec. 2009. http://shakespearelinkcanada.ca. Path: Artistic Team; Kennedy C. Mackinnon.

Mojica, Monique. Personal interview. 15 June 2009.

– Personal communication to the author. 26 Oct. 2009.

– and Ric Knowles, eds. Introduction. *Staging Coyote's Dream: An Anthology of First Nations Drama in English*. Toronto: Playwrights Canada Press, 2003.

Moll, Sorouja. "*The Davin Report*: Shakespeare and Canada's Manifest Destiny." *Canadian Adaptations of Shakespeare Project*. University of Guelph. 2007. Accessed 26 Dec. 2009. http://www.canadianshakespeares.ca/essays/davin.cfm

– and Marion Gruner, co-directors. *What Means This Shouting? Canadian Adaptations of Shakespeare Project*. University of Guelph. 2007. Accessed 26 Dec. 2009. http://www.canadianshakespeares.ca/multimedia/video/what_means_this_shouting.mov

Native Earth Performing Arts Inc. "About Us." 2008. Accessed 25 Dec. 2009. http://nativeearth.ca/en/index.php?option=com_content&view=article&id=2&Itemid=2

Nolan, Yvette. "Death of a Chief." Unpublished draft script, 27 Jan. 2008.

– "Notes to Production of *Death of a Chief*." Unpublished draft script, 27 Jan. 2008.

– Personal interview. 8 Nov. 2008.

– Personal communications to the author. 26 June and 28 July 2009.

– "*Death of a Chief*: An Interview with Yvette Nolan." Interview with Sorouja Moll. Toronto. 12 Mar. 2006. Accessed 26 Dec. 2009. http://www.canadianshakespeares.ca/i_ynolan2.cfm

– and Kennedy C. MacKinnon, directors. *The Death of a Chief*. Robert Gill Theatre, University of Toronto. Feb. 2006.

– *The Death of a Chief*. Macdonald Stewart Arts Centre, Guelph, Oct. 2006.

– *The Death of a Chief*. Buddies in Bad Times Theatre, Toronto, 2008. National Arts Centre, Ottawa, 2008.

– "Death of a Chief." In Ric Knowles, ed., *The Shakespeare's Mine: Adapting Shakespeare in Anglophone Canada*. Toronto: Playwrights Canada Press, 2009, 381–427.

Shakespeare, William. *The Tragedy of Julius Caesar*. Ed. Stephen Greenblatt. 2nd ed. London: Norton, 2008.

– Workshop presentations by Native Earth Performing Arts. Dir. Kennedy Catherine MacKinnon and Yvette Nolan. Perf. Monique Mojica and Jani Lauzon. Native Earth Performing Arts. Dancemakers Studio, Toronto. Sept. 2005. http://www.nativeearth.ca/en/index.php?option=com_content&view=category&layout=blog&id=3&Itemid=17&limitstart=4

PART FIVE

Performing Translation

29

1974: The Weimar Republic Comes to Gay Toronto[1]

Brian Mossop

In the September/October 1974 issue of *The Body Politic*, a gay liberation newspaper published in Toronto, the following words appeared in capital letters across the bottom of page 2: "THE LIBERATION OF HOMOSEXUALS CAN ONLY BE THE WORK OF HOMOSEXUALS THEMSELVES" –KURT HILLER, 1921.

In the October 1975 issue of the paper, Hiller's words were moved to the paper's masthead, and they continued to appear there as a sort of motto until the final issue in 1987. The importance attributed to Hiller's idea is also evident from a poster that was produced at the time showing a gay rights march that took place in Winnipeg in the summer of 1974, with Hiller's words underneath (see Figures 29.1 and 29.2).

Some fifty years earlier, in May 1921, soon after a democratic republic had emerged from the November 1918 revolution that had brought an end to the German monarchy, the following text appeared in a journal published in Leipzig:

> Ihr wisst, Homosexuelle, was es mit den Gründen und Beweggründen eurer Gegner auf sich hat; ihr wisst auch, dass eure Führer und Sachwalter seit Jahrzehnten unermüdlich an der Arbeit sind, die Vorurteile zu zerstreuen, die Wahrheit zu verbreiten, euer gutes Recht euch zu erstreiten (und ganz ohne Erfolg sind diese Bemühungen ja nicht geblieben); aber schließlich müsst ihr es euch selber erkämpfen, schließlich fällt euer Recht euch einzig als die Frucht eigener Anstrengungen in den Schoß. Die Befreiung der Homosexuellen kann nur das Werk der Homosexuellen sein. (*Jahrbuch für sexuelle Zwischenstufen* 21: 55)

Figure 29.1

Masthead of *The Body Politic* Issue 20 (Oct. 1975).

The Body Politic
Gay Liberation Journal

No. 20 September-October 1975

"The liberation of homosexuals can only be the work of homosexuals themselves."
Kurt Hiller 1921

FEATURES:

DEPARTMENTS:

Cover: Some of the more than 200 participants in the Gay Rights march on Parliament Hill on June 30 following the National Conference.
Photo: Gerald Hannon.

EDI

Editor

One strugg

The National Gay Ri
held in Ottawa at the
accomplished even more
hard-working organize
Delegates not only re
sus on a comprehensiv
programme for the new
tional Gay Rights Coa.
so dealt wisely with
ial issue of age of c

The Body Politic en
mands hammered out at
ence, demands which c
areas of discriminati
employment and law en

The arguments which
majority of the deleg
for revocation of all
laws must now be repe
panded upon for the e
rest of the gay commu
have called the conce
ual rights of youth p
the fight for gay rig

We must see that se

Figure 29.2

Poster showing a gay rights march that took place in Winnipeg in the summer of 1974.

Here is the translation that appeared in *The Body Politic* in 1973:

> Homosexuals, you know what the reasons and motives of your opponents amount to; you know, too, that for decades your leaders and advisers have been working tirelessly to destroy prejudices, spread truth, and achieve justice for you. But in the last analysis, you must carry on the struggle yourselves. In the final analysis, justice for you will only be the fruit of your own efforts. The liberation of homosexuals can only be the work of homosexuals themselves. (10: 17)

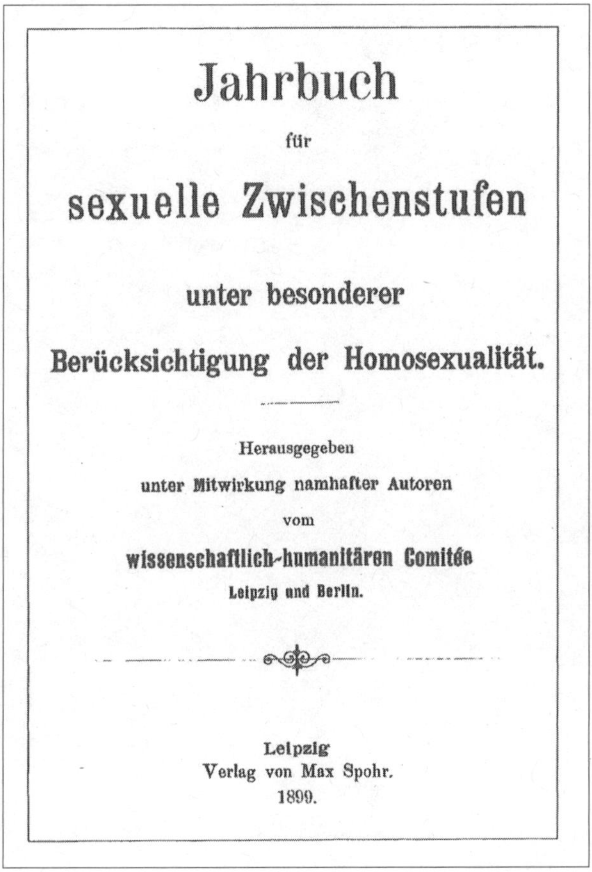

Jahrbuch

für

sexuelle Zwischenstufen

unter besonderer

Berücksichtigung der Homosexualität.

Herausgegeben

unter Mitwirkung namhafter Autoren

vom

wissenschaftlich-humanitären Comitée

Leipzig und Berlin.

Leipzig

Verlag von Max Spohr.

1899.

Figure 29.3 Cover of the first issue of the *Jahrbuch* 1899.

Figure 29.4

Cover of Issue 1 of *The Body Politic*, 1971

How did a text from the Weimar Republic end up on a poster and on the masthead of a gay liberation newspaper in 1970s Toronto? (See Figures 29.3 and 29.4.) The translator of the above passage, James Steakley, was an American gay activist at Cornell University, where he was a doctoral student of German. While in Berlin in 1971–72, he became involved in the new German gay liberation movement and decided to write his thesis on a gay author. He considered Thomas Mann, but then discovered the *Jahrbuch* in the library and decided to write on the movement for the rights of homosexuals that had existed in Germany in the late nineteenth and early twentieth centuries. Back at Cornell, he was in contact with Canadian students involved in *The Body Politic*. He moved to Toronto for a year, where he became a member of the paper's editorial collective. In 1973–74, the paper published three lengthy articles by Steakley describing that early movement in Germany. Naturally, they contained a considerable number of translations from the original German sources, including the one cited above. The three articles were subsequently published in the United States as a book (Steakley, *The Homosexual Emancipation Movement*; see Figure 29.5).

The German Source Text

The journal in which our source text appeared, the *Jahrbuch für sexuelle Zwischenstufen* (Yearbook for Sexual Intermediates) was published by an organization called the Wissenschaftlich-humanitäres Komitee (Scientific-Humanitarian Committee),[2] probably the world's first gay rights organization, founded in 1897.[3] The editor of the *Jahrbuch*, and leading figure of the committee, was Dr Magnus Hirschfeld (1863–1935). The *Jahrbuch* reported on the medical research of Hirschfeld and others concerning sexuality, but it also reported on the committee's political activities.

The source text comes from an item in the *Jahrbuch* for 1921 entitled "Aus der Bewegung" ("From the Movement"), which includes a call from the "Aktionsausschuß für die Beseitigung des § 175" ("Action Committee for the Repeal of Paragraph 175," the section of Germany's penal code that outlawed homosexual acts).[4] The call is signed by Hirschfeld and eleven others, including lawyer Kurt Hiller (1885–1972). The wording of the call was attributed to Hiller by translator Steakley on stylistic grounds (Personal communication with the author).

Figure 29.5

Front cover of Issue 9 of *The Body Politic*, in which the first of the three articles by James Steakley appeared. It shows a cartoon from the magazine *Jugend* at the time of a homosexual witchhunt in 1907; Kaiser Wilhelm II (left) and his close friend and adviser Prince Philip of Eulenburg (right).

The idea expressed by the text, that homosexuals had to free themselves, was based on the well-known socialist concept that the working class had to free itself. By 1921, this notion had been a political commonplace in Germany for several decades. The first document in which it was expressed was perhaps this one:

Considering: that the emancipation of the working classes must be conquered by the working classes themselves, that the struggle for the emancipation of the working classes means not a struggle for class privileges and monopolies, but for equal rights and duties, and the abolition of all class rule. (*Marx Engels Gesamtausgabe* 20: 13)

This is the opening passage of the *General Rules of the International Workingmen's Association*, sometimes called the First International, founded in 1864 in London. The *Rules* were drafted by Karl Marx in English. The idea of self-emancipation is repeated in Frederick Engels' preface to the 1888 English edition of the 1848 *Manifesto of the Communist Party*:

Socialism was, in 1847, a middle-class movement, "Communism" a working class movement. Socialism was, on the Continent at least, "respectable"; Communism was the very opposite. And as our notion, from the very beginning, was that "the emancipation of the working class must be the act of the working class itself," there could be no doubt as to which of the two names we must take. (*Marx Engels Gesamtausgabe* 31: 119)

In Engels' preface to the 1890 German edition of the *Manifesto*, which seems to be based on the above English, the quotation marks make it clear that the notion of self-liberation was already familiar to German readers:

Und da wir schon damals sehr entschieden der Ansicht waren, dass "die Emanzipation der Arbeiter das Werk der Arbeiterklasse selbst sein muss," so konnten wir keinen Augenblick im Zweifel sein, welchen der beiden Namen zu wählen. (*Marx Engels Gesamtausgabe* 31: 258)

The idea of self-liberation thus appears to date from some time before 1848 and to have been first expressed in print, in a form recognizably similar to our source text, in English in 1864. At some point, it entered German socialist culture and was eventually adapted by Kurt Hiller, with a change from "muss" ("must") to "kann nur" ("can only"): "das Werk der Arbeiterklasse selbst sein muss" ("must be the work of the working class itself") became "kann nur das Werk der Homosexuellen sein" ("can only be the work of homosexuals"). This was, in turn, rendered by Steakley, with even more emphasis on the role of homosexuals in their own liberation, as "can only be the work of homosexuals themselves."

Translation at *The Body Politic*

The translation under discussion here is far from the only one that appeared in the pages of *The Body Politic*. The paper was the very opposite of a parochial publication, or one where "international" coverage meant including the United States. It developed a readership in many countries and a special effort was made to gather news of the doings of gay men and lesbians around the world. In line with this, translated materials as well as reviews of translations from several European languages (and of original works in French) appeared frequently.

The entire front page of issue 8 (spring 1973) was devoted to a translation by André Stein of a "long-suppressed gay poem" by Paul Verlaine, side-by-side with the original French. In issue 19 (July–August 1975), I myself reviewed a book of translations of essays by the left Freudian Wilhelm Reich. Issue 12 (March–April 1974) contained translations by Ken Popert (a member of the editorial collective) of several homoerotic poems by the early twentieth-century Russian poet Mikhail Kuzmin (1875–1936), along with commentary. Issue 14 (July–August 1974) contained two reviews of Quebec playwright Michel Tremblay's *Hosanna*. One of these reviews, by Jean Le Derff (author of *Homosexuel? Et Pourquoi Pas!*, the first book-length Canadian work with a gay liberation perspective, published in 1973) concerned the performance in French that had premiered in Montreal in May 1973 at the Théâtre de Quat'Sous. The other review, by Gerald Hannon (yet another member of the editorial collective), concerned the Toronto performance in English translation, which opened at the Tarragon Theatre in May 1974, starring Richard Monette as the drag queen Hosanna.

All the reviewers were highly critical of the works they were considering. Le Derff wrote:

Tremblay [...] specializes in the scum, the wretched of the earth, and he does it beautifully. Nevertheless, we gays must realize that in so doing, he helps perpetuate the old stereotypes, by which we are viewed as basically sick and unhappy, to be pitied at best, if not scorned or laughed at. (*The Body Politic* 14: 12)

And Popert argued:

Although Kuzmin's writing, like much homoerotic literature, is permeated by escapism and cloying sentimentality, it is not slavishly derived from heterosexual romantic literature. His work reveals a certain degree of gay consciousness [...] this consciousness though falls short of being political. (*The Body Politic* 12: 14–15)

Such comments were typical of the reception, in the gay liberation milieu at that time, of any writings that were seen as expressing self-oppressive conceptions of homosexuality, such as the notion that perhaps there is, indeed, something wrong with homosexuals, but society should treat us nicely because it isn't our fault. Writings (from any era) were judged not so much on their merits but on their potential for contributing to the efforts of what was then a tiny group of gay activists.

This need to bend the past to present purposes may have influenced the way James Steakley translated our source text in 1973. This can be seen if that first translation is compared with the following rather different re-translation that he prepared two decades later for a scholarly anthology:

You know, homosexuals, what the reasons and motives of your enemies portend; you know too that your leaders and advisers have been tirelessly at work for decades to dispel the prejudices, to spread the truth, to win for you due justice (and these efforts have not been entirely without success). Yet ultimately you must secure justice by struggling yourselves, for ultimately it will be yours only as the fruit of your own labors. The liberation of homosexuals can only be the work of homosexuals themselves. (Trans. James Steakley, quoted in Blasius and Phelan 170–1)

This translation follows the wording of the German more closely. The 1974 translation uses simpler vocabulary ("amount to" rather than "portend") and syntax ("achieve justice for you" rather than "win for you due justice"). The 1974 translation also gets more quickly to the point by omitting the parenthetical remark, and it creates drama by splitting part of a very lengthy German sentence into two short sentences with parallel structure ("But in the last analysis, you […] In the final analysis, justice for you […]"), whereas the later translation has a single sentence that is reflective in tone rather than dramatic, and thus does not call readers to action.

Reception of the English Translation in the Target Culture

In 1972–74, Pierre Trudeau was heading a Liberal minority government in Ottawa kept in power by the social-democratic New Democratic Party. The Royal Canadian Mounted Police admitted its first uniformed female members, and the Le Dain Commission of Inquiry into the Non-Medicinal Use of Drugs recommended that marijuana should be decriminalized. In the international headlines were the Watergate hearings that forced the resignation of President Richard Nixon, the ongoing US war in Vietnam, and a sudden energy crisis caused by OPEC's raising the price of oil. In Toronto, construction began on the CN Tower, and a reform city council under the new mayor David Crombie was placing strong limits on property developers.

In contrast with the Reagan-Thatcher era, which would begin a few years later, there was a high level of optimism in society about the possibility of social changes of the sort favoured by the left. The new left and the youth countercultures were still going strong. The counterculture aesthetic can be seen in the layout and artwork of *The Body Politic*, and the anti-fascist theme in new left thinking can be seen in the name given to the press that published the paper – Pink Triangle Press: the last of Steakley's three articles revealed for the first time that gay men incarcerated in Hitler's concentration camps had been forced to wear triangular pink badges. The liberation theme of the counterculture was reflected in the main tendency of thinking in the gay movement, which sought not so much equal legal rights as sexual liberation – the former being seen not as an end in itself but as something that would help people to come out of the closet in order to achieve the latter.

The gay movement was just beginning to make itself felt in Canada at this time, mostly in the big cities. While there had long been gay bars and social circles, there were no gay villages and no gay listings in the telephone directory or in tourist guides. By the fall of 1973, the oldest openly gay social and political organizations had existed for only three or four years.[5] It was ten years before AIDS would be heard of, twenty years before the advent of Queer Theory, and thirty years before gay marriage.

In 1969, Pierre Trudeau's government had decriminalized certain sexual acts between two adults aged 21 or over in private, but this had not by itself changed much in the everyday lives of homosexuals. For example, there was no protection in human rights codes (the first of many demonstrations demanding this took place in Toronto in 1971, but the Ontario Human Rights Code was not amended until 1986). Much more importantly, the reigning ideas about homosexuality had yet to be challenged – a task taken up by *The Body Politic* when it began publication in 1971.

The translation of the sentence that later became the paper's motto appeared in the second of James Steakley's articles, in the fall of 1973. Like every issue of the paper, this one included a wide variety of materials, such as classified ads, a community events listing, letters to the editor, book reviews, and most importantly, news. As it happens, the cover story in this issue was the first legal victory of the organized gay movement in Canada – the passage on 10 October 1973 by Toronto City Council of a resolution directing that the city not discriminate against its employees on the basis of their sexual orientation. It seemed that the liberation of homosexuals was not only the work of homosexuals themselves after all!

The collective that produced *The Body Politic* explained Kurt Hiller's use of "only" thus:

A pacifist and women's rights advocate, Hiller was obviously not opposed to alliances between the gay struggle and other forces for social progress.[6] But he warned gays against relying on liberal "friends" for their rights and saw that autonomous gay organization was a prerequisite to gay liberation. (*The Body Politic* 16: 2)

A previous generation of homosexuals in Canada had occasionally appealed to society at large to be more understanding, but they had mostly remained in the shadows, relying on sympathetic heterosexuals to make their case, with little success. There had been no real attempts at "autonomous gay organization." This quiet approach was rejected by many of the younger generation. Quite suddenly, militant and openly gay organizations appeared. Marches were held at which people chanted, "Out of the closet and into the streets, gay liberation now!" and "Two four six eight, gay is just as good as straight!" Public interventions took place in Canada's major cities: kiss-ins in public places, pairs of men dancing together at public events, demonstrations against the police, conservative churches, and psychiatric institutions – to combat the previously unchallenged ideas that gays were criminal, sinful, or sick. All this public presence of unapologetic homosexuality was completely new in Canadian society. Political parties, churches, and the media – of the left as well as the right – had great difficulty overcoming the received negative ideas of the past that had maintained a near monopoly on public discourse and had often been accepted by homosexuals themselves.

In order for activists to operate in the new situation, gut feeling, outrage, and spontaneous self-expression were not enough. We needed ideas to set goals, organize to achieve them, and address other homosexuals and society at large in a new way. The positive public discourse about homosexuality that exists today was unknown; it had to be invented. From where could ideas be drawn, that is, ideas about sexuality and about how things could be changed? The answer was twofold: older writings about sex, and gay history.

In Toronto, reading groups of gay activists in the mid-1970s discussed works about sexuality from the late nineteenth and early twentieth centuries, for example, writings by Sigmund Freud,[7] Wilhelm Reich, Alexandra Kollontai, and Edward Carpenter. Much of the reading material was, of course, translation, mostly from German. A pamphlet describing the courses to be given in the fall of 1975 by a Toronto organization known as the Marxist Institute included the following:

Gay Liberation and Marxism
The course will apply a Marxist analysis to questions of Gay Liberation. We will discuss experiences of sexual oppression, the division

of labour and the rise of gender roles, psychology and gay oppression, the homosexual rights movement from 1900 through revolutionary upheaval to the present, the relation of gay and feminist movements, modern strategic questions.

The course leader, Tim McCaskell, was a member of *The Body Politic* editorial collective and later its international news editor. Activists in the gay movement in Toronto in the 1970s were disproportionately socialists of one sort or another (social democrats, left liberals, Marxists, communists, left libertarians, anarchists). Thus, the socialist origin of the Hiller translation resonated strongly; it was highly "receivable" in the target environment. Like the working class, we gay men and lesbians would liberate ourselves. Indeed, many believed in a link between the two: the heterosexual nuclear family was an important institution for the reproduction of the capitalist order, and that was why homosexuals were oppressed. Others believed that we were bringing about a cultural revolution in the field of sexuality, overthrowing the reigning views grounded in Judaeo-Christianity. *The Body Politic* was the leading voice of these "liberationist" ideas within the gay movement.[8]

Lessons from Weimar Germany

Naturally, it was of the greatest interest, in early 1970s Toronto, to discover – through translation – that we were living not only through the second wave of the women's movement but also through the second wave of the gay movement, the memory of the first having been all but expunged by the Nazi regime. That is perhaps the significance of the fact that the translation of the Hiller quote is always accompanied by the date of the source text, 1921. We were continuing the work of our predecessors, and the past could perhaps provide guidance about how to proceed, or not proceed, in the present.

Hirschfeld's main aim, law reform, was never achieved, even though the Scientific-Humanitarian Committee's petition to the Reichstag had thousands of names of prominent people on it (e.g., Thomas Mann, Sigmund Freud, Albert Einstein, Rainer Maria Rilke, Gerhard Hauptmann, and Martin Buber). The previously mentioned committee formed to change the law in 1921 was unsuccessful. In 1929, a coalition for the reform of the sexual crimes code almost succeeded: a Reichstag committee approved a penal reform bill by a vote of 15 to 13, but the bill was tabled in the aftermath of the stock market crash of that year, and the matter was never taken up again.

It seemed that the whole idea of a humanitarian appeal grounded in scientific arguments for the naturalness of homosexuality, to be endorsed by prominent people, did not work. Hirschfeld believed in self-organization, but only of professionals like himself; the idea of mass mobilization of ordinary people seems never to have occurred to him. As a result, when anti-gay witch hunts began in 1907, and charges were laid against high government officials and military officers, no one was ready to defend homosexuals, and the Scientific-Humanitarian Committee simply went into decline for several years. In Toronto, a different approach was used, and things turned out very differently. When the state launched a series of attacks on the gay community in the period 1977–82, conducting numerous police raids on gay men's baths and bringing criminal charges against three members of *The Body Politic* collective for distributing "immoral, indecent and scurrilous" material, the gay community was ready to fight back, and it did so successfully, with big public meetings and militant demonstrations of thousands.

Despite the Scientific-Humanitarian Committee's lack of mass organizing, it did enjoy tremendous success in the area of public education, that is, in spreading positive ideas about homosexuality. There were huge numbers of publications and public lectures, and Hirschfeld and the Committee became extremely well known. Still, some people felt that the Committee had an overly academic orientation, and thus lacked broad appeal. After the First World War, another more popular organization was formed called the Deutscher Freundschaftsverband (German Friendship Association). It operated a gay community centre in Berlin, sponsored dances, and published a magazine that was sold on newsstands in all major cities and carried news and classified ads. However, Hirschfeld and others were critical of organizations that simply organized social events and put out purely cultural publications, with no political content.

All this – revealed by Steakley's articles – resonated very strongly in early 1970s Toronto, where there was constant debate about the relative roles of mass organization, political work, culture, and social activities (dances, baseball leagues, and the like). There was debate because it was not obvious how to proceed. It is important to realize that no one at the time expected the relatively rapid successes of campaigns for gay legal rights in Canada, and the fairly widespread tolerant attitude towards gays and lesbians that arose towards the end of the twentieth century. For all we knew in the mid-1970s, we would have no more success than the gay organizations of the Weimar Republic. While the final defeat of the gay movement in Germany came with the advent of the Nazi dictatorship in 1933,[9] the movement had operated under reasonably open conditions both under the pre-war monarchy and under the democratic republic of the 1920s. It was, therefore, vital to determine why it had failed, so that we could do things differently.

Aside from a lack of mass organizing, the history of the early German movement perhaps confirmed a feeling among many activists that it was necessary to be bold. Petitioning for law reform would not be enough. We had to simply proclaim that gay is good and on that basis loudly demand our rights. In order to be loud, it was necessary – and this became the central goal of the movement – for large numbers of people to come out of the closet in order to create a mass openly gay and lesbian presence in society rather than continuing to live in the shadows. In other words, first there would have to be an ever larger open presence of gays in society, and only then would there be further law reform and, more importantly, a change in attitudes and behaviour towards homosexuals. And this is, in fact, by and large what happened. The considerable progress that has been made by homosexuals in Canada has not come about mainly through legal change but, rather, through the individual and collective effort of coming out. It has been, in the main, the work of homosexuals themselves, as Kurt Hiller had predicted.

Notes

1 I would like to thank James Steakley and Ken Popert for their comments on earlier versions of this essay.

2 "Zwischenstufen" (literally "inter-steps") reflected the view that homosexuals are an "intersex," a sex "in-between" men and women. Like bisexuals and hermaphrodites, they were thought to be part of a natural continuum of sexual

types ultimately grounded in chemical substances that determine gender and sexual orientation, and are present in different ratios in different individuals.

3 The Committee was founded at a meeting attended by five people, but by 1915, it had 1,500 members. It eventually had international branches in Amsterdam, Vienna, and London.

4 Paragraph 175, first passed in 1871, continued through the Third Reich in strengthened form, and this Nazi version remained in effect in the Federal Republic of Germany (West Germany), although some limitations were added in 1969 and 1973; it was not finally repealed until after German reunification in 1994. In the German Democratic Republic (East Germany), the pre-Nazi version was used, made more lenient in 1968, and then repealed in 1988.

5 An organization called the Association for Sexual Knowledge, established in Vancouver in 1964, published a newsletter in the mid-1960s. However, as its name suggests, it was not openly gay.

6 Page 2 of the previous issue contained a somewhat confused initial statement of this explanation of Hiller's "only" but was otherwise devoted entirely to a lengthy editorial denouncing the 18-month jail sentenced imposed on abortion rights advocate and provider Dr Henry Morgentaler on 25 July 1974. It read, in part: "abortion laws and the laws that oppress gays are cut from the same cloth [...] as long as society fails to understand that the sexual drive is essentially recreative and not procreative, we will have failed to validate our sexual orientation and free society from sexual misery. And women, too, will have failed to validate their humanity and escape domestic imprisonment" (*Body Politic* 15: 2).

7 Issue 33 of *The Body Politic* contained translations by Steakley of four recently discovered documents by Freud showing the "founder of the psychology called psychoanalysis, which has been used for decades to oppress homosexuals, to have been himself consistently opposed to the oppression of homosexuals" (8–9).

8 *The Body Politic* was not the only Canadian gay publication interested in the early German movement. In November 1976, the Vancouver journal *Gay Tide* published a translation by American gay activist John Lauritsen of a speech prepared by Hiller and read by Hirschfeld to the World Congress of Sexual Reform (Copenhagen 1928), another organization created at Hirschfeld's initiative. Interestingly, the Congress took the new Russian legal approach to sexual matters as a model: under the Bolshevik government, the criminal code of 1922 had eliminated the tsarist ban on consensual same-sex relations between adults.

A 1923 pamphlet on "the sexual revolution in Russia" by a Russian delegate
to the Congress, Grigorij Batkis, director of the Moscow "institute for social
hygiene," was translated from Russian into German by Stefanie Theilhaber
(*Die Sexualrevolution in Russland*), and a few pages of this German version
were later translated into English (Lauritsen and Thorstad 63–4). The "sexual
revolution," as it turned out, was short-lived: homosexual acts were recriminal-
ized in 1934 as the Stalin period got under way. Whatever the reason for the
change in the law in 1922, it was not the presence of any gay political self-
organization in either pre- or post-revolutionary Russia (Healey 109, 138).
The German movement seems to have been unique.

9 Incarceration of homosexuals in labour/death camps began in 1934. Hiller was
briefly sent to a camp, but was released and survived the Nazi era. On 6 May
1933, soon after Hitler came to power, Hirschfeld's Institute for Sexual Science
in Berlin was stripped by the Nazis, and on 11 May, the contents were burned
in a public ceremony. Hirschfeld had come back to Europe from an international speaking tour in 1932 but decided that, being a Jew, it would not be
wise for him to return to Germany. He died in exile in France in 1935.

Works Cited

Batkis, Grigorij. *Die Sexualrevolution in Russland*. Trans. Stefanie Theilhaber.
    Berlin: Fritz Kater, 1925.
Blasius, Mark, and Shane Phelan, eds. *We Are Everywhere: A Historical Source
    Book of Gay and Lesbian Politics*. New York: Routledge, 1997.
Healey, Dan. *Homosexual Desire in Revolutionary Russia*. Chicago: University
    of Chicago Press, 2001.
Jahrbuch für sexuelle Zwischenstufen. Leipzig: Verlag von Max Spohr, 1899–1923.
Karl Marx Friedrich Engels Gesamtausgabe. Berlin: Dietz-Verlag, 1992.
Lauritsen, John, and David Thorstad. *The Early Homosexual Rights Movement,
    1864–1935*. Novato, CA: Times Change Press, [1974] 1995.
Steakley, James D. *The Homosexual Emancipation Movement in Germany*. New
    York: Arno Press, 1975.
The Body Politic. Toronto: Pink Triangle Press, 1971–87. http://archive.org

30

1986: Interpreting Effects: From Legislative Framework to End Users

Andrew Clifford

Introduction: Interpreting in Health Care

Imagine that you have arrived on the shores of a distant land, only to find that you are ill. You make your way to a hospital and are seen by a host of different health care practitioners. "Di-a-bet-es" the people around you keep saying, but you don't speak the local language, and you can't really follow much more of the conversations around you than this. You can tell there is something wrong with your left foot and leg – it is numb and ulcerated. In fact, you are very worried that you may have gangrene. One of the health care practitioners confirms your worst fear, and through a very awkward pantomime, you come to understand that they want to perform an amputation. You are asked to sign a piece of paper. You can't read what it says, but you have a family member with you who knows a bit of the local language. He struggles to make sense of the form, and you have a short discussion.

"I can't remember the word for 'left' in their language," he says. You worry together for a moment, before he does his best to fill in the form with the correct information. You both hope for the best and hand the completed paper back to a nurse. The formalities now aside, you begin to think about the surgery. You are practically nauseated by the thought of what is about to happen to you, yet you understand that it is necessary.

The day of your surgery comes. While you are waiting to go into the operating room, a doctor comes to you and starts asking questions. He asks your name, your address, and then gestures at your good leg. Your mind flashes back to your relative, and the form he filled in for you. The frustrations of the language barrier are horrifyingly overwhelming at this point. You point wildly to your left leg, the gangrenous one. The doctor points a few more times at your healthy leg, the right one, and you try even harder to shift his focus to the left. After a few minutes, a look of understanding seems to come over his face, but you're not entirely certain. Doubt gnaws at the back of your mind as you are wheeled into surgery.

As you come to after the operation, you slowly begin to become aware of the room around you. The world seems hazy, and you are extremely disoriented. You're in great pain, which only adds to the confusion. Some nurses notice you stir and up your pain medication. Slightly more lucid, you cast your eyes downward. With an alertness that belies the grogginess you felt mere moments before, you make the sickening realization that your gangrenous left leg is intact, and your healthy right one is now missing.

Errors such as this are, unfortunately, not confined to the realm of imagination. They take place in real life when communication between patient and health care practitioner is complicated by a language barrier, and when no appropriate steps are taken to overcome it.[1] What is more, the scenario outlined above clearly demonstrates the effects that interpreting can have on the people involved. A simple mix-up between the words "right" and "left" were egregious and life altering. If the confusion had revolved around questions such as, "Do you have allergies to any medications?" or "Are you currently taking any drugs, prescription or otherwise?" the effects could just as easily have been fatal. Indeed, this is one of the hallmarks of health care interpreting: the effects associated with error can be catastrophic.

Another hallmark of health care interpreting is the lack of importance placed on it. In the scenario above, the health care professionals were content to relay messages through a family member. This person had absolutely no training as an interpreter, nor did he even have a solid command of the languages involved. The practitioners made use of him not because they had any reason to believe he was good, but simply because he was there. And yet the final effect of their casual selection does not need to be as grave as unnecessary amputation for us to see why it is wrong to call upon family members to interpret. All we need do is think about a few circumstances where vulnerabilities and power relationships between family members have an effect on communication such as:

- A bruised and battered woman stares with fear and incomprehension as a health care professional invites her still-seething husband into the examination room to interpret.

• A teenage boy is put in the position of asking his mother about her sexual partners and practices in an STD clinic.

• A little girl under the age of eight has to persuade the domineering patriarch of her family – who only begrudgingly agreed to consult a doctor – that the medication being prescribed cannot be taken with the alcohol that is a part of his cultural upbringing and that has accompanied every meal for as long as he remembers.

In each of these cases, those who have the power to shape the outcome of the health care encounter have failed to consider the importance of interpreting. In so doing, they have set up situations where compliance or disclosure is in doubt, and where the risk of harm is elevated. Indeed, the specific effects of interpreting in these instances would most likely include a continuing spiral of spousal abuse, an inaccurate assessment of high-risk sexual behaviours and subsequent spread of communicable disease, and a potentially fatal drug interaction. In short, to call upon family to interpret is to fail to understand the importance of interpreting quality, and this lack of quality will be a direct cause of negative patient outcomes.

A Second Opinion: Conference Interpreting

As we have seen, serious problems in health care can be caused by the casualness with which interpreters are selected, and by an inattention to the quality of an interpreter's work. It is a situation that is clearly unacceptable, and one that seems even more stark when it is held up against another type of interpreting. This time, we turn to examine an instance of conference interpreting.

Imagine now that you are a qualified conference interpreter. You have lived your entire life in two cultures and in two languages. You completed primary school in one language, secondary in another. This bilingual pattern was repeated as you earned an undergraduate university degree – most likely at a recognized professional school that taught written translation – and eventually even a graduate degree. You are highly educated and extremely well read in both your languages.

You make the decision to earn another graduate degree, this time in conference interpreting, something you have seen in clips from the United Nations, or perhaps from the floor of the Canadian House of Commons.

You have been fascinated for a long time by the challenges of listening in one language, and speaking simultaneously in another. You sit a gruelling aptitude test and beat out scores of other candidates to secure yourself a spot in a training program. With the start of the school year, you slowly grind through that program, not-so-quietly grumbling that the discipline and rigour needed make the experience a kind of bilingual boot camp for the mind. Many of your classmates are asked to leave as they one-by-one fail batteries of exams that come with numbing regularity. Only a fraction of the original students remain as you gear up for an exam that will determine whether you successfully exit the program and earn your degree. When the exam results come, you are elated to learn you have passed, but crestfallen to find out that several of the few remaining classmates who took the exam with you did not.

Despite the fact that you have earned a degree in conference interpreting, the trials and tribulations are not over. You are hired by an in-house government interpreting service, and until you pass another test – this time a form of professional accreditation – you will be constantly monitored by a senior colleague. Each day, you take the microphone for 30 minutes at a time. At the end of that half hour, and when another interpreter takes over, your senior colleague exits the booth with you, and then proceeds to give you a thorough critique of everything you said over the course of your turn on the microphone. And so it continues until that fateful day when you take and pass your certification test.

Elated, you now have earned the right to interpret without constant monitoring by your peers. You show up to your first assignment as a newly accredited professional. You are interpreting a meeting of accountants, who have gathered to discuss the fine-grained differences between accrual and cash accounting. It's a marathon day, and you reach your fifth half-hour turn convinced that no human mind can sustain for that length of time the heightened levels of concentration required for simultaneous interpreting. As you fight your persistent mental fatigue, a French-speaking delegate stands to ask a question about "la comptabilité d'exercice," which, in your wearied state, you mistakenly render as "cash accounting." The person who will answer the question is an anglophone, and she is dependent on your interpretation to understand. However, she isn't confused by your mistake. She removes her headphones when it is her turn to talk, and quite rightly responds to the query with mention of "accrual accounting."

You're not sure how it happened, but you thank your lucky stars that the experts gathered in that meeting were not confused by your error. Somehow – through knowledge of context perhaps? – they were able to disregard what you actually said and, instead, attend to what you should have said. You've avoided a potentially embarrassing moment.[2]

This second scenario highlights some of the important differences between community and conference interpreting. First, despite some situational similarities, the interpreting effects are not the same. It is true that both scenarios revolve around a word-based distinction that was at the heart of the communication between the parties involved. In the hospital setting, the distinction between "left" and "right" could not have been more germane; in the meeting of accountants, the difference between "cash" and "accrual" was likewise central to their discussions. Furthermore, in both instances, the interpreters, whether ad hoc or professional, confused one word for its opposite. Yet the consequences of the interpreting errors could not be more unlike. The confusion in the hospital likely dealt a heavy blow to the professional reputation of the surgeon, and it was most certainly life altering for the patient, who now has to cope with the trauma of mutilation. However, the mix-up in the conference hall seemed to go unnoticed. Indeed, the expert-to-expert communication that took place there seemed to be able to sidestep the error entirely.[3] This is not to suggest that conference interpreting is in some way easy, or that conference interpreters can rest on their laurels and assume that the quality of their work is unimportant. Just the opposite is true – the technical and cognitive demands of conference interpreting often push the human mind to the limits of its ability, and the interpreter's clients pay good money to receive high-quality service. It is simply that the clients of the conference interpreter are not typically laying either their well-being or their lives on the line.

Second, the level of importance accorded to each type of interpreting seems to be inversely proportional to the severity of the effects of error. We have already seen how importance has an effect on interpreter training. As we outlined above, it is unfortunately not uncommon to ask family members – even when they are children – to interpret in health care. These people do not make effective interpreters because they are not impartial parties in the interpreted encounter, because they rarely have any kind of instruction in interpreting, and because they often lack the necessary command of the languages involved. It is true that many health care institutions are recognizing the dangers of using ad hoc family interpreters, and that they and other stakeholders are making a concerted effort to push for professional health care interpreters. However, in those instances where professional interpreters are used, it is all too clear that their work is undervalued. To see that this is true, we need only examine the training that supports that work, and the remuneration that rewards it. Most of the training available to health care interpreters is offered by individual interpreting service agencies or health care institutions, and it rarely goes beyond 40 hours (i.e., a little longer than the length of a single postsecondary course). In Ontario, a number of community colleges are offering a certificate program in interpreting that is 180 hours (i.e., it is made up of five postsecondary courses). In neither case, however, do trainees ever receive instruction on how to improve the interpreting they do between their working languages. In other words, they are never called upon to actually interpret before an instructor who is able to assess the quality of their output. With regard to remuneration, most health care interpreters struggle to earn a livelihood from interpreting alone. It would be rare for someone to earn as much as $30,000,[4] and many have to take additional full-time or part-time work to make ends meet. It happens all too often that economic forces push an interpreter into other career paths.

To understand the notion of value, it is useful to compare health care interpreting with conference interpreting. As we noted before, most conference interpreters in Canada go through a four-year undergraduate degree in translation before competing for a spot in a very rigorous interpreter-training program at the graduate level. The training program is intense, with over 360 hours of classroom instruction, followed by countless hours of group and individual practice. After completion of the degree, interpreters hired in-house would typically continue training with their employers for as long as a year before passing an accreditation exam. And along the way, all the training interpreters receive is language-specific. That is, the interpreters practice and are taught the specifics of their work between a given pair of languages by someone who shares those working languages. Monetarily, too, there is a stark contrast. An accredited in-house interpreter could expect to earn between $65,000 and $80,000 plus benefits. In the Canadian free-lance market, it would not be unreasonable for a conference interpreter to earn from $80,000 to perhaps as much as $120,000.

Effects of and on Interpreting: The Legislative Framework

Up until this point, we have seen that errors in interpreting can have varying effects, depending on the context in which they occur. A straightforward mix-up with a word pair in the conference setting had a negligible impact and was nearly invisibly corrected in the minds of the listeners, yet a similar mistake in the health care setting had absolutely devastating consequences. We have also seen that the value placed on each type of interpreting seems unrelated to the effects of error. Health care interpreting, despite the risks it poses, does not seem to have elicited the same concern for training and overall quality that conference interpreting has. Conference interpreters must be able to meet very intense training requirements, and there are multiple stages at which the quality of their output is tightly controlled. The same simply cannot be said to be true in the health care sector.

This situation raises an important question – why does the disparity between the two types of interpreting exist? In other words, what are the factors that have had an effect on interpreting such that it, in turn, produces the differential effect on its users that was outlined above? We would argue that one of the factors that explains the differential is the effect of the legislative framework that surrounds each kind of interpreting.

In Canada, the legislative instruments that have had the greatest effect on conference interpreting are without a doubt the Official Languages Act and the Canadian Charter of Rights and Freedoms. Together, these two pieces of legislation are the cornerstone of official bilingualism in Canada, and they jointly support the existence of two separate interpreting services within the Government of Canada.

To begin with, section 16 of the Charter declares that English and French are the official languages of Canada, and that they enjoy equal status, rights, and privileges within the Parliament of Canada. This principle is echoed in section 4(1) of the Official Languages Act, and it is further developed in section (2), which stipulates that "facilities shall be made available for the simultaneous interpretation of the debates and other proceedings of Parliament from one official language into the other." To uphold these provisions, the Government of Canada operates the Parliamentary Interpreting Service, and it is responsible for interpreting the proceedings of the House of Commons, of the Senate, and of all House and Senate committees. The Service was not actually created by either piece of legislation – its inception preceded the Act by ten years and the Charter by twenty-three years – but the advent of the Act and the Charter meant that the provision of conference interpreting was enshrined in some of this country's most fundamental legislative instruments.

The Charter and the Act do not merely have an effect on interpreting in Parliament. They also contain provisions that govern interactions with the public and with employees. For instance, section 20 of the Charter, and section 21 of the Act indicate that members of the public have a right to communicate with and receive services from federal institutions in the official languages. In addition, section 34 of the Act establishes English and French as the languages of work in all federal institutions. The Act indicates that obligations towards the public and towards employees mainly affect the National Capital Region, or other designated regions where both languages are widely spoken, but there are stipulations that concern so-called unilingual regions as well. What all this means is that when government departments or agencies hold either internal meetings or organize public events, particularly in certain parts of the country, they have an obligation to ensure that access is provided to speakers of both official languages. The Act does not explicitly indicate the means of doing so; however, it is common practice to provide access through simultaneous conference interpreting. To meet the resulting need, a second group of interpreters – the ambiguously named Conference Interpreting Service – was formed within the government, this time to interpret a variety of conferences and other gatherings, big and small, internal and public, all across the country.

The Imperfect Frame: Negative and Positive Effects

It must be said that, despite the intent of the Act and the Charter, the provision of conference interpreting does not always have its desired effect. In some instances, the uneducated use of interpreting not only does not promote the use of both official languages, but instead winds up establishing English alone as the language of interaction. This comes about in two ways.

First, some conference organizers hold the false impression that all they need do to meet official language needs is ensure the presence of interpreters. Consequently, they do not actively promote the use of French on the conference floor. The plenaries, presentations, or moderated discussions all take place in English, and francophones simply decide to accept this turn of events by at all times speaking English themselves. Their decision may come about because they feel self-conscious being the only person in the room wearing headphones (and thus listening to the interpretation) or because they are comfortable listening to English. (In the National Capital Region, it often seems that the bulk of bilingual positions are staffed by francophones who speak English, as anglophones with a solid command of French appear to be few and far between.) The end result is that no one in the room is actually listening to the interpretation. In situations like these, interpreters often feel tremendously discouraged, as they are essentially being asked to expend great amounts of mental energy providing quality service in vain. When faced with assignments like these, many conference interpreters, in frustration, simply turn off their microphones and stew.

The second scenario comes about when anglophones are ignorant about the conference interpreting service that is provided to them. It is often the case that the conference interpreting is seen as a service intended for francophones only, and many English-speakers seem not to even notice the headset and receiver sitting at their place on the conference table. On the odd occasion when a francophone actually makes a point of saying something to the group in French, a great hew and cry will frequently go up from the masses. "What is he saying?" someone will invariably ask testily, and the francophone will be interrupted by a random English-speaker with some limited French, who takes it upon himself or herself to suddenly become an ad hoc interpreter. The francophone will then be instructed to speak in short sentences, while the would-be linguistic mediator begins his or her turns at talk by saying things like, "I think what he's getting at is …" or "If I get the gist of what he's saying …" The meeting attendees put up with this situation for a time, blissfully unaware that a much simpler solution would be to simply pick up the headsets on the table and put them on their ears. If they were to do so, they would hear the professionals in the booth interpreting the entire farcical scene – relaying the francophone's choppy sentences into English, and the armchair interpreter's utterances back into French. Needless to say, the whole turn of events has two predictable effects – it drives the conference interpreters' blood pressure into the stratosphere, and it actively discourages the francophone from ever daring to speak in French in public again. It also explains the origin of scenario number one.

Still, even when events unfold as they did in the scenarios above, the interpreting is nevertheless *present*. Clients may choose not to use it, or they may not know to use it, but it is provided regardless. In other words, the mere availability of interpreting is a kind of minimal condition that upholds the letter – if not the spirit – of the most basic laws of the land. To understand the importance of this minimal condition, we need only think about the televised coverage of the proceedings in the Canadian House of Commons, which feature the voice of a House interpreter whenever a Member of Parliament says something in the other official language. The coverage will clearly not be leading the television ratings anytime soon, but the interpretation allows Canadian citizens to tune into Parliamentary proceedings at any point they see fit to do so, and to follow what transpires despite potential language barriers. If the interpretation were no longer available to the public, then a major obstacle would prevent millions of citizens from monitoring and participating in the political process. As things stand now, interpretation may be often underutilized, but it is, nevertheless, an important safeguard for Canadian democracy. For this reason, it may be that the best metric for interpreting is not the number of people who actively use it, but rather the effects on the lives of citizens when it is taken away from them.

It is also important to point out that interpretation is not always underutilized. Indeed, there are many instances when the interpreters' hard work is both sorely needed and greatly appreciated. It is not uncommon for even the most hard-nosed public servants to make their way to the interpreting booth after a meeting has ended, in order to thank the interpreters for their efforts. Clients such as these often acknowledge that they spent the day with their headphones firmly clamped over their ears, because without the interpretation, they would have been unable to follow or participate in conference proceedings. Similarly, Parliamentary debate attracts a significant audience during an election campaign, as the party leaders square off on national television to try to win over voters. In Canada, it has become tradition to hold two debates per campaign: one in English, and one in French. Thanks to interpreting, each debate is broadcast in both official languages (e.g., the French-language debate is broadcast on the French television networks, and an interpreted version is broadcast on the

English networks). The interpreted versions usually draw the attention of the political pundits, and mention of the interpreters seems to regularly work its way into the media reports.[5]

At this point, what should be apparent is that the federal legislative framework in Canada may have its shortcomings, but that it by and large has allowed high-quality interpreting services to be offered to clients who need them. What is more, the structure of that legislative framework is also significant. It consists of an iconic foundational document – the Canadian Charter of Rights and Freedoms – that is, undeniably, part of the political and social fabric of the nation, and also of a more precise instrument – the Official Languages Act – that builds upon the foundation document and makes specific mention of interpreting as a much needed service.

The Claim to Frame: Health Care Interpreting

If we turn once again to health care interpreting, we will find that a similar legislative framework is not present in Canada – at least not in its entirety. It can be argued that there is an iconic foundational document, in the form of the Canada Health Act. The Act is most certainly a part of our political and social fabric. Its key principles of comprehensiveness, universality, portability, and accessibility inform public debate over the nature of our system of health insurance, which is touted by many as one of the aspects of Canadian society that distinguishes us from our neighbours and, therefore, that helps to establish our national identity. Section 3 of the Act is often cited by proponents of health care interpreting, as it stipulates that "the primary objective of Canadian health care policy is to protect, promote and restore the physical and mental well-being of residents of Canada and to facilitate reasonable access to health services without financial or other barriers."

The key wording is obviously the mention of "other barriers," and a growing movement is currently seeking to have language considered such a barrier. To do this, it is likely that a second legislative instrument would be necessary. In the same way that the Official Languages Act has sustained two interpreting services within the federal government, a companion piece of legislation that reinforced the interpretation of language as a barrier and that made mention of interpreting as a solution would have a tremendous effect on the state of health care interpreting and, in turn, on the acceptability of patient outcomes.

To see the forms that such companion legislation could take, we need only look south of our border to the United States, where a number of instruments have been put in place. In 2000, then-President Clinton signed Executive Order 13166 (Executive Order on Limited English Proficiency), which called for improved access to health services for people with limited English proficiency. It led to the creation of the National Standards for Culturally and Linguistically Appropriate Services (CLAS) that required federally funded health care institutions to provide language services – including interpreters – free of charge to patients in need. Although the CLAS standards were subsequently watered down, it can be argued that they, nevertheless, created a climate where other measures could be introduced. As such, section 1259 of the California Health and Safety Code requires general acute care hospitals to call upon either interpreters or bilingual professional staff to ensure "adequate and speedy communication between patients and staff." Likewise, the bill recently passed by the California Senate (Bill 853) requires medical insurance companies to provide interpreters for non–English-speaking patients. Both of the Californian provisions have come into effect only recently, and so it is far too early to see the effect that they will eventually have on interpreting and, in turn, on patients. Yet it seems likely that they will be highly useful models for study that may eventually help us here in Canada create a legislative framework for health care interpreting similar to the one that has allowed conference interpreting to provide quality services to those that both need it and are entitled to it.

Conclusion: Parallel Frames, Parallel Effects

In this essay, we have shown how similar errors of interpreting can have very different effects upon the clients of health care interpreters and of conference interpreters, respectively. It was argued that the effects of error seem to be inversely proportional to the importance accorded to each profession. Conference interpreters have very exacting training and respectable remuneration, yet their slip-ups are rarely life altering; conversely, health care interpreters are underpaid and undertrained, yet their mistakes can be disastrous. To better understand how such an ironic dichotomy came to be,

we have looked at one significant factor, the legislative framework associated with each type of interpreting. In conference interpreting, the combination of a foundational document and specific follow-up legislation has
not had entirely positive results, but it has ensured that interpreting services
are provided to politicians, to government employees, and to members of
the public. In health care interpreting, a foundational document exists, but
it lacks the companion piece to focus interpretations of it. As a result, there
is no mandatory provision of health care interpreting. However, examples
of interesting models abound, most notably in the United States.

It would be helpful if future attempts to alter the status quo began by
completing the legislative framework for health care interpreting. Such a
framework would see the provision of interpreting expressly outlined in
companion legislation, and this companion legislation would expand upon
the principles of the Canada Health Act. This type of scenario would go a
long way towards recreating the conditions that have allowed conference
interpreting to reach its current state of development in Canada. In short,
the legislative framework would have its effect upon health care interpreting, and health care interpreting, in turn, would have its subsequent effect
upon its ultimate users. The end result would be a more uniform profes-
sionalization in interpreting as a whole, and a more equitable effect on
those who rely on it to communicate. When it comes right down to it,
shouldn't the quality service currently provided to our political leaders also
be offered to health care patients? Shouldn't we try to ensure that the effects
of interpreting are fair?

Notes

1 The amputation error is, unfortunately, a true-life story ("Limited English Is
   a Barrier for Many Asians in the US").

2 In this scenario, the pathway we outlined through training is typical of many
   conference interpreters in Canada. The interpreting error described, however,
   was one made by the author alone.

3 It is true that errors of this type are not always so benign in conference interpreting. There is an often-told story of a fatigued interpreter working at an
   international political forum who relayed "La France demande une réponse"
   ("France asks for a response") as "France demands a response," and in so
   doing nearly caused an international incident. However, the author would

argue that the majority of conference interpreters in Canada work in settings where tension is considerably lower, and the stakes not as high.

4 In 2004, the author participated in a study of health care interpreting in Vancouver, Toronto, and Montreal. In-depth qualitative interviews were conducted with over 150 stakeholders in health care interpreting, many of whom were interpreters. In only one instance did we hear of an interpreter who reached an income of $30,000. The person in question worked as a full-time staff interpreter for a provincial ministry of health. Positions such as these are few and far between.

5 One parliamentary interpreter, in particular, seems to get singled out somewhat consistently during the English-language debates because of his Australian accent ("The Lighter Side of the French TV Debate").

Works Cited

California Health and Safety Code. Accessed 26 June 2009. http://law.onecle.com/california/health/1259.html

California State Senate. 2003. Bill No. 853. Accessed 26 June 2009. http://info.sen.ca.gov/pub/03-04/bill/sen/sb_0851-0900/sb_853_bill_20031009_chaptered.pdf

Canada Health Act. R.S.C. 1985, c. 6. Accessed 16 Dec. 2009. http://laws.justice.gc.ca/eng/C-6/page-1.html

Canadian Charter of Rights and Freedoms. Part I of the Constitution Act, 1982. R.S.C. 1985. Accessed 16 Dec. 2009. http://laws.justice.gc.ca/en/charter/1.html

Executive Order on Limited English Proficiency 13166. 11 Aug. 2000. Accessed 26 June 2009. http://www.usdoj.gov/crt/cor/Pubs/eolep.php

"The Lighter Side of the French TV Debate." *Daily Observer*, 2 Oct. 2008. http://www.thedailyobserver.ca/2008/10/03/the-lighter-side-of-the-french-tv-debate

"Limited English Is a Barrier for Many Asians in the US." *China Post*, 7 Aug. 2008. Accessed 16 Dec. 2009. https://www.chinapost.com.tw/life/detail.asp?id=168963&sY=discover/2008&sM=08&sD=07&sN=Limited-English&GRP=Q&sPeriod=30

Official Languages Act. R.S.C. 1985, c. 31. Accessed 24 June 2009. http://laws.justice.gc.ca/PDF/Statute/O/O-3.01.pdf

31

1997: The Supreme Court of Canada Rules that the Laws of Evidence Must Be Adapted to Accommodate Aboriginal Oral Histories

Sophie McCall

In 1991, Chief Justice Allan McEachern of the Supreme Court of British Columbia wrote his Reasons for Judgment, *Delgamuukw* v. *British Columbia*, which denied the claim of the Gitksan and Wet'suwet'en plaintiffs to the ownership and jurisdiction of their territories on the northwest coast of British Columbia. In 1997, the Supreme Court of Canada stated that there were "palpable errors" in the judgment (*Delgamuukw* v. *Canada* [scc] par. 7).[1] Chief Justice Antonio Lamer wrote that McEachern had not given adequate weight to the oral histories presented in the court and determined that future trials must include oral traditions as evidence. "The laws of evidence must be adapted in order that they [oral histories] can be accommodated and placed on an equal footing with the types of historical evidence that courts are familiar with, which largely consists of historical documents," wrote Lamer. Otherwise, "an impossible burden of proof" would be placed on groups who do not have written records (par. 87). Only by using oral traditions, as opposed to written records from the past, do First Nations plaintiffs have a chance to contest colonial and racist assumptions about the "vanishing Indian" or the "noble savage" that inform the official history of contact. However, although the Supreme Court decision officially recognized oral traditions as evidence, the court cases since 1997 demonstrate that profound difficulties of transcription and translation remain. What does it mean to place oral histories "on an equal footing with" written, historical documents? What is involved in "adapting" the "laws of evidence" to "accommodate" oral history? The main source of trouble in translating oral histories in the courtroom is their status as mediated knowledge. As a form of mediated knowledge, oral history dangerously approaches the untrustworthiness of hearsay. Yet hearsay, an out-of-court statement by someone other than the witness, is another way of describing the transmission of oral history through a chain of storytellers that stretches back in time. Although oral history falls under the formal exceptions to hearsay rulings, its status as an exception places it in a separate epistemological category that potentially compromises its credibility. This widens the culturally loaded division between writing and orality and, concomitantly, sharply distinguishes "authentic" oral traditions from what are considered impure or contaminated. In considering the "translation effects" of *Delgamuukw* in land claims cases since 1997, it is clear that oral history, as a form of mediated knowledge, defers the kernel of truth that the courts attempt to reify.

Lamer's injunction to place oral traditions "on an equal footing with" written evidence recalls a liberal Canadian notion of perfect translatability that underpins official bilingualism but remains in contradistinction to the realities of unequal language exchange (Simon 12). Thus, the *Delgamuukw* ruling continuously attempts to efface or downplay the role of mediating layers of translation while buttressing the stability of evidence. Reading oral traditions for hard evidence of territorial ownership misses the point that storytelling is an embodied performance, a series of situated tellings, a moment or event in which interlocutors mutually shape meaning through communication. Thus, in the context of interpreting Aboriginal oral testimony in the courtroom, translation is most usefully understood as a process and as an act, rather than as a product or outcome. Such an approach addresses the multiple layers of translation, cultural or linguistic, at work in a land claims case. Each layer of translation mobilizes asymmetries of power, culturally loaded sets of assumptions, and persistent binary oppositions. The stakes are high in moving from oral performance to written document, from Aboriginal languages to English, from witnesses' statements to stenographic notes (which, in turn, are translated into the court's official transcripts), and from out-of-court statements by cultural bearers and their interpreters to expert witness reports. These layers of translation are implicated in Aboriginal peoples' ongoing struggles over land, resources, jurisdiction, and autonomy in a settler state such as Canada. A layered approach to translation, which clashes with the court's tendency to fracture knowledge into bites of information, demonstrates the complexity of intersecting relations of power at work in the courtroom. In a land claims case, acts of translation are deeply embedded in cultural and social contexts that defy the legal procedures of decontextualizing and recontextualizing moveable pieces of data.[2] Theorizing the translation of oral traditions as evidence of Aboriginal rights in a court of law must take into account the degree to which oral history is fundamentally changed by moving from one cultural context to another. A dramatic context-shift is the move from an Aboriginal system of law, such as the Gitksan or Wet'suwet'en feast hall, to a key arena of colonial rule: the settler's court of law. In essence, as Cree/Saulteaux/Dunneza legal scholar Val Napoleon claims, *Delgamuukw* was about one legal system (the Canadian judiciary) judging another (the Gitksan and Wet'suwet'en feast hall) (154).

The 1991 *Delgamuukw* Trial in the British Columbia Supreme Court

The *Delgamuukw* trial began in May 1987, and ended on 30 June 1990, after 374 trial days. Chief Justice Allan McEachern released his reasons for judgment on 21 March 1991, which found that no Aboriginal title or rights had pre-existed European settlement. McEachern went further and said that, even if there had been Aboriginal rights, they had been extinguished by the assertion of sovereignty by Great Britain: "It is the law that aboriginal rights exist at the 'pleasure of the Crown,' and they may be extinguished whenever the intention of the Crown to do so is clear and plain [...] The plaintiffs' claims for aboriginal rights are accordingly dismissed" (*Delgamuukw* [BCSC] ix). The plaintiffs, the Gitksan and Wet'suwet'en First Nations, appealed the decision, and in 1997, ten years after the trial began, the Supreme Court released its landmark decision.

The 1991 *Delgamuukw* trial was the first in Canada that depended primarily upon Elders, scholars, House Chiefs, and other community members as expert witnesses. The plaintiffs argued that, in performing their oral traditions, they were enacting both title to and jurisdiction over land.[3] "My power is carried in my House's histories, songs, dances and crests," says Ken Muldoe, who held the Gitksan name Delgam Uukw at the time of the trial. "It is recreated at the Feast when the histories are told, the songs and dances performed, and the crests displayed" (Gisday Wa and Delgam Uukw 7). Similarly, Gyologyet (Mary McKenzie), a Gitksan House Chief who has jurisdiction over three large territories, describes the importance of the *adaawk* as it relates to her knowledge of her territory: "*Adaawk* in Gitksan language is a powerful word describing what the house stands for, what the chief stands for, what the territory stands for [...] And it's the most important thing in Gitksan [...] Without *adaawk* you can't very well say you are a chief or you own territory" (quoted in Monet and Skanu'u 28). In performing the adaawk, the Chiefs assert territorial ownership and ancestral connections to land. In both Gitksan and Wet'suwet'en cultures, each community member is associated with a House, and each House owns and has jurisdiction over a given territory.[4] The expressions of ownership of these territories come through the Gitksan adaawk, the Wet'suwet'en kungax, and the ceremonial regalia (Monet and Skanu'u 26; Cruikshank, "Invention" 35). The plaintiffs argued that the adaawk and kungax – the collections of stories, songs, and histories that had never before been performed outside the feast halls – provide evidence of title and rights to the disputed territory.

However, the Gitksan and Wet'suwet'en legal team faced a difficult challenge to present the Elders' testimony as statements of land ownership in ways that the court would accept. First, neither the adaawk nor the kungax express land ownership through concrete descriptions of land boundaries. The Gitksan and Wet'suwet'en witnesses defied the province's "colour-coded maps," which sought to define land in units (Gisday Wa and Delgam Uukw 63). Second, the adaawk and kungax mostly describe travels through land, not settlements in the land. According to Gyologyet, adaawk is "not a story, it's just how people travelled is *adaawk*" (quoted in Monet and Skanu'u 28). Travel, land ownership, and the exchange of stories are closely related concepts; Gisday Wa (Alfred Joseph) describes the Wet'suwet'en kungax as "a song or songs about trails between territories" (*Delgamuukw* [BCSC] 179). The performative and narrative movement of the adaawk and kungax imbue place with fluidity and movement that defy Euro-Canadian legal understandings of land ownership. Third, the adaawk and kungax are highly performative oral genres that enact meaning through feasting. Performing and listening to the adaawk at the feast hall confirms and enacts a House's claim to territory. As Delgam Uukw states, "The histories of my House are always being added to. My presence in this courtroom today will add to my House's power [...] Through the witnessing of all the histories, century after century, we have exercised our jurisdiction" (Gisday Wa and Delgam Uukw 8). Regardless of the outcome of the trial, Delgam Uukw implies, repeated tellings of the oral histories, including those recited in the courtroom, expand the House's histories, and bring about the possibility of negotiating the land settlement on the Gitksan and Wet'suwet'en people's own terms.

While the passing on of information through time and through different people is part of the process of oral transmission, "retelling" is a characteristic of hearsay. In a sense, the oral tradition is hearsay – an "ear" witnessing that attends to the out-of-court voices of ancestors sounding in the present.[5] Thus, the process of verifying oral traditions conflicts with the process of verifying standard forms of evidence. In order to take the plaintiffs' evidence seriously, the court needed to consider how to listen to the adaawk and kungax. Indeed, hearing oral traditions as evidence of Aboriginal rights is a challenge. In legal processes of interpretation, a high degree of decontextualization occurs in determining what is true and what is false. Yet the treatment of testimony as bits of moveable text in a legal proceeding is anathema to the treatment of testimony in oral history. Julie Cruikshank, an anthropologist who has written extensively on the challenges of textualizing oral history, and who has worked collaboratively with three Athapaskan Elders/storytellers to produce a critically acclaimed collection of life narratives, *Life Lived Like a Story* (1990), argues that oral history does not occur in a vacuum; it is situated and contextualized in a moment of telling. The audience plays a role in the shaping of the narrative. Even when the same words are used in the telling of a story, each performance is irreducibly particular. At the same time, narratives are fluid, transformative, and intersubjective, connecting the past, present, and future.[6]

The many layers of mediation that make up court documents render translation a fraught process. During the trial, interpreters translated the testimony told in the Tsimshian languages,[7] spelling out words letter by letter; meanwhile, stenographers recorded the translations in shorthand. At the end of each day, court employees converted the shorthand back into prose. The judge and lawyers then consulted the transcripts for the purpose of cross-examining witnesses, sometimes months after the witnesses gave their initial testimony. The continuous process of decontextualizing and re-contextualizing the court testimony has a profound effect on how the stories generate meaning. Leslie Pinder, a legal consultant for the plaintiffs in the *Delgamuukw* case, highlights the dangers of decontextualizing testimony in the process of making arguments either for or against: "In court cases, we word-search transcripts to reassemble evidence; it doesn't resemble anything that was said, by anyone. We cut the words, even our written words, away from the environment, and hold them up as pieces of meaning, hacked up pieces of meaning" (11–12). Moveable text, cut and pasted into new contexts, warps and changes the possible range of meanings that a testimony produces. Pinder's graphic description of the violence of interpretation, in which re-membering testimony is closer to dismemberment, is particularly relevant to the problem of translating Aboriginal oral traditions and languages. The courtroom, a symbol of Euro-Canadian dominance over Aboriginal epistemologies and languages, is saturated in colonial discourses that virtually foreclose the possibility of accurate or fair interpretations of the adaawk and kungax. Moreover, the transcripts emerge from the severely binarized relations of legal contest, in which the Crown and the plaintiffs attempt to annihilate one another's arguments by whatever means necessary. In the cross-examinations, the Crown lawyers sought to discredit the reliability of the adaawk and kungax. The plaintiffs' lawyers, on the other hand, asserted that the adaawk and kungax were definitive statements of land title, even though some of the stories do not explicitly describe territory at all. Although McEachern does not adequately take into account the performative dimension of the adaawk and kungax, readers of his Reasons for Judgment have few means to recreate that performance in order to revise his interpretations.

Although McEachern officially admitted oral tradition as a legitimate form of evidence, his Reasons for Judgment shows that he got stuck on the question of its validity. Cruikshank argues that the judgment reflects the idea that transcribed oral traditions are equivalent to archival documents ("Invention" 38). Yet the relations of address in oral storytelling have much greater importance than McEachern allowed. McEachern's response to the testimony of Antgulilibix (Mary Johnson), a Gitksan Chief who claims to own and have jurisdiction over a large portion of the territory under dispute, reveals the difficulty of using oral traditions in a courtroom without first changing what the plaintiffs have to prove: "Mrs Johnson [...] did not have a clear understanding of the boundaries of her House, but she spoke comprehensively about its legends. When asked about the adaawk of her House she related several stories which I would have classified generally as mythology" (*Delgamuukw* [BCSC] 51). For McEachern, territorial boundaries belong to the realm of visible proof and concrete evidence, while legends exist beyond time or place or measurement. He concludes, "I am not able to accept adaawk, kungax and oral traditions as reliable bases for detailed history" (75); "the adaawk are seriously lacking in detail about the specific lands to which they are said to relate" (58). But the Gitksan and Wet'suwet'en were determined to use their oral traditions to challenge the nature of proof in an effort to decolonize legal definitions of Aboriginal title and ownership.

Translation Effects: After *Delgamuukw*

The Supreme Court of Canada's 1997 *Delgamuukw* decision, which ruled that the trial judge "gave no independent weight" (par. 98) to the Gitksan-Wet'suwet'en oral traditions, has become the leading case on the admission and interpretation of oral histories in Aboriginal rights litigation.[8] Yet, while the Supreme Court's legitimization of the use of oral history is potentially groundbreaking, scholars have argued that definitions about the evidentiary nature of oral tradition have actually narrowed since 1997, and oral history has come to be used in ever more circumscribed ways in courts.

Although *Delgamuukw* was initially celebrated as a victory in Aboriginal rights litigation, particularly in media representations,[9] a number of legal scholars have since expressed strong scepticism. Candace Metallic and Patricia Monture-Angus argue that Lamer's recommendation to adapt the rules of evidence amounts to "no more than a bit of tinkering" (par. 24). This tinkering allows First Nations appellants to become "'white' at law," leaving the existing paradigm intact (par. 24). Val Napoleon contends that although the Supreme Court of Canada declared McEachern in error and ordered a new trial, the process of litigation, nonetheless, "filtered and altered" the oral histories of the Gitksan and Wet'suwet'en people, producing "a distorted legal truth" about oral histories that now powerfully shapes the discourses of Aboriginal rights (125). The most far-reaching critique is that of John Borrows, who focuses on Lamer's qualification that any adaptation of the rules of evidence "must not strain the Canadian legal and constitutional structure" (*Delgamuukw* [SCC] par. 82). Borrows objects to this caveat, arguing that if Aboriginal oral histories are taken seriously, "the very core of the Canadian legal and constitutional structure" may be called into question (25). For Borrows, Lamer's ruling aims to incorporate Aboriginal oral history into the process of litigation without, in effect, changing the rules of the game. For this reason, he is quite critical of the decision and questions the extent to which it may be considered genuinely "groundbreaking" (which continues to be a common descriptor of the case in both popular and scholarly writings).[10]

Part of the problem lies in the fact that Lamer offers little guidance on how the multiple processes of translating oral histories should unfold. The decision is reflective of the Court's circumspection regarding mediated knowledge, which stands in opposition to direct, immediate truth. This becomes clear in Lamer's working definition of oral history, which he derived, to a large extent, from the 1996 final report of the Royal Commission on Aboriginal Peoples. The commissioners' approach to oral history, as described in the first volume of the report, *Looking Forward, Looking Back* (32–3), is cited in Lamer's decision. Following the lead of the RCAP, Lamer emphasizes the "difference" that oral tradition represents – it is subjective, embodied, cultural, and communal, as opposed to writing which is objective, abstract, scientific, and individualistic.[11] Although Lamer's apparent intention is to encourage trial judges to take oral history seriously, he risks isolating it as an exception for which the courts will adjust nominally their usual criteria. Thus, the standards of evidence themselves go unexamined. Moreover, Lamer's prescription encourages future judges to follow one set of criteria for written documents and another for oral histories. This binary opposition between writing and orality risks spawning other value-laden dichotomies, such as civilized vs. savage, and contaminated vs. authentic.

In litigation relating to Aboriginal rights after *Delgamuukw*, in an attempt to clarify how to interpret and verify oral history evidence, judges have asserted increasingly rigid boundaries between written and oral documentation. The narrowing of the admissibility and interpretation of oral histories in trials relating to the defence of Aboriginal rights is evident in *Mitchell* v. *M.N.R.*, a case that, like *Delgamuukw*, goes to some lengths to clarify an appropriate approach to Aboriginal oral histories for the courts to adopt. In this Supreme Court decision, which considered whether the Mohawk First Nation at Akwesasne have the right to bring goods into Canada from the United States for collective use and trade with other First Nations without paying customs duties, Chief Justice Beverley McLachlin affirms the need to give "due weight" to oral histories. However, she cautions against giving too much weight to oral histories, which could potentially lead to the "negation" of general evidentiary principles (*Mitchell* par.

38). She states: "There is a boundary that must not be crossed between a sensitive application and a complete abandonment of the rules of evidence" (par. 39). Although she clarifies the role of oral histories in court, her interpretation of *Delgamuukw* has been used more often to dismiss, rather than to affirm, Aboriginal oral histories as evidence.[12]

Another key effect in the aftermath of *Delgamuukw* is the emergence of a fairly strict notion of what counts as an "authentic" body of oral traditions. Despite McEachern's dismissal of the oral histories at trial, the Gitksan adaawk and the Wet'suwet'en kungax are now becoming the standard for legitimate oral traditions, and other First Nations oral histories are being discredited for not matching this imagined standard. Lamer's attempt to valorize the Gitksan and Wet'suwet'en oral histories is contributing to the establishment of increasingly regimented criteria for determining what constitutes "genuine" oral traditions. Val Napoleon points out that in the Court of Appeal of *Benoit* v. *Canada* (2003), a case in which Cree and Dene plaintiffs argued that the 1899 Treaty 8 included a tax exemption for the signatories, the oral histories of the Cree and Dene people were explicitly compared to those of the Gitksan and Wet'suwet'en people, and found lacking. Quoting from the *Delgamuukw* decision (*Benoit* par. 93), Justice Marc Nadon described the Gitksan adaawk and the Wet'suwet'en kungax as "sacred 'official' litany" which recites "the most important laws, history, traditions and traditional territory of a House" (par. 109). In contrast, according to Nadon, the oral history presented in *Benoit* was "of a substantially different nature in that it was passed on from individual to individual in an informal manner" (par. 109). The court concluded that the oral history presented by the Cree and Dene people in this case "could not be considered as reliable as that presented in *Delgamuukw*" (par. 109). Yet passing down stories "from individual to individual" is precisely what the perpetuation of oral history involves.

Not only do the courts remain undecided about the translatability of oral history; the role of cultural translators themselves – from "outsider" expert witnesses to "insider" cultural experts, such as Elders – also remains unresolved. Brian Thom, an anthropologist and treaty negotiator for Coast Salish peoples from southeast Vancouver Island, argues that "Lamer's decision [...] keeps expert witnesses in a limbo and promotes oral histories as highly credible, if not the only, admissible evidence" in Aboriginal title cases (21). For example, in *Lac La Ronge Indian Band* v. *Canada* (2000),[13] the court argued that the claimants' oral histories "should have been put forward by the elders themselves and not filtered through a third party," who in this case were deemed by the court to be political activists (quoted in Lovisek 261). As a result, little weight was given to the oral history (260). The controversy in *Lac La Ronge Indian Band* v. *Canada* over who should present oral history evidence suggests that the courts are struggling with how much weight to assign the testimony of "insiders" vs. "outsiders." On the one hand, evidence should not be "filtered through" a third party, compromising the court's privileging of "first-hand" knowledge. On the other hand, Elders or tradition bearers are often subjected to a process of scrutiny, in which their credibility as experts becomes the foremost question, rather than the evidence they present. John Borrows maintains that while cross-examination is difficult for most people, for Elders, it can amount to discrediting their standing in their community (32).

Borrows explains that as keepers of wisdom, Elders are ethically bound by a set of moral and spiritual laws that in some cases cannot be fully articulated in a foreign court of law. Aggressive questioning, which seeks to discover *how* an Elder knows something, may come into conflict with the laws to which the Elder is primarily responsible. The process of decontextualizing evidence, and, through analysis, shattering it into ever tinier pieces, can become tantamount to debasing an Elder's knowledge. Borrows argues, "The wisdom they [Elders] have attained and the struggles they have endured in acquiring this knowledge demand that they be shown the highest honour and deepest respect" (32). This honour and respect, in turn, demand a different process of legitimization and verification than that of decontextualizing "bites" of information.

Because of the courts' ambivalent reliance upon, and suspicion of, both "insiders" and "outsiders" in the production of knowledge, judges are increasingly taking on the role of cultural translator, deciding themselves which oral traditions are authentic and which are not (Napoleon 136). Perhaps unwittingly, Lamer has assigned the courts a greater share in the responsibility of interpreting oral traditions, traditions they likely have had little or no exposure to before the trial. This renders vulnerable the precedent established by the *Delgamuukw* trial, in which Gitksan and Wet'suwet'en witnesses were primarily responsible for the presentation of the evidence. It is vitally important that Aboriginal people maintain their roles as cultural translators of their own traditions and participate in the interpretation of their oral histories in the Canadian judicial system. As Borrows argues, Aboriginal peoples' responsibility for interpreting their traditions is not limited to their role as witnesses in court; they must also more fully participate in the running of the legal system, as lawyers, judges, and other legal experts in positions of control. Only with this kind of change in the Canadian legal system can the Court ensure more nuanced interpretations of Aboriginal oral histories.

Notes

1 Hereafter, the Supreme Court of Canada decision will be cited as *Delgamuukw* [scc], and the British Columbia Supreme Court decision as *Delgamuukw* [bcsc]. Full citations are found in the Works Cited.

2 Anishinaabe legal scholar John Borrows argues that the transmission of oral traditions in numerous Aboriginal societies "is bound up with the configuration of language, political structures, economic systems, social relations, intellectual methodologies, morality, ideology and the physical world [...] Oral tradition does not stand alone but is given meaning through the context of the larger cultural experiences that surround it" (8). See also Cruikshank's work on the role of social and cultural contexts in understanding Aboriginal oral traditions.

3 In their legal arguments, the plaintiffs stressed the interdependence of *title* and *jurisdiction* of land: "The uniqueness of the Gitksan and Wet'suwet'en action lies in the statement of claim. Not only are we seeking recognition of title to the territories, but we are further seeking recognition of jurisdiction of our people over their own lands" (Gisday Wa and Delgam Uukw 1).

4 For more detail on the function of the House system in Gitksan and Wet'-suwet'en cultures, see Napoleon; Cruikshank, "Invention"; and Gisday Wa and Delgam Uukw.

5 Lamer identifies the difficulty that oral histories pose in relation to the hearsay rule: "oral histories [...] largely consist of out-of-court statements, passed on through an unbroken chain across the generations of a particular aboriginal nation to the present day. These out-of-court statements are admitted for their truth and therefore conflict with the general rule against the admissibility of hearsay" (*Delgamuukw* [scc] par. 86). His argument, that the laws of evidence must be adapted to accommodate Aboriginal oral histories, on the one hand,

legitimizes the plaintiffs' testimonies; on the other, it reasserts the status of these testimonies as exceptions, setting them apart from what is considered standard evidence.

6 See Cruikshank, *The Social Life of Stories: Narrative and Knowledge in the Yukon Territory*, for more discussion of the complexity of what she calls "various" or "layered tellings" (25–45).

7 The Gitskan people speak Gitsenimx and the Wet'suwet'en people speak Witsuwit'en. These are two distinct but closely related languages.

8 John Borrows provides a list of cases, from Canada, the United States, and Australia, which have considered Aboriginal oral history as evidence from 1971 to 2001 (22, 62n). In the Canadian context, the relevant cases include *Hamlet of Baker Lake* v. *Minister of Indian Affairs and Northern Development* (1979), 102 D.L.R. (3d) 513 (F.C.T.D.); *Attorney General for Ontario* v. *Bear Island Foundation* (1984) 49 O.R. (2d) 353; *R.* v. *Van der Peet* (1996) 2 S.C.R. 507; *R.* v. *Gladstone* (1996) 2 S.C.R. 723; *Delgamuukw* v. *Canada* [1997] 3 S.C.R. 1010; *Mitchell* v. *M.N.R.*, 2001 SCC 33, [2001] S.C.J. No. 33; and *Benoit* v. *Canada* [2002] F.C.J. No. 257, 2002 FCT 243.

9 For example, on 12 December 1997, the day after the decision was released, the *Globe and Mail* published a feature (by Robert Matas et. al.) entitled "Natives Win on Land Rights." The provocative tone of the article, suggesting that Native people hereafter will use their ancestral lands "almost entirely as they wish" and compromise the potential of the mining and lumber industries of British Columbia, is detectable in other newspaper articles published in the weeks and months following the decision.

10 Although both Drew Mildon and Peter Grant likewise argue that in the *post-Delgamuukw* period the Crown has attempted to challenge and narrow reliance on oral histories, they both offer a more optimistic interpretation of a recent case in the British Columbia Supreme Court, *T'Silhqot'in* v. *British Columbia and Canada* (2007), in which the Xeni Gwet'in First Nation used oral histories to prove long-term occupation in a claimed territory (Mildon 89–94; Grant par. 14–15).

11 The excerpt from *Looking Forward, Looking Back* reads as follows: "The Aboriginal tradition in the recording of history is neither linear nor steeped in the same notions of social progress and evolution [as in the non-Aboriginal tradition]. Nor is it usually human centred in the same way as in the western scientific tradition, for it does not assume that human beings are anything more than one – and not necessarily the most important – element of the natural

order of the universe. Moreover, the Aboriginal historical tradition is an oral one, involving legends, stories and accounts handed down through the generations in oral form. It is less focused on establishing objective truth and assumes that the teller of the story is so much a part of the event being described that it would be arrogant to presume to classify or categorize the event exactly or for all time" (quoted in *Delgamuukw* [scc] par. 85).

12 For example, in *Benoit* v. *Canada* (2002), Justice Nadon discusses extensively the Mitchell decision to disqualify the evidence presented by the Cree and Dene plaintiffs (*Benoit* pars. 100–16). He calls the evidence "hearsay," and describes it as "ambiguous and inconclusive" (par. 116, no. 10).

13 In this case, the Lac La Ronge Indian Band of Saskatchewan, as signatories to Treaty 6, claimed that their land entitlement was not being honoured.

Works Cited

Benoit v. *Canada* [2002] F.C.J. No. 257. 2002 FCT 243.

Borrows, John. "Listening for a Change: The Courts and Oral Tradition." *Osgoode Hall Law Journal* 39: 1 (2001): 1–38.

Cruikshank, Julie. "Invention of Anthropology in British Columbia's Supreme Court: Oral Tradition as Evidence." *BC Studies* 95 (1992): 25–42.

– in collaboration with Angela Sidney, Kitty Smith, and Annie Ned. *Life Lived Like a Story: Life Stories of Three Yukon Elders*. Lincoln: University of Nebraska Press; Vancouver: UBC Press, 1990.

– *The Social Life of Stories: Narrative and Knowledge in the Yukon Territory*. Lincoln: University of Nebraska Press, 1998.

Delgamuukw v. *Canada* [scc] 3 S.C.R. 1010, 1997.

Delgamuukw v. *The Queen* [bcsc] Western Weekly Reports 3, 1991.

Gisday Wa and Delgam Uukw. *The Spirit in the Land: The Opening Statement of the Gitksan and Wet'suwet'en Hereditary Chiefs in the Supreme Court of British Columbia, May 11, 1987*. Gabriola, BC: Reflections, 1989.

Grant, Peter. "The Anniversary of *Delgamuukw* v. *The Queen*: Two Legacies." 10 Dec. 2007. Accessed 26 Feb. 2009. http://www.thecourt.ca/2007/12/10/the-anniversary-of-delgamuukw-v-the-queen-two-legacies/

Looking Forward, Looking Back. Vol. 1. *Report of the Royal Commission of Aboriginal Peoples*. *Goverment of Canada*. Ottawa: Minister of Supply and Services, 1996.

Lovisek, Joan. "Transmission Difficulties: The Use and Abuse of Oral History in Aboriginal Claims." *Papers of the 33rd Algonquian Conference.* Ed. H.C. Wolfart. Winnipeg: University of Manitoba Press, 2002, 251–70.

Matas, Robert, Erin Anderssen, and Sean Fine. "Natives Win on Land Rights." *Globe and Mail,* 12 Dec. 1997. Accessed 26 Feb. 2009. http://sisis.nativeweb.org/clark/dec12git.html

Metallic, Candace, and Patricia Monture-Angus. "Domestic Laws versus Aboriginal Visions: An Analysis of the *Delgamuukw* Decision." *Borderlands* 1: 2 (2002): par. 1–64. Accessed 26 Feb. 2009. http://www.borderlands.net.au/vol1no2_2002/metallic_angus.html

Mildon, Drew. "A Bad Connection: First Nations Oral Histories in the Canadian Courts." *Aboriginal Oral Traditions: Theory, Practice, Ethics.* Halifax: Fernwood, 2008.

Mitchell v. *M.N.R.* [2001] SCC 33; [2001] S.C.J. No. 33.

Monet, Don, and Skanu'u (Ardythe Wilson). *Colonialism on Trial: Indigenous Rights and the Gitksan and Wet'suwet'en Sovereignty Case.* Gabriola, BC: Reflections, 1992.

Napoleon, Val. "*Delgamuukw*: A Legal Straitjacket for Oral Histories?" *Canadian Journal of Law and Society* 20: 2 (2005): 123–55.

Pinder, Leslie Hall. *The Carriers of No: After the Land Claims Trial.* Vancouver, BC: Lazara, 1991.

Simon, Sherry. "Translation and the Making of Canadian Culture." *Traduire depuis les marges / Translating from the Margins.* Quebec City: Nota bene, 2008, 11–24.

Thom, Brian. "Aboriginal Rights and Title in Canada after *Delgamuukw*: Part One, Oral Traditions and Anthropological Evidence in the Courtroom." *Native Studies Review* 14: 1 (2001): 1–26.

32

20 October 2008: Translating Reconciliation[1]

David Gaertner

On 10 May 2006, following from models provided by Argentina, Chile, and South Africa, among others, the Canadian federal government approved a Truth and Reconciliation Commission (hereafter, TRC) to both acknowledge and document the injustices and harm committed against Native Canadian children as a direct result of residential school programs. In 1920, attendance at these schools was made compulsory for Aboriginal children between the ages of seven and fifteen. By 1931, there were eighty residential schools open and operating in Canada. It was not until 1996 that the last residential school, the Gordon Residential School, closed in Saskatchewan. On 20 October 2008, only six months after receiving the appointment, Harry Laforme, an Ontario Court of Appeal judge, resigned from his position as chairman of this Commission.[2] Laforme's reason for leaving was, ironically, his inability to reconcile his opinions on the matter at hand with his two commissioners, attorney Jane Brewin Morley and Native health expert Claudette Dumont-Smith. According to the Canadian Broadcasting Corporation, Morley and Dumont-Smith wanted to focus on "uncovering and documenting truth," while Laforme wanted the emphasis to be on "reconciliation between aboriginal and non-aboriginal Canadians" ("Chairman Quits Troubled Residential-School Commission"). Because the commissioners failed to recognize the ultimate authority of the chair, Laforme asserted, the TRC was no longer able to move forward. "At the heart of it is an incurable problem," he wrote in a letter to Indian Affairs Minister Chuck Strahl. "The two Commissioners are unprepared to accept that the structure of the Commission requires that the Commission's course is to be charted and its objectives are to be shaped ultimately through the authority and leadership of its Chair" (quoted in ibid.).

Laforme's authoritative position on the TRC is indicative of the general character of the TRC and its mandates. By emphasizing the role of the leader and authority, he underscored the fact that reconciliation can only have one direction or meaning in order to be effective. While one sympathizes with the judge's need for decision, reconciliation in Canada, a country that bases a large portion of its identity on diversity and multiculturalism, cannot be addressed as singular. This is due to the very slippery quality of language, a point that is demonstrated to us most succinctly through Translation Studies. It is not simply that reconciliation means different things to different people but, rather, that the very idea of "reconciliation" is altered whenever it is conveyed into another language and sociopolitical context. Languages are constellations in which every node or word is connected and defined by those around it in an irreducible system of meaning making. Therefore, translating a word – moving it into another constellation – radically reconfigures its very character. Murray Ironchild points out the difficulties of translating "reconciliation" into Canada's Aboriginal population alone: "there are over 600 First Nations communities and each one has a different approach [to reconciliation] [...] What does reconciliation mean in each one of these languages? Everyone's understanding and interpretation of reconciliation will be different, and perhaps this is something we need to look at" (408). As Ironchild is suggesting here, rather than attempting to hold "reconciliation" within a singular definition, an idea that becomes problematic as soon as one tries to disseminate it, Canada needs to start looking at how reconciliation is shaped through language. In this sense, "reconciliation" itself becomes an issue of translation, of appreciating the differences that arise when this word is evoked in new linguistic contexts. Indeed, perhaps it is in the very act of translating (or talking about translation) that Aboriginals and non-Aboriginals can be brought together. Understanding how translation is accommodated in Canadian TRC documents, such as those that define the Commission's mandate, is thus a way to understand Laforme's resignation as an effect of translation while also pointing us in the direction that reconciliation must take in Canada in order to be realized.

Since President Nelson Mandela established a Truth and Reconciliation Commission in South Africa in 1995, TRCs have been established all over the world. Some of the most prominent include the Gacaca Court in

Rwanda, the Sierra Leone Truth and Reconciliation Commission, and South Korea's Truth and Reconciliation Commission. And since Barack Obama's election as president of the United States, there has also been heightened talk of an American TRC to deal with US-sponsored torture in Iraq and elsewhere. Although few of these Commissions have seen the success of Mandela's project,[3] TRCs have become an important part of the way nations and politicians resolve conflict arising from historical injustice, civil unrest, war, and dictatorship. These commissions provide a forum for both victims and perpetrators to share their stories and bear witness to historical harms and injustices in an open, public forum. In order to encourage truth, in a manner that is sharply differentiated from the Nuremberg Trials after the Second World War, the "criminals" are often given amnesty and encouraged to plainly state their side of the story. The South African TRC, which, due to its perceived success, is most often used as the model on which new Commissions base themselves, is widely viewed as a triumph because of its ability to identify the events and emotions surrounding the apartheid regime, while also positively influencing the state's political and economic circumstances. Books such as *Country of My Skull* and *A Human Being Died that Night*, movies such as *In My Country*, and the heavy media coverage during the proceedings made the South African TRC an international event, solidifying the Commission's paradigm as the new way to deal with human rights grievances in a world increasingly concerned with apology.[4]

The Canadian TRC is the first to ever be conducted in a country not recently subject to war or other tragic experiences. TRC events will take place across Canada that will encourage residential school survivors to share their stories in supportive, but public, forums. While it would be imprudent to suggest that all residential schools were sites of immeasurable violence and cruelty, it is irresponsible not to acknowledge the harm done to thousands of Native children under the pretence of education. Multiple cases of rape and sexual abuse have been reported (Ross); children were stripped of their culture, forbidden to speak their language. As Kevin Annett argues, many children died as a direct result of the schools, through tuberculosis and physical maltreatment. W.J. Chisholm, inspector of Indian Agencies in Ontario in 1905, is recorded as saying: "what is unfortunately too certain is that whatever good the children may receive through residence in a boarding school will be at the expense of the health of all and the lives of others" (quoted in Annett 12). Fred Kelly, a former Anishinaabe chief and member of Midewewin, the Sacred Law and Medicine Society of the Anishi-naabe, shares one story that will serve to inform our understanding of this history:

> I was literally thrown into St Mary's Residential School at four years of age [...] My very first memory of my entry into the school is a painful flashback. For whatever reason I am thrown into a kneeling position. My head is bashed against a wooden cupboard by the boys' supervisor. Instant shock, the nauseating smell of ether, more spanking, then numbness; sudden fear returns at the sight of the man. (14)

Testimony like Kelly's will go towards building a report for the Government of Canada on "the effects and consequences of the IRS [Indian Residential School] system" ("Our Mandate"). An archive of these stories will be collated and made available for research and private study. Most specifically, however, the Canadian TRC was established to "contribute to truth, healing and reconciliation" ("Our Mandate") between Native and non-Native groups in Canada. The "Mandate" for the Truth and Reconciliation Commission further states: "this is a profound commitment to establishing new relationships embedded in mutual recognition and respect that will forge a brighter future. The truth of our common experiences will help set our spirits free and pave the way towards reconciliation."

These goals, and the route to be followed to achieve them, are laid out in the Commission's mandate, which is recorded in "Schedule N" of the TRC's documentation (and in the "Our Mandate" section of the TRC's website from which all the citations in this section are drawn). While the TRC is not a formal legal process, insofar as it does not hold subpoena powers and cannot compel attendance or participation, both "Schedule N" and the Commission that follows from it are highly regimented, official instruments that follow very specific rules and regulations. "Schedule N" was written in direct response to a class action lawsuit filed on 20 August 2007 by the Honourable Frank Iacobucci, National Chief Phil Fontaine, and legal representatives of both former Indian residential school students and the churches involved in running those schools. The Commission itself has been given seven "Goals" which it has been mandated to complete "within five years."[5] Within that five-year mandate there are both two-year and five-year timelines to be followed, which cover everything from the "preparation of a budget" to the "completion of [...] statement taking / truth sharing." The mandate itself is broken down into eleven sections, almost all of which have individual subsections and some of which have further sub-subsections. The entire document is twelve pages long and includes three footnotes.

As it stands, the legal documentation surrounding the TRC mirrors Laforme's position. Like the judge, these documents take a singular, authoritative position. This can be established by looking at how "aboriginal principles," as they are deemed in the Commission's mandate, are translated into (English) government documents. Indeed, what has been a concern for some critics is the way in which "Schedule N" and the Commission work to contain this delicate process within a highly regimented and restrictive (English) structure (although it should be mentioned that "the possibility of a six-month extension" exists for the two-year time frame). The implementation of authoritative legislation and autocratic politics stifles diversity and emulates colonial repression. A Commission that wants to address reconciliation without denying the rights and opinions of certain communities, therefore, must be willing to accommodate an open-ended system and overturn the definitions its discourse is built upon. Failure to do so ignores Canada's colonial past and reaffirms (Eurocentric) top-down politics.

The limitations placed on Native languages within "Schedule N" are most clearly indicated in one of the three footnotes included in the document. Section (c) of the TRC's goals (listed in full in the footnote above) states that the Commission will "witness, support, promote and facilitate truth and reconciliation events at both the national and community levels." Next to the word "witness" in this line is a tiny number referring the reader to the bottom of the web-page (paper page, or back of the book, depending on which format you are consulting).[6] It reads: "This [witness] refers to the Aboriginal principle of 'witnessing.'"

By relegating this "Aboriginal principle" to a footnote, "Schedule N" economizes its narrative by limiting community response and thus maintaining and reproducing a singular colonial discourse. Indeed, the form of the footnote itself already designates "Aboriginal principles" as excess, an idea that cannot be translated into the body of the text itself. Despite its relegation to a footnote, or perhaps because of it, the stakes of this particular translation are quite high. How "witnessing" is translated becomes an important aspect of how the TRC will be conducted, and thus how reconciliation will be achieved. As Todd Wise suggests, "When the radical difference of the testimonial witness is ignored, colonization and harm continue through the sanctioning powers of academic intention" (28). In other words, if "witnessing" is not translated properly to allow for its "radical difference," the TRC could be seen as a further act of colonization.[7] This requires a careful study of what Fred Kelly calls the "nuances and intricacies" of Aboriginal languages and their relation to law in order for the TRC to proceed responsibly. The Cree word for "witness," *sehtoskakew*, provides a place to begin such a study.

"Sehtoskakew" – "a person who testifies to a certain observation" – is included in the "New Terms" section of the *Alberta Elders' Cree Dictionary*. As the editor of this dictionary, Dr Earle Waugh, points out, legal terminology, and its definition, has taken on particular importance in the Cree language. Waugh writes, "We have paid special attention throughout to terms that are commonly used in government, court and social institutions" (xiv). It can be argued that "special attention" is necessary because Western legal terminology does not always translate into Cree, and it is necessary to generate an Aboriginal understanding of the system. For example, The *Alberta Elders' Cree Dictionary* includes a Cree statement of commitment, "because Cree has no concept of swearing an oath" (xiv). By translating the oath, this dictionary is not simply transferring meaning from English to Cree, but reformulating it as a Cree principle. Indeed, as the authors of this statement themselves make sure to point out, the translation cannot be guided by vocabulary alone, because that vocabulary does not always exist. For example, "there are no legal equivalents in Cree for the terms" of "guilty" and "non-guilty" (561). As Waugh is suggesting, we, as citizens of Canada, need to start recognizing how Cree conceptions of the law can inform the state, rather than always assuming that the state must inform Cree conceptions. Obviously, this idea needs to be explored in the terms of the legal terminology being put to use today in documents like "Schedule N." Because of the tension located around the word "witnessing," and its translation into Aboriginal principles, it serves as an important starting point.

Before we can even begin to consider an "Aboriginal principle" of witnessing, however, we need to locate the borders that demarcate a "Western principle." In Canadian law, "witness" is assumed to be a stable term. For example, the *Aboriginal Law Handbook* makes the following statement about "The Trial":

> At the trial, the accused person is presumed to be innocent of the charge. It is the Crown Attorney's task to prove beyond a reasonable doubt that the accused person is guilty. The Crown will try to do so by calling *witnesses* and bringing in physical objects. The accused person has the opportunity to refute the Crown's evidence by questioning the Crown *witnesses* and presenting evidence that shows his or her side of the story. The Crown also has the opportunity to question the accused person's *witnesses* to reveal further information or discrepancies. (345, emphasis added)

"Witness" is the stable term around which this legal definition of the trial turns. At no point in the section on "The Trial" (or in the entirety of the *Aboriginal Law Handbook* for that matter) is "witness" further defined. In other words, a witness is a witness; no new information is added to the definition to stabilize it. Through this (empty) tautological gesture, legal discourse defends itself against the slippage of language implicit to the symbolic order; it provides the stepping stone from which a definition of something such as "the trial" might begin.

Despite what the courts might like to infer, "witness" is not some sort of transcendental signifier. It is not beyond the play of language and differences that grant a word its identity. By first acknowledging that "witness" has no stable meaning, we can begin to search for the terms that support it, that make it meaningful.

Further clarity is granted to a legal definition of "witness" or "witnessing" when we stabilize it with a supplemental term. A quick look through Canada's legal history illustrates that "hearsay" is the obvious choice for this position. According to *The Law of Evidence in Canada* "hearsay" is defined as:

> Any evidence that is offered by a *witness* of which they do not have direct knowledge but, rather, their testimony is based on what others have said to them. The evidence may be admissible to show that an-

other person's statement was made, but not of the truth of what was contained therein. (Emphasis added)

In other words, a proper witness in Canada, one who can testify to the "truth" of an event, has direct knowledge of the event in question (as opposed to having heard of the event). The "proper" witness is thus always the (eye) witness. Using this doctrine of the witness, Canadian courts have historically discredited Aboriginal testimony and rights on the terms "that the memory of what we have *heard said* is less reliable than the memory of what we have *seen done*" (Chamberlin 75).[8]

In Cree, however, the time and space of the witness flows out of a different paradigm. Sight is, of course, still important, but how it is defined challenges the English definition. Take the Cree word *wapatam*, which can be loosely translated to "she (or he) sees it."[9] Etymologically, *wapatam* is closely related to the inanimate noun *wapamon* (mirror) and the transitive verb *wapamiw* ("She (or he) looks in the mirror and sees herself (or himself)").[10] In making these connections between seeing and reflection, we begin to establish what might be a fundamental difference in a Cree definition of "witnessing," inasmuch as a witness "sees" an event.

The etymological connection between *wapatam* and *wapamon* suggests that seeing is always already a matter of reflection; in the same manner, reflection is always intimately connected to sight, inasmuch as both words share an etymological root. If we can take reflection as our starting point, then – as the paradigm from which we are always already working – we are confronted not with the potential for a *loss* of meaning in witnessing, but with a powerful augmentation of it – *as when one mirror is held to another*. It is here, in reflection, in stories, in sharing, in *mekinawewin,* and in the transfer of energy, that *sehtoskakew* defines itself and its difference can begin to be explored.

This argument can be supported through a critical reading of the long poem *Blue Marrow* by the Cree poet Louise Bernice Halfe. In this moving historical text, which itself bears witness to colonial violence, particularly that committed against Aboriginal women, Halfe locates the difference of Cree witnessing in the relationship between colonizer and colonized. The author asks her reader to consider what witnessing might entail when no one is left to testify to the crime or where, because of fear or anger or repression, the stories have been both suppressed and repressed for so many years. In the following passage, *acimowinis*, writing from the "present," acts as a witness to a violent chase scene involving *kimiwan-piysis* and the "redcoats," or British colonialists:

> *kimiwan-piysis*, Raining Bird
> ran with Spirits in his feet,
> redcoats behind him.
> He swam the *sohkeciwani-sipiy*,
> the Fast Flowing River,
> heart stronger than the cold
> swell of water.
>
> I hold his eyes in my fist,
> and when *yotin-napesis*, Windy Boy,
> sweeps the earth,
> my fist uncurls. (46)

What makes this scene so visceral is the location of the eyes. As the first line of the second stanza reveals, *acimowinis's* re-telling of her ancestor's history cannot be clearly delineated from *kimiwan-piysis's* own experience. As such, a legal delineation between "seeing" and "telling" only serves to relegate a Canadian truth outside the limits of sanctified history. Halfe writes, "I hold his eyes in my fist," suggesting that her own "reflection" on the events is, in fact, the source of her strength (46). It is by taking *kimiwan-piysis's* sight, by literally gripping it in her hand, as one might a pen or pencil, that *acimownis* is able to give the story to her reader, passing it from her hand to our own; and with these eyes in our hands at this powerful moment of reflection, we become *sehtoskakew* to colonial violence, not merely seeing it but becoming it, allowing it to become part of who we are as Canadians.

In legal discourse, "'reconciliation' implies a judicial balancing process that 'takes into account the Aboriginal perspective [*sic*] while at the same time taking into account the perspective of the common law'" (Grant and Ross 9). Implicit in this definition is the constant deferral of any singular authority or designation for what reconciliation "is." Rather, reconciliation becomes about the *act* of "balancing," weighing both Aboriginal principles and common law. Translating Aboriginal words such as *sehtoskakew* into common law itself is a way of participating in this act at a fundamental level, unsettling the colonial ground it rests on and opening up a space in which Aboriginal and European principles can be compared and contrasted on equal ground. Insofar as "witnessing" acts as a pivotal term in the Canadian TRC mandate, it plays an important role in how reconciliation itself can be translated, whether into Cree or into any one of the other six hundred Aboriginal languages that Ironchild identifies.

Laforme's resignation from the TRC can be seen as an effect of translation insofar as he refused to acknowledge the fundamental role translation plays in the very definition of what reconciliation is, and must be, in Canada. With over six hundred Aboriginal languages to contend with, the TRC cannot hope to design an inclusive model without ignoring the ideas and hopes of some, probably most, groups. Successful reconciliation is, then, a paradigm that constantly unsettles itself, that opens its definitions to a multitude of translations that continually shift and alter its very structure. The actual force behind this idea can be located in reconciliation discourse, such as "Schedule N." Although Iacobucci and Fontaine attempted to contain the disruptive force of translation by relegating "aboriginal principles" to a footnote, while at the same time responding to the need to accommodate non-European ontologies in the definition of the TRC's mandate, a close examination of the footnote begins to unravel the very discourse "Schedule N" is built on. In this sense, insofar as it serves as the foundation of the TRC, Canadian reconciliation must be seen as having the potential for disruption built into it. As the case of Laforme indicates, in a Canadian context, reconciliation as a paradigm cannot support a mode of thinking that does not take into account the problem of translation.

By ignoring translation in his drive for a singular, authoritative Commission, Laforme was, therefore, not simply struggling against his commissioners, but more importantly, he was struggling against the very meaning of the project. Reconciliation remains an ambivalent concept in Canada, and Canadians must learn how to embrace this problematic formulation if it is to be successful.

Notes

1 I would like to thank Louise Bernice Halfe for the kindness and wisdom she offered to me while I was considering how to approach this essay. My reflections on *sehtoskakew* would not have been possible without her guidance and beautiful writing. Her long poems, *Blue Marrow*, which I will be discussing briefly at the end of this essay, and *The Crooked Good*, both played a large role in shaping this essay, *kinanaskomitin*.

2 Since writing the initial draft of this essay, a new commission was announced by\ Minister of Indian and Northern Affairs Chuck Strahl (11 June 2009). Murray Sinclair, an Ojibway judge from Manitoba, heads the new commission. Joining him are Wilton Littlechild, the Alberta regional chief for the Assembly of First Nations, and Marie Wilson, a former regional director of CBC North. Since its inception, the new commission has worked to produce an Interim Report (2012), detailing its activities since its appointment. The Interim Report includes a number of conclusions on the effects of residential schools in Canada and makes a series of recommendations for improvements. National reconciliation events have also been staged across Canada, including Winnipeg, MB, June, 2010; Inuvik, NT, 28 June to 1 July 2011; an Atlantic National Event, 26–9 Oct. 2011; Saskatoon, SK, 21–4 June 2012; Montréal, QC, 24–7 April 2013; Vancouver, BC, 18–21 Sept. 2013. As of this writing, one future event remains to be held in Edmonton, AL, 27–30 March 2014. There will also be a national closing ceremony in Ottawa. The new commission continues to build out of the work started by early activists and those who first made the trauma of residential schools public. The Interim Report ends with a quotation from former National Chief Phil Fontaine (who made his residential school story public on the CBC in 1980): "As Assembly of First Nations National Chief Phil Fontaine observed when he accepted Canada's apology in June 2008, 'Together we can achieve the greatness our country deserves.' Our challenge and opportunity will be to work together to achieve that greatness" (27). The TRC's five-year mandate is scheduled to end in the spring of 2014.

3 The South African TRC is often viewed as being successful due to its ability to facilitate forgiveness in victims, whereas other commissions have failed. According to Tristan Anne Boer, "The Commission deserves credit for having changed the lives of those who were able to forgive and apologize and for those whose experiences with the Commission did result in healing, its lack of an ex-

plicit mandate to do so notwithstanding" ("Reconciling South Africa or South Africans?" 33).

4 With recent public statements made to residential school survivors, Chinese Canadians, and families of the Komogata Maru tragedy, Canada and, in particular, the Conservative government, seem to have a special investment in apology (for more on this, see Jeffrey Simpson, "Sorry to Say but the Apology-Seeking Industry Is Thriving").

5 The goals are as follows:
(a) Acknowledge Residential School experiences, impacts and consequences;
(b) Provide a holistic, culturally appropriate and safe setting for former students, their families and communities as they come forward to the commission;
(c) Witness, support, promote and facilitate truth and reconciliation events at both the national and community levels;
(d) Promote awareness and public education of Canadians about the IRS system and its impacts;
(e) Identify sources and create as complete an historical record as possible of the IRS system and legacy. The record shall be preserved and made accessible to the public for future study and use;
(f) Produce and submit to the parties of the agreement a report including recommendations to the Government of Canada concerning the IRS system and experience including: the history, purpose, operation, and supervision of the IRS system, the effect and consequences of IRS (including systemic harms, intergenerational consequences, and the impact on human dignity) and the ongoing legacy of the residential schools;
g) Support commemoration of former Indian Residential School students and their families in accordance with the Commemoration Policy Directive.

6 See "Our Mandate: Schedule N" available online, as well as an independent document disseminated by the government and Aboriginal groups and as part of *From Truth to Reconciliation*, published by the Aboriginal Healing Foundation (Castellano et al.).

7 No translation of "Schedule N" in an Aboriginal language is publicly available. A French translation can be found online at http://www.trc-cvr.ca/overview_f.html

8 The most important Canadian case that makes use of this judgment is, of course, *Delgamuukw* v. *The Queen* (1987). For more on the relations between

hearsay and Delgamuukw, see J. Edward Chamberlin's "Doing Things with Words"; see also Sophie McCall's contribution to this volume.

9 All of my translations here are from the *Alberta Elders' Cree Dictionary*.

10 I am very grateful to Louise Bernice Halfe for pointing this connection out to me.

Works Cited

Aboriginal Law Handbook. 2nd ed. By Shin Imai. Scarborough: Carswell, 1999.

Annett, Kevin. *Hidden From History: The Canadian Holocaust*. Vancouver: The Truth Commission into Genocide in Canada, 2005.

Alberta Elders' Cree Dictionary / Alperta ohci kehtehayak nehiyaw otwestamâke-wasinahikan. "Appendix A: A Legal Oath." Nancy LeClaire, and George Cardinal. Cree consultants, Emily Hunter et al. Ed. Earle Waugh. Edmonton: University of Alberta Press / Duval House, 1998.

– "Sehtoskakew," "Wapatam," "Wapamiw," and "Wapamon." In *Alberta Elders' Cree Dictionary*. Edmonton: University of Alberta Press/Duval House, 1998.

Borer, Tristan Anne. "Reconciling South Africa or South Africans? Cautionary Notes from the TRC." *African Studies Quarterly* 8: 1 (2004): 19–38.

Castellano, Marlene Brant, Linda Archibald, and Mike DeGagne, eds. *From Truth to Reconciliation*. Ottawa: Aboriginal Healing Foundation, 2008.

"Chairman Quits Troubled Residential-School Commission." CBC.ca. CBC News. 20 Oct. 2008. Accessed 27 Dec. 2009. http://www.cbc.ca/canada/story/2008/10/20/truth-resignation.html

Chamberlin, J. Edward. "Doing Things with Words." *Talking on the Page*. Ed. Laura J. Murray and Keren Rice. Toronto: University of Toronto Press, 1999, 69–90.

Grant, Peter R., and Michael Lee Ross. The Supreme Court of Canada's Decision in *Marshal* and *Bernard*: Its Implications for Aboriginal Title in British Columbia. 2005. Accessed 27 June 2011. http://www.grantnativelaw.com/pdf/Marshal landBernard_TitleImplications.pdf

Halfe, Louise Bernice. *Blue Marrow*. Saskatchewan: Coteau, 2004.

"Hearsay." *The Law of Evidence in Canada*. 2nd ed. Ed. John Sopinka. Toronto: Butterworths, 1999.

Ironchild, Murray. "Sidebar." *From Truth to Reconciliation: Transforming the Legacy of Residential Schools*. Ed. Marlene Brant Castellano, Linda Archibald, and Mike DeGagné. Ottawa: Aboriginal Healing Foundation, 2008, 408.

Kelly, Fred. "Confession of a Born Again Pagan." *From Truth to Reconciliation: Transforming the Legacy of Residential Schools*. Ed. Marlene Brant Castellano,

Linda Archibald, and Mike DeGagné. Ottawa: Aboriginal Healing Foundation, 2008, 11–40.

"Our Mandate: Schedule N." *Truth and Reconciliation Canada*. Accessed 27 Dec. 2009. http://www.trc-cvr.ca/overview.html

Ross, Rupert. "Telling Truths and Seeking Reconciliation." *From Truth to Reconciliation: Transforming the Legacy of Residential Schools*. Ed. Marlene Brant Castellano, Linda Archibald, and Mike DeGagné. Ottawa: Aboriginal Healing Foundation, 2008, 143–62.

Simpson, Jeffrey, "Sorry to Say, but the Apology-Seeking Industry Is Thriving." *Globe and Mail*, 20 May 2008. http://www.theglobeandmail.com

Sinclair, Murray. Marie Wilson, Wilton Littlechild. "Truth and Reconciliation Commission of Canada: Interim Report." Winnipeg: Truth and Reconciliation Commission of Canada, 2012.

Waugh, Earl. Preface. *Alberta Elders' Cree Dictionary / Alperta ohci kehtehayak nehiyaw otwestamâkewasinahikan*. Edmonton: University of Alberta Press / Duval House, 1998.

Wise, Todd. "Speaking Through Others: *Black Elk Speaks* as Testimonial Literature." *The Black Elk Reader*. Ed. Clyde Holler. Syracuse: Syracuse University Press, 2000, 19–39.

CONTRIBUTORS

PIERRE ANCTIL is a full professor in the Department of History at the
University of Ottawa. His recent publications include *Trajectoires juives
au Québec*; *Les communautés juives de Montréal, histoire et enjeux
contemporains* (in collaboration with Ira Robinson); *Religion, Culture
and the State: Reflections on the Bouchard-Taylor Report* (co-edited
with Howard Adelman); and a biography entitled *Jacob-Isaac Segal
(1896–1954), un poète yiddish de Montréal et son milieu.*

HÉLÈNE BUZELIN holds a PhD in French language and literature from
McGill University. She teaches translation theory and practice at
Université de Montréal. Her areas of interest and specialization include
post-colonial theories, literary translation, and sociological as well as
ethnographic approaches in Descriptive Translation Studies. She has
conducted research on translation practices in different sectors of the
publishing industry, such as literary and higher education publishing
and is the author of *Sur le terrain de la traduction*. In collaboration with
Deborah Folaron, she co-edited an issue of *Meta* on "Translation and
Network Studies" (2007). She has published contributions in *Canadian
Literature, Target, The Translator, TTR: Traduction, traductologie,
rédaction*, and *Meta*.

ALESSANDRA CAPPERDONI teaches modern and contemporary literature
in the Department of English at Simon Fraser University. She specializes
in Canadian and anglophone literatures, feminist poetics and translation,
avant-garde studies, post-colonialism and diaspora, modernism and
psychoanalysis, and critical theory. She is currently working on a book
manuscript, "Shifting Geographies: Poetics of Citizenship in the Age of

Global Modernity." Her essays have appeared in *Cultural Grammars of Nation, Diaspora, and Indigeneity in Canada*; *Translating from the Margins / Traduire des marges*; *Convergence and Divergence in North America: Canada and the United States*; and the journals *Canadian Literature, Open Letter, TTR: Traduction, traductologie, rédaction,* and *West Coast Line.*

PHILIPPE CARDINAL lives in Whitehorse where he works as a freelance translator, a French teacher for federal and territorial government officials, and as a language consultant.

ANDREW CLIFFORD is director of the Master of Conference Interpreting program at York University. He has worked as a community interpreter, a translator, a technical writer, and as a conference interpreter. His recent publications include "Is Fidelity Ethical? The Social Role of the Health-care Interpreter" and "Healthcare Interpreting and Informed Consent: What is the Interpreter's Role in Treatment Decision-Making?" both of which appeared in *TTR: Traduction, traductologie, rédaction.*

BEVERLEY CURRAN teaches linguistic, cultural, and media translation in the Department of Media, Communication, and Culture at International Christian University in Tokyo. Her current research focuses on hybrid cultural productions and bi- or multilingual graphic narratives. Her recent publications include *Theatre Translation Theory and Performance in Contemporary Japan: Native Voices, Foreign Bodies*; "*The Gull*: Intercultural Noh as Webwork," in *Words, Images and Performances in Translation*; and "Nogami Toyoichir 's Noh Translation Theory and the Primacy of Performance," in *Theatre Translation in Performance.*

RENÉE DESJARDINS is an adjunct professor at the School of Translation at the University of Ottawa and a full-time editor at the Royal College of Physicians and Surgeons of Canada. She recently obtained a PhD in Translation Studies and Canadian Studies. Her doctoral research focused on broadening the definition of translation in Canada using the Bouchard-Taylor Commission as a case study. She also recently explored translation's role in the formation of culinary identities; she has published a study of menu translation in a special issue of *Cuizine* (co-edited by Desjardins and Marc Charron).

RAY ELLENWOOD is a retired professor of English (York University), and author of ten books of translation (French-to-English), mostly of Quebec literature, including the manifesto, *Refus global*, by the Montreal Automatist Movement, and works by associated writers such as Thérèse Renaud, Claude Gauvreau, and Gilles Hénault.

LUISE VON FLOTOW teaches at the School of Translation and Interpretation at the University of Ottawa. Her research interests include women and translation, audiovisual translation, and translation in cultural diplomacy. She is also a literary translator working from French and German. Her most recent academic book is *Translating Women*.

DAVID GAERTNER is a postdoctoral fellow in the First Nations Studies program at the University of British Columbia and a sessional instructor at Simon Fraser University. His research is on Indigenous literature and film, with special focus on discourses of reconciliation. He has published work in *Psychoanalysis, Culture and Society*, *Bioethical Inquiry*, and *Essays in Canadian Studies*. He has presented his research internationally, including at the Global Reconciliation Summit in Amman, Jordan. With Jason Starnes, he has edited a special issue, "Here Comes the Neighbourhood," of *West Coast Line* (2012).

CHANTAL GAGNON is an assistant professor at the Université de Montréal. Her academic research has focused on the translation of political speeches in Canada, and she has published several articles and book chapters on the subject, in Canada and abroad. She earned a doctorate in Translation Studies at Aston University in the United Kingdom.

PATRICIA GODBOUT is a professor of translation at the Université de Sherbrooke. She has published a book and articles on the history of literary translation in Canada. Her current research project is on the figure of the translator in Quebec novels. She is also a translator, mainly of books of literary criticism.

HUGH HAZELTON is a writer and translator who specializes in the comparison of English-Canadian and Quebec literatures with the literature of Latin America. His most recent academic book is *Latinocanadá: A Critical Study of Ten Latin American Writers of Canada*. He is a professor emeritus of Spanish translation and Latin American civilization at Concordia University in Montreal and is co-director of the Banff International Literary Translation Centre.

JANE KOUSTAS is a professor in the Department of Modern Languages and Literatures at Brock University, where she also directed Canadian Studies, and Craig Dobbin Professor of Canadian Studies at University College Dublin in 2005–06, 2010–2011, and spring 2012. She is the author of *Les belles étrangères: Canadians in Paris* and continues to work on the theatre of Robert Lepage.

GILLIAN LANE-MERCIER is an associate professor in the Département de langue et littérature françaises at McGill University. She is the author of *La parole romanesque* and co-author of *Faulkner: Une expérience de retraduction*. She has published numerous articles on theories of the novel, translation studies, and Canadian novelists/translators.

LOUISE LADOUCEUR is a professor at the University of Alberta. Her publications include *Making the Scene: la traduction du théâtre d'une langue officielle à l'autre au Canada* and *Dramatic Licence: Translating Theatre from One Official Language to the Other in Canada*, translated by Richard Lebeau. She also co-authored *Plus d'un siècle sur scène! Histoire du théâtre francophone en Alberta de 1887 à 2008*. She is French associate editor of *Recherches théâtrales au Canada / Theatre Research in Canada*.

GEORGE LANG taught French and Comparative Literature for twenty years at the University of Alberta and then served as dean of Arts at the University of Ottawa until his retirement. He is the author of *Entwisted Tongues: Comparative Creole Literatures* and *Making Wawa: The Genesis of Chinook Jargon*.

REBECCA MARGOLIS is an associate professor in the University of Ottawa's Vered Jewish Canadian Studies program. Her research centres on Canadian Jewish culture, in particular, as it relates to Yiddish. Her most recent publication is *Jewish Roots, Canadian Soil: Yiddish Culture in Montreal, 1905–1945*.

SOPHIE McCALL teaches contemporary Canadian and Indigenous literatures at Simon Fraser University. Her recent publications include *First Person Plural: Aboriginal Storytelling and the Ethics of Collaborative Authorship* and *Cultural Grammars of Nation, Diaspora, and Indigeneity in Canada*, co-edited with Christine Kim and Melina Baum Singer. She has published articles in *Essays on Canadian Writing*, *Canadian Review of American Studies*, *Resources for Feminist Research*, *Canadian Literature*, and *C.L.R. James Journal*.

JULIE McDONOUGH DOLMAYA teaches in the School of Translation at York University's Glendon Campus. She obtained a PhD in Translation Studies from the University of Ottawa. Her research interests range from political translation and oral history to crowdsourcing, blogs, and web translation, and she has published articles on these topics in international journals such as *Meta*, *The Translator*, *Translation Studies*, and *Linguistica Antverpiensia*. She blogs about her teaching and research at www.mcdonough-dolmaya.ca.

DENISE MERKLE is a professor of Translation at the Université de Moncton. She is interested in the history of, primarily, literary translation, psycho-sociological theories of translation, the translating subject, and censorship. In addition to co-editing collected volumes, she edited the *TTR: Traduction, traductologie, rédaction* issues on "Censorship and Translation" (15: 2, 2002; 23: 2, 2010) and the issue on "Comparative Literature and Literary Translation Studies" (22: 2, 2009).

KATHY MEZEI is professor emeritus in the Department of Humanities at Simon Fraser University and life member at Clare Hall, Cambridge. She is one of the founding editors of *Tessera*; her most recent publication is *The Domestic Space Reader*, co-edited with Chiara Briganti.

SOROUJA MOLL is a PhD candidate in the Humanities (Media, Shake-speare Studies, and Nineteenth-Century Canadian Print Culture) at Concordia University in Montreal.

BRIAN MOSSOP has been a translator in the Canadian federal govern-ment's translation service since 1974. He is also an instructor at the York University School of Translation and the author of the widely used text-book *Revising and Editing for Translators*.

GLEN NICHOLS is director of Drama at Mount Allison University. He has published articles on theatre history, theatre translation, and Acadian theatre, as well as a collection under the title, *Angels and Anger: Five Contemporary Acadian Plays in Translation*. He has served as president of the Association of Theatre Research in Canada and as editor of *Theatre Research in Canada*.

DAISY NIEJMANN holds a PhD from the Vrije Universiteit Amsterdam, and has published widely on Icelandic-Canadian literature and culture, twentieth-century Icelandic fiction, and war and memory. She teaches at the University of Iceland and is a researcher with the Edda Centre of Excellence.

JOSEPH PIVATO is a professor of Literary Studies at Athabasca Univer-sity. He has published six books including *Contrasts: Comparative Essays on Italian-Canadian Writing* and *Echo: Essays on Other Literatures*, and edited *The Anthology of Italian-Canadian Writing* and *Africadian Atlantic: Essays on George Elliott Clarke*.

GREGORY J. REID is a retired professor of English and Comparative Lit-erature from the Université de Sherbrooke. He was a co-founder of the Great Canadian Theatre Company in Ottawa, co-editor of *The Bibliog-raphy of Comparative Studies in Canadian, Québec and Foreign Litera-tures*, and author of *A Re-Examination of Tragedy and Madness in Eight Selected Plays from the Greeks to the 20th Century* and *The Cunning to Be Strange* (a collection of short stories). With Pamela Grant, he has translated Anne Hébert's play *Le Temps sauvage*, published as *The Savage Season* in the *Anthology of Québec Women's Plays in English*

Translation, vol. 1, *1966–1986* and *La Cage* in *Two Plays: The Cage and L'Île de la Demoiselle.*

DEBORAH SHADD is completing a PhD in Translation Studies, with a specialization in Canadian Studies, at the University of Ottawa. Her research focuses on the role of language and education policy in the formation of cultural identity among linguistic minority groups in Canada. She is a lecturer in the Applied Linguistics Department at Trinity Western University in Langley, BC.

ROBERT SCHWARTZWALD is a professor of English Studies and director of Graduate Programs in International Studies at the Université de Montréal, and the 2008 recipient of the Governor General's International Award for Canadian Studies. His numerous publications focus on the relations between notions of literary, cultural, and national modernity, often with particular attention to sexuality.

SHERRY SIMON teaches in the French Department at Concordia University. Among her publications are *Translating Montreal* and *Cities in Translation: Intersections of Language and Memory.* She is a member of the Royal Society of Canada and of the Académie des lettres du Québec.

TRISH VAN BOLDEREN has a Bachelor of Fine Arts in Dance from York University and a Master of Arts in Translation from the University of Ottawa. A PhD student in Translation Studies (University of Ottawa), she is researching self-translation practices in Canada.

CHRISTINE YORK is a lecturer in the Département d'études françaises at Concordia University. She is completing a PhD at the University of Ottawa and has an MA from Concordia University. Her current research focuses on audiovisual translation and museum translation.